# THE MAHARAJAH'S BOX

# THE
# MAHARAJAH'S
# BOX

*An Exotic Tale of Espionage,*
*Intrigue, and Illicit Love*
*in the Days of the Raj*

# CHRISTY CAMPBELL

THE OVERLOOK PRESS
WOODSTOCK & NEW YORK

*For Clare, Katy, Maria and Joe*

First published in the United States in 2002 by
The Overlook Press, Peter Mayer Publishers, Inc.
Woodstock & New York

WOODSTOCK:
One Overlook Drive
Woodstock, NY 12498
www.overlookpress.com
[for individual orders, bulk and special sales, contact our Woodstock office]

NEW YORK:
141 Wooster Street
New York, NY 10012

Library of Congress Cataloging-in-Publication Data

Campbell, Christopher.
The Maharajah's Box : An exotic tale of espionage, intrigue, and
illicit love in the days of the raj / Christopher Campbell.
p. cm.
Includes bibliographical references and index.
1. Duleep Singh, Maharajah, 1838-1893. 2. Punjab (India—Politics and government.
3. Punjab (India—Kings and rulers—Biography. 4. Punjab (India—Biography. I. Title.
DS485.P87 C36 2002    954'.5503'092—dc21  [B]    2002025222

Printed in the United States of America
FIRST EDITION
ISBN 1-58567-293-9
1 3 5 7 9 8 6 4 2

# CONTENTS

# Contents

## Appendices

# ILLUSTRATIONS

'Ranjit Singh'. *Musée des arts asiatiques-Guimet, Paris. © RMN-Arnaudet*
'The Court of Lahore'. © *Princess Bamba Collection, Lahore Fort*
'Maharajah Ranjit Singh listening to the Granth being recited near the Golden Temple, Amristar'. © *Princess Bamba Collection, Lahore Fort*
'Rani Jindan seated on a cushion'. © *Princess Bamba Collection, Lahore Fort*
Maharajah Duleep Singh as a 10-year-old. © *National Army Museum,* 1999
Maharajah Duleep Singh, 23 August, 1854. *The Royal Archives* © *Her Majesty The Queen*
Maharajah Duleep Singh, 7 June, 1856. *The Royal Archives* © *Her Majesty The Queen*
'Duleep Singh, Maharajah of Lahore' by Franz Xaver Winterhalter. © *The Bridgeman Art Library*
Maharani Bamba.
Ludwig Müller. © *Ancient House Museum, Thetford*
Mulgrave Castle. © *Whitby Archives*
Tennis party. © *Princess Bamba Collection. By kind permission Maharajah Duleep Singh Centenary Trust Collection*
Elveden Hall. © *Ancient House Museum, Thetford*
Elveden's 'eastern' interior. © *Ancient House Museum, Thetford*
Prince Victor. © *Ancient House Museum, Thetford*
Princesses Bamba and Catherine, c.1878. © *Ancient House Museum, Thetford*
Royal hunting party at Elveden Hall, 8 December, 1876. *The Royal Archives* © *Her Majesty The Queen*
Elveden gamekeepers, c.1883. © *Ancient House Museum, Thetford*

The Maharajah's abandoned youngest children, Edward and Sophia, at a fancy dress party, c.1888. © *Ancient House Museum, Thetford*

Maharani Bamba with Princes Victor and Frederick, Princesses Bamba
and Catherine and the infant Sophia, c.1878. © *Princess Bamba
Collection. By kind permission Maharajah Duleep Singh Centenary Trust*
Maharani Bamba in mid-life, c.1878. © *Princess Bamba Collection. By
kind permission Maharajah Duleep Singh Centenary Trust*
Prince Victor, c.1878. © *Princess Bamba Collection. By kind permission
Maharajah Duleep Singh Centenary Trust*
Prince Frederick, c.1883. © *Princess Bamba Collection. By kind permission
Maharajah Duleep Singh Centenary Trust*
The Maharajah, c.1887. *By kind permission Maharajah Duleep Singh
Centenary Trust*
Prince Edward. © *Ancient House Museum, Thetford*
Princess Bamba, c.1887. © *Princess Bamba Collection, Lahore Fort*
Lina Schäfer. © *Princess Bamba Collection. By kind permission Maharajah
Duleep Singh Centenary Trust*
Princess Catherine, c.1889. © *Ancient House Museum, Thetford*
Princess Catherine, Bamba, Sophia and Prince Edward, c.1886.
© *Ancient House Museum, Thetford*
'Hush! (The Concert)' by James Jacques Tissot, 1875. *Manchester City
Art Galleries.* © *The Bridgeman Art Library*
The Maharajah, 1883. © *Princess Bamba Collection. By kind permission
Maharajah Duleep Singh Centenary Trust*
'Fillaloo! Ould India For Ever!' © *Punch*
Juliette Lamber (Madame Adam). © *Harlingue/Roger-Viollet*
Elie de Cyon. © *The British Library*
Mikhail Katkov. © *The British Library*
General Charles Carrol-Tevis. © *US Military Academy Library,
West Point, NY*
British Sikhs gather for the unveiling of the equestrian statue of the
Maharajah Duleep Singh, Thetford, August 1998. © *M. Roberts*

# AUTHOR'S NOTE

## SPELLINGS

'What is the proper spelling of the Maharajah's name?' asked Sir Henry Mortimer Durand, Foreign Secretary of the government of India in August 1886. 'He spells it Duleep. We have in the papers about him Dhulip, Dulip, Dhalip, and other forms. Is there an h after the d, and is the succeeding vowel a or u?'

His secretary replied: 'The correct spelling is "Dalip". There is no h after the d and the succeeding vowel is a not u.'

'Spell accordingly,' Sir Henry ordered. Thus, in most official British documents he is 'Dalip Singh'. To *The Times* he was variously 'Dhuleep' or 'Duleep'. His story is indexed in contemporary records in a multitude of spellings. But in his own autograph, he was always 'Duleep Singh, Maharajah', and thus he is in this narrative.

The 'Panjab' or 'Punjaub' is styled in modern references as 'Punjab'.

## ALIASES

This is a story of conspiracy and espionage; thus, in the original documentation, many of the key participants have codenames and often several aliases. I have striven to identify them just as did the competing intelligence agencies of the period.

For the sake of clarity they are reprised here with real names given first – except in the last two instances – although I have chosen to keep the identity of 'Our

Correspondent', the British-paid spy in Paris, concealed until the end of this narrative.

**Maharajah Duleep Singh**: Covername in Paris was 'Reginald Lorraine'; for his journey to Russia he was 'Patrick Casey'. Referred to by the Moscow conspirators as 'The Traveller'. Ada Wetherill, travelling as his wife, variously changed identities to Madame Lorraine, Madame Casey, etc.

**Abdul Aziz-ud-Din**: Detective in pay of government of India Foreign Department. Known as 'Lambert's Man', later codenamed 'L.M.'. He penetrated the Lahore government-in-exile in Pondicherry calling himself 'Ali Muhammed'.

**Amrik Singh**: Sikh detective loyal to government of India. Covernames were 'Bhaghat Singh' and 'Jaswant Singh'. Known to his controller at the Department for the Suppression of Thugee and Dacoity (Indian police Special Branch) as agent 'A.S.'. He was also styled 'Father of the Turban'.

**Arur Singh**: The Maharajah's servant and ambassador. Travelled to India as 'Partab Singh'.

**Ilya Fadeevich Tsion**: Physiologist and journalist, chief operative in Paris of Mikhail Katkov, proprietor of the *Moscow Gazette*. Referred to throughout as 'Elie de Cyon'. Appears in correspondence as 'E.C.'.

**Abdul Rasul**: Islamic conspirator in service of the Ottoman Empire (and others) who attached himself to Duleep Singh. Alias 'Abdul Effendi'.

**Queen Victoria**, Queen of Great Britain and Ireland, Empress of India: travelled to France, where she met the Maharajah, under the title 'Countess of Balmoral'. Also referred to as 'Mrs Brown'.

**General Francis F. Millen**: Irish-American Fenian dynamite conspirator; travelled New York–Paris under alias 'Mr Muller'. Referred to by British Foreign Office first as 'James Thompson', later as 'X' and by the Commissioner of Scotland Yard in his memoirs as 'Jenks'.

**Inspector J. C. Mitter**: Calcutta detective who wrote anonymously to the Maharajah in Moscow posing as a clandestine supporter. Referred to as 'My Unknown Friend'.

**Colonel Yellow**: British agent and forger in Paris in pay of Home Office, later employed by *The Times* newspaper. Real name Captain Stuart Stephens.

**'Un Officier Russe'**: Author of conspiratorial pamphlet 'L'Alliance Franco-Russe'. First identified as General Evgenii Bogdanovich, later as the journalist-spy Nicholas Notovich.

After flying the Trondheim and Warnemunde missions, I went to the mission debriefing at Third Air Division Headquarters, at Elveden Hall, past Bury St Edmunds in Suffolk.

At Elveden Hall, I was in a palace. I learned that it was once the English home of one of the richest Maharajahs of India. When we arrived, we were directed to the rear, where we left the car and walked up huge stone stairs. Along with several quartets of fliers, we walked down a long hall with high, ornate ceilings and into what was probably once the Rajah's dining room.

The pictures were gone, but the curtains, the chandeliers and the oriental rugs were stored and forgotten in the basement.

*A Wing and a Prayer*, by Harry H. Crosby
(US Army Air Force bomber pilot 1943–44)

# PREFACE

THERE WAS wild drumming. Khalistan! The name of a non-existent country was rapturously shouted over loud-speakers booming round a municipal playing field outside the English town of Thetford on a high summer's day in 1998. The Lord-Lieutenant of Norfolk munched microwaved curried puffs in a marquee with veteran Duffadars, Sikh soldiers in blazers and turbans who had defended the British Indian Empire against the Japanese. 'Bravest men I ever knew,' said an elderly Englishman in a Garrick Club tie held by a regimental pin. 'I am a Sikh you know.' The British Army had come to try and recruit their great-grandchildren. Boys peered suspiciously at the close-fitting infantry helmet held by a sergeant. The turban thing could be got round, he seemed sure.

Teenage Sikhs dressed in black waved the orange banners of Khalistan – a dreamt-of reunited, independent Punjab. The coaches kept arriving and the field filled with families. Things ran late. Officials of the Maharajah Duleep Singh Centenary Trust who had sponsored the event began to look concerned. Later in the afternoon, the pilgrims were due to move in their thousands to visit a gothic Victorian grave in a Christian church nearby. At some signal the crowd went quiet, women and children sitting in a huge circle. Balloons rose, lifting the covering veil from a statue in bronze, a stern man on a horse carrying a sword.

He was the Maharajah Duleep Singh, last King of the Sikhs. I already knew a little bit about him. Once he and his family had lived in a great house, Elveden Hall, a few miles up the road across the county border in Suffolk. He was buried in the churchyard there – that was why we had all come to sleepy Thetford on a summer's day to see the statue which had been paid for by the subscriptions of the Anglo-Sikh diaspora.

The previous winter, I had tried to visit Elveden Hall. The house was shuttered and empty, its stonework crumbling, girt with Keep Out signs. It had an unusual history. Just over a century ago it hosted the grandest shooting parties in England. Half a century later, olive-drab Packards swept up the drive, bearing the US Army Air Force commanders who, from its mirror-glass saloons, directed the American bomber fleets that took off each day to wreck Nazi Germany from end to end.

In the churchyard on the fringe of the Hall's grounds there were three graves in a discrete plot, the Maharajah's, his wife's and his son's. On that winter's day, a gaggle of mournful Sikhs stood reverentially by them. 'We have come from Wolverhampton,' one said, 'to see our Maharajah.'

Duleep Singh had already planted himself in my life. In the summer of 1997, I had stumbled by journalistic accident on a quirky clue about the fate of the Indian King who had somehow 'rebelled' against England. One of his daughters, Princess Catherine, last heard of living in a village in wartime Buckinghamshire, had an unclaimed Swiss bank account, evidently untouched for decades. Banking officials were asking descendants of the original owner of this, among many other accounts, to come forward. Duleep Singh had once owned the Koh-i-Noor, the 'mountain of light', probably the most famous diamond in the world. The safe deposit box, if that was what it was, might be stuffed with jewels. There was a deadline of a year for claims to be resolved. I set out to learn more about father and daughter and found many other things on the way.

I had embarked on parallel journeys in space and in time. I could only wait for claimants to the account to make their case and for Swiss lawyers to deliberate. In the meantime, where could I find out more about the Maharajah and his family? The Kingdom of Lahore had been extinguished for a century and a half. The Punjab was divided, Lahore its temporal capital had been suborned into Muslim Pakistan for the last fifty years. There were discoveries to be made in Amritsar, the spiritual capital of the Sikhs. And I found consuming passion for the last Maharajah in England. Documents were passed to me by young Sikhs in clothing factories in the East End of London, research clues given provenance by Punjabi businessmen in plush Midlands suburbs. Information began to arrive from Dublin, Paris, Moscow and Birmingham. I dug in the Royal Archives at Windsor, the Public

Record Office and the records of the India Office preserved in the British Library. Empires that retreat in reasonable order keep their archives in reasonable order. As did the British in India. In London I found something remarkable: the sequential reports of a spy at the heart of the matter.

Maharajah Duleep Singh's rebellion was real. It was taken very seriously at the highest level of the British government. The Queen Empress was told what she needed to know but much was left untold. The Maharajah's rebellion embraced a conspiracy which had little to do with India or the 'mountain of light'. It destroyed him. And Princess Catherine Hilda Duleep Singh of Colehatch House, Penn, Bucks, may have had a very good reason for forgetting all about a Swiss bank account.

I started out on a treasure hunt and found a love story. This is the true tragedy of the last King of Lahore.

ST PETERSBURG

Gatchina

Moscow

Baltic Sea

*Europe 1887*

Verjbolovo/Weidballen

RUSSIAN EMPIRE

Kiev

Budapest

UNGARIAN

EMPIRE

Odessa

Black Sea

ROMANIA

Belgrade

SERBIA

OSNIA-
RZEGOVINA

MONTE
NEGRO

BULGARIA

Sofia

OTTOMAN

CONSTANTINOPLE

EMPIRE

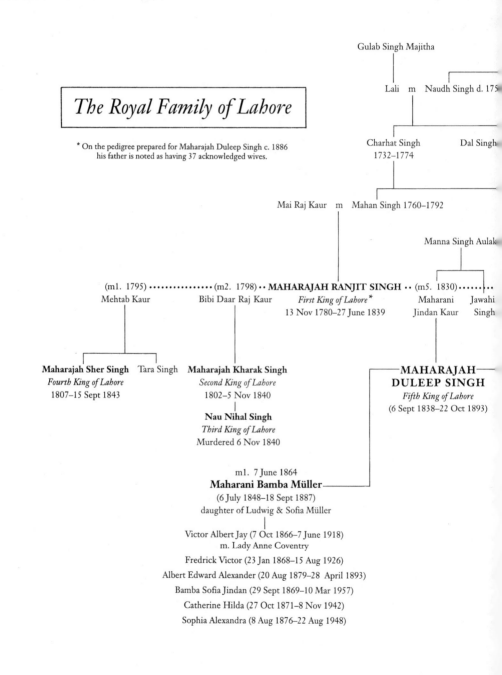

# The Royal Family of Lahore

* On the pedigree prepared for Maharajah Duleep Singh c. 1886
his father is noted as having 37 acknowledged wives.

Gulab Singh Majitha

Lali   m   Naudh Singh d. 175⬛

Charhat Singh      Dal Singh⬛
1732–1774

Mai Raj Kaur   m   Mahan Singh 1760–1792

Manna Singh Aulak⬛

(m1. 1795) ⋯⋯⋯⋯⋯⋯ (m2. 1798) ⋅⋅ **MAHARAJAH RANJIT SINGH** ⋅⋅ (m5. 1830)⋅⋅⋅⋅⋅⋅|⋅⋅
Mehtab Kaur      Bibi Daar Raj Kaur     *First King of Lahore**      Maharani    Jawahi⬛
                                                 13 Nov 1780–27 June 1839     Jindan Kaur    Singh⬛

**Maharajah Sher Singh**   Tara Singh    **Maharajah Kharak Singh**               **MAHARAJAH**⎯
*Fourth King of Lahore*                *Second King of Lahore*                      **DULEEP SINGH**
1807–15 Sept 1843                        1802–5 Nov 1840                        *Fifth King of Lahore*
                                        **Nau Nihal Singh**                      (6 Sept 1838–22 Oct 1893)
                                        *Third King of Lahore*
                                        Murdered 6 Nov 1840

m1. 7 June 1864
**Maharani Bamba Müller**⎯⎯⎯⎯⎯
(6 July 1848–18 Sept 1887)
daughter of Ludwig & Sofia Müller

Victor Albert Jay (7 Oct 1866–7 June 1918)
m. Lady Anne Coventry

Fredrick Victor (23 Jan 1868–15 Aug 1926)

Albert Edward Alexander (20 Aug 1879–28 April 1893)

Bamba Sofia Jindan (29 Sept 1869–10 Mar 1957)

Catherine Hilda (27 Oct 1871–8 Nov 1942)

Sophia Alexandra (8 Aug 1876–22 Aug 1948)

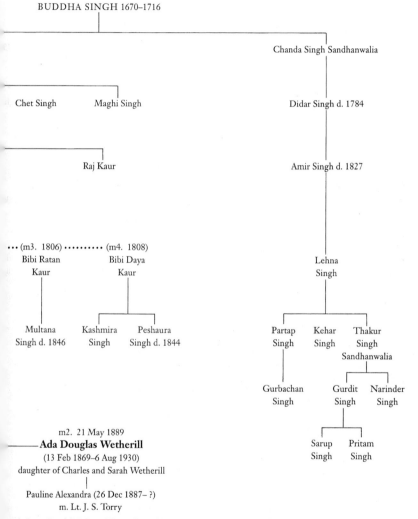

BUDDHA SINGH 1670–1716

Chanda Singh Sandhanwalia

Chet Singh     Maghi Singh            Didar Singh d. 1784

Raj Kaur                    Amir Singh d. 1827

••• (m3. 1806) •••••••• (m4. 1808)          Lehna
Bibi Ratan      Bibi Daya           Singh
Kaur          Kaur

Multana     Kashmira    Peshaura         Partap    Kehar    Thakur
Singh d. 1846    Singh    Singh d. 1844       Singh    Singh    Singh
                                         Sandhanwalia

Gurbachan      Gurdit    Narinder
Singh           Singh     Singh

m2. 21 May 1889
**Ada Douglas Wetherill**
(13 Feb 1869–6 Aug 1930)
daughter of Charles and Sarah Wetherill

Sarup    Pritam
Singh    Singh

Pauline Alexandra (26 Dec 1887– ?)
m. Lt. J. S. Torry

Ada Irene Beryl (25 Oct 1889–14 Sept 1926)
m. M. P. Villament

# Part One

'Russia has an unlimited command of secret service money. England has, for the service of foreign affairs all over the world, just 15,000 a year, a sum so small as to be practically worthless.'

The Marquis of Salisbury to Queen Victoria, 24 August 1886

# The Maharani of Tunbridge Wells

∾❦∾

*Golders Green Crematorium, London, 9 August 1930*

FOR THE FUNERAL of an empress it was a modest affair. Just two sombre Armstrong-Siddeley limousines followed the gondola-black hearse bearing Ada, Maharani Duleep Singh, last Queen of the Punjab, up through the suburbs of north London on an August day in 1930. The cortège swung into the red-brick court-yard of Golders Green Crematorium, established in the first year of King Edward VII's reign, when burning the dead had at last been made legal. Queen Victoria had abominated the practice, so un-English, so un-Christian. Even now, in polite society, cremation seemed faintly scandalous.

The little party of mourners – the Maharani's daughter and step-daughter, Nurse Spain (the deceased's companion), Mr Harrold Farrer (the loyal family solicitor), a certain Miss Maude and a few neighbours from respectable Madeira Park, Tunbridge Wells – gathered in the funerary chapel built in the style of a Lombardic palace by the architect of Claridge's Hotel. The top-hatted staff of Messrs H. Pink ('complete house-furnisher and undertaker, cremations arranged') bore in the coffin as the Reverend Herbert Trundle said the Anglican obsequies and the boys of the London College of Choristers sang 'Abide With Me'. A little before luncheon, Queen Ada sailed on rollers into the gas-fired flames.

The two princesses, half-sisters Sophia and Pauline, were the chief mourners – elegant under black veils, olive-skinned, still beautiful in mid-life. Sophia Alexdrovna, older by ten years, had been born into grandeur; her nursery was in the great house of one of the finest shooting estates in England, Elveden in Suffolk. The Prince of Wales had patted her long, dark childhood tresses and news of her scholastic progress was regularly sent to Queen Victoria. Pauline had been delivered in a boarding-house in a Moscow midwinter, where their father slept with two dogs growling at the door and a revolver under his pillow for fear of assassination.

The two elder sisters, the princesses Catherine and Bamba, declined to attend their step-mother's funeral. They preferred to forget everything to do with 'Queen' Ada. Princess Bamba loathed her and would go to her own grave believing that Ada Douglas Wetherill was the cause of her beloved father's destruction. Old and frail, she would tell the curious who sought her out in Lahore before her own death just over a quarter of a century later that Ada was all along a British spy.

*The Times*'s obituarist thought it all rather quaint. 'The death of Ada, Maharani Duleep Singh, which took place last Wednesday, severs one of the last personal links with events of early Victorian days,' he wrote. 'She was the widow of the Maharajah Duleep Singh, who as a child of five was placed on the throne of Lahore by the Sikh Khalsa* on the doubtful grounds that he was the son of the famous Maharajah Ranjit Singh.'

*The Times*, ungracious even in death, could not resist implying that the Maharajah was a bastard. The reporter had looked up the cuttings to breathe some fleeting life into the events of long ago. Maharajah Duleep Singh, born Lahore, 6 September 1838, died Paris, 23 October 1893. The files were bulging: furious letters to the editor from the Maharajah demanding 'magnanimity from the great Christian British Empire', toweringly scornful leaders studded with pompous Latin in reply. All this plus a campaign of salacious tales stoked by its long-departed Paris and St Peterburg correspondents to make him look as ridiculous as possible. *The Times* and the Maharajah had never got on. But as a summation of the dolours of the last King of the Lahore, *The Times*'s account was efficient enough.

> On the death in 1839 of Ranjit Singh, the 'Lion of the Punjab', six years of storm and anarchy ensued in the kingdom. Duleep Singh the son of Jindan Kaur, an ambitious dancing girl, was proclaimed Maharajah. The Khalsa compelled Jindan Kaur and her counsellors to authorize the invasion of British territory by crossing the Sutlej river. The first Sikh war

---

* Khalsa: 'The Pure', synonym for both the Sikh national identity and the Sikh Army.

resulted and by the Treaty of Lahore large cessions of territory were made to the British.

The government of the Punjab was to continue in the hands of the youthful Maharajah under the supervision of Sir Henry Lawrence who was appointed Resident. The arrangement did not work satisfactorily, the semi-independent governor of Mooltan revolted and the second Sikh war in 1849 was followed by annexation.

The boy Maharajah was required to resign for himself, his heirs and his successors all rights, title and claim to the sovereignty of the Punjab or to any sovereign power whatsoever.

The deposed Maharajah was placed under the guardianship of Sir John Login of the Bengal Army and brought to this country. All his personal effects and jewels were made over to his guardians and the famous Koh-i-Noor diamond was presented by the East India Company to Queen Victoria.

Duleep Singh was liberally treated, having a pension of five lakhs* of Rupees (then the equal of £50,000) settled on him. He embraced Christianity and purchased a large estate at Elveden in Suffolk and settled down as a country gentleman. On public occasions he appeared in Oriental costume and decorated with magnificent jewels. He married at the British consulate at Alexandria an Egyptian Christian lady by whom he had a large family.

The Maharajah's extravagance necessitated an inquiry into his debts. Seeking permission in the late 'eighties to visit India, he re-entered the Sikh pale and had wild visions of the restoration of his kingdom which were promptly dispelled.

As they went back to their depository in Printing House Square, the yellowing cuttings spoke no more of Ada – no date of birth, no details of parentage, no early life. She had a walk-on part in a minor drama long ago.

But the report still breathes a sense of high imperial indignation over 'wild visions' of a kingdom's restoration and 'ambitious dancing girls' – as if the Indian subjects of the Crown were naughty children

---

* One lakh = 100,000.

prone to excess. Even after ninety years *The Times* had felt it necessary
to point out again that the annexation of the boy Maharajah's kingdom
had been somehow to rescue the natives from their own wickedness.
The reason for making such an implication was on the imperial doorstep in that summer of 1930; India was getting uppity again.

For a month the papers had been full of the imprisonment in Poona
of the troublesome Mr Gandhi after his 'salt march' to the sea. On
5 April, at Dandi beach, the Mahatma and several thousand followers
had picked up crystals of salt left by the waves, symbolically breaking
the government's hated tax-raising monopoly. Within a month the
whole of India was in revolt, newspapers were censored, thousands of
political offenders were gaoled. As Ramsay MacDonald's government
wrung their hands in London, the Maharani's death was a perfect
excuse to reprise years of British self-righteousness about India.

*The Times*'s report concluded: 'The Maharajah's turbulent mother
Jindan Kaur had died in a London suburb in 1863 and his wife, much
troubled by his vagaries, died in 1887. He married two years later,
in Paris, Miss Ada Douglas Wetherill, the lady whose death is now
announced. Her husband died of a paralytic seizure in Paris in 1893
– and in the intervening 37 years his widow has lived a quiet life in
the country . . .'

In the India Office in London, the great department of state from
where the sub-continental empire was effectively run, another file was
being closed and returned to the vaults: Ada Douglas Wetherill, The
Maharani Duleep Singh, born 15 January 1869, at No. 10 Oval Road,
Kennington, Surrey.* She seemed to have done little more exciting
in the last twenty years than ask for a loan to buy a hat shop, but
longer-memoried inhabitants of the Italianate building overlooking
St James's Park might choose to dig deeper – back into the late 1880s
and the leatherbound volumes of the Political and Secret Department,
the London-based intelligence department which kept an eye on the
empire's frontiers and the 'Princely states'. It was then run with exemplary gusto by Sir Owen Tudor Burne and his successor Sir Edward
Bradford who had once been a dashing Indian Army cavalryman until
his left arm was bitten off by a tiger. Aging civil servants might look

---

* Now Kennington Road, Lambeth, south London. Before the establishment of the County
of London in 1888 it was in Surrey. The houses of Oval Road, circumscribing the famous
cricket ground, vanished beneath an LCC housing estate in 1926.

too into the forty-year-old secret dispatches of the Department for the Suppression of Thugee and Dacoity, responsible for sniffing out political crime in India itself, run from Simla, the summer capital set in agreeably cool hills, by another ex-cavalryman, Colonel Philip Durham Henderson.* He too became a dedicated Ada-watcher.

The really knowing bureaucrats might have also amused themselves by reading the voluminous reports of a spy known simply as 'Our Correspondent'. This agent, based in Paris, was obsessive when it came to Ada Wetherill. For three years he wrote breathless dispatches detailing her latest condition to be sent that night in cipher code for the urgent attention of the India Office and Lord Salisbury, who was both Prime Minister and Foreign Secretary.

Ada of the quiet life had posed as the wife of an Irish republican revolutionary, 'Madame Patrick Casey', to outfox British diplomats and embark on a wild railway journey into imperial Russia. She was detained at the border where the Czar's frontier gendarmes thought she was a fortune-teller from a circus.

A Muslim spy in British pay was sent to Cairo to track down her movements: 'The Maharajah intends installing her as the cockney empress of India,' he reported. She was, so it was claimed, the subject of a guru's prophecy that such a thing would come to pass. Queen Victoria was distinctly concerned. To save Her Majesty's sensitivities, she was told that Ada was the 'daughter of an English general officer', but the Queen was shrewd enough to see a different truth.

At least Sir Robert Morier, Her Britannic Majesty's ambassador at St Petersburg, got his facts right when he cabled an urgent dispatch to the Prime Minister on 11 December 1887: 'I may mention that my last news from Moscow establishes that the lady who is living at Billo's Hotel with Duleep Singh ... is English, good looking, aged twenty and *enceinte*.'

Ada was not a walk-on, but the leading actress in 'the most serious danger the British perceived within India in the later 19th century.' Maharani Ada, late of Tunbridge Wells, as I was to discover, was not at all what she seemed. Like so much else in this story.

---

* The original 'Thagi and Dakaiti' department had been formed in 1835 to suppress the Thug strangling cult and dacoits (bandit gangs). In 1877 it was reorganized as a central department of the government of India to collect political and secret intelligence, reporting via the Foreign Secretary. In 1887 it began to be referred to as the 'Special Branch'.

# 2

# The Diamond

## ❦

IT BEGAN, like all good treasure hunts, with a clue: one line, including the misspelled name of a dead princess. I found it, unromantically perhaps, not on an ancient parchment but twinkling on a computer screen in a newspaper office. It said simply: 'Dulecp Singh, Catherine (Princess), last heard of in 1942 living in Penn, Bucks.'

Sunday journalists know the terror of Thursdays: talked-up stories falling down, nothing to write, deadlines looming. In early August 1997, the London media were transfixed by the rumoured romance of Diana, Princess of Wales, and Mr Dodi Fayed. I had little to contribute. That Thursday morning came an electronic deliverance. The Swiss Bankers' Association published a list of names on the Internet. The mysterious Princess Catherine was on it. She was listed among more than 1,800 holders of so-called 'dormant accounts', deposits of cash, valuables and who knew what else, made long ago in the vaults of exquisitely secretive Swiss banks and untouched since the end of the Second World War. The list's publication, the unaccustomed openness, was part of a national Swiss shriving for complicity in bankrolling the Third Reich. The journalistic shorthand was 'Swiss Nazi Gold'. 'Sounds like a radio-station,' said a cynical photographer colleague.

It was an idea for a story. Perhaps I could reunite a family with their inheritance. Claimants had until January 1998 to come forward, their provenance would be assessed by an international committee and, supposedly, eight months later, they would be handed the keys. (In this case, the deadline was to slip substantially.)

First I had to find some living heirs; the original account-holders must surely be dead. The names were theoretically those of Holocaust victims, Jews, enemies of the Reich, individuals who had managed to get their valuables to a place of safety only to be brutally extinguished themselves. In fact, the list was impenetrable, including counts and barons, Spanish fascists, black-marketeers, collaborators, anyone with something to hide. The accounts were 'dormant' for a reason: no one had dared go back to them. The Nazi-hunters at the Jewish Documentation Centre founded by Simon Wiesenthal in Vienna described the list to me as 'an insult'. There were more names of murderers than their victims, they said.

At least fifty named account-holders had last been heard of living in Britain. This was closer to home. I began to dig. There was that one name that intrigued me: 'Dulecp Singh, Catherine (Princess).' Who was she? Why was this Indian-sounding lady living in an English village in wartime? What reason could she have to possess a numbered Swiss bank account and why did she seem to have forgotten about it? The Buckinghamshire telephone directories* for March 1939 disclosed this name: 'Duleep Singh, Princess C. Hilda, Colehatch ho. Penn 2154.' Could the computerizing transcribers of a Swiss bank-clerk's copperplate ledger entry have made a simple spelling mistake?

I rang the local librarian in Buckinghamshire, who searched county records. 'There was a Catherine Duleep Singh, double-e, in the electoral register in the 1930s,' he said. 'She lived at Colehatch House, it's on the village outskirts, then Hilden Hall. Have you tried looking at the wills at Somerset House?'

A leatherbound volume creaked open. ' "Probate granted Llandudno, May 1943" – that's all we need,' said a dusty custodian. A copy of the will arrived, for a fee of 25 pence. It was made in 1935: 'I, Princess Catherine Hilda Duleep Singh desire to be cremated and the ashes buried at Elveden in Suffolk. I give my gold jewellery, my long pearl necklace and my wearing apparel to my sisters Princess Bamba Sophie Jinda Sutherland and Princess Sophia Alexandrowna Duleep Singh.' In a codicil she asked for a quarter of her ashes to be 'buried as near as possible to the coffin of my friend Fraulein Lina Schäfer at the Principal Cemetery at Kassel in Germany'. Who were these exotic characters?

---

* Telephone directories are preserved at the British Library in London.

I searched the wills of the other sisters. The last, Princess Bamba, had died aged eighty-eight in Lahore, Pakistan, in March 1957. She had married but had no children, evidently leaving her worldly goods to her secretary, a Mr Pir Karim Baksh Supra. Could there be no descendant-heirs at all?

There was no mention of a Swiss bank account in Catherine's will, nor in Princess Sophia's (she died in England in August 1948), nor in Bamba's, and nothing that might be deposited in a Zurich vault. But Elveden sounded familiar. It was a country house, once the home of Lord Iveagh, head of the Guinness family – now apparently empty and shuttered. There was a church listed in *Crockford's Clerical Directory*, St Andrew's and St Patrick's. The rector was helpful: 'We think her ashes are here and her father is buried in the graveyard. He was Maharajah Duleep Singh, the last emperor of the Sikhs – the one who gave the Koh-i-Noor diamond to Queen Victoria.'

The Koh-i-Noor, the 'mountain of light', the most celebrated diamond in the world. Wars were fought for it, brother killed brother for it, and ill-luck was supposed to befall any male ruler who wore it. It had been the jewel in the crown of Britain's sovereigns for almost a century and a half. But what of the Indian king who had once owned it, this mysterious Duleep Singh?

'There's a very proper historical trust in the Maharajah's memory,' the rector of Elveden told me, 'run by a Mr Trilok Singh Wouhra.' Mr Wouhra lived in Birmingham. A beneficent, BMW-driving millionaire in his sixties, he met me off the Euston train to entertain me to a Punjabi lunch in his boardroom above a warehouse packed with sacks of rice and jars of spices. What did he think about the Swiss account and could he help me find an heir?

'The discovery of this bank box is very exciting,' Mr Wouhra said. He thought the 'box' might contain jewels, or perhaps the private papers of Princess Catherine's father. Did I know who he was? I confessed I knew little beyond what the rector and a few cuttings had told me.

He outlined the life of Maharajah Duleep Singh. It was the most extraordinary story I had ever heard.

'Now you understand why Sikhs revere their last king,' said Mr Wouhra when he had finished. 'He both loved England and hated her.' It seemed extraordinary, I said, that the Maharajah's children had no children themselves. He had six children with Queen Bamba, the girl he married in Cairo, and two with the 'European he married in Paris', Ada Douglas Wetherill, about whom little seemed to be known.

'Ah yes – why no grandchildren,' he replied. 'That is the curse of the tenth guru.' He outlined a popular myth: the Sikhs' greatest spiritual leader, Guru Gobind Singh, had had a golden box of treasure buried on his death. The line of whoever touched it would 'vanish from the light', the guru is supposed to have prophesied. 'But Ranjit Singh [Duleep Singh's father] dug it up, to build a monument to the holy man. That is why all Duleep Singh's children died childless.' So that was it; there was no heir to open the vault. 'Don't worry,' Mr Wouhra said, 'there will be many, many cousins. Write your story and someone is bound to come forward.'

'Nazi Gold Fortune Awaits the Heirs of Maharajah' ran the headline of my *Sunday Telegraph* story published on 3 August 1997, which summarized the Swiss bank's declaration for claimants to come forward and what little I knew of the family history. It repeated Mr Wouhra's suggestion that the box might contain documents. But if they did prove that Duleep Singh had somehow been defrauded out of his kingdom, where would that leave 150 years of subsequent history? The Punjab was divided between India and Pakistan in 1947 on independence – Lahore on one side of the border, Amritsar on the other. The descendants of the once-ruling family had been brutally driven out along with millions of other Sikh refugees.

Within a few days the story was on the front page of papers all over India. 'Koh-i-Noor in a Swiss Bank vault?' asked the *Lahore Tribune* on 5 August. 'Diplomatic row likely over Duleep's Swiss "box",' proclaimed the *Hindustan Times* a day later, darkly hinting that the British Foreign Office had prior knowledge of my story and were 'concerned' that the Indian government might force the 'deposit safe to be opened'. Pakistan would say it was theirs, the paper reported; even Iran might lay claim to the Koh-i-Noor 'on behalf of the Moghul empire . . . This discovery could lead to war.' This was not my intention. The stories kept rolling in: 'Heir makes demand on Queen Now,' proclaimed the *Indian Express*. 'Indian Prime Minister rejects plea for Koh-i-Noor.' 'Crown Jewel controversy engulfs Königin Elisabeth,' said *Die Welt*.

I had no clue what might be in Princess Catherine's dormant account, whether it was a safe deposit at all. No matter, as far as millions of Sikhs around the world seemed concerned, I had stumbled on the existence of the Maharajah's Box.

There were more letters and faxes. An English woman of tantalizing anonymity wrote to say she had known Princess Bamba in Lahore, Pakistan, shortly before her death. 'She showed me the residue of the Duleep Singh jewels remaining in the family after a century of sale and gifts,' she recalled. 'The magic box was brought from her strong room in her house and as the trays were filled they seemed to my child's eyes the extravagant equivalent of an Aladdin's cave. They may have been small beer to the grand-daughter of the mighty Sikh warrior who, after Indian independence was signing herself "Bamba Shahzadi, Rightful Queen of the Punjab and Kashmir." I suggest the Swiss box contains little more than locks of Duleep Singh's hair.'

'A Pandora's box has been opened,' proclaimed the *Hindustan Times*. 'A host of family descendants will say it's theirs.' The newspaper was right. Mr Wouhra's Birmingham phone began to ring. He listened to his callers on crackly lines from India, and then he got back in touch with me. 'I think we have found some heirs for you. There is a gentleman in Amritsar, a Mr Sandhanwalia, and a princess who lives in Delhi. You might want to meet them . . .'

The story had taken wings. I flew to India as soon as I could.

# 3

# The Heirs

❦

THE FRONTIER MAIL express from Delhi to Amritsar, holy city of the Sikhs, trundled across the north Indian plain for eight hours, pausing sporadically for cows on the line. The battered metallic carriage with its TV-sized darkened windows looked like a 1950s refrigerator. It seemed to get hot or cold at random. At Ludhiana, turbanned railway police in battle order boarded, strewing loaded Sten-guns and vintage Lee-Enfield rifles on the plastic seats as they chatted over mugs of sweet tea. We arrived at Amritsar station at midnight. Pools of yellow light illuminated beggars, holy men and more soldiers. Lahore, the historic capital of the Punjab where so many of the events of this story took place, was twenty miles further up the line. Sealed behind the heavily militarized border with Pakistan, it could have been on the moon.

A swarm of cyclo-rickshaws greeted the train in a backlit haze of two-stroke fumes. A handsome Sikh aged about thirty in a neatly pressed shirt pushed them aside and beckoned me to his tiny Suzuki car. 'I am Gurpartap Singh, a lawyer,' he said. 'The people in Birmingham told me you were coming to meet Mr Sandhanwalia.'

We dined at two in the morning in the Amritsar Ritz, a Soviet-built concrete box – 500 rupees a night. International phone calls were banned, certainly no Internet modems were allowed. 'They can be used by the ISI, the Pakistani Inter-Service-Intelligence,' it was explained. 'There are enemy spies everywhere.'

'Have you read Rattigan?' asked my host.

'*The Browning Version?*'

'Sir John Rattigan, the English judge of the Lahore High Court who compiled the great book on Punjabi customary law a hundred years ago. It is very important in this case – when someone dies childless, his property reverts up the line of ancestry. It is also very common for orphans to be adopted, the elders of the village meet and it is agreed, it all becomes legal – that has happened over and again with Ranjit Singh's descendants. We will talk about it when we meet Mr Sandhanwalia in the morning.'

The bedside phone rang at dawn. 'Is the coast clear?' whispered a well-spoken Indian voice, not my host from the night before. 'You must not be tricked by those cheats from the so-called Maharajah's Trust.'

I descended to find the Ritz hotel's shabby lobby filled with animated men in turbans. My mysterious caller was a thin, elderly man in a baseball cap.

'I am an attorney,' he said. 'The family have asked me translate. Your discovery of the Maharajah's box has caused great excitement,' he said. 'There are many, many false people who want to claim it as for themselves – who will say the Koh-i-Noor is theirs.'

There were. My original host appeared looking sheepish. They argued loudly for ten minutes. 'Did I ever claim the box for myself?' said Gurpartap Singh. 'Tell them, all I wanted to do was help you find the truth – all that these people want is a visa to come to England.'

'Come with us,' said his mysterious rival. 'You will meet the only true heir of the Maharajah.' There seemed little choice.

I bounced through the back-streets of Amritsar on the pillion of a motor-scooter. A pair of Indian Air Force MiG-29 fighters on morning border patrol lit their afterburners, startling a flock of buzzards.

In a breeze-block house on Amritsar's Central Jail Road there waited a very tall, elderly Sikh with a white beard and yellow turban. He spoke no English so his son, Sukhdev Singh, a schoolteacher, translated. 'This is Mr Beant Singh Sandhanwalia,' he said, 'the great-great-grandson of Maharajah Ranjit Singh – and he is claiming the Koh-i-Noor diamond from your Queen.'

The letter of petition which the elderly Sikh had written to Buckingham Palace came straight to the point. 'Your Majesty,' it said, 'with utmost reverence for the Crown, I bring to your kind notice the gravest injustice meted out to my family by your then government. I am the sole legal descendant of the heir to the Lahore Durbar of the late Maharajah Duleep Singh.

'I have requested your most worthy Prime Minister, Mr Tony Blair, for the restoration of our property. I renew my claim to the plume of Guru Gobind Singh, the Golden Throne of Maharajah Ranjit Singh,* the Koh-i-Noor diamond and the treasure and documents which were locked in a Swiss bank vault. Your Majesty is known for righting many a wrong.' The palace stayed silent. When the Queen made a politically turbulent visit to Amritsar in October 1997, the Sandhanwalias were threatened with arrest by the Indian police but managed to present their petition to accompanying British officials. A diplomat said merely that it would be 'looked into'. There was no reply.

Was he serious? 'Very serious,' said his son, who produced a metal chest full of letters from the princesses and a complex pedigree made by a Victorian engraver, continuing in a scrawl of handwriting encompassing thirty generations. Beant Singh Sandhanwalia was certainly the great-grandson of Duleep's cousin Thakur Singh. There was a poignant letter dated 1909 from Duleep's third daughter, Princess Sophia, offering to pay for the education and upbringing of Mr Sandhanwalia's father – a custom that, in the Punjab, amounts to adoption. Indeed, Sophia's will, as well as asking that 'a full band should play the funeral march from Götterdämmerung', left Mr Sandhanwalia's father a small legacy; it also bequeathed £3,500 to the Battersea Dogs' Home.

'I was born in 1926,' the old man said. 'I knew I was from a royal family from very young ... as I grew I hated the Britishers, who wouldn't? But we were helpless and poor. All our lands had been confiscated for Thakur Singh's rebellion. I was a schoolboy at Khalsa college in Amritsar and I loved hunting. I fell from a horse and was unconscious for a week. That was the end of my learning.' He had worked as a truck driver.

As a child, Sandhanwalia had visited the invalid Princess Bamba, Duleep Singh's eldest daughter, in Lahore. 'She was paralysed by a stroke and unable to talk; she just sat there simply staring at me. She gave my father lots of things, a gold watch, silver and gold utensils –

---

* The throne is in the Victoria and Albert Museum in London; the plume or 'kalgi' is missing – many Sikhs believe it is in some secret British collection.

she knew we were the last of the family.' Bamba died in 1957. A neighbour in Lahore Model Town had recorded: 'Old "Princess" Sutherland, widow of an English Army doctor, last descendant of the Maharajah Ranjit Singh, complained she could not get a seat on the bus – when all of the Punjab should have been hers. The old lady spent her days dreaming of her ancestral glory.'

But what, I asked, could be in the Swiss vault? 'We are in complete ignorance,' said the son. 'But Duleep Singh was surrounded by British spies – he would have put his papers in a bank and his last jewels from Lahore, the ones the British never got their hands on, then left it to his daughter without her knowing – that is what we must find.'

Might Duleep Singh really have arranged for his papers to be placed in safe-keeping in a Zurich bank? The Swiss had started the system of anonymous numbered bank accounts in the 1870s to suit the needs of uneasily crowned heads as revolutionaries primed their bombs. He had been one of the richest men in England, prone to reward Drury Lane chorines with admiring emeralds. His will left just £7,328. 7s. 6d. – his family estate encumbered and bankrupt. The money had gone somewhere.

And the Koh-i-Noor diamond? The son was adamant. 'It belongs to us – it is our "Adam", our origin for all Sikhs. We will put it in the Golden Temple at Amritsar; it is a holy relic, and the people will worship it.'

## Delhi, September 1997

The Delhi-bound Boeing 737 took off from Amritsar in shimmering heat, decanting its passengers into the heaving chaos of Indira Gandhi airport ninety minutes later. A driver beckoned me to another tiny white Suzuki, and we were soon heading for an apartment block in the southern suburbs of the capital.

An elegant Sikh woman in a royal-blue sari welcomed me. She introduced herself as Ranjit Kaur, Mr Wouhra's second correspondent, a childhood refugee from the partitioned Punjab. Her air-conditioned apartment was a cool relief after the heat of Amritsar, and full of books on Sikh history. 'I am the great-great-great-granddaughter of

Maharajah Ranjit Singh,' she said as we settled down to a glass of cold beer supplied by a manservant. 'My family were prosperous farmers and traders – with rents from the bazaar in Lahore. I knew we were a royal family; I am descended from Maharajah Sher Singh, the king who was assassinated, and his Queen the Rani Prem Kaur.' She had a family tree to prove it.

There were some dresses in her wardrobe, wrapped in tissue paper. An embroidered jerkin, cut low at the neck, was laid on the bed. It had a fugitive perfumed scent.

'This is from the court of Ranjit Singh,' she said. 'A dancing girl's costume. Look at all that tinsel.' Tinsel? It was encrusted in skeins of pure gold wire and flowed with rivulets of pearls.

'I was never brought up as a princess. We were rich, united and happy. Then came partition in 1947 and we had to get out of Pakistan,' she said. 'We thought we were all going to be massacred. My father had a 1936 Rolls-Royce, a vis-à-vis with passenger seats facing each other. I used to play in it all the time. My grandmother escaped in it, we got out in a truck. Growing up in Lahore, nobody really resented the Britishers. Some of us loved them. My great-grandfather was aide-de-camp to the British Lieutenant-Governor of the Punjab and he was very loyal.' A picture of her forebear in scarlet coat and imperial trappings stood on her sideboard. One of her uncles had visited the court of Queen Victoria in London: 'At the age of ninety he would say to me: "Tell the people who we are – the descendants of Ranjit Singh".'

She offered a vivid account of how her mother had seen Duleep's daughters at first hand. 'My mother, Mohinder, remembered going as a child to the Shalimar gardens outside Lahore some time in the early '20s. Something amazing was happening, two ladies were there, crowds were gathering, shouting wildly: "The princesses, the princesses are here, the daughters of Maharajah Duleep Singh!" It was true – Sophia and Bamba had come home. The British authorities did not like it one bit. Sardars [Sikh noblemen] were weeping openly. "We are with you, we will give you the world," the crowd cried.

'My mother remembered exactly how the princesses looked, one in bottle-green, the other in a maroon sari in fine French georgette, a kind of chiffon, both fringed with gold and precious stones. They wore exquisite traditional Kundan jewels – long earrings of pure gold faced with enamel encrusted with diamonds. My mother cried; they looked so beautiful, our cousins, come here after so many years.

'The princesses cried too. They could not bear it. They could speak no Punjabi; they had to speak through translators with the fine English accents they had been taught. They were cut off from their inheritance, unable even to talk with their people. Then the police broke up the crowd. It was too dangerous, politically. My mother never saw them again.'

Ranjit Kaur paused, then said: 'What if the vault stayed shut? It could have the real story of Maharajah Duleep Singh inside, not the stuff we've had to learn from the British. They took away our kingdom and blamed us for it. They claimed to be the guardian of a little boy then made him sign away all his property. They took the Koh-i-Noor and said it was a gift.'

She gave me an exquisitely illustrated book to bear back to London. It was a window on the wild, baroque kingdom of Lahore on the eve of its destruction exactly 150 years earlier.

# 4

# The Lion

❦

TODAY HE WOULD be a photographer for *National Geographic*, slung with Nikons, bouncing along in a Mahindra jeep. On the eve of photography's invention, an itinerant painter travelled by mule around the 'native' courts of India, capturing his princely subjects in oils.

August Theodor Schoefft, a cheroot-smoking Hungarian, was thirty years old, talented and ambitious. Tired of capturing stuffy Magyar nobles he sought more exotic, perhaps more generous, patrons and in 1838 he arrived, with his wife, in Bombay. He painted the last Mughal emperor, Shah Zafar, in Delhi before toiling with easel and brushes north-westwards towards the fabled Punjab. He was greeted with excitement, filling his notebooks with portraits and sketches of his proud sitters to bear them back to Europe and set them within Canaletto-like depictions of the Punjab's capital and its holy city. His masterpiece, the huge painting the 'Sikh Darbar at Lahore',* was created retrospectively, and at one time hung on the great staircase in Elveden Hall.

Although he had reached the Punjab in 1841, two years after the great Maharajah's death, Schoefft chose to make an outsize scene of the Darbar at its glittering zenith. He depicted Ranjit Singh himself, his princes – Kharak Singh and Sher Singh – his ministers, his grandson Nau Nihal, Hira Singh and the gifted Muslim foreign minister Aziz-ud-din, his European mercenary officers in their sub-Napoleonic magnificence, all gathered for the festival of Dusherra in the marble

---

* Darbar: (Persian) 'doorway to a court' – synonym for government.

*baradari*, the audience pavilion, of Lahore Fort. It looks like a high-Hollywood film poster. When Herr Schoefft's painting was unveiled it was the sensation of the Vienna salon of 1855. By then the epic was over, the cast swept away by treachery, murder and war, the Kingdom of Lahore itself extinguished.

Scholars have interpreted the painting as much more than a gorgeous crowd scene. Its groupings and spatial relationships show the jealousies that would tear the Punjab court apart. Rivals for the succession stare each other down or cluster conspiratorially. Cavalrymen muster behind their ambitious general. 'The artist deliberately composed the picture to reflect the paradox inherent in the Sikh kingdom,' wrote an art historian, 'the circumstances under which Muslims and Hindus served a Sikh Maharajah which the Sikhs themselves could not rival. Their loyalty attached to his person only.'

The artist made another posthumous painting showing Ranjit Singh having the *Granth* (book of scriptures) read to him at Amritsar. Smaller in scale, spectacular in its depiction of the temples and palaces of the holy city reflected in the great reservoir, it is also filled with metaphor. The Maharajah sits on a cushion, the Koh-i-Noor diamond set in an amulet in his right arm. Beside him are his favourite courtier, Hira Singh, and his eldest son and heir to the throne, Kharak Singh, who also sit as a mark of privilege. Sher Singh, the Maharajah's ambitious second son (whose legitimacy was never fully acknowledged in Ranjit's lifetime) stands behind them, partly obscured. A group of Akalis, guardians of the temple, look on suspiciously. A boy-child plays with a hawk in the foreground.

By the time August Schoefft made his reverential royal family snapshot, in Vienna around 1850, three of the principles in the composition had been murdered, the boy-child (interpreted by some scholars as Duleep Singh, although the painter must have altered his age) was an exile, and the great diamond was in new ownership. 'The break-up of the Punjab will probably begin with murder,' Lord Ellenborough, the Governor-General of India told the Duke of Wellington on the eve of the catastrophe, 'it is their way.' Thus it was.

Maharajah Ranjit Singh, the 'Lion of the Panjab', died of a stroke in his capital on 28 June 1839. He went to his funerary pyre borne in a golden ship 'amid his people's lamentations. Four of Ranjit's

Queens* elected to burn alive with their dead husband. Five slave-girls accompanied them into the flames in the act of sati. The Sanskrit word means 'perfect wife'.

The unified kingdom was his creation. With its conquered provinces of Jammu and Kashmir, the Sikh Empire stretched in a broadening triangle from the baking plains of Sind at its apex to the Khyber Pass in the north and the foothills of the Himalayas in the north-east. Its long southern flank on the Sutlej river faced British India. It would outlast its creator by barely ten years before being swallowed in digestible chunks by an empire of greater ambition.

Duleep Singh, the Maharajah's fourth acknowledged son, was born on 6 September 1838, of Rani Jindan, a favourite dancing-girl, a Punjabi from Gujeranwala. She was twenty-one, the sexually precocious daughter of a kennel-keeper. There were great rejoicings at the birth: 'When the Sirdar sat, surrounded by his warriors and nobles, when the court bards chanted shabads, guns boomed, bands played, and the ladies in the palace joyously sang.'

Nine months later Ranjit Singh lay paralysed and speechless. He gestured to his priests to give his greatest treasure, the Koh-i-Noor diamond, as penitent alms to the Hindu temple of Jagannath. The worldlier courtiers demurred. 'Three times the name of God was spoken in his ear – he repeated it twice with his lips and his soul departed.'

The cremation took place the following day. Double ranks of black-clad infantrymen lined the capital's streets. 'The corpse of the late Maharajah, placed upon a splendidly gilt car, constructed in the form of a ship, with sails of gilt cloth to waft him into paradise, was borne upon the shoulders of soldiers, preceded by a body of native musicians, playing their wild and melancholy airs,' recorded William Osborne, a British emissary to Lahore.

The royal widows were carried behind in gilded chairs, each preceded by a large mirror and a golden parasol, symbols of their rank. The slaves walked. The Maharajah's elder sons and the nobles of the court followed in white robes, bare-footed. The women were to burn

---

* According to Duleep Singh's own account given to a French newspaper in 1889, his father had forty-four acknowledged wives by the time of his death. His entourage also included his favourite catamites and Kashmiri dancing-girls; he maintained a whole royal bodyguard of them, attired in tinselly armour and armed with pretty toy bows.

in the act of self-immolation on the funerary pyre of a dead husband that the otherwise reforming Sikh religion had carried from its Brahminic root.* There was no coercion, a widow would elect to die in the flames; it was the gateway to paradise.

'Four wives, all very handsome, burned themselves with his body, as did five of his Cachmerian slave girls, one of whom, who was called the Lotus, or Lily, I often saw last year in my first visit to Lahore,' recorded Osborne writing in July 1839. 'Everything was done to prevent it, but in vain. They were guaranteed in their rank and in all their possessions, but they insisted upon it; and the accounts from the European officers who were present, described it as the most horrible sight.

'The four wives seated themselves on the pile with Ranjit Singh's head upon their laps; and his principal wife desired Kharak Singh, Ranjit's son and heir, and Dhian Singh, Prime Minister, to come to her upon the pile, and made the former take the Maharajah's dead hand in his own, and swear to protect and favour Dhian Singh as Ranjit Singh had done.'

The men departed the pyre as the nine women made a canopy of Kashmiri shawls around themselves. Wild drumming rose. Ghee and sulphur had been applied to the sandalwood to fuel the pyre into a superheated fireball and consume the bodies. Opiates were another mild mercy. 'The favoured wife set fire to the pile with her own hands, and they are dead – nine living beings having perished together without a shriek or a groan.' The next day Kharak Singh, an 'imbecile with a passion for opium', was proclaimed Maharajah.

Rani Jindan chose not to burn alive. She had the ten-month Duleep Singh to protect and his cause to advance. She had no doubt it was her son who was born to be king. In a few years' time she must find him a suitable bride.

For the rulers of British India the death of the Great Maharajah was of more than peripheral concern. For over thirty years the powerful homogeneous state he had forged in the north-west, the historic overland invasion route since Alexander the Great (the European

* Sati was made illegal in the East India Company's dominions in 1829. It was proscribed in the Punjab in 1847 by the British resident in Lahore acting in the name of the boy-king Duleep Singh.

22

conquerors came by sea), had been of signal strategic utility. Ranjit Singh had signed a treaty of friendship with the Honourable East India Company in 1806; three years later the Treaty of Amritsar sealed 'perpetual friendship between the British Government and the State of Lahore'. The spectre had arisen (not for the last time) of a Franco-Russian invasion of India which, mounted through Asia Minor, must knock on the door of the Punjab. That threat faded when Napoleon turned on his ally to reach for Moscow itself, but thereafter, just as the British had a powerful ally bottling up the mountain tribes of Afghanistan, so the Lion had had a free hand to push his own frontiers into the high, fruitful valleys of Jammu and Kashmir.

The Sikh Empire had grown into an independent state of conspicuous wealth and power. Its army, tutored by mercenary officers – Prussian, French, American and Spanish – had become the most formidable fighting machine outside British India. With Ranjit Singh dead it began to look dangerous. Scarlet-coated emissaries to Lahore had already begun to note the Khalsa's strengths and weaknesses, the number of men needed to subdue it, the invasion routes, the river crossings, potential collaborators . . .

In that diffident way British India was assembled – an opportunistic treaty of protection here, a punitive expedition there – as the infant Duleep gurgled in the Zenana, the Punjab looked ripe for another casual takeover. All that was needed was an excuse. The Sikhs themselves would provide it.

# The Governor-General

⚜

*Reading Room, British Museum, London, March 1882*

VISITORS TO the British Museum in the spring months of the early 1880s would have seen an unusual figure striding purposefully each morning from his carriage to a particular desk in the great circular reading room. Scholars toiled in the library's daylit quadrants as an Indian gentleman turned obsessively to the so-called 'Punjab Papers' – the collection of correspondence and government documents which dealt with the two Anglo-Sikh wars and the final annexation of the Punjab in 1849. A turbanned servant scribbled furiously beside him, transcribing Prinsep's *History of the Sikhs* and Bosworth Smith's *The Life of Sir Henry Lawrence*. Maharajah Duleep Singh wanted his childhood back. What had happened to him?

He wrote eagerly to Queen Victoria of his Bloomsbury epiphany. 'Had I been aware, My Sovereign, of the true state of things, the knowledge of which was carefully kept from me by the late Sir John Login, a creature of Lord Dalhousie,* a very different provision both for the maintenance of myself and my children would have been made.

'But even now I do not despair as having by accident discovered providentially preserved the official dispatches connected with the Punjab in their entirety at the British Museum and feeling certain that Your Majesty at the head of this great nation will cause justice to be done to me some day or other.'

---

* James Andrew Brown Ramsay, 1st Marquis of Dalhousie, Governor-General of India 1848–56. For narrative purposes I have included material in this chapter from *Private Letters of the Marquess of Dalhousie* (Edinburgh, 1910) as well as from *Papers Relating to the Punjab 1847–1849 Presented to both Houses of Parliament by order of Her Majesty, May 1849*.

Like the litigants in the interminable Dickensian chancery court case, *Jarndyce* v. *Jarndyce*, the Maharajah believed he was the victim of a monstrous injustice, inflicted upon him as a child. Now, so he thought, he had the means to prove it.

Buoyed up by his discoveries in the reading room, on 28 August 1882 he wrote a voluminous letter to the editor of *The Times*.

'Sir, As the era of doing justice and restoration appears to have dawned, judging from the recent truly liberal and noble act of the present Liberal Government, headed now by the great Gladstone the Just, I am encouraged to lay before the British Nation, through the medium of The Times, the injustice which I have suffered.'

The Maharajah précised the events of his childhood as he now saw them. 'When I succeeded to the throne of the Punjab, I was only an infant and the Khalsa soldiery, becoming more and more mutinous and overbearing during both my uncle's and my mother's regencies, at last crossed the Sutlej and attacked the friendly British Power; and was completely defeated and entirely routed by the English Army,' he wrote.

'Had, at this time, my dominions been annexed to the British territories, I would have now not a word to say, for I was that time an independent chief at the head of an independent people, and any penalty which might have been then inflicted would have been perfectly just. But that kind, true English gentleman, the late Lord Hardinge, in consideration of the friendship which had existed between the British Empire and the "Lion of the Punjab", replaced me on my throne, and the diamond Koh-i-noor on my arm. (*Vide* PUNJAB PAPERS at the British Museum).'

The Maharajah had certainly got his facts right thus far. Sir Henry Hardinge, grizzled veteran of the Napoleonic wars, had arrived at Calcutta as Governor-General in 1844. There was the bogey of supposed French military intrigues in the Punjab to deal with, but far more serious was the descent into murderous chaos of the warrior state on the north-west border of British India which had followed the death of Ranjit Singh.

Kharak Singh, the 'imbecile Maharajah', had lasted fifteen months, deposed and poisoned by his wife Chand Kaur and son Nau Nihal Singh acting in collusion. The new reign spanned one day. Nau Nihal Singh was crushed by a conveniently falling parapet while returning from his father's cremation. The Rani and her supporters, the Sandhanwalia clan, were soon under siege in Lahore Fort with Ranjit's second son, Sher Singh, at the head of a vengeful, turbulent army camped at the gates.

The Rani was promptly dislodged. Sher Singh with the Khalsa's backing was placed on the golden throne in January 1841. The anglophile Maharajah, who liked to collect English musical-boxes, shrewdly gave the Sikh troops two years back pay. Chand Kaur got a different reward: she was crushed to a pulp in her bath by rock-wielding slave-girls. The profitless Sandhanwalia clan and their ambitious young chieftain Ajit Singh sulked and plotted.

On the 'crimson day', 15 September 1843, Sher Singh was watching wrestlers in the garden at the Shah Bilaal. Ajit Singh Sandhanwalia (who had been sent into exile for supporting Chand Kaur, and then allowed back after British lobbying) approached him with a presentation double-barrelled pistol and shot him dead through the chest. His twelve-year-old son Partap Singh was slashed to pieces in the gardens outside minutes later. Rajah Dhian Singh, the Vizir, was promptly cut down outside Lahore Fort. The murderous Ajit Singh Sandhanwalia shut himself up in the citadel and declared the infant Duleep to be king with himself as First Minister.

His tenure did not last long. The slain Vizir's heir, Hira Singh, exacted swift revenge. The moment before his mother hurled herself into her husband's funeral pyre, Hira Singh placed the heads of the assassins at the sati-garlanded widow's feet. The Lahore bloodbath overflowed. Hira Singh was in turn cut down by agents of Queen Jindan's brother Jawahir Singh while fleeing laden with treasure to the hills of Jammu.

At last in December 1844 Rani Jindan became regent, guarding her son as each Borgia-like demise brought him closer to the throne. She declared her brother as Vizir. According to a salacious English account: 'The Rani's mind had become seriously affected by her profligacy; from being clever and lively, she had become stupid and imbecile. The Sardar and his low favourites, each supplied with a bottle of brandy, set out on an excursion. They returned drunk, and sent for dancing girls – and Jawahir Singh, emulating the worst traditions of Rome in its decline, dressed himself as a dancing girl.'

The Khalsa army bided its time until the Vizir was implicated in

the death of Peshaura Singh, another of Ranjit's sons. The consequences were recorded by an American eye-witness:*

> Jawahir Singh was summoned before the army. He came out
> on an elephant, holding in his arms his nephew, the young
> Maharajah Duleep Singh. The Maharani Jindan accompanied
> him on another elephant. Jawahir Singh had an escort of 400
> horsemen, and two elephant-loads of rupees with which to
> tempt the army.
>
> Duleep Singh was received with royal honours: his mother,
> the Maharani Jindan, in miserable terror for her brother, was
> seated on her golden howdah dressed in white Sikh clothes
> and closely veiled.
>
> As soon as the procession reached the middle of the line,
> one man came forward and cried out, 'Stop.' A tremor ran
> through the host: many expected a rescue on the part of the
> French brigade.†
>
> The Military Council was still sitting on the right of the line.
> Four battalions were now ordered to the front, and removed
> Jawahir Singh's escort. Then another battalion marched up
> and surrounded the elephants of the royal personages. The
> Rani's elephant was ordered to kneel down, and she herself
> was escorted to a small tent.
>
> The Rani was dragged away, shrieking to the army to spare
> her brother. Jawahir Singh was next ordered to descend from
> his elephant. A tall Sikh slapped his face and took the boy
> from his arms, asking him how he dared to disobey the Khalsa.
> Duleep Singh was placed in his mother's arms, and she, hiding
> herself behind the walls of her tent, held the child up above
> them in view of the army, crying for mercy for her brother in
> the name of her son. She flung the child away in an agony of
> grief and rage . . . he was caught by a soldier.
>
> A soldier had gone up the ladder placed by Jawahir Singh's
> elephant, stabbed him with his bayonet, and flung him upon

---

* Alexander Haughton Gardner (1785–1877), an American adventurer, joined Ranjit Singh's
army as an artillery officer in 1832. He was banished to Kashmir by the Council of Regency
in 1845. His memoirs are full of drama but many commentators regard them as flights of
the imagination.
† Khalsa troops commanded by the French mercenary officers.

the ground, where he was despatched in a moment with fifty more.

For weeks afterwards Jindan wandered accompanied by her slave-girls through the streets of the capital with 'long dishevelled hair' to weep at her brother's samadh (funerary monument). The Lahore court became deeper coiled in its licentious camarilla. After her recovery, Jindan had taken as a lover Lal Singh, son of a Brahmin shop-keeper the new Vizir, whose name had been drawn by lots by Duleep's chubby fingers. Mangala, her favourite slave-girl, functioned as 'minister of pleasure and riot' (a British description from 1888). Within the Khalsa, the *Panches* – the pious, puritanical elected military committees – in between slashing disapproved-of vizirs to pieces, maintained a discipline which General Monck would have recognized. They looked with deepening disgust at the Lahore debauch.

The pleasure-seekers in the palace had the means to continue the revels. The Khalsa could be distracted by an enemy at the gates – the British Army which was conveniently piling up military pressure on the border. The Vizir and Tej Singh, nominal commander-in-chief of the army, embarked on a baroque conspiracy. They secretly corresponded with the buccaneering British political agent, Major George Broadfoot, established just across the frontier at Ludhiana, to engender a war they knew they would lose. Thus the Khalsa would be cowed. In return the conquerors would make them rulers of a dependent kingdom.

The plot worked. British troops decamped from Ambala on 6 December and marched towards the frontier. In Lahore, Lal Singh, clad in knightly armour, exhorted the Khalsa committees to act like warriors. The first Sikh patrols crossed the Sutlej on 12 December, the great elephant-drawn artillery train four days later. They were advancing into what, on the treaty-drawn map at least, was nominally their own territory – the 'Cis-Sutlej Sikh states'. Sir Henry Hardinge immediately declared them forfeit but still seemed doubt-ridden. 'Will the people in England consider this an actual invasion of our frontier and a justification for war?' he asked a young political officer. The sought-for war had come.

The first encounter was at Mudki. The Sikh Army was led by Lal Singh who swiftly vanished from the field. In a battle fought by dim starlight, the losses were heavy on both sides. A British general was killed. At Ferozshar on 21 December 1845, the Khalsa were entrenched behind elaborate fortifications (their artillery and engineering skills were exemplary) and mauled an assaulting British division. Tej Singh arrived at dawn with the Sikh reserve but ordered them to stand in their saddles. The regimental commanders cursed but obeyed. It was a situation unique in military history; a battle against invaders by a proud army led by commanders who sought nothing more than their own defeat. The Khalsa were subsisting on raw carrots, their powder and shot locked up in the arsenal of the capital. The British (or those of them who knew) were laughing up their scarlet sleeves.

A delegation of 500 soldiers from the *Panches* were dispatched to Lahore to demand food and ammunition. Little Duleep peeped fearfully from a chair set before his mother's purdah screen as wild-eyed soldiers prowled the palace.

'Give us powder and shot,' the delegates demanded. Jindan rolled up her petticoat and threw it over the screen crying, 'Wear that, you cowards. I'll go in trousers and fight myself.' The effect was electric. The deputation shouted: 'Duleep Singh Maharajah! We shall go and die for his kingdom and the Khalsa.'

They died by the thousand. The finale came on 10 February 1846 at Sobraon, a heavily fortified village on the east side of the Sutlej linked to the Punjab bank by a bridge of boats. Emissaries from the conspirators had already imparted the layout of the Sikh entrenchments. When General Sir Hugh Gough's artillery began a two-hour bombardment, the conspirators fled. The Sikh Army was routed. As the broken regiments fled back, the pontoon collapsed. British gunners switched from rampart-pounding ball-shot to man-killing grape and canister. The floundering survivors were flayed in the river-bed. The Sutlej foamed with blood. Lord Hardinge (he was made a viscount after Sobraon) wrote of the Sikh enemy: 'Few escaped, none of it may be said surrendered.' The battle was hailed in London as an 'Indian Waterloo'. Two hundred and fifty captured Sikh howitzers were dragged by elephant in triumph all the way to Calcutta. The British entered Lahore ten days later.

Seven Sikh chiefs, including Tej Singh and Lal Singh, signed the two Treaties of Lahore on 9 and 11 March 1846. Jammu and Kashmir were to be dismembered from the Punjab and granted to the slippery

Dogra* Rajah Gulab Singh in return for 68 lakhs of rupees (he took the money from the Lahore treasury) and a British force was to be stationed in the capital.

A council of regency was to be established, consisting of the eight elders at court. The British pressed further for a resident to be installed at its head and given wide powers – a move fought vociferously by Rani Jindan. But now she could only hiss in rage. The powers of the Mai Sahiba (Queen Mother) to seduce or cajole her opponents by hurling her undergarments had been extinguished. By the Treaty of Bhyrowal, signed on 16 December, everything was granted. The British government became the sole guardian of the person and property of the boy-king – a plump, pampered puppet, wide eyes blinking beneath a turban dripping with gems.

Toiling over the Punjab Papers in the British Museum over thirty years later, the Maharajah's childhood memories returned in a rush of colour and sounds: the terrors of the 'crimson day', his mother padding fearfully through the Shish Mahal, the glass palace. They were mixed with a dreamlike recall of absolute indulgence. 'We have heard from Punjabi gentlemen who had seen him in England that he had forgotten nothing of his early life,' the *Lahore Tribune* reported many years later. 'He loved to talk of the old days and his eyes were often filled with tears as he spoke of his playmates, his favourite horses and his own gorgeously uniformed regiment of infantry, consisting of the cadets of the noblest houses in the Punjab.'

Duleep's letter to *The Times* picked up at this point in his story:

> The Council of Regency, which had been created to govern the country during my minority, finding that it was not in their power to rule the Punjab unaided, applied for assistance to the representative of the British Government, who after stipulating for absolute power to control every Government department, entered into the Bhyrowal Treaty with me, by which was guaranteed that I should be protected on my throne until I attained the age of sixteen years, the British also

* *Dogra*: Hindus from the hills between Punjab and Kashmir. Gulab Singh's Dogra descendants remained rulers of the largely Muslim Jammu and Kashmir until partition in 1947. Incorporation into Pakistan was vetoed.

furnishing troops both for the above object and preservation of peace in the country, in consideration of a certain sum to be paid to them annually by my Durbar, for the maintenance of that force.

Thus the British nation, with open eyes, assumed my guardianship, the nature of which is clearly defined in a proclamation subsequently issued by Lord Hardinge's orders on the 20th of August, 1847, which declares 'that the tender age of the Maharajah Duleep Singh causes him to feel the interest of a father in the education and guardianship of the young prince' [*Vide* PUNJAB PAPERS].

If the young Duleep was now a ward of the British government, what was his mother's role? The Maharajah ploughed on furiously through the musty papers in the reading room, finding Lord Hardinge's description of his own first act of rebelliousness, and of the day the soldiers came to take the Mai Sahiba away.

The Sikh war was won. It was time to reward the treacherous Tej Singh.* Colonel Sir Henry Montgomery Lawrence, the newly installed British resident, proposed making him a Rajah. The ceremony was fixed for 7 August 1847 in the Tuklitgah ('the place of the throne') of Lahore Fort. The resident reported what happened: 'All went off well, except for a momentary check, occasioned by the refusal of the Maharajah to make the saffron "teeka" on the Sirdar's forehead. At first I thought it might be dislike to wet his finger in the saffron paste, but when he was begged to comply, His Highness folded his arms and shrank back into his velvet chair.' Colonel Lawrence was surprised, as the boy, 'for an hour before had been affable and good humoured . . . sending for singing birds from his play-room to show us. There cannot be any doubt that the young Maharajah had been carefully schooled by his mother, not to take part in the ceremonies,' he concluded. 'I look for no contentment for the Maharani – money is not enough for her, she must have power, and free scope to satisfy her lusts.'

---

* Tej Singh received a British pension and died in 1862, but the vizir, Lal Singh, objected to the British-engineered transfer of Kashmir to the newly-raised 'Maharajah' Gulab Singh of the Dogra clan and ordered the province's Muslim governor to resist. The British resident in Lahore sent troops to enforce the deal, put Lal Singh on trial, found him guilty and in December 1846 exiled him from the Punjab.

Sir Henry Hardinge agreed. 'He is a very fine little fellow and grows more intelligent every day,' he wrote. 'There is a general feeling amongst the Council and Sardars that these systematic efforts on the Maharani's part in training up the child to counteract the Government and make him hate all the chiefs who deprived her of power as regent, can only be prevented by separating the mother from the son.'

Hardinge was not the first or the last to perceive Jindan as a malign influence on her son. The 'Lahore news-writers' began a campaign of besmirchment. She was a libertine who, at the age of thirteen, had bewitched the old Maharajah while pleasuring half the court and the stable-hands besides with the sexual athleticism of a Roman empress. When her lover Lal Singh was exiled, she called for portraits of the British garrison officers with a view to a matrimonial alliance. She took a particular interest in one, declaring 'he must be a lord'. Old India hands were reading these saucy accounts of the 'Messalina of the Punjab' (Lord Hardinge's coining) years later with undimmed excitement.

The news-writers' work had a two-fold purpose: to damn Jindan politically and imply Duleep was not Ranjit Singh's legitimate heir. A salacious contemporary pamphlet, 'The Reigning Family of Lahore', recorded: 'The young lady was brought to Lahore to enliven the night scenes in the palace ... her business being to put to shame all, both men and women, who were in any degree less depraved or less shameless than herself.

'Numerous were the amours in which she was now engaged, some with, others without the knowledge and consent of the Maharajah. To detail her affairs would be an outrage on common decency; suffice it then to say, that Runjeet actually encouraged the amours of this woman, who passed as his wife, with a person known as Gulloo Moskee – formerly a bhisti [water carrier] of the palace – and that in nine or ten months afterwards the present Maharajah Duleep Singh was born.'

Sir Henry returned to the business at hand: getting rid of her. Soon after the throne-room indignities he wrote:

> The half measures of restricting the Ranee to the Palace and the gardens according to Eastern custom, would not answer the end in view. But to deport Ranjit Singh's widow across the Sutlej, and the mother of the prince to be denied all access to

her son for this exercise of her spite in affronting those whom she considers her enemies, would, if made the sole ground of her expulsion from Lahore, savour of injustice. Last November, I stated that the Ranee must be deprived of all power, and there can be no doubt that it is for the Boy's interest that he should be withdrawn from the evil example of his mother which is too notorious to require any comments. Her power of obstructing the Government by constantly making the mind of the Boy to hate those who are endeavouring to save the Raj must be effectively prevented.

It is a measure more required for the welfare of the Boy under British guardianship than for the convenience of the Government – although in this respect a deposed Regent in the Eastern court, known to be bold and clever woman, would at any time be a serious obstacle. She is the person towards whom all eyes are directed who wish for change and think it may be brought about by a person of her well known experience in acts of astute intrigue.

Sir Henry Lawrence had his mandate and, on 9 August 1847, he locked Jindan in the Samman Tower of Lahore Fort. There was no trial; she was a 'political offender'. She wrote impassionately to her gaoler: 'I had entrusted my head to your care. You have thrust it under the feet of traitors. You have kept no regard of the friendship of the Maharajah. You have caused me to be disgraced. You have not even remained true to treaties and agreements. Rajah Lal Singh was true and faithful to me. He was loyal. Having levelled charges against him, you sent him away.

'Myself, the Maharajah and twenty-two maidservants are imprisoned in the Samman. All other servants have been dismissed. We are in a very helpless condition. Even water and food are not allowed to come in. Now that you persecute us in this way, it is better that you hang us instead.'

Ten days later the moment came. Jindan was 'pulled out by her hair' and Duleep was led away to the groves of the Shalimar Garden a few miles outside the city. That night his mother was spirited from her capital to the fortress of Sheikhupura. According to dispatches in the Punjab Papers, he reacted to the separation with 'complete indifference'. He would not see her again for thirteen and a half years.

Jindan wrote imploringly to Sir Henry Lawrence: 'You have snatched my son from me. For ten months I kept him in my womb. Then I brought him up with great difficulty. In the name of God you worship, and in the name of the king whose salt you eat, restore my son to me, I cannot bear the pain of this separation.

'My son is very young. He is incapable of doing anything. I have left the kingdom. I have no need of kingdom. There is no one with my son. He has no sister, no brother. He has no uncle, senior or junior. His father he has lost. To whose care has he been entrusted?'

As he completed his education in the gloom of late-Victorian London, two ideas came to obsess the Maharajah. They smacked more of mid-life hubristic greed than the motivations that psychologists might ascribe to an infant torn from his mother. First he had been bundled off his throne in return for a pension but had been short-changed. Second, the private property of the 'subverted dynasty of the Singhs' – the salt-mines, the estates, the *jagirs* (rental income from agricultural estates) – had been pocketed by the government or by the offspring of avaricious rival ranis.

Lord Hardinge, it seemed, was blameless in the Maharajah's eyes. The story had one towering villain of the deepest black: James Andrew Brown Ramsay, Tenth Earl and First Marquis of Dalhousie, the Governor-General of India 1848–56.

The fate of the independent Punjab was effectively sealed when, in January 1848, the thirty-six-year-old Dalhousie stepped ashore at Bombay as newly appointed Governor-General, the youngest in the history of British India. Railway-builder, modernizer and annexationist, his vision of his dominion's bounds did not stop at the Sutlej river.

In April 1848 Dewan Mulraj, governor of the south-western district of Multan, had risen in revolt in the cause of the exiled Queen Mother. Two English officers were killed by an angry mob. No British troops were sent to restore order (as they should have been under the Treaty) because of the 'approaching hot weather'. The delay was cynical. The turbulence spread. On 15 May, Jindan, 'the rallying point of rebellion' as the new resident at Lahore, Sir Frederick Currie, called her, was again abstracted from confinement and bundled out of the Punjab altogether to Chunar Fort in the United Provinces. In August, Chutter Singh Attariwala, governor of Hazara district, was accused by the British resident, Captain Abbot, of 'conspiring to expel the British forces from Lahore'. A month later Chutter Singh's son, Rajah Sher Singh, raised the Sikh standard against the 'oppression, tyranny and violence of the *feringhees* [foreigners]'. Lord Dalhousie saw his opportunity.

On 9 November 1848 the British Army crossed the Sutlej for the second time.

The Maharajah had been old enough to remember vividly what happened next. He was in Lahore Fort guarded by red-coated soldiers of the 53rd Regiment of Foot when the banners and bugles of the main British force arrived at the Akbari Gate, sixty-nine-year-old General Lord Gough at the column's head. The Irish-born veteran of the Peninsular War (he too had been made a viscount after Sobraon) admitted later that he did not know 'whether he was at peace or war or who it is we are fighting for'.

Was he there to topple Duleep or to put down his rebellious subjects? The boy-king squeaked with excitement at the sight of the scarlet ranks. They had come to save him. Seventeen Sikh cannon boomed a salute of welcome from Lahore Fort on the resident's orders. Sweetmeats and garlands were presented to the smiling English soldiers as they quietly took over the city, bayonets fixed to their Enfield muskets.

In London there was intense political unease. Dalhousie damned the faint-hearts in Whitehall wringing their hands with guilt. 'There are many objections,' he wrote in December 1848, 'but the minority of the Maharajah is the feeblest. That old women and young ladies should say "poor little fellow" is all very well ... it is inconceivable that such a principle [the Maharajah's minority] should be recognised in the case of Duleep Singh – a child notoriously surreptitious, a brat begotten of a Bhisti and no more the child of old Ranjit Singh than is Queen Victoria.'

Duleep was a bastard, said Dalhousie. The 'Lahore news-writers' and the salacious pamphleteers were right. Many years later, the Maharajah was more charitable towards his nemesis. 'Finding only a helpless child to deal with, and the temptation being so strong, Lord Dalhousie annexed the Punjab,' wrote Duleep in his letter to *The Times*. 'Instead of carrying out the solemn compact entered into by the British Government at Bhyrowal; his Lordship sold almost all my personal, as well as all my private property, consisting of jewels, gold and silver plate, even some of my wearing apparel and household furniture, and distributed the proceeds, amounting as prize money among those very troops who had come to put down a rebellion against my authority.

'If one righteous man was found in the two most wicked cities of the world, I pray God that at least one honourable, just, and noble Englishman may be forthcoming out of this Christian land of liberty and justice to advocate my cause in Parliament, otherwise what chance have I of obtaining justice, considering that my despoiler, guardian, judge, advocate, and my jury is the British nation itself?'

*The Times* puffed itself up in scornful response in its editorial, run the same day as the Maharajah's broadside:

> We print elsewhere a somewhat singular letter from the Maharajah Duleep Singh. He puts forward an impassioned plea for the consideration of his claims. On a first glance, his letter reads as if he demanded nothing less than to be replaced on the throne of the Punjab.
>
> His real object, however, is far less ambitious. It is to prefer a claim for a more generous treatment of his private affairs at the hands of the Indian Government. All that he has hitherto succeeded in obtaining from the Indian Government is an arrangement, lately sanctioned by Act of Parliament, whereby he will receive an addition of £2,000 to his annual income on condition that his estates are sold at his death in order to liquidate his liabilities, and provide for his widow and children. It is really against this arrangement that the Maharajah appeals.
>
> If his pecuniary claims were settled to his satisfaction, he would doubtless be content, and more than content, to die, as he has lived, an English country gentleman, with estates swarming with game. For a long time he preferred a claim for the Koh-i-noor, of which he alleged that he had been wrongfully despoiled. Now it is his private estates in India which he declares have been confiscated without adequate compensation.
>
> The Maharajah's claim of sovereignty is merely intended to

cover his claim for money. An argument which starts from the sovereign claims of the son of the 'Lion of the Punjab,' ends, somewhat ridiculously, though not without a touch of pathos, with the sorrows of the Magnificent Squire of Elveden.

It is, no doubt, the duty of every man to live within his income and yet if the Maharajah has failed to acquire a virtue rare indeed among Eastern princes there is no Englishman but would feel ashamed if he or his descendants were thereby to come to want.

The Magnificent Squire of Elveden could only fume with rage. He returned to his labours in the reading room. The dispatches of the dead marquis (he had died of cancer in 1860) regarding the second Anglo-Sikh war and its denouement were the final stations of the Maharajah's *via dolorosa*.

# 6

# The Fall

*The Punjab, January–March 1849*

'UNWARNED BY PRECEDENT, uninfluenced by example, the Sikh nation has called for war – on my word, sirs, they shall have it,' Lord Dalhousie told his officers on 10 October 1848. The second Sikh war followed the line of the first, but this time the Khalsa's commanders were not plotting their own army's destruction. The British Army marched out of Lahore, leaving the boy-king with a bodyguard of cavalry. On 16 November 1848, General Gough led his forces across the Ravi, the second finger on the hand of the five rivers.

On 13 January 1849, at Chillianwala, Gough's troops collided with Sher Singh's forces and were soundly beaten. The British lost 2,331 men in a morning. In London, the eighty-four-year-old Duke of Wellington offered to go to India to repeat his successes half a century earlier against the Mahrattas. A week later Multan, where the rebellion had begun, fell to the British besiegers after a mortar shell ignited the defenders' powder magazine. The resident in Lahore ordered a twenty-one-gun salute to greet the victory over the rebels. The end came at the battle of Gujrat on 21 February 1849. A huge artillery duel smashed the Sikh gun line. The British infantry assault was driven in with intense bravery. The Khalsa broke and was extinguished.

On 12 March at Rawalpindi, Sher Singh and 16,000 survivors kissed their swords and placed them reverently on the earth. They were marched into Ferozepore camp, 1,000 at a time, and laid down their firearms as they passed between the lines of British troops. Forty-one artillery pieces were captured. Dalhousie wrote exultingly to the Queen: 'Your Majesty may well imagine the pride with which British officers looked on such a scene, and witnessed this absolute subjection of so powerful an enemy.* How deeply the humiliation was felt by the Sikhs themselves may be judged by the report which the officers who were present have made – that many of them, and especially the grim old Khalsa of Ranjit's time, exclaimed as they threw their arms down upon the heap: "This day Ranjit Singh has died!"'

There was nothing left to do. On the morning of 29 March 1849 the fawning regency council led the boy-king into the throne room. Henry Elliot, Foreign Secretary and annexationist zealot had been deputed to Lahore to perform the final act. Sir Henry Lawrence was by now considered too sensitized to his Sikh hosts to present the Dalhousie-drafted document: 'Terms granted to and accepted by the Maharajah Duleep Singh. He must resign for himself, his heirs, his successors, all right, title and claim to the sovereignty of the Punjab or to any sovereign power whatsoever, the confiscation of all state property, and the surrender of the Koh-i-Noor diamond.' In return he would get a pension of 'not less than four and not more than five lakhs of rupees.' He would bear the title 'Maharajah Duleep Singh Bahador' and continue to receive 'all respect and honour'.

The Punjab Papers revealed Dalhousie's *raisons d'état* in brutal starkness. A dispatch of 7 April to the East India Company's secret committee read: 'I cannot permit myself to be turned aside from fulfilling the duty which I owe to the security and prosperity of millions of British subjects by a feeling of misplaced and mistimed compassion for the fate of a child. We must resolve on the entire subject of the Sikh people and on its extinction as an independent state.'

The little boy gazed upwards at the Englishmen in their red coats and fine plumed hats. They all smiled at him. Where was his mother? Where were his uncles? He signed 'with alacrity'. He was aged ten and a half.


## Lahore Fort, Punjab, December 1849

The British were absolute masters of the Punjab. The rebels – Dewan Mulraj, who had raised the flag of revolt at Multan, Chutter Singh, the governor of Huzara, and his son Sher Singh, who had laid

---

* The rebel Sher Singh died in a Calcutta prison in May 1858.

down his sword after Gujrat – were incarcerated in Lahore Fort.

Every town and village in the Punjab was placarded with notices demanding the surrender of arms. More than 120,000 stands of match-locks and swords were collected. A mournful muster of the Khalsa's remnants was called at Lahore. A small number of troops were retained; the rest were disbanded. All defences – and practically every Punjabi village was a miniature fortress – were levelled.

In Lahore the Bengal Army surgeon, Dr John Login, was declared Killah-ki-Malik, 'Lord of the Citadel', with 'all stores, magazines, state prisoners and harems of the late Maharajah' under his control. The dour Presbyterian doctor was made 'Superintendent' of the dethroned king.

The new masters were naturally eager to inspect the most glittering prize of all – the Koh-i-Noor, held in a specially imported British-made Chubb safe under guard in the Toshakhana (treasure house) of the palace.

On 3 May 1849 they were ushered in by Misr Makraj, the treasurer, whose family had been hereditary custodians of the Koh-i-Noor since its acquisition by Ranjit Singh in 1809 from the fugitive Shah Sujah-ul-Mulk, deposed ruler of Afghanistan.

A British officer, Colonel Robert Adams, breathlessly described the Toshakhana's wonders. 'I wish you could see it,' he wrote to Mrs Lena Login, his cousin, 'the vast quantities of gold and silver; the jewels not yet to be valued, so many, and so rich – and the Koh-i-noor, far beyond what I had imagined. Runjeet's golden chair of State; his silver pavilion; Shah Soojah's ditto; relics of the Prophet; the Khalgi plume of the last Sikh guru, the sword of the Persian hero Rustum and, perhaps above all, the immense collection of magnificent Cashmere shawls, rooms full of them, heaped up in bales.'

There were tents, carpets, elaborate purdahs, jewel-embossed saddles, harnesses for elephants, armour, illuminated manuscripts, rings strung together like 'rows of buttons'. In one corner Login found a portrait of Queen Victoria. Aided by some sergeants of Horse Artillery, four European writers, and 'several moonshees and mutsuddies', (clerks) the doctor diligently catalogued the haul. His first estimate of the jewels alone, exclusive of the Koh-i-Noor, was little short of a million pounds. It was all forfeit.

Lord Dalhousie saw scant need for justification as the 'old women' in London tut-tutted at his rapacity. A week after the treaty's signature, the Governor-General wrote to a confidante: 'The confiscation of the Lahore crown property was quite necessary for two reasons: One, that means of mischief hereafter might not be left to the Maharajah. Two, that of the great debt which is due to this Government, something of the expenses of the war may be diminished by the amount of this property.

'Whatever my affectionate friends in London-hall may think . . . [I] regarded the Koh-i-Noor as something by itself, and with my having caused the Maharajah of Lahore, in token of submission, to surrender it to the Queen of England. The Koh-i-Noor has become in the lapse of ages a sort of historical emblem of conquest in India. It has now found its proper resting place.'

Referring to the boy-king he said: 'I am sorry for him, poor little fellow, although it is a superfluous compassion. He does not care two pence about it himself – he will have a good and regular income all his life, and will die in his bed like a gentleman.' The Maharajah would indeed die in his bed, alone in a Paris hotel, but not quite a gentleman.

Lord Dalhousie was brutal but perceptive in his analysis of the diamond's power. The Toshakhana was part state treasure house, part reliquary, part Ark-of-the-Sikh-Covenant, with the Koh-i-Noor at its glittering heart. Remove the gem and the fires of resistance in the Punjab would be extinguished for ever. That is what happened.

Dr Login could not resist the diamond's temptations. In the shimmering heat of that first summer of Lahore's subjection, he would, under the advice of its displaced hereditary guardian, show the gem to curious visitors with the strings securing it as an armlet twisted firmly around his wrist. The doctor's sense of theatre had developed by the time the cool weather arrived and Lord Dalhousie with it from Calcutta to see for himself. Login displayed the 'mountain of light', 'on a table covered with black velvet, the diamond alone appearing through a hole cut in the cloth, thrown up by the blackness around it'.

Lord Dalhousie was also enraptured. For many years a legend persisted in England that the resident, Sir Henry Lawrence, had diffidently placed the diamond in his waistcoat pocket at the moment of the signature of the treaty. But the extraction of the totemic gem from Lahore was anything but casual. Just before his due departure, Lord

Dalhousie visited Login in his marble-lined quarters in the palace. With him he had a small silk bag which had been, according to his own account, specially crafted by the nimble fingers of Lady Dalhousie.

They proceeded to the treasury. The safe swung open. Still set in its armlet, the Koh-i-Noor glinted within. Dalhousie placed the gem in her ladyship's bag. The other members of the board of administration appeared as Dalhousie made out a receipt which read: 'I have received this day from Doctor Login into my personal possession, for transmission to England, the Koh-i-Noor diamond, in the presence of the members of the Board of Administration, and of Sir Henry Elliot, K.C.B., Secretary to the Government of India. Signed Dalhousie. Lahore, December 7th, 1849. Signed H. M. Lawrence. C. G. Mansel. John Lawrence. H. M. Eliot.' They all duly applied their personal seals.

The Governor-General fumbled with his waistcoat and breeches, shackling the silken bundle to an elaborate double-stitched money-belt with two running chains round the waist and round the neck. In this bizarre halter, he departed for the coast with utmost dispatch. The diamond was lodged in the Bombay treasury. Later, in great secrecy, it was placed aboard HMS *Medea*. On 6 April 1850 the Royal Navy steam-sloop sailed for England.*

The new masters of Lahore were not conquistadors looting Inca plate to be sent to Cadiz, however. There was a great dominion to run, 15 million new subjects to be enlightened, and their labour and property turned to profit. Even the fighting power of the Khalsa, the toughest enemy the British ever fought in India, could be turned to good account. Empire-building was a high-risk business; it could end in death at the end of a Sikh spear or in a fever bed, or with riches and titles all round.

---

* Lord Dalhousie was well appraised of the sceptral power of the 'mountain of light'. He was to write in 1858: 'When Runjeet Singh seized the diamond from Shah Shoojah he was very anxious to ascertain its real value. He sent to the merchants at Amritsar, but they said its value could not be estimated in money. He then sent to the Begum, Shah Shoojah's wife. Her answer was thus: "If a strong man should take five stones, and should cast them, one east, one west, one north, and one south, and the last straight up in the air, and if all the space between those points were filled with gold and gems, that would not equal the value of the Koh-i-noor." Runjeet Singh then applied to Shah Shoojah. The old man's answer was: "The value of the Koh-i-noor is that whoever holds it is victorious over all his enemies." And so it is.'

Acting like good housekeepers, the cost of the Punjab's annexation were made self-liquidating. The board embarked on a series of auctions held by Messrs Lattey Brothers of Lahore. There were eight sales in all of the so-called 'Lahore Confiscated Property' from December 1850 to February 1851. Extraordinarily, the full revenue was never officially recorded. A Sikh historian has reckoned the total raised as 'more than five lakhs of rupees'. The Maharajah would later send Queen Victoria one of the sale catalogues as proof of English perfidy; it still sits in a buckram box in Windsor Castle.

With the diamond on its way to England, it was its former owner's turn for removal. The eleven-year-old seemed trusting enough of his new British friends, diligently completing an illuminated book on falconry, his great new passion, writing the text himself in Persian with court painters depicting his beloved raptors.

In December 1849 Mrs Helen Mackenzie, wife of an East India Company officer, visited the 'little prince'. 'A box of toys had just arrived from Sir F. Currie,' she wrote, 'and the little Maharajah anxiously waited to see its contents . . . boxes of figures, some with music such as blacksmith hammering, a cobbler drawing his thread, very baby toys for a boy of eleven. The little Maharajah looked very handsome with a sirpesh or aigrette of diamonds, and wreaths of pearls in his turban. His hawk is always in the hall, and when he drives out he carries it on his wrist. It is a mark of royalty.'

In February 1850 the Maharajah was removed on Dalhousie's instructions from the Punjab to Futtergarh in the United Provinces, taking with him a casket of jewels charitably picked out from the treasure house by Dr Login. His guardian was instructed: 'Take him to Agra, to Delhi – wherever you like – and eventually to England.'

The miniature ex-king was fleetingly allowed a miniature court; he was accompanied in his carriage or on his elephant with its silver howdah by a detachment of Skinner's Horse in their saffron-coloured uniforms.

The Maharajah was eager to present more gifts to his new friends. He wrote to Lord Dalhousie: 'Having heard that Your Lordship is about to present some Indian arms to Her Most Gracious Majesty the Queen, I gladly avail myself of the opportunity to ask your Lordship to permit a suit of my small armour and arms to accompany them for the purpose of being presented to H.R.H. the Prince of Wales.' Lahore was being effectively looted.*

At Futtergarh, a young Brahmin at the American Mission School named Bhajun Lal (not himself a Christian convert) became his guide to the strange beliefs of the *feringhees*. Duleep was settled down with the Bible, haltingly deciphering its seventeenth-century verse in his newly learned English. According to Bhajun Lal, the Bible was not his only reading material: 'It was sometimes Bible, sometimes a few conjuring tricks of which he was very fond, sometimes games in the "Boy's Own Book"† and all he did, he did of his own wilful will.'

It took two years and three months to get final permission from the Court of Directors of the East India Company for his baptism. The growing boy was well instructed in the Christian religion. 'I asked him many questions,' said Archdeacon Brett, 'which he answered very clearly and fully. He made statements on the doctrine of the Trinity, the person of our Lord, His two Natures, His offices, of Prophet, Priest and King which he explained.'

The ceremony was performed on 8 March 1853 in Duleep Singh's own house at Futtergarh. The signatures of Dr and Mrs Login and Colonel Alexander were affixed. The ceremony was felt to be 'very touching and impressive'. More than thirty years later Lady Login wrote: 'I well remember the earnest expression on the young boy's face, and the look, half-sad, half-curious, on those of his people present by their own wish.' He cut off his Sikhly hair to 'be like other boys' and gave it to her. She found it 'as long and abundant as a woman's'.

By now even Lord Dalhousie was showing some sympathy towards him. The Governor-General saw Christianity and tea-parties as denaturing. 'My little friend Duleep has taken us all aback lately by declaring

---

* The letter in the Royal Archives is accompanied by a: 'List of armour Selected by the Most Noble the Governor-General of India from the late Lahore Durbar for her Majesty Queen Victoria: Maharajah Shere Singh's helmet (topee), breastplate and arm piece. Shield inlaid with gold: Maharajah Ranjit Singh's – sword, bow, quiver, powder horn, matchlock (double barrelled) and shield. Maharajah Kharak Singh's khalgi, armour and sword.'

† *The Boy's Own Book*, a splendid volume first published in 1849, was given to the young Duleep by Dr Login. It was 'A complete encyclopedia of all the diversions, athletic, scientific and recreation of boyhood and youth.' Its contents explain much of the Maharajah's later adult obsessions: 'The Fancier: How to keep singing birds, talking birds, domestic fowls, pigeons, rabbits, guinea pigs, mice, silkworms and bees. Photography, magnetism, electromagnetic amusements, conjuring, puzzles, riddles and codes', and how to make 'lilliputian artillery' with gunpowder.

his resolution to become a Christian,' Dalhousie wrote to his old friend, the Bengal civil servant Sir George Couper, in March 1851. 'The pundits, he says, tell him humbug – he has had the Bible read to him, and he believes the sahib's religion.

'Politically we could desire nothing better, for it destroys his possible influence for ever. But I should have been glad if it had been deferred, since at present it may be represented to have been brought about by tampering with the mind of a child.

'This is not the case – it is his own free act, and apparently his firm resolution. "He will be a Christian," he says; "and he will take tea with Tommy Scott," [the playmate son of a schoolmaster at his new home in the hill station of Mussoorie] which his caste has hitherto prevented!' Dalhousie thought this last highly comic.

The Governor-General was becoming almost paternal. 'I look on him, as in some sort, my son,' he wrote in March 1853. 'He told me he is dying to see Europe and all its wonders. He told me he used to dream every night he was visiting the Duke of Wellington.' So be it, let him go to England, it had long been the plan to get the boy out of India. Dalhousie gave him a Bible inscribed 'you have gained a richer inheritance' before ushering him under the watchful eye of Dr and Mrs Login towards a berth on the P&O steamer SS *Hindustan*, departing Calcutta on 19 April 1854.

After a break in Egypt to inspect both the pyramids and the American Mission School at Cairo, the Christian prince arrived in Southampton in May and was taken to London where he was ensconced in Mivart's (Mrs Claridge's) Hotel, Mayfair. The streets of London teemed with wonders; he became one of them in his aigrette-plumed turban, cashmere tunic, pearl necklace and emerald earrings. Queen Victoria bundled him into the bosom of the royal family. He was no longer 'poor little Duleep' but a questioning, bumptious adolescent. His majority was approaching; according to the Treaty of Bhyrowal it would fall on his sixteenth birthday, 6 September 1854. Dalhousie had a practical solution: postpone it by two years.

The Maharajah wrote from Claridge's to the Chairman of the Court of Directors of the East India Company in December, with the first hint of the storms to come. 'Having at the early age of ten years been required to resign the throne of the Punjab ... I readily consented, believing the conditions to be as fair and liberal as under the circumstances could be obtained,' he said. 'I trust, therefore, that in considering the subject of my future settlement . . . such provision may be assigned to me as may appear liberal, considering my former rank, my present recognized position, and the expenses necessary for its proper and dignified maintenance.'

Queen Victoria agreed. She added her voice with that mixture of motherly protectiveness and imperial pragmatism that was to inform her relationship with the Maharajah for so long: 'The Queen has seen the Memorandum which she thinks very fair and reasonable, and she trusts that the East India Company will be able to comply.

'As we are in complete possession since 1849 of the Maharajah's enormous and splendid kingdom, the Queen thinks we ought to do everything (which does not interfere with the safety of her Indian dominions) to render the position of this interesting and peculiarly good and amiable Prince as agreeable as possible.'

An essential part of an Englishman's education was proposed – the Grand Tour of the Continent. With the Logins, and his Oxford under-graduate friend Ronald Leslie-Melville (the future Lord Leven), the party set off by train for the newly fashionable Riviera. There were soirées in Nice and a grand cultural progress via Florence to Rome – where the Maharajah twice declared himself to be 'in love' – and on to Venice, where he contracted malaria.

The Maharajah was convalescing in Switzerland when news reached London of a riot by sepoys (native troops) on 10 May 1857 at Meerut, forty miles north-east of Delhi. The city was captured within a day. A month later the whole Ganges valley, Oudh and central India were in open rebellion. The Punjab stayed loyal.* The great mutiny of 1857 passed the Maharajah with scarcely a ripple, other than the looting of his old residence at Futtergarh and the slaughter there of his English

---

* The loyalty of the Sikh troops was instrumental in suppressing the mutiny. The Maharajah wrote to Lord Salisbury in 1886: 'As my subjects, the Sikh army, had ten years previously given the English much trouble, so did they in 1857 take a noble revenge on their former foes, by being instrumental in preserving for the English their Indian Empire during the memorable Mutiny of that year. If the Sikhs had not responded to Sir John Lawrence's appeal, the English might have lost India.' He was right.

The India Act of August 1858 abolished the powers of the Honourable East India Company, transferring its authority to the Crown and its troops to the British Army. The post of Secretary of State for India (based in London) was created with an India Council of fifteen members. The Governor-General (in Calcutta) was given the title Viceroy. By the Royal Titles Act, Queen Victoria was proclaimed Empress of India on 1 January 1877.

steward and young family. On his return to England Duleep seemed more interested in setting his hawks on quivering rabbits. His 'callous' attitude was commented on at court.

The pious Login saw his work slipping away. 'I am a little disappointed that he showed such indifference to the cruelties in India and has scarcely abstained from the gaieties of the season. I have been reluctantly obliged to forebear the hope that he would take a foremost part in enlightening the people of India,' he wrote.

The Queen was less utopian. 'It was hardly to be expected that he should pronounce on so painful a subject, naturally still possessing . . . an eastern nature.' But she could not think him personally cruel. With the horrors of the well of Cawnpore and the drama of the siege of Lucknow filling the London prints, she wrote on 20 December 1857: 'The Queen fears that people who do not know him well have been led away by their present very natural feelings of hatred and distrust of all Indians . . . We have known him for three years (our two boys intimately), and he always shuddered at hurting anything, and was peculiarly gentle and kind towards children and animals, and if anything rather timid; so that all who knew him said he never could have had a chance in his own country.'

Expressing a sentiment she would return to in the future, she added: 'What he might turn out, if left in the hands of unscrupulous Indians in his own country, of course, no one can foresee.'

# 7

# The Shoot

❦

*Elveden Hall, Suffolk, October 1883*

IF THE REVEREND Dr Antonius Tien, rector of the Church of the Holy Trinity, Milton, next-Gravesend, Kent, is to be believed, there were once Russian spies lurking in the hedgerows of Victorian Suffolk.

The clergyman felt compelled to seek an interview with Sir Owen Tudor Burne, secretary of the Political and Secret Department of the India Office. The rector, who seemed to have mixed the care of his Thames-side flock with some amateur secret-agenting, had read newspaper reports of the Maharajah's rebellious intentions and had information of the highest importance. The meeting took place on 24 November 1886 but it concerned events three years earlier, in the autumn of 1883. Sir Owen felt it urgent enough to write a memorandum for his colleagues on the India Council immediately.

'The Reverend Dr. Tien, who is acting pro tem in charge of Sheikh Hassan-bin-Jaffar, of Muscat,* informed me today that a fellow countryman of his, a Bayrouti, is now serving in the Intelligence Branch of the Russian Foreign Office,' Sir Owen minuted. 'He came over to England some three years ago from St Petersburg to see Duleep Singh with promises to restore him in course of time as Ruler of the Punjab if he would place himself in Russian hands and go to Central Asia when they required it.

'Duleep Singh consented. Dr. Tien promised to give me a great deal more information on this and other subjects connected with the

---

* The Sheikh was the Sultan's master of horse, come to Britain to present Queen Victoria with a gift of six Arab stallions. In return, Lord Cross at the India Office gave the Sultan 'a costly gold tea-service for the ladies at the Sultan's harem'.

Russian Foreign Office, but as I have only known him within the last few days I deemed it best to show no anxiety in the matter, although he has, I think, a good deal to say. He possessed a Russian cipher now used in the Russian Foreign Office. Dr. Tien was formerly an interpreter in the Crimea, is a Knight Commander of the Medjede and author of many Arabic grammars.'

The file on the mysterious Levantine-Russian agent ends there. The Reverend Tien might have been making it all up, but it is entirely believable that an emissary from Russia (not necessarily from the imperial government) should have sought out the squire of Elveden to discuss some highly secret matters of state at the time Dr Tien indicated.

By then the Maharajah had long been firing his broadsides at the London newspapers and growling his complaints around the Garrick and the Carlton. The club bore may have emptied the smoking room sharpish, but someone was listening. To the enemies of England, the grumpy Maharajah suddenly looked very useful.

The arrival of a mysterious stranger by the Great Eastern Railway at Thetford station's oil-lit platform would not have been remarkable. There had been all sorts of comings and goings of Eastern gentlemen lately, heading in closed carriages the few miles up the London road from the sleepy town to the gates of the Maharajah's estate just across the border in Suffolk.

Elveden Hall had been a strange place since the Maharajah's arrival in 1863, at which time he began its transformation. The plain, Georgian country house, once home to Admiral Keppel, was rebuilt from the ground up in red brick and Ancaster stone, sprouting ornate wings and a Tuscan portico. Outside it looked more like a grand railway hotel than a country house. Inside, a very English architect, John Norton, a notable restorer of East Anglian churches, worked from photographs of Lahore's marble-lined palaces and the watercolours of August Schoefft to re-create a flamboyantly mock-oriental interior, scalloped Agra-style arches, shards of convex glass embedded in coloured plaster, ornamental foliage growing like jungle fronds to smother some ancient temple.

Elveden was further exoticized. Carrion birds flapped in its aviary. Marsupials hopped beneath the spreading cedars. Apes patrolled the kitchen garden. Missions were sent to India to return with hawks for the mews; falcons were brought from Iceland and Norway, buzzards from Holland. 'The house was full of curious parrots which would fly down in shouts of hoarse laughter at the Maharajah and his Indian servants,' ran a contemporary account of the high days at Elveden. There were rumours that the Maharajah had sent for an elephant to amuse his guests. It was best not to gossip too much about how and whom he entertained within – the Prince of Wales for one. Perhaps the Russian visitor was a grand duke. All sorts came to Elveden for the sport.

The screech of peacocks may have disturbed the Russian as he and his host pored over maps and papers in the library lined with gold-embroidered Kashmiri shawls, but it would not have bothered another arrival that winter at Elveden who had also travelled far. He had come from the Punjab bearing stories of lost greatness, fantastic riches and of the miraculously ever evolving Guru's prophecy, part of which now ran: 'When the Russian troops invade the country, agitation will prevail in London, and the British army will march to India.' The Indian visitor and Dr Tien's mysterious Russian emissary would have had a lot to talk about. An amazing plan was being hatched in Elveden's mirrored halls.

The conspiracy's origins would be painstakingly inquired into much later by Donald McCracken, an inspector of the Punjab police Special Branch. He compiled a voluminous report which traced the intrigue's root to Thakur Singh Sandhanwalia, Duleep's cousin. The Maharajah had summoned Thakur Singh to England by telegram in September 1883 but because he was under a bankruptcy order he could not leave the Punjab without permission. It was withheld for a year. Thakur Singh was already fingered by the police as a potential source of trouble.

He had conceived a claim of breathtaking ambition and had written to Duleep in November 1883: 'The Government had given to or allowed to be taken away by relatives of your deceased mothers [sic], the Maharanis of the great Maharajah, an enormous property both movable and immovable to which you were the rightful owner – lands, houses, villages, garden and jagirs.'

A huge list followed of 'nice and large palaces', including one with treasure supposedly buried underground by one of Ranjit's queens.

'Other Maharanis had died or were about to die,' according to Thakur Singh, 'and their property has been done away with by relatives or unlawful adopted sons. You are the rightful owner.' The way ahead was simple: the Maharajah must take Pahul (Sikh baptism) and re-embrace the abandoned faith of his birth. Then he must come to India and reclaim his lost kingdom. There was one problem: the Punjab had been an apparently loyal part of British India for the last thirty-four years.

As if he knew his letter would be intercepted and read by unfriendly eyes, the Maharajah's cousin had added: 'I know that you are the well-wisher of and loyal to the British crown and would not do any-thing against the wishes of her most august Majesty the Empress, which is right and proper.'

Harkishen Das, who was the son of the Prohit (hereditary priest) of Maharajah Ranjit Singh's family, had also been summoned to Eng-land by telegram in September 1883 and had made the long journey from Lahore to Elveden. On his return to the Punjab the following spring, so McCracken reported, the priest had been deputed by the Maharajah to offer *karah parshad* (a sweetmeat paste of sugar, flour and ghee) at the Golden Temple at Amritsar and at the samadh of Ranjit Singh at Lahore. In return the priests had offered prayers for Sikhi-dan, 'the blessing of the Sikh faith to fall on him'. Duleep was sloughing off his English skin.*

He resolved that autumn, despite everything, to show everyone just what a fine sporting English gent he was. He would stage one last great hunt before he went off to India. The Sikh priest and the Russian visitor must have looked on in astonishment. It was late October 1883, the pheasant season was already three weeks run. Bearded, spatted, plumply clad in baggy tweeds and Tyrolean hat, Duleep looked just like his noble neighbours. The Maharajah was the fourth-best shot in England and he could take out his frustration on the birds, blasting away with his matched pair of hammerless Purdey shotguns firing new breech-loading centre-fire cartridges with Schultz smokeless powder.†

---

* The Maharajah dispatched a London solicitor, Mr Talbot of Farrers and Co., to the Punjab in March 1884 to inquire into his 'family estates'. Talbot trudged the country with Harkishen Das for three months as the authorities in Lahore grudgingly produced old land deeds. The eventual report added greatly to the Jarndycian coils of the Maharajah's claim.
† I am grateful to Nigel Beaumont of James Purdey and Sons for this information.

How grand it had once all been. Mr L'Aigle Cole of *The Field* recalled a battue* at Elveden in the 1870s: 'Lunch was served each day in a large marquee, where the Maharani, and other ladies joined the party, and crowds of people went daily to see the shooting. A wand, with card attached, told each guest his place, and then Duleep Singh sounded a bugle, and the battue began.

'During that day over 3,000 head of game were killed, two carts, each drawn by a pair of strong horses, being filled with the spoil. This sounds like absolute slaughter, but remember it was on one of the finest and most highly-preserved sporting estates in England.'

Reading the press reports of the last great hunt in October 1883, Lord Kimberley, the new Secretary of State for India, noted with disgust: 'It did not help matters for the public to read that this "distressed prince" has just had a shooting party at which many thousands of heads of game were killed.'

The Queen offered a glimmer of charity – she minuted on a cross letter about the conspicuous slaughter she had received from Lord Ripon, the Viceroy: 'She is sorry for the shooting and he ought to be informed of it . . . but he sells his game.'† The Queen would always forgive the Maharajah.

Queen Victoria had been forgiving the Maharajah for years. Money was the problem. The Suffolk pleasure-dome was colossally expensive. Messrs Coutts had advanced £40,000 to sustain it. From 1878 onwards, stiff letters began to arrive from the patrician bankers at no. 59 Strand: 'although it is our desire to consult your convenience in every way . . . arrangements for liquidation . . . early date . . . considerable reduction . . .' The Maharajah's response was to send them to the India Office with copies to an ever sympathetic Queen.

In August 1878, 'to avoid the scandal of exposing the Maharajah to the mercy of his creditors', a discreet inquiry had been mounted into his financial affairs. Colonel William Sackville-West went through the books and absolved the Maharajah of most things except poor accounting. Sums were advanced to keep the bailiffs from the door.

---

* Battue: a 'hunt' in which birds are driven by beaters over the gun-line, a technique then becoming fashionable.
† The Maharajah took out a game dealer's licence in 1882, a deliberate move to humiliate himself by going into 'trade'. Messrs Baily of Mount Street, Mayfair, sold Elveden's produce.

The Maharajah's pleading letters had a new edge. He began to mention 'his private estates in India illegally held'. In 1880 he made first mention of the Koh-i-Noor which, he felt honoured to say, 'was in the possession of my most gracious sovereign'. There were more advances, more debt write-offs, more pleading letters ... and so it went on. He sent the Queen the latest Coutts statement. It amounted to £44,000, of which the money was spent: '£448 on life annuities, £8,000 on Elveden, £23,000 on rebuilding the Hall, £7,000 on furnishing it and £700 as a loan that I obtained for an old play-fellow in India Major Tommy Scott.

'Thus, my sovereign, there only remains the sum of £882 to be put down to the credit of my extravagance. Besides, my sovereign, I have been spending some £2,000 annually in restoring the church and repairing cottages for the poor. I must employ perhaps a rather vulgar Indian phrase saying that every hair of my body is full of gratitude.'

The Queen had told her ministers in September 1880: 'He may have and indeed has been very extravagant but that was most natural for an oriental and he is very truthful and straightforward and loyally disposed, rare qualities in his race.'

An interest-free loan of £44,000 had been brokered to clear the Maharajah with Coutts at least, contingent on Elveden being sold on his death to repay the government's 4 per cent loan and to provide pensions for his family. The Maharajah stormed and fretted but had little choice. The arrangement was enshrined by Parliament as the Duleep Singh Estates Act, 10 August 1882. It was to be a 'final settlement', but not as far as the Maharajah was concerned. He could not even leave his land to his children. His Englishness was on a mortgage. The Sikh and the Christian inside him were struggling for ascendancy. So too were the absolute monarch and the English gentleman (a staunch Conservative, member of the Carlton Club, former prospective parliamentary candidate, pillar of respectable society, and justice of the peace). His father had had a harem full of slave-girls. He had a hatchery full of pheasant eggs. He would quit Elveden entirely rather than see the dynasty of Ranjit Singh subverted out of his 17,000-acre East Anglian kingdom of conifers and blowing sand.

He rattled his gilded cage. The threats he sent to the India Office became ever wilder. In 1881 he had resolved to 'hire a house in Holland Park and reside there with my family as economically as possible' (he took the house but did not leave Elveden). Next he would 'lay aside his rank and go into business as a diamond-merchant'. Then, he 'hated the sight of Elveden, the Government must take the estates off my hands', adding in a postscript: 'As I presume I am now a naturalised Englishman there is no legal difficulty in my returning to the Punjab.' There was immense legal difficulty. Clause V of the 'Terms Granted 1849' stated: 'he shall remain obedient to the British Government, and shall reside at such a place as the Governor-General of India may select.'

The sympathetic writer and journalist Major Evans Bell* was commissioned to compile a statement of woes in book form and Duleep announced he would stand for parliament to articulate them. An Irish MP, Mr Mitchell Henry, had taken up his case.†

The Maharajah told the Queen in April 1883: 'I have learned by now nearly thirty years residence in this country that the only chance there may be of obtaining a hearing is to make as much noise as possible like for example the Irish.' Interesting connections were being made.

Duleep then embarked on an extraordinary new wheeze, bringing political pressure via the saleroom. In July 1883 Sir Henry Ponsonby was startled to receive an embossed invitation. 'Messrs. Phillips Son & Neale respectfully invites ... to the private view of The Valuable Casket of Jewels and the 25,000 of Chased Silver Gilt and other Plate, Indian Shawls and Embroideries &c of his Highness The Maharajah of Lahore Duleep Singh G.C.S.I. (preparatory to his leaving England for India) on Thursday July 19th.'

The newspapers woke up. 'The Maharajah is making preparations for a journey in state in the style of Indian magnates to his native country ... £20,000 is the sum to be realised,' reported *The Times*.

---

* Major Evans Bell: a former assistant commissioner at Nagpur, dismissed for insubordination, he was an early champion of Indian nationalism. The two books articulating the Maharajah's case were published in 1883–84 with English public opinion in mind. In many other works (such as *Our Vassal Empire* or *The Oxus and The Indus*) he attacked the Indian government which regarded him as a 'paid agitator'. He died in 1887 and after his death was (wrongly) suspected of being a Fenian sympathizer and key player in the Duleep Singh conspiracy.
† Mitchell Henry MP: a sporting Manchester magnate who had been drawn to the west of Ireland by the salmon fishing. He built the spectacular gothic Kylemore Castle in Connemara in 1868 and stood as Home Rule MP for Galway. The Maharajah stayed in correspondence with him throughout.

Notable items included a huge silver elephant tablepiece and 'an abundance of unpolished pearls, singularly beautiful in their native dusky hue, like the veiled beauties of Lahore and Cashmere'.

But he was going nowhere near Lahore without the government of India's permission. Lord Ripon, the Viceroy, telegraphed Lord Kimberley, Secretary of State at the India Office, in August 1883: 'Having consulted Punjab Government we consider Maharajah cannot be allowed to visit Punjab or to go north of Allahabad.'

The Viceroy followed by letter: 'It is little more than 40 years since Ranjit Singh died and the Khalsa was supreme in the Punjab. Many men, indeed, almost an entire generation, are still alive who remember that great ruler who took a leading part in the events which followed his death and it is quite impossible to say what might be the effect of the appearance of the son of their great Maharajah, Christian though he be, in the country of the five rivers.'

Then there was the matter of the prophecy: 'Rumours among Hindus and Mohammedans alike point to the current year as a season of trouble,' said the Viceroy. 'Among the Kukas* especially there exists much uneasiness and an unusual movement. The predictions in their religious book lead them to expect civil commotion – and they are reported to be performing the same ceremonies as were observed by Guru Gobind† before his revolt against the Mohammedan power.'

The Punjab Special Branch reported at the height of the Duleep Singh scare: 'Guru Ram Singh's followers have resolutely refused to believe in his death and still maintain that he is alive, and will return to restore the Khalsa kingdom. This hope is founded on some prophecies contained in the spurious Sakhis (i.e. book of prophecies) attributed

---

* Kukas ('shouters') was a disparaging name for the revivalist Sikh Namdhari sect founded in the Punjab in the late 1840s by Balak Singh. He was succeeded by the mystic Ram Singh around 1863. British power was spurned by a boycott on salt (in the manner that Gandhi would use sixty years later) and a violent outbreak in 1872 was brutally suppressed when sixty-eight Namdharis were blown from British cannon. Ram Singh died in exile in 1885.
† The Sikh religion was founded in northern India at the end of the fifteenth century by the wandering mystic and teacher Nanak. 'Sikh' is Punjabi for disciple or learner. The holy book the *Granth* was compiled from the teachings of Nanak and other gurus.
   Gobind Singh (1675–1708) became the tenth guru at the age of nine and developed a mission to reanimate the pacific faith of Nanak as a brotherhood of spiritual warriors by founding the 'Khalsa', with a common surname 'Singh', meaning 'lion'. The first such Sikh baptism (Pahul) took place on 30 March 1699. He proclaimed himself the last guru – it was the *Granth* that was to be revered after his death.

to Guru Gobind Singh. Ram Singh claimed to be the twelfth guru alluded to in these prophecies, who, with the help of the Russians, is to expel the English from India, and afterwards re-establish the Khalsa Raj. Hence the Kukas look forward to the advent of Russia, and agents of the sect are continually being deputed to Central Asia: some of them are known to have had interviews with the Russian authorities.'

Of the Maharajah himself the Viceroy telegraphed: 'It might even be found necessary to have recourse to personal restraint.' Lord Dalhousie would have recognized the sudden glint of steel. Duleep had found the lever he would bend to breaking point. The Punjab bubbled with sign and portents. The more dangerous his presence in India looked, the greater the leverage he could bring in England. Conjure up a Russian threat . . . and he would be unstoppable.

# 8

# Regina Imperatrix

❦

*Balmoral Castle, Aberdeenshire, Scotland, 18 September 1884*

AUTUMN ALWAYS SEEMED to come earlier at Balmoral; a diligent geographer might have pointed out that the Scottish granite castle, the gift of Prince Albert to his beloved wife, was two degrees of latitude north of Moscow. On this damp morning General Sir Henry Ponsonby, Queen Victoria's private secretary, entered the gardener's cottage in the grounds within which Her Majesty had taken to doing the morning's official business.

The Balmoral mail train had arrived at Ballater station bearing a particularly vexatious communication. Sir Henry handed it to her mournfully. It was addressed with courtly correctness to 'The Queen of England and Empress of India, Balmoral Castle, North Britain.' The crest on the stiff, creamy paper was familiar, depressingly so – a lion in gold surmounted by a starry crown, its paw resting on a most Christian emblem, a crusader's shield. Indeed, her late consort had designed it himself in happier times for the letter's author. But now, it had to be said, the Maharajah Duleep Singh was becoming a bit of a bore.

The letter blew a hot presaging wind from the plains of north-west India into Balmoral's saloons. It spoke of a far-away kingdom, the swindling of a royal inheritance, of a guru's prophecy, the reinvigoration of a martial religion and of the writer's manifest destiny to be its deity incarnate. Between expressions of servility, there was a distant rumble of gunfire. It rambled on in swirling copperplate for five pages, and is preserved in the Royal Archives at Windsor Castle. The following is a précis:

My Sovereign. Like as a dog participates in the joys as well as sorrows of his master so do I humbly share whatever affects Your Majesty. What all the British cannon, though they can blow me to pieces, could not make me say now that I know my true position viz. I yield Your Majesty's boundless graciousness towards me. I hope always to remain, as I am at this moment, Your Majesty's most loyal subject – unless the persecution of the Government will compel me to seek an asylum beyond the bounds of Your Majesty's dominions.

As Your Majesty is the only true and disinterested friend I possess in the world I did not wish that you, My Sovereign, should hear from any other source but myself of the possibility of my re-embracing the faith of my ancestors.

I have since sent for a Bhaee or Brother to come with a copy of the Holy Book of the Sikhs to teach me to read it. When lots were cast before the Holy Book of the Sikhs to selecting a name for me, 'Dleep' came up – which was afterwards corrupted by my English and Persian tutors into 'Duleep'.

Shortly after I ascended the throne of the Punjab it was found written in the book of Sikh prophecies called Sakheean that a man of my name would be born, who, after becoming entirely dispossessed of all he inherited and residing alone for a long period in a foreign country, would return to be the eleventh gooroo of the Khalsa, or 'Pure'.

I suppose from the similarity of the two names and what has taken place regarding me – this prophecy is believed by millions of Punjabis who have long been looking forward to its fulfilment and wonder that if I am the right man, why I do not return?

I myself was told of it when only six or seven years of age and so much did I believe at the time that I was the person to whom this prophecy applied, that I had a cage constructed and placed every night near my bed to carry away in it a favourite pair of pigeons which as a child I prized beyond all the contents of my Treasury.

The Maharajah again, how tiresome. The Queen read on, reaching for a purple crayon to scribble terse notes.

I did not remember until last year when I was about to leave England against my will of all this apparently nonsense nor think of the words until a short time before her death by my mother on one occasion while discussing the prophecy with her I jeeringly remarked, 'But, mother, how can all this come to pass if I do not return to India at all?' She replied, 'Mark my words my child, I may not live to see the day but when the right moment arrives. Circumstances will so shape themselves that thou will be compelled to quit England against thy will' and Your Majesty perhaps recollects how nearly this was brought about by the India Council and may yet be fulfilled. I hope Your Majesty will pardon me if I have begun to believe in the force of destiny.

Your Majesty is now fully acquainted with the treatment I have received from the Christians who spend vast sums annually to teach the heathen to do justice, love mercy and walk humbly with God and to do unto others as you would wish them to do unto you.

Lord Dalhousie wrote in a Bible he presented me the following inscription. 'This Holy Book, in which he has been led by God's Grace to find an inheritance richer by far than all earthly kingdoms, is presented with sincere respect and regard by his faithful friend.'* Or, in other words, having deprived me of my inheritance which was in his power to let alone, he hoped as my friend that I may acquire another birthright which was not in his power to bestow.

My Sovereign, such vile hypocrisy of the Christians has made me wish to resort to the faith of my forefathers which is simple trust and belief in the great architect of the Universe. I have the honour to remain My Sovereign, Your Majesty's humble and most loyal subject – Maharajah Duleep Singh.

* The Bible presented on the eve of his departure from Calcutta.

This was most unfortunate. Had he not been more than justly treated? The Maharajah had been a boy, it was true, when his ministers had treacherously made war on the British, but his armies had been defeated in battle. He had converted to Christianity, been brought to England and given a decidedly generous pension.

Then there was that extraordinary business last July when the Maharajah wrote to Sir Henry Ponsonby, enclosing a paper knife, apparently a souvenir from a trip to Naples, which was to be laid symbolically at Her Majesty's feet with the message: 'There is a terrible storm gathering in India and I hope to render such service as to compel the responsible ministers of the Crown to recognise my just claims which under the present circumstances they may be disinclined to admit. I know that the advent of Russia is hailed with immense joy both by the people and Princes of India in their secret hearts . . . and they are all prepared to rebel as soon as the power advances a little nearer.'

Russia was a beastly place. Now there was this hocus-pocus about a prophecy revealed by his mother, Rani Jindan, the disreputable woman there had been all that scandal about. Her Majesty felt compelled to scribble a note on her heavily black-bordered paper: 'extraordinary and half-cracky'.

The Queen's reply was taken by the mail-gig to catch the four o'clock messenger express: 'My dear Maharajah, as your friend and perhaps the truest you have, I would strongly warn you against those who would lead you into trouble. Do not use threats or abusive language, for it will not be the means of obtaining the impartial hearing of your claims that you desire. Above all I most earnestly warn you against going to India where you will find yourself far less independent and far less at your ease than here.'

He wrote back from Elveden with equal dispatch: 'I humbly beg to be pardoned for causing Your Majesty pain . . . but my own history is such a painful one. I often ask myself, am I in my right senses or am I mad?'

## Buckingham Palace, London, 1854

The Maharajah's history had indeed been painful, but it was for true sovereigns to endure misfortune with dignity.

The Queen remembered their first meeting. It had been thirty years ago, at Buckingham Palace, not a place of which she was otherwise overly fond. He was fifteen, she was thirty-five, but her journal for that day, 1 July 1854, gushed with girlish enthusiasm: 'After luncheon to which Mama came, we received the young Maharajah Duleep Singh, the son of Runjeet Singh who was deposed by us after the annexation of the Punjaub. He has been carefully brought up and was baptised last year so he is a Christian. He is extremely handsome and speaks English perfectly, and has a pretty, graceful and dignified manner. He was beautifully dressed and covered in diamonds. The Koh-i-Noor belonged to and was once worn by him. I always feel so sorry for these poor deposed Indian princes.'

How exotic this prince had been, how extraordinary his story. There was a dinner at the palace a week later and she sat Duleep at her right hand. Sir Charles Wood, secretary to the India Board, had told her that 'The young man had been horrified by the cruelties he had witnessed', and Lord Hardinge, the former Governor-General, had confided that 'the Maharajah had been in the arms of Jawahir Singh [his maternal uncle] when the latter had been shot; his mother the Ranee was a very violent woman, who now lived in Nepaul.' The Queen had recorded it all in her journal.

A month later she had felt compelled to write about her new acquaintance to the Governor-General of India, with the same mixture of flirtatious interest and maternal concern: 'The Queen wishes to tell Lord Dalhousie how much interested and pleased we have been in making the acquaintance of the young Maharajah Duleep Singh. It is not without mixed feelings of pain and sympathy that the Queen sees this young prince, once destined to so high and powerful a position, and now reduced to so dependent a one by her arms; his youth, amiable character, and striking good looks, as well as his being a Christian, the first of his high rank who has embraced our faith, must incline everyone favourably towards him, and it will be a pleasure to us to do all we can be of use to him, and to befriend and protect him.'

There it was, that slight prickling of guilt, like a burr beneath the saddle – a sense that somehow the prince had been displaced from his splendid kingdom by her over-eager servants. The Queen would return to the uncomfortable sentiment many times in her journal and letters.

On a long-ago visit to Osborne, the Italianate house on the Isle of Wight, another splendid inspiration of Albert's, she had quizzed the Maharajah on his childhood. 'We took a drive out towards Carisbrooke & came back by Cowes & over the ferry,' she had confided to her journal. 'The Maharajah sat next to me, very handsomely dressed and with his jewels on. We spoke of Heera Singh, whom the Maharajah remembered well, saying, "my uncle murdered him." I observed that he must have seen many terrible things. "Oh, your majesty I have seen dreadful things. I am certain they would have murdered *me* too," he replied. This thought reconciles me to having had to despoil his kingdom, & he is convinced of the wisdom of this himself.'

The Queen had written to the Governor-General again in October 1854: 'This young prince has the strongest claims upon our generosity and sympathy; deposed, for *no* fault of his, when a little boy of ten years old, he is as innocent as any private individual of the misdeeds which compelled us to depose him, and take possession of his territories. He has besides since become a Christian, whereby he is for ever cut off from his own people ... he was not even a conquered enemy, but merely powerless in the hands of the Sikh soldiery.'

That winter the Maharajah had come on several occasions to 'dine and sleep' at Windsor. He had worn 'beautiful clothes ... a golden coat lined with fur'. He attempted to skate and expressed a desire to learn to dance. The young man joined the royal family at worship in the royal pew, 'which seemed like a dream', the Queen's journal recalled. Castle Menzies in Perthshire was taken for a season's shooting, the Maharajah amusingly bestriding the heather in a kilt and alarming his companions by setting his falcon on hapless grouse and unsportingly shooting a crofter's cat. Was he especially cruel? Perhaps it was his 'eastern nature', perhaps the terrors of his childhood. The Queen was sure that something could be done.

The question of his continuing education had arisen. 'He had learned nothing from books until he left Lahore,' the Queen's journal recalled. 'Albert took him into the library and showed him the collection of Indian illuminated books in which he was most interested.'

Her husband did not add that one of the gorgeous volumes in the Persian script had been lifted from an Afghan Khan's fortress by his own guardian, Dr John Login. 'We took great care to avoid showing him the Sikh cannon sent by Lord Gough,'* the Queen also noted.

How unfortunate it was that Prince Albert was no longer at her side to offer guidance. It was Albert who had taken such an interest in the young Maharajah's welfare, had appointed his tutors: Professors Bentley and Becker for science and German, Dr Edward Rimbault and W. G. Cousins for music, for which, so everyone said, the Maharajah showed considerable talent. It had been agreed that a public school or university education for the young man 'would not do at all'.

Lord Dalhousie had been highly suspicious of the notion of sending him to Eton. Appraised of Queen Victoria's apparent infatuation, the marquis had written gruffly to Sir George Couper: 'It is very good for the Maharajah to have seen the Royal family. But I am a little afraid that this exceeding distinction will not be for his future comfort. If he is to live and die in England, good and well, but if he is to return to India, he is not likely to be rendered more contented with his position there by being so highly treated in England. After breakfasting with queens and princesses, I doubt his much liking the necessity of leaving his shoes at the door of the Governor-General's room, when he is admitted to visit him which he will certainly be again required to do.'

At Government House, Calcutta, an educated native looked far more dangerous than he did at Osborne. Duleep should either be left in ignorance or completely denatured. 'The "night-cappy" appearance of his turban is his strongest national feature,' the Marquis had added. 'Do away with that and he has no longer any outward and visible sign of a Sikh about him.' The letter had been brutal but it was prescient.

There had also been the question of a suitable bride. By then, 1855, the Maharajah was rising sixteen. In the Punjab he would have been betrothed aged five.† There had been overtures to the ex-Rajah of Coorg for a marriage to his elder daughter, but then Duleep was baptized a Christian. Conveniently, the thirteen-year-old Princess

---

* The cannon was captured by Lord Gough at the battle of Sobraon and shipped to England as a trophy of war.
† The Maharajah was betrothed in Lahore aged eight to the daughter of Chutter Singh Attariwala. The engagement was broken on the insistence of the British-dominated Council of Regency.

Gouramma also became a convert; a god-daughter of Queen Victoria herself, with the same baptismal name, she lived with suitably respectable guardians in Scotland.

The Queen had written to Lord Dalhousie in that same first flush of concern. 'She thinks such a marriage between these two most interesting young Christians most desirable. The young people have met and were pleased with each other, so that the Queen hopes that their union will, in the course of time, come to pass. Her little god-daughter has been here lately, and though still childish for her age, is pretty, lively, intelligent, and going on satisfactorily in her education.'

Her journal recorded how Albert had told the young man: 'A good wife would be the best companion for him.' The Maharajah had replied: 'He did not wish to be hurried, that he did not wish to marry until he was 23 or 24. He could not marry a heathen and an Indian who would become Christian only to please him would be very objectionable.' He told Albert that he liked Princess Gouramma 'very much as a friend but not as wife'.

The Maharajah's spurning of Victoria Gouramma may have been provident after all. She turned out to be, in the Queen's words, 'over-excitable'. There had been a dalliance with a stable-boy and, after a change of guardians, she had fallen in love with an under-butler to whom she sent volumes of poetry. The princess had been shockingly caught with her coat over her nightgown, evidently in the act of elopement. She was expeditiously married to an Englishman, Colonel John Campbell (Lady Login's brother), thirty years her senior. After bearing a daughter, she died aged twenty-three.

Thus it had been decided that, like an exotic bloom, the transplanted Maharajah was to be nurtured in a hot-house of his own. John Login, the Orcadian doctor who five years earlier in the conquered Punjab had been made the infant king's 'superintendent', in the summer of 1854 had been given both a knighthood and responsibility for his further education.

The Maharajah's relationship with the royal family had blossomed. The Queen remembered happily how he and the Prince Consort would potter for hours with the photographic apparatus of which the Queen's husband was so fond. Together they had made splendid portraits of her sons, Albert Edward (Bertie), the Prince of Wales, and Prince Alfred (Affie), Duke of Saxe-Coburg-Gotha, wearing Indian costume.

Her journal for 22 August 1855 recorded: 'Osborne. A beautiful morning. Breakfast in the alcove with the truly amiable young Maharajah who is so kind to the children playing so amiably with them.' That day they all enjoyed a trip on the royal yacht, the *Victoria and Albert*. 'I had a most interesting conversation with the Maharajah about his motives for becoming a Christian, entirely at his own wish, and with what determination in the face of great opposition, he carried it through. I was much touched by his fervent and strongly religious turn of mind ... We only came back at 8.'

There were wheelbarrow races and boisterous games of leap-frog, and blind-man's bluff in which the Maharajah would carry poor, sickly Prince Leopold in his arms with such tenderness.* Far away in the Crimea the Queen's soldiers toiled towards the bulwarks of Sebastopol; the sunlit gambols were a most welcome distraction from the vexations of Czar Nicholas of Russia.

The princesses had also much enjoyed the company of their 'amiable young visitor' and the royal children would play happily, baking cakes for dollies' tea-parties in the kitchen of the Swiss Cottage in Osborne's grounds. There were presents from the Maharajah every birthday: a cage of fifty birds was sent to the Prince of Wales, for example, and a puzzle-ring to Prince Alfred. There were gifts of Sikh armour, native dresses and hangings all richly embroidered in gold and silver thread. In return, the Queen sent a horse from the royal stables, and, at Christmas, an agreeable mincemeat pie, a case of tangerine oranges and a roe deer shot by the Prince Consort.

Thirty years later, amidst the mourning monochrome of Balmoral, the Queen sadly considered the lost innocence of long ago. On cluttered royal what-nots there were plentiful tokens of familial affection, photographs, sketches and watercolours in her own hand.†

The most splendid memento of all, though, was the portrait of the Maharajah the Queen had commissioned from Franz Xaver

---

* Queen Victoria's fourth son, Prince Leopold, Duke of Albany, suffered from haemophilia. He died from its complications, aged thirty-one, in 1884. Queen Victoria sent the Maharajah an enamelled photograph as a memento.

† A bust of the Maharajah in marble by Baron Marochetti RA, later tinted by Sir John Millais, stood in a place of honour at Osborne. The Italian sculptor had crafted the funerary monument for Albert's mausoleum at Frogmore, with, at her insistence, an effigy of the young Victoria lying beside him in sure and certain hope of their reunion at the Resurrection.

Winterhalter, the celebrated court painter of Frankfurt. It was hanging in the drawing room at Osborne, dark eyes blazing from a girlishly beautiful face smudged with adolescent masculinity.

The Queen's journal for 10 July 1855 recalled its creation: 'Went to see our dear Winterhalter painting where we found the Maharajah in full dress. Winterhalter was in ecstasies at the beauty and nobility of the young Maharajah.' The fashionable painter deliberately gave his subject the height he thought he would attain when he reached full manhood. Duleep Singh never grew any taller.

The sittings took place at Buckingham Palace. The Maharajah was then barely seventeen years of age, and a 'very handsome youth, slight and graceful', clad for the portrait in the splendour of an Eastern chieftain. The effect was both effeminate and martial: a sumptuous string of pearls coiled around his neck, with a miniature portrait of the Queen mounted on the fifth row like a choker, two enormous gold earrings, a sword dangling from his waist and, on his un-Sikhly shorn head, a brocade turban dripping with emeralds. In the background the artist conjured, like an Italian renaissance hill-town, the lofty pavilions of Lahore. So remarkable were the results that a lithograph of the portrait had been made for popular sale to raise money to buy comforts for soldiers in the Crimea.

There was also the matter of the Koh-i-Noor. The subject of the irksome diamond came up during the Winterhalter sittings. The Maharajah may have been dripping with gems shimmering on the canvas in a thousand droplets of titanium white, but the 'mountain of light' was not among them. It was safely lodged in the jewel house of the Tower of London after its recutting in the multi-faceted style by Dutch glypticians using a steam-powered engine. Prince Albert and the Duke of Wellington had gone to see the work. It was not part of the English crown jewels; it was the Queen's personal property.

On a July afternoon in 1855, the Queen had attended a sitting in the White Drawing Room, which had been equipped as a studio, where the subject would stand stock-still on a raised wooden platform for two hours at a time. Sir John and Lady Lena Login had accompanied the Maharajah from their grace-and-favour home, Church House in Kew, Surrey. The great painter was concentrating on his subject's spectacular gemstones. Something was missing. The atmosphere became brittle.

'Her Majesty took the opportunity to speak to me aside on the subject of the Koh-i-Noor,' recalled Lady Login in her memoirs. 'She had not yet worn it in public, and, as she herself remarked, had a delicacy about doing so in the Maharajah's presence. "Tell me, Lady Login, does the Maharajah ever mention the Koh-i-Noor? Does he seem to regret it, and would he like to see it again? Find out for me before the next sitting," the Queen said.' According to Lady Login, 'there was no other subject that so filled the thoughts and conversation of the Maharajah, his relatives and dependants' as the forsaken diamond. 'For the confiscation of the jewel which to the Oriental is the symbol of the sovereignty of India, rankled in his mind even more than the loss of his kingdom, and I dreaded what sentiments he might give vent to were the subject once re-opened.'

Lady Login and the Maharajah were in the habit of taking morning rides in Richmond Park. The English woman casually asked her companion if he was curious to see the Koh-i-Noor in its new form. 'Yes,' he replied, 'I would give a good deal to hold it again in my own hand. I was but a child, an infant, when forced to surrender it by treaty . . . now that I am a man, I should like to have it in my power to place it myself in Her Majesty's hand.' The diamond, it seemed, was safe.*

The next day the Queen 'came across at once' as Lady Login entered the studio. The Maharajah was on the platform, posing for the artist. In a huddle of crinolines his intended magnanimity was vouchsafed. The Queen signalled to the Prince Consort who was engaged in conversation with Herr Winterhalter at the other end of the room. 'They held a hurried consultation in whispers, despatching one of the gentlemen-in-waiting with a message.' A half-hour later there was a 'bustle at the door' and a halberd-wielding escort of yeomen warders from the Tower entered dramatically with a frock-coated official bearing a small casket.

'This Her Majesty opened hastily,' Lady Login recorded, 'and took therefrom a small object which, still holding, she showed to the Prince, and, both advancing together to the dais, the Queen cried out,

---

* Challenged on the legitimacy of the Koh-i-Noor's original seizure, Lord Dalhousie wrote in 1856: 'I do not recollect that any subject has fallen on the good fortune of sending so precious and so storied a trophy of war to England. I was unquestionably within my competency to do as I did. The Punjab was conquered, the dynasty destroyed, and all state property therefore confiscated.'

"Maharajah, I have something to show you!"' Duleep Singh stepped hurriedly down to the floor. Before he knew what was happening, he found himself once more with the Koh-i-Noor in his grasp, while the Queen was asking him 'if he thought it improved, and if he would have recognised it again?'

The Maharajah walked towards the window, turning the gem to let the sooty London light fall upon its facets. 'For all his air of polite interest and curiosity, there was a passion of repressed emotion in his face ... evident, I think, to Her Majesty, who watched him with sympathy not unmixed with anxiety.' For a quarter of an hour the Maharajah paced up and down, peering at the glittering, shrunken thing, the gem of emperors and amirs with which he had played as a childish bauble. The ruler of Afghanistan, Shah Sujah-ul-Mulk, had swallowed the enormous stone rather than surrender it to the Maharajah's father.* What would he do?

'At last, as if summoning up his resolution after a profound struggle, he raised his eyes from the jewel,' Lady Login recorded. 'I was prepared for almost anything – even to seeing him, in a sudden fit of madness, fling the precious talisman out of the open window by which he stood. My own and the other spectators' nerves were equally on edge – as he moved deliberately to where Her Majesty was standing.'

This had been the moment, more than the conversation on the Cowes ferry, which had shriven the Queen. She may have shamelessly stage-managed the encounter and have been forewarned of its likely outcome, but she had to be somehow absolved. The Maharajah had bowed low, placing the diamond in her hand and saying with circumlocutional pomp: 'It is to me, Ma'am, the greatest pleasure thus to have the opportunity, as a loyal subject, of myself tendering to my Sovereign – the Koh-i-Noor.'

This had all happened long ago. How noble and handsome the Maharajah had been; how tragic were his present delusions. What had brought him to this pass? The Queen thought she knew: the bad advisers and unsuitable friends she had warned of. News of the Maharajah inviting 'rascally cousins' to England had lately reached her.

She went on believing for a while – at least until the Maharajah

---

* The Shah was placed under guard and some hours later 'gave the gem up'.

became really dangerous – that she herself could return him to the paths of righteousness. It was that prickle of guilt again; she must move to protect him even against his own 'eastern nature'. How mortified she would have been to know that the Maharajah was already growling a different name for his most beloved sovereign through his brindled beard. To those of his unsuitable sporting friends at the Union Whist Club who would still listen, he was calling her 'Mrs Fagin'.

# 9

# The Green-room

*34 King Street, Covent Garden, London, Autumn 1884*

FOR A VICTORIAN sporting gentleman to keep a mistress was no surprise; for a former oriental monarch, however piously Christian, it was to be expected. The thing was not to have a government department scrutinizing the bills. That, perhaps, was Duleep's mistake.

The 'Magnificent Squire of Elveden' had always sought more metropolitan diversions. He was clubbable (the Garrick, the Carlton,* the Marlborough, the East India, the Oriental,† blackballed by White's) and libidinous. He was an ornament of the court and of fashionable London salons. He pops up in Victorian society paintings of the period like a spot-the-Maharajah contest. William Frith depicted him in 1863 leading the delegation of 'foreign princes' in the gorgeously crowded 'Wedding of the Prince of Wales'. Twelve years later, Duleep lurks bare-headed, accompanied by two turbanned servants, in the audience of Jacques Tissot's 'Hush! (The Concert)' as a chokered young lady takes up her violin in a glittering drawing room. 'Spy' of *Vanity Fair* drew him portly, frock-coated, sporting a cigarette in a holder.

There were other ways to spend the evening: cards at the Union Whist Club (the 'shirt shop' on Jermyn Street), discreet (and illegal) games of Baccarat, or little trips to the most flamboyant of London's theatres, the Alhambra on Leicester Square, home of the can-can,

---

* The Maharajah was put up for the staunchly Tory club in 1873 by the Duke of Richmond, seconded by Lord Walsingham. It was proposed he should stand in the Conservative interest for the seat of Whitby, held by Gladstone's son, Herbert. The Queen disapproved and the plan was dropped. Duleep Singh's entry in the Carlton membership book that survived the club's destruction in the London Blitz has been scratched out.

† The Maharajah complained about the quality of the club's curry. He recommended his own supplier, an enterprising Bengali spice-merchant of Talbot Road, Bayswater.

*opéra bouffe* and tinselly ballets. The theatre, built à la Elveden in a mock-Moorish taste, was 'a temple of that type of ballet in which everything is expressed in terms of pretty girls', according to a contemporary memoir. 'One night it might be a tableau – "the ingredients of a salad," (including ten young ladies as slices of boiled-egg), the next, "the armies of all nations".' Particularly well received by Fleet Street critics was 'The Press', as girls, as scantily dressed as the Lord Chamberlain would allow, depicted the great organs of public opinion.

In December 1882 the Alhambra burned down. The fire-hose water froze overnight. The ruins were described, the icicle-clad morning after, as looking like a 'Russian winter palace'. It was to be rebuilt and reopened two years later in even more splendour as the Alhambra Theatre of Varieties.* Elderly gentlemen remained quite besotted by certain of the chorines. So too, it seems, was the Maharajah.

Direct evidence of the Maharajah's dalliances is scanty, but enough survives in official files, the Royal Archives, letters (sent interestingly enough to William Ewart Gladstone), and in contemporary memoirs, to work out what was going on. First a memoir. A minor author of the 1880s called Donald Shaw published a pamphlet called 'Advice to the Stout', a diet-book extolling wholemeal bread and licorice powder. Perhaps that is how he met the by-now rapidly expanding Maharajah. Mr Shaw was also an Alhambra-habitué. In 1908 he published his memoirs anonymously. 'The Maharajah Duleep Singh was in nightly attendance and never failed to bring some gimcrack which he displayed in the Alhambra green room with the enquiry: "What nice little girl is going to have this"?

'This however was before he had concentrated his affections on pretty Polly Ash,' continued Mr Shaw's saucy memoir. 'Polly, however, was not devoid of common sense, and retired some time later to a sumptuous flat in Covent Garden and an annuity that survived the donor.'†

More clues are divulged in a letter from Elveden to Gladstone dated 22 March 1882. 'Will you kindly grant me an interview for a few minutes one day next week?' the Maharajah wrote to the Prime Minister. 'I shall not return to town till Monday next when my <u>certain</u>

---

* Today the Odeon Cinema, Leicester Square, built in 1936.
† Miss Ash never got top billing. She flits through playbills of the Alhambra 1879–80 season as a dancer in the 'grand pantomimic spectacular, The Carnival of Venice', and seems to have retired thereafter; perhaps the Maharajah wanted to keep her for himself.

address always is 34 King Street Covent Garden where I go to write the music of my opera every day.'* He installed two grand pianos in the capacious apartment above a publisher's office, a short stroll from the Alhambra stage door on Charing Cross Road. It was that dual personality again. As the Maharajah toiled in the British Museum by day over his Punjab Paper polemics, by night he poured his romantic anguish into music, Miss Ash reposing elegantly at his side. His wife stayed in Suffolk purdah.

It was hard to keep the beautiful Miss Polly Ash a secret. As the Maharajah made more public noises over his grievances, the society whispers intensified. At Eton, his son, Prince Victor, was evidently being bullied by top-hatted tormentors. The Maharajah told Sir Henry Ponsonby for the Queen's ears in early 1883: 'He strongly denied having any political intrigue in India, he protested against the false stories repeated against him – thus for instance his son, coming from Eton, told him it was being said he had lost £20,000 last year in gambling. The truth was he never played for high stakes and what he had lost last year was twenty pounds. Other stories of gifts given to actresses were utterly untrue and unfounded.'

Sir Owen Burne at the India Office minuted tartly to Windsor Castle in response. 'I am bound to say that the India Council are inclined to have less sympathy with the Maharajah by some apparently well founded rumours which have reached them that he has settled £2,000 a year on a Miss Ash who he has taken into his keeping. I am unable to say whether this rumour is true or false.'

Miss Ash was to have a rival. How the Maharajah met and fell in love with the girl who would share his last extraordinary adventure begins to emerge from another anonymous memoir published in 1926. Called *Uncensored Recollections*, it was by Julian Osgood Field, a minor playwright and author who wrote some spectacularly bad gothic novels under the pseudonym 'XL'. In his dissolute youth, Field had been a masher, a gambler, a gentleman of the turf. He had been stranded, broke, having lost all his money at the races, in Dieppe some time in early autumn of 1886 (he mentions being on his way to the Jubilee of the Grand Duke of Baden – which fell on 4 September).

---

* The libretto was given to Lady Login but seems to have been lost. In her bowdlevised memoirs, the pianos were installed in the family house in Holland Park. Today 34 King Street is a Mexican restaurant.

I accepted a loan of the money I needed (I blush to say) from a lady of questionable repute, the fair and aristocratic-looking 'Marini', the chère amie of Duleep Singh and originally a chambermaid at an hotel in Knightsbridge.

The Prince was so much in love with her that she had to send a wire twice a day to Elveden to tell him how she was getting on!

Duleep Singh was not a bad chap, and in every way superior to his eldest son Victor who was by no means a pleasing youth, and who certainly had not a good influence on Lord Caernarvon, who died only the other day.*

The Koh-i-noor rightly belonged to Duleep Singh – it had been taken when he was a child from his father's palace at Lahore, and he once laughingly spoke to me of Queen Victoria as 'Mrs. Fagin,' for, he said, 'she's really a receiver of stolen property'.

Sharp-eyed civil servants at the India Office were already keeping track of the Maharajah's urban pursuits. They simply had to look at the bills he regally sent them. This, for example, from October 1880:

> Statement from Farrers to the India Office looking for an advance to pay pressing debts.
> Claridges Hotel – £128 4s. 0d.
> Cox's Hotel – £94 11s. 0d.
> Savory and Moore (chemists and perfumiers) £45 16s. 11d.
> Private loan to pay off pressing bills £2000
> Plus: 467 sheep at 65 shillings each which died last winter £1502 5s. 0d.

Claridge's was an old favourite and doubtless highly respectable, but Cox's Hotel at 54–5 Jermyn Street was another matter. The raffish area south of Piccadilly was a gentleman's playground, home of high-quality shirt-makers, flashy card clubs and discreetly bohemian hotels. The Maharajah was unabashed enough to keep up a correspondence with Gladstone from 1882 onwards on Cox's Hotel letterhead (his outraged letters to Tory politicians were sent from the Carlton Club).

* Sponsor of the ill-fated expedition that discovered the Egyptian tomb of Tutankhamun.

The disreputable Mr Field's memoirs provide the thinnest thread of proof, but there is enough supporting evidence to make a direct presumption. Sometime around 1884–5, the Maharajah was entranced by a pretty chambermaid in his favoured London hideaway (Cox's Hotel on Jermyn Street is not quite 'Knightsbridge' but is near enough). He fell obsessively in love with a girl who was little more than a child. He was already calling her his queen. He would abandon everything for her.

Mr Field says in his memoirs that he met the Maharajah and his Channel-crossing *chère amie* again in Paris on his journey back from Baden – say, in late September 1886. 'When I told him how Marini had helped me out of my scrape at Dieppe, he was greatly amused,' he recorded. 'Marini (no doubt originally 'Maharanee') was, as I said, once a chambermaid, but in appearance she looked like the typical patrician English girl, the descendant of countless earls . . .

'But when she spoke the charm vanished. Her manners were admirable, but her voice had the unmistakable Whitechapel accent, and her pronunciation and the expressions she used were, to say the least, abnormal.' She also seemed to like knocking back brandy and soda with her breakfast.

That unmistakable accent would soon be heard in places a long way from Whitechapel. And it came from Newington Butts, not Bow Bells. The voice belonged to one Ada Douglas Wetherill.

# The Guru

❦

*53 Holland Park, Kensington, London, December 1884*

THE MAHARAJAH HAD opened a new front in his interminable grumble with the India Office. He had decamped to no. 53 Holland Park, a fine oil-painted stucco house in a fashionable corner of Kensington in west London.* His wife Bamba stayed in the country.

It was a convenient base from which to make his enlightening visits to the British Museum, for forays to King Street, and a cab-ride away from St James's to bore everyone senseless at the Carlton. By the winter of 1884 it had become the command headquarters for incipient rebellion against the British Empire.

After a year of bureaucratic anguish, the Punjab government had finally allowed Duleep's 'rascally cousin' to take ship for England with two of his sons and three servants. The report of Inspector McCracken of the Punjab Special Branch takes up the story: 'On the 28th September 1884, Sardar Thakur Singh Sandhanwalia left Amritsar and proceeded to his father-in-law's house at Dadri, in the Jhind state, where he stayed about a month. Then, on pretence of his son's marriage expenses, he obtained Rs. 12,000 and started for England. He was accompanied by Gurmukh Singh,† Gurdit Singh, and Partab Singh. Nothing is known of the first named, but Gurdit Singh and Partab Singh are brothers the former being the elder, and they live near the Kaulsar tank in Amritsar city. Partab Singh is a "Granthi" a reader of the Sikh scriptures i.e., a Sikh Priest, taken to England to read the

---

* He first took the lease in 1881 at £350 a year when threatening to abandon Elveden. The government advanced £4,000 to furnish it.
† The inspector was mistaken – the emissary was Thakur Singh's son Narinder.

"Granth" to Maharajah Duleep Singh.' (He was the 'Bhaee' or brother mentioned in the 'prophecy' letter to Balmoral.)

Every day the *Granth* was read. Every night in the shuttered Holland Park house Thakur Singh would talk of the lost riches of the Punjab, poring over lists of private estates and Mr Talbot's report. But Thakur Singh had carried with him to England something much more potent than a list of lost property. He bore the keys to the whole kingdom in the form of the prophecy, the intimation of which was so perplexing Queen Victoria as she read the stream of 'half-cracky' letters in autumnal Aberdeenshire. The prophecy had now taken on a fantastic new dimension. As well as Duleep, it seemed, the Czar of Russia was having visions of the marble pavilions of Lahore.

McCracken's report continued:

> In April 1884 a Kuka named Chanda Singh was found to be reciting an inflammatory poem at the Baisakhi cattle fair at Amritsar, which is largely attended by the Sikhs. Towards the end of the poem, the following lines occur:
>
> 'The Sat Guru (True Guru) remarked that the martyrs had already been sent by him to fetch Russia, with instructions to deliver the order of God to her, and compel her to obey it.
>
> 'Having delivered the written order to the messenger, the Guru told him to deliver the following message to Russia. "Thou art ordered by God to conquer Lahore for us." When the Czar held his court, he called his Minister and offering him a seat, told him that in the night he had seen the Khalsa in a vision at which he was alarmed, as they had asked him to march on Lahore.
>
> 'The Minister reflected on the arduous and hazardous nature of the journey, but finally ordered preparations to be made for the army to march, with drums beating. When the Russian troops invade the country, agitation will prevail in London, and the British army will march to India. Many battles will be fought, and there will be much lamentation, mothers will weep for their sons, and wives for their husbands.
>
> 'When the Russians enter the Punjab, famine will rage and make waste the country. People will die in terrible numbers and crime will be without limit. He alone will be saved, who

will seek the protection of the guru and devote his whole attention to God.

'The Sat Guru will then return to the Punjab and disestablish all former systems and set up new standards, causing the name of God to be repeated by everyone even the demons.'

The return of the True Guru meant the return of Duleep Singh – as king and deity.

The Maharajah was in conflict. He was Christian, the Sikh doctrine of his childhood smothered under years of Anglican piety. The teaching of Guru Gobind Singh was that no other guru should follow. This was a double heresy; he was doubly sceptical. The Maharajah told his cousin: 'He perfectly remembered the prophecies being designedly altered by his maternal uncle [Jawahir Singh], and therefore did not attach any weight to them.'

Thakur Singh would not give up. He wrote urgently to his eldest son, Gurbachan Singh, in the Punjab to obtain written statements from the principal Sikh priests on the prophecies' veracity. These were sent signed and sealed to Elveden. There would be no more doubts.

The Maharajah was to relay the revelations a year later in a grumbling letter to a startled Lord Randolph Churchill, Secretary of State for India:

> Being asked upon an occasion by his disciples whether he would ever again visit the world, Gooroo Gobind Singh replied in the affirmative adding that he will take birth again in the household of Sikh who will marry a Mohammedan wife, and that his name will be Deep Singh, of which Duleep Singh is a corruption. [His father Ranjit had a Muslim wife.]
>
> The Gooroo went on to say that this Deep Singh, after becoming dispossessed of all he had inherited, residing for a long time alone in a foreign land, will return and correct the errors in which the Sikhs have fallen ... but that before the latter comes to pass Deep Singh will suffer much persecution and will be reduced to absolute poverty.
>
> The Gooroo further predicts that Deep Singh will marry a Christian wife, and his children by her, the Gooroo calls 'Englishmen' in the prophecy.
>
> The Gooroo foretells that there will be a war between the

two dogs Boochoo and Dultoo (presumably the bear and the bull-dog) in which Deep Singh will take part, but that he will be defeated and will take refuge at certain village (the name of which cannot at present be identified) and when there self-knowledge will be revealed to him.'

[The Maharajah finished the letter in Gurmukhi script:] *Des bech utth jaen Farangi, Tau gajenge mor Bhujangi* – The English after selling the country will quit the land. Then will thunder my snakes.

The symbolism was obvious, it could have been plucked from a Punch cartoon: England was the bull-dog, Russia the bear.

Perhaps it was cheek, perhaps it was that internal conflict, but before their return to the Punjab laden with seditious plans, Duleep was anxious for Thakur Singh Sandhanwalia to meet the Queen Empress herself. On 12 May 1885 he wrote to Sir Henry Ponsonby: 'My cousins who are to be presented at court tomorrow are very anxious that they should not miss seeing their Empress of whose graciousness they have heard so much from me.

'They are extremely poor for their station in life and hence their appearing before Her Majesty in peasant costumes. It is most painful for me to think what these blood relatives of the Lion of the Punjab have come down to – but who can resist the force of destiny?' Sir Henry minuted on the letter: 'The Queen saw them at the drawing room and saw the servants at the Palace.'

It seems to have been an uncomfortable encounter. On 15 August 1885 Lord Randolph Churchill received a memo from Sir Henry: 'The Queen commands me to inform you that she fears the financial difficulties of the Maharajah Duleep Singh are rendering him desperate, that he is consequently susceptible to the intrigues of evil counsellors who are calling him to come to the Punjab.'

There is no doubt whom she meant. Had she not warned long ago of the Maharajah falling into the hands of 'bad advisers'? This was worse – they were Indians. The Russian Army was knocking on the door of Afghanistan. The time for the snakes to thunder was growing near.

# The Guru

## HM Legation, Tokyo, Japan, May 1885

The Hon. Francis Plunkett, Her Majesty's Envoy Extraordinary to Japan, peered through his binoculars. A large Russian merchantman, the *Vladimir*, was in Tokyo Bay, its agents buying all the Welsh steam-coal in the port. The envoy was convinced the ship was a commerce raider about to embark on a predatory cruise in the Pacific as soon as war broke out with Britain. But there was other, more secret, business to conduct. On 2 May a cipher telegram arrived from Sir Philip Currie at the Foreign Office in London. It read: 'Private. Would you mind wiring to General Tevis reminding him of conversation with you of May 'eighty-three, and ask, if of the same mind, he would allow agent to call on him. Strictest secrecy guaranteed.'

The veteran diplomat understood. It referred to a very confidential approach made to him two years earlier when Plunkett was first secretary in Paris – and Whitehall was alarmed by Irish-American republican plots being cooked up in France. Someone had discreetly offered his services as a double-agent. Now in 1885 the threat had returned, tinged with the prospect of an imminent Anglo-Russian war. It was time to renew an old acquaintance.

Plunkett cabled back: 'To whom is the General to send answer? If he agrees he will no doubt expect some compensation.' Currie replied: 'General had better send his answer to you as he might be shy about writing to an unknown person. Could you ascertain what compensation he would expect and ask him for card or password which agent could give when he communicates with the General, by which latter could recognise him?' Plunkett did as he was asked – a letter from Japan crossed the world via the American mail to the French capital. By the same route the mysterious 'General' agreed. Her Majesty's Foreign Secret Service had recruited an agent in Paris whom no one (especially rival departments in Whitehall) could possibly have sight of. A trap was set.

## Elveden Hall, Suffolk, Summer–Autumn 1885

The Maharajah was desperate to get to India. He would use any means, any excuse. The Russian advance towards Afghanistan provided it. On 21 April 1885 he suddenly wrote to the Secretary of State: 'I beg of you kindly to inform the British government that it is my intention to join the British Army as a volunteer unfortunately should war break out between England and Russia and to proceed for Bombay via Karachi and Bolechestan to Afghanistan and thus avoiding passing through the Punjab.

'My father was an ally of the British crown and I myself have had the honour of being styled as such and although my Christian guardian has thought it fit to oppress and ill-treat me yet I am determined to prove my loyalty to my sovereign. I shall leave my family as hostages in your Lordship's hands.' He wrote to the Queen: 'I humbly hope my sovereign will not forget my prayer . . . and grant me the privilege of wearing her uniform like the other princes of India and thus identifying me in the eyes of all the disaffected in India with the British "Raaj".'

The answer was most definitely no; the Maharajah might suddenly do a runner. The Duke of Cambridge himself, commander-in-chief of the British Army, had lately dined with the Maharajah at Euston Hall, the Norfolk seat of the Duke of Grafton. As they discussed grand strategy, manoeuvring Russian mustard pots across the dinner table towards the fruit bowl of Herat, the Maharajah's motives seemed unconvincing. The Duke of Cambridge wrote to Ponsonby: 'Depend on it, while he is harmless here, he is dangerous there [India] and I think he is disposed for mischief!'

The Queen's cousin was perceptive. The Maharajah had already opened a burgeoning correspondence with his potential partisans in the Punjab, especially the dispossessed of the good old days (or, rather, their children, the average life expectancy for a male Punjabi being under forty). The Indian Police Special Branch intercepted a poignant letter to Hera Khan, the Mohammedan son of a former courtier.

ELVEDEN HALL, THETFORD, NORFOLK.
OCTOBER 7TH, 1885

I am aware that your father was a favourite servant of my father. I also recollect that your father was sitting on the neck of the elephant when my uncle was shot before me, and I myself recollect him perfectly well and often think of his faithful services.

You must be content with the lot that God has placed you in. I greatly regret to say that there is no possibility of the Government rendering me justice, and therefore I shall leave England on the 16th December next and take up my residence quietly at Delhi for I am also poor now:

I send you Salam Alaikum for I now follow the precepts of Baba Nanak who considered all religions to be alike before the Almighty or we are all His servants.
(sgd) Duleep Singh.

PS You will be surprised to hear that I know a little Arabic and have read the Koran, translated into the English language. La illa il l lilla Muhammad ul Rasul ulla, and that is quite true. You see I am not a bigoted Sikh, but am a lover of all God's creatures.

The messianic talk in Lahore of a second coming meanwhile made the government of India more nervous. Inspector McCracken reported: 'The vernacular newspapers have begun to discuss the Maharajah's return to India, and congratulate Sardar Thakur Singh on his success in prevailing on His Highness to re-embrace the religion of his forefathers.'

Across the Punjab the portents and rumours were multiplying. Letters were circulating with the message: 'The time is close at hand when the white and red-faced "Malech"* will be swept away and the beloved of the Guru, your comforter, will arrive.' More letters were intercepted at the travelling post office at Amritsar with 'a small piece of black ribbon pinned at the top, below which was written in English: India

---

* McCracken explained: 'Malech – abomination, a term applied to eaters of beef and particularly to the English by the Kukas.'

for the Indians only. Wear this and let it be the sign of brotherhood and friendship. Be true to our race as Indians. Strike now or never. Maharajah Duleep Singh ki jai! (May Maharajah Duleep Singh be victorious!)'

When the Maharajah and his family's names appeared on the passenger list of the P & O steamer SS *Paramatta*, Bombay-bound from Gravesend departing 28 October 1885, officials in India went into near panic. If he could not be stopped in England, he could be detained en route. It was only practical politics to set a spy on him.

Mr George Forbes, junior under-secretary at the Foreign Department, wrote to London urgently from Simla: 'The question for consideration concerns the regulation of the Maharajah's movements on his entering Indian territories. As soon as the vessel carrying His Highness puts into Aden harbour, the Viceroy has, under the treaty of Lahore, the right to declare and assign the Maharajah's place of future residence.' It was an exquisite piece of civil-service drafting. Mr Forbes had spotted something. Indian-bound British steamers made landfall at Aden, broiling colonial outpost and coaling station. Aden came under the Viceroy's legal remit under whiskery legislation. Collar the Maharajah there and he and his family would vanish into an Arabian limbo. The memorandum was filed and noted.

The clever Mr Forbes continued: 'His adherents and well-wishers have been circulating pamphlets favourable to his pretensions – and prayers offered for himself in the temple at Amritsar. Should therefore the Maharajah make the journey which he has advertised and come out to India, it might be well to stop him at Aden and intern him there.'

He added: 'I presume the Secretary of State has taken steps to have His Highness's movements watched, and that it is not necessary to remind on this point.'

Lord Randolph Churchill had tried to wash his hands of the Maharajah, telling him curtly by letter that the Viceroy would deal with him as he saw fit if he should set foot in India. It was time to remind Lord Randolph of England's iniquities, the revelations of the Punjab Papers and the latest from the guru. They were falling into his trap. The Maharajah replied:

# The Guru

I cannot tell Your Lordship how pleased I am to learn that the Government have determined the very course which I have all along desired should be followed towards me on my arrival in India in order to help forward my destiny.

I welcome the persecution which awaits me in India, for it has been foretold by the last Sikh Gooroo that I shall suffer in this manner, and that when I shall have been reduced to absolute poverty then my prosperity is to commence.

What effect this ill-treatment, foretold by Gooroo Gobind Singh, of one so intimately connected by prophecy with Sikh Faith as I am, will have on the mind of my countrymen I am not able to imagine, but doubtless seeing all predictions come literally to pass in my case, they will not unnaturally look forward to the fulfilment of the rest of the prophecy shortly.

I feel very proud indeed of the fact that the buzzing of a wretched little gnat should have disturbed the repose of the mighty British Lion, and in consequence the India Government should think it necessary as it were to 'set out to seek a flea'.

Another august personage was subjected to similar bombardment in those last months of 1885. 'May I invite myself tomorrow for a cup of tea?' the Maharajah wrote to Sir Robert Montgomery, former Lieutenant-Governor of the Punjab, who still had influential connections at the India Office. Sir Robert would rather not meet quite yet. The Maharajah thanked him for his 'cold tone'; this, he felt sure, was because he was 'afraid of betraying the real feelings of his noble and kind heart. You do not know how I value at this moment when I am broken-hearted a kind word or a kind thought from one who knew the old Punjab. Would he take tea at five o'clock on Saturday – which I trust Lady Montgomery will not refuse me and you are liberty to shut the door in my face?'

Duleep duly called at 5 p.m. at Sir Robert's Hyde Park house. The master was out. He tried again on Tuesday. Tea was taken. The Maharajah had at least one unwilling ally in Whitehall. Poor Sir Robert would soon be bombarded with demands for more than cups of tea.

The government of India budged a little, agreeing that he would be allowed at the discretion of the Viceroy, Lord Dufferin, to reside at Ootacamund, in the Madras presidency, a sleepy hill station far distant from Lahore. With its half-timbered houses and temperate climate it was supposed to be 'just like Leatherhead'. The Maharajah would have none of it and returned to his barrage aimed at Lord Randolph. He wrote on 2 December:

> I have the honour to acknowledge the receipt of Your Lordship's letter conveying to me perfectly unnecessary information as to my place of residence in India.
>
> I have already on several occasions informed the India Council that I intend on reaching Bombay to proceed to Delhi, and His Excellency the Viceroy has only to have me put under arrest ... for I am quite prepared to suffer any persecution from the most immoral and unjust British Government.
>
> For the verification of the above assertion, I refer Your Lordship to the Punjab Papers, 1848–49, in which it will be found stated that the British nation constituted itself my guardian under the Treaty of Bhyrowal, but finding the obligations contracted under that document inconvenient ... not only deprived me most unjustly of my kingdom, but also appropriated to its own use all my private property.

Lord Randolph despaired. 'He pesters this office with either violent or cringeing letters,' he memoed. 'I have read the history of his case very carefully and am irresistibly led to the conclusion he is a "very bad lot".'

It was time to get tough. Not only was a detective from Scotland Yard discreetly dogging the Indian gentleman's footsteps,* his by-now bulging dossier became the responsibility of the hard man at the India Office, Colonel Owen Tudor Burne.

Burne summed up the bizarre letters to his minister as 'breathing

---

* There is no direct archival evidence for this assertion. It is based on the note to Churchill – 'I presume he has taken steps to have H.H. watched' – and the fact that would emerge later, the Indian Police were being fed information on the Maharajah's movements in London.

with the malice and vexation of impotent rage'. The question was what to do next. Was the Maharajah playing a venal game of blackmail (and thus might be bought off)? Or had his mind been seized by this mumbo-jumbo about gurus, destiny and the Koh-i-Noor? The Queen must be protected from an appalling scandal.

Sir Owen* wrote in his memoirs: 'Duleep Singh's affairs came under the supervision of my department, in consequence of which I had unceasing difficulty with him . . . although our personal relations were always studiously friendly.

'In fact, Duleep Singh was a man of perfect manners, and even grumbled and snarled in quite a pleasant way. His principal trouble was, as with all asiatics, money. A few years before his death the Maharajah claimed the Koh-i-noor, as to which I had to give detailed explanations to the Queen, which quite satisfied her of the baselessness of the demand, and added, I think, to her gracious regard for myself.'

Duleep was getting close to the brink. In Calcutta, urgent official papers were being circulated. Sir Henry Mortimer Durand, the India government's Foreign Secretary, minuted: 'The Maharajah intends leaving England on the 20th January. He cannot be allowed to intrigue freely on the Punjab. His arrival in Bombay will, I am afraid, be a sure proof that he means to give as much trouble as he can.'

A dovish colleague on the India Council, Sir Theodore Hope, minuted back: 'I am strongly disposed to deal liberally with the Maharajah. I would rather pay his debts and give him a fresh start on a reasonable income in England than run the risk of the scandal and political difficulties of his returning to India.'

But the hard men seemed to be winning. 'The moment we show any willingness to treat, we place ourselves in the Maharajah's hands. It is a very dangerous game for us to play. "Chantage" lives on fear, and we shall form no exception to the rule,' wrote Sir Arthur Godley, permanent under-secretary of state at the India Office.

On 16 January 1886 the Maharajah wrote from Elveden to the

---

* Sir Owen Tudor Burne (1837–1909) would be the most important official figure in the Maharajah's life. Secretary of the Political and Secret Department 1874–87, he later became trustee of the Maharajah's abandoned family. He expressed his own unwavering *raison d'état* views on Duleep's case in a confidential memorandum for Queen Victoria's private secretary in 1882: 'The terms which D.S. had to swallow on the Annexation were perhaps a little hard on him. But he <u>had</u> to fall because his subjects broke out in open rebellion and it was hard on him.'

Marquis of Salisbury (the Conservative peer had displaced Gladstone as Prime Minister on 24 June 1885). The immense document reprised the double-barrelled broadsides to *The Times* of four years earlier; he was still banging away about money at the iniquities of the Treaty of Lahore. 'I do not aspire to be reinstated on the throne of the Punjab,' he insisted. What he desired above all was an investigation of his claims by the 'highest legal authorities of Your Lordship's House'.

## *India Office, St James' Park, London, January 1886*

A sudden political crisis opened a crack in the door. The Salisbury administration fell on 26 January 1886. The Earl of Kimberley arrived back at the India Office for a six-month Gladstonian interregnum. The Maharajah had received a reply from the Conservative Prime Minister, written on his last day in office, which seemed to offer a glimmer of hope. It had ended: 'The Secretary of State for India and his Council have both the power and the wish to arrive at a just decision in regard to these controverted matters.' The next morning, 28 January, he stormed round to the India Office clutching the letter to see Sir Owen Burne in person.

The secret-civil servant greeted his visitor and opened proceedings speaking in Punjabi, making a joke about being late for his train; the Maharajah found it amusing. They got down to business, Duleep Singh rehearsing his well-worn fiscal claims. The Pind Dadan Khan salt-mines, 'which belonged to him', alone were worth a staggering £400,000 a year.*

Sir Owen recorded the meeting in the form of a conversation. 'Your claims are enormous and visionary, my dear Maharajah,' he said. 'My own Department is filled with correspondence on your case, which would prove that, year after year, you have thankfully accepted the concessions given to you, and finally agreed to an Act of Parliament which it was hoped at the time would put an end to all further disagreements.'

---

* A British visitor to the disputed mines in Ranjit Singh's time witnessed scenes of biblical cruelty. 'Mothers and their infants, children and old men – all with cadaverous looks and stifled breathing, toiling amidst the beautiful red salt crystals that formed the cave. The pay was one rupee for 2,000 pounds of salt.'

The Maharajah replied: 'This was true enough, but I had done it all in ignorance of my real position, that I have only recently realised.' He was referring to the Punjab Papers again. 'One of the highest legal authorities in England has assured me that my claims are all perfectly just. I am a King and ought to be treated as such.'

Sir Owen had other matters to attend to. He rushed away, top-hatted, to the smoky tunnels of the District Railway, agreeing to continue the conversation the following day.

The contentious dialogue began again next morning.

'Well, Maharajah, I have read your memorial to Lord Salisbury. This I see as labour thrown away. I will merely speak of your claims as they strike me personally as one who is a true friend to you. They are preposterous. I cannot comprehend how a person in your position can court rebuff by making demands which no Government in its sense can even consider, much less satisfy.'

The Maharajah replied: 'I like your frankness, Sir Owen, and appreciate it. But I can assure you that nothing short of their recognition by the Government, and adequate compensation, will satisfy me. Why cannot the Privy Council, or the House of Lords, adjudicate on my case?'

'That is impossible,' said Sir Owen. 'You will never get any Government to agree to so direct an interference with the powers of the Government of India, in its dealings with the native princes and their pensions.'

Now he came to the point. Breaking the Treaty of Lahore would challenge the legal basis on which the whole empire in India had been built.

The Maharajah knew he was caught, but his outraged royal dignity would not let go: 'Will not the Government of India give me this full inquiry? They have treated me like an animal; they are now trying to goad me to desperation; they forget I am a King.'

Sir Owen changed tack. His visitor had 'wind in his head'. He appealed to him to 'view the matter in a business-like way': 'On your part, Maharajah, you signed away your kingdom with alacrity; you could say nothing at the time against the justice then dealt out to you; you have since then thankfully accepted from year to year, until lately, all that the Government of India have done for you.'

'I acknowledge all this. But I now see, that I have been a fool. It is only lately that I have learnt to realize my position as a King.'

There was no way round the Maharajah's regal illusions. Perhaps money would help after all.

'Suppose I was a benevolent Secretary of State and were to say that you shall have £25,000 a year, clear for all charges, would that be acceptable?' Sir Owen ventured. It was not.

'Well, Maharajah, I see that benevolence won't do. Picture me, therefore, as an austere Secretary of State,' said Sir Owen. 'Suppose I were to say to you: "You are disobeying our wishes by going to India. You will therefore be seized when you get there, you will be deprived of your stipends and be made to reside in some spot selected by Government of India," what then?'

'I should laugh at you. This is just what I want. You must at any rate feed and clothe me and my family, and my income will be then more than made up by subscriptions from every *ryot* [peasant village] in the Punjab.'

Sir Owen was perplexed. 'What on earth are you going to India for?' he asked. 'I cannot quite understand why a nobleman like you, who has embraced Christianity . . . should want to go to India.'

'I have already taken the first step to abjure Christianity, because I no longer believe in so-called Christian Governments,' the Maharajah replied. 'If they touch me, it will shake the Punjab, if not now, at any rate later. My friends advise me to stay on to see if I can get an inquiry, and, moreover, there is now a change of Government, and I think Lord Kimberley will befriend me.' Perhaps by now he was snarling in the pleasant way that so amused Sir Owen.

The incoming minister was just as unmoved. Lord Kimberley met the Maharajah at the India Office on 8 February and told him his claims were 'preposterous'. His offer to serve in the British Army in Afghanistan had been turned down because his loyalty 'was not of a nature to inspire the Government of India with confidence'.

The interview was clearly at an end. The Maharajah seemed crestfallen. He replied limply: 'I see it is all of no use, but I shall wait a few days to see whether I can get any satisfaction. If not, I shall go broken-hearted to India.'

# 11

# Bamba

❧

*Elveden Hall, Suffolk, Autumn–Winter 1885–86*

QUEEN BAMBA'S CONDITION was a delicate one. Her husband had seemingly immured himself in Holland Park. His infrequent returns to Elveden were stormy. The children were listless: the princes Victor and Frederick were now aged nineteen and sixteen; the princesses Bamba and Catherine were becoming questioning adolescents; Sophia was nine; little Prince Albert was proving sickly.

Elveden was decaying around them. The hatcheries went untended. Pheasant eggs were no longer dispatched to be sold in Mayfair for ninepence a dozen. The menagerie was empty. The tumbling pigeons had flown and the parrots refrained from flying comically at grand visitors; they merely mimicked the guttural oaths of the absent Maharajah.

The Rector of Elveden, the Reverend St George Walker, felt compelled to write to the India Office about the great fall. His letter was copied to Queen Victoria and is in the Royal Archives at Windsor.

ELVEDEN RECTORY, 11 SEPTEMBER 1885

As the rector of this parish and having I trust the temporal as well as the spiritual care of my people, may I be allowed to inform you of what probably you may not yet be aware of . . . viz that everything here is at a standstill if not in a state of collapse.

His Highness the Maharajah Duleep Singh has lately declared his intention of at once giving up to the Government his estates here in England and proceeding forthwith to India.

Notices to this effect have been issued to servants and the tenantry generally and directions given for all labour to cease and an immediate sale of stock.

The consequence is that numbers have been thrown out of employment and others are preparing to quit their cottages. As a matter of course the able-bodied of the parish have been compelled to seek employment elsewhere – but what will become of the afflicted, the aged and the extreme poor I know not.

We in the neighbourhood are indeed sorry and in a measure surprised at that very serious turn which affairs have now taken, it being generally supposed that His Highness having proved the justice of his claims, the Government would at once redress his grievances and so prevent the deplorable troubles and privations which now threaten this and the surrounding parishes.

I hope that you will pardon the liberty in thus addressing you but a sense of duty to my poor helpless parishioners prompts me to do so.

On his rare Suffolk visits the Maharajah was impossible – brooding obsessively in the library with his box of transcripts of the Punjab Papers, cursing at every new rebuff. He was drinking heavily. Bamba too began to seek increasing solace from the sideboard. How could he uproot her from all she had come to know? What about the children? She wept and prayed. Bamba was ill; she had never been quite right since a fall while skating eight years ago. The nanny, Miss Date, had left when Bamba first became 'difficult'.

Bamba remembered her first meeting with the Maharajah in the spring of 1864 at the American Mission School in Cairo. She was fifteen, he was twenty-four. The circumstances of his arrival were extraordinary enough. His mother's body, six months dead, lay in a lead-lined casket in the hold of a ship in Alexandria harbour. The Maharajah was taking Rani Jindan's remains to India to be cremated according to Sikh rites. Soortoo, her mother's favourite slave-girl, travelled with him.

This was the same mission school that he had visited eighteen years before on his first voyage to England, when 'he had been interested to see so many orphan girls being educated in the Christian religion'.

This time he was a grand personage, invited to present prizes to the most diligent pupils. He was no longer the slim-hipped adolescent of the Winterhalter portrait made nine years before; he was becoming pudgy, but looked fetching enough.

One pretty girl caught his eye: Bamba Müller, the daughter of Herr Ludwig Müller, a German banker, and Frau Sofia Müller, a Coptic Christian. The Maharajah had shrugged off the consorts that Prince Albert had pressed on him; here was a pretty Christian bride. 'I love you – will you be my wife?' he asked on his first outbound encounter. Bamba did not understand a word, she spoke only Arabic. A dragoman (interpreter) was summoned. She gave him an embroidered handkerchief and 'kissed his hands'. How could she marry one so grand? He sailed on to India with his mother's corpse.

He clearly loved her. He wrote from Bombay to Mrs Dales, wife of the American head of the Cairo Presbyterian Mission: 'I know how dearly you love Bamba, it is natural you should feel pangs at the thought of losing her. I sympathise with you cordially but you must pardon my selfishness in being delighted at the hope of possessing that Precious Pearl which is invaluable to me. I feel I am not worthy of her. She is such a spiritually minded girl – it will indeed be a source of great pleasure to me to secure her happiness in every way.'

The Maharajah wrote from Bombay to English friends announcing his engagement. Her name was 'Bamba' which meant 'pink', he explained.

On his return to Egypt, she was waiting for him. She had changed her mind.

'She is the illegitimate daughter of a wealthy merchant' so the India Court of Directors were privately informed. The Maharajah already knew it and also knew that she had been 'adopted by her father'. He told the Queen by letter of the fact on the eve of the wedding: 'It is her birth that has prevented me from telling you of this sooner, knowing that there is such an objection to it in England,' he explained.

The story stayed in the India Office for decades, like a ghost in the machine. An odd cycle of letters is appended to the copious Duleep Singh family papers: in 1909 a Lieut.-General Frederick Lance of 'The Laurels', Roehampton, wrote to the India Office enclosing a long deposition sent to him by a Mrs A. A. Johnson of Oberlin, Ohio, USA.

Her letter, dated 8 December 1903, was composed aboard the Nile steamer SS *Rameses the Great* and titled: 'The story of the marriage of Maharajah Duleep Singh, as told to me by a member of the American Baptist Mission, Cairo.' General Lance felt he should lodge it with the government as 'it may be of interest'.

An Abyssinian woman of attractive appearance and supposed to be of rank in her country was proposed for sale as a slave in Cairo with other captives.

The utter dejection and shame she displayed so affected a gentleman (a German savant who happened to be in Cairo) that he bid for her. This gentleman made an arrangement for her care, with the intention of sending her back to her country when opportunity offered. But he was taken seriously ill and died, but before his death he made the woman over to a friend, a German banker.

The banker betrayed his trust, and a female child was born whom he made over to the American [Baptist crossed out] Presbyterian mission in Cairo to be brought up.* The girl was educated and grew to be very beautiful – with a sweet disposition, but she was brought up as a native that she might be employed in mission work in Abyssinia.

The Maharajah Duleep Singh when quite a young man was detained at Cairo on his way to dispose of the ashes of his mother. In the mission school he saw the Abyssininan girl and was much struck by her beauty and manner. He was determined not to marry one of his own race (because she would be a heathen and uneducated) nor a native of that country who had deprived him of the throne of his father. He had been so struck by the beauty of this girl he was desirous of marrying her.

The missionaries strongly objected . . . (it was they who told the Maharajah of the girl's parentage as a reason not to marry her) . . . and the girl felt quite unable to accept the offer. The Maharajah, much disappointed, continued on his voyage. The

---

* Mrs Johnson noted on the letter that the father did not make the child over, as her informant stated, but 'the mother came and lived near the Mission that her daughter might be educated by them. She died with the cholera.'

girl became ill at ease, a marked change came over her . . . it was clear that she regretted her answer.

The missionaries wrote to the Maharajah, and he at once sent a sum of money for her and a request that she taken into the missionaries' house to be taught European manners.

The missionaries informed the girl's father . . . who said it was impossible for the girl to fill such a position, and that the marriage was sure to turn out unhappy, and thoroughly objected. He however thought it right to tell his wife of the whole affair. The wife at once insisted that no obstacles be put in the way of the girl's marriage – and moreover caused the Maharajah to be told the story of the girl's true parentage.

The Maharajah being told replied that his 'father had three wives and I am the son of the last one taken. I have no reason to compare my parentage with hers – for I have nothing of which to boast.'

These papers, clearly indicating that Bamba was the illegitimate daughter of a slave bought in the Cairo market, were dryly considered by an India Office official. 'There is nothing in them inconsistent with their relating to the Maharajah's marriage with his first wife, the mother of Prince Victor etc,' he reported. 'There is nothing otherwise than to the credit of all parties concerned in the story now told, but the publication of them could not but give offence. There is no guarantee of their accuracy . . . I have buried them in the archives of the Dept. from which, let us hope, they will never have to be disinterred.'

Bamba and the Maharajah were married in a civil ceremony at the British consulate in Alexandria. The *Times of India* reported: 'The marriage of the Maharajah Duleep Singh was conducted on the 7th June, in the presence of a very few witnesses. The young lady who has now become the Maharani is the daughter of an European merchant here. Her mother is an Abyssinian.

'She is between fifteen and sixteen years of age, of a slight but graceful figure, interesting rather than handsome, not tall, and in complexion lighter than her husband. She is a Christian, and was educated in the American Presbyterian Mission School at Cairo; and it was during a chance visit there, while on his way out to India, that the Prince first saw his future bride, who was engaged in instructions in the school.'

The Maharajah wore European costume for the wedding, 'excepting a red tarboosh'. The bride's dress was also European, 'of white moire antique, a fichu pointe d'Alencon with short lace sleeves, orange blossoms in her dark hair, with, of course, the usual gauze veil. She wore but few jewels; a necklace of fine pearls, and a bracelet set with diamonds, were her only ornaments.'

The British consul went through the wedding formalities. Bamba made her vows in Arabic, in 'a low but musical voice'. A Christian ceremony was performed afterwards by one of the American ministers at Herr Müller's summer villa at Ramala. After a month in Egypt, the couple embarked for England via Marseilles and Paris.

They put up first at Mrs Claridge's Hotel, then in August took a train for Scotland. The first child came quickly, a boy, but he is not noted in any contemporary memoir. He lived for one day. There is a grave in Kenmore churchyard, Perthshire, seventeen miles from Auchlyne House, a favoured shooting lodge on the estate of Lord Breadalbane. The small headstone reads: 'To the memory of the infant son of the Maharajah Duleep Singh, late ruler of the Sikh nation, Punjab, India and the Maharanee his wife, born 4 August 1865, died 5 August 1865.'

Just as Duleep had been uprooted, denatured and reconstructed by his English mentors, so Bamba would be his clay. She was sixteen when she became mistress of Elveden, purchased by the Maharajah in September 1864. A governess, Miss Hart, was appointed to teach her English before she came out in society. Lady Sophia Leven, mother of Duleep's friend Ronald Leslie-Melville, wrote to her Roehampton neighbour, Lady Login, of the social novelty: 'She is not the wonderful beauty that my son supposed; but she is remarkably nice-looking, with very fine eyes, and a sweet expression. In that respect she is better-looking than Gouramma, and a size larger.

'She looked simple and quiet, and rather dignified. I asked the Maharani if her head was turned by her marriage? And he said that she knew nothing of her position, and did not care for her jewels when the Maharajah showed them to her . . . I fancy she is entirely occupied with him. She is most submissive, and if asked if she would like to do anything, answers: "Maharajah wish – I wish!" '

The Maharajah fussed over his doll-like bride, pushing her into the voluminous crinolines then so modish. According to Lady Leven he wanted her to look 'like other people' but insisted 'that her dresses were cut short'. Her seamstresses despaired. A solution was found: she would dress in daring faux-Egyptian taste.

'Her costume had a full skirt, and Turkish jacket with wide sleeves; on her head was a jaunty cap, like a fez, made of fine large pearls, worn on one side with a long tassel of pearls hanging almost to her shoulder,' Lady Leven wrote in gushing letters to her friend. 'Her hair was plaited into several long, tight plaits, hanging straight down all round. This had rather a curious effect. She wore this only on state occasions. Ordinarily, her hair was coiled on her head in an immense plait of course, she was loaded with jewels besides.'

Just before Christmas 1865, the Maharajah and Bamba were invited to 'dine and sleep' at Windsor, a signal social honour, where her 'native costume' proved a fashion sensation. 'Her Majesty and the Princesses were exceedingly kind and immensely interested in her and her toilette,' Lady Leven recorded. 'The Queen kissed her, as an acknowledgment of her rank, and pleased the Maharajah very much by her complimentary speeches; and the two Princesses made her sit between them all the evening, cross-questioning her about her life.'

The second child, Prince Victor Albert Jay, was born in July 1866. The bond with their royal friends seemed complete when, on 20 March 1867, he was baptized in the private chapel at Windsor Castle with Queen Victoria and the Reverend William Jay, the Rector of Elveden, as sponsors. The Queen wrote in her journal: 'I never beheld a lovelier child, a plump little darling with the most splendid dark eyes, but not very dark skin.'

The Maharajah had embarked on Elveden's transformation. He filled the house with builders while Bamba filled it with children. She corresponded piously with Mrs Lansing, an old friend from the American Mission in Cairo: 'All the building of the house is finished now, but we have not begun to decorate it yet as the walls are not perfectly dry enough for painting,' she wrote in May 1871. 'Baby now talks a little and it is so pretty to hear him. The Maharajah has been talking much about going to India next winter but will not go if he does not let out his farms well. I am expecting another baby next October.'

A year later she wrote: 'The Lord has been very merciful and brought me safely through my confinement. I am able to nurse myself which

is a great comfort. Victor and Freddie have had very bad colds. Bamba
has been very well and can speak nicely. We find the house very
comfortable, a great deal has been done but the painting and furnishing
is not finished yet. Baby's name is Catherine Hilda.'

Victor went to Eton. He seems to have been miserable, tormented
by stories of his father's profligacy. Fragmentary letters survive. His
father wrote: 'Cheer up old chap. I am looking forward to your coming
home for the holidays and our going out together to shoot the "long
tails".' Bamba told him: 'Dearest Vickie, Avoid every mischievous and
bad way, give no trouble to your kind tutor so that dear Papa may
have not trouble. By the first train was sent to you this morning two
partridges, one pheasant and a dozen eggs.'

'Our little ones are on the whole dear good children, still one sometimes sees the old nature rising up,' she wrote to her old mission
friend. 'I pray that they may be the Lord's true servants.' The 'old
nature' – Bamba, so Christian, sensed, even in her own infant children,
the call of something wild. The house was turning into an oriental
palace of mirrors. Its owner had embarked on his own transformation.


## Elveden Hall, Suffolk, Spring 1886

The Maharajah seemed, if it were possible, even more obsessive. He
had abandoned his Christian devotions. Benevolent subscriptions to
the poor of Elveden parish and the American Mission at Cairo had
ceased. When he was at the Hall he would only pore over that heathen
prophecy. Even hunting seemed to hold no charms.

Mr Frederick Bonnet, the estate message-taker, would arrive with
daily telegrams from Thetford post office. Some would make the Maharajah growl in rage. Others, with a London dispatch mark, he would
pocket with a smirk. Bamba's destiny seemed to have been shackled
to a lunatic's.

These were things to put in order before the great *démarche*. The
Maharajah wrote brusquely to the India Office: 'I desire also that
my stipend continues to be paid into Messrs Coutts & Co's Bank as
heretofore, and that the following life pensions be deducted from it
and disbursed by the India Office Treasury: To Lady Login, at the
rate of £500 per annum, to Mrs James Oliphant, at the rate of £500

per annum [widow of Colonel Oliphant, the original comptroller of his household], to my old Scotch gamekeeper, John Peebles, at the rate of £40 per annum, to my English gamekeeper, James Mayes, at the rate of £70 per annum.'

Messrs Phillips, the London auction house which had knocked out the 'dusky native pearls' three years earlier, were instructed to value Elveden's contents: its 'gorgeous' state bedrooms, the drawing-room suite of gilt carved wood covered in green satin, the sandalwood chairs covered with Indian needlework, an ebony suite inlaid and mounted in ormolu, 'enormous mirrors'. The brokers-men were in, prying into Bamba's knife-drawers, sizing up her bedroom linen, cheeking the servants.*

The Maharajah could still do things in style. Madame Flarie, dressmaker, of Bruton Street and Mme Smith, outfitter, were commissioned to make hot-weather outfits for Bamba and the four elder children. The account for £1,102. 5s. 6d. was never paid. She would later send the bill to the India Office where it was endlessly batted around by outraged civil servants. They would eventually decide: 'Secret: The Political Committee are of opinion that the scale of outfit provided by the Maharani Duleep Singh was of an extravagant character and they recommend that £600 only be sanctioned by the Secretary of State for India in Council towards payment.'

The Maharajah made a final plea to 'the Just and the Good' Gladstone: 'Grant me an independent court which the late Prime Minister out of fear of Lord Randolph Churchill denied me,' he wrote on 24 February. 'We poor Indians, I have now learned (though rather late in the day), have no hope from the wicked Tories and our political freedom must come from the Liberals and men like yourself.' Mr Gladstone was unmoved.

Passage to India was booked, on the Peninsular and Orient steamer the SS *Verona*, due to depart Tilbury on 31 March. There was their reception in Bombay to organize – a suite was booked at the Hamilton Hotel and carriages ordered to bear his supporters to the quayside. As a king he must return in pomp (like the bill for Bamba's outfits, the

---

* The sale took place in May 1886 following the Maharajah's departure. *The Times* reported exultingly on how cheaply everything had been sold, concluding: 'Elveden Hall has been so transformed from an old red-brick mansion into a sort of oriental palace, that it would have to be considerably restored back to its English garb to suit most tastes.'

hotel account was sent to the India Office). His partisans in the Punjab must be prepared. Letters were drafted in the style of royal proclamations. There were telegrams to send. In Thetford's sleepy post office the telegraphist tapped out a stream of Morse code to be carried over thousands of miles of copper wire to the heart of India.

The agents of the state began to wake up. The diligent Mr McCracken of the Punjab Special Branch noted: 'On the 12th May 1886 the secretary to the Punjab Government furnished the Deputy Commissioner of Delhi with the necessary order, under the Telegraph Act, to enable him to see any messages passing through the Delhi Telegraph Office, relating to the movements of Duleep Singh or of any persons who appeared to be in correspondence with the Maharajah.' The mail-openers were already at work. A stream of intelligence reports began to arrive in Calcutta and London.

ABSTRACT OF POLITICAL INTELLIGENCE, PUNJAB POLICE No 10, 13TH MARCH 1886

Sardar Thakur Singh Sandhanwalia has received a letter from Maharajah Duleep Singh, announcing his departure for India and his intention of staying 25 days in Egypt at his father-in-law's house.

Chirag-ud-din, a postal peon at Lahore, stated that his father had a letter from the Maharajah, enclosing a copy of his photograph. His Highness wrote that he remembered Chirag-ud-din, with whom he used to play as a child, and requested that the likeness he sent should be kept until he came out to India.

The Maharajah's arrival is daily expected at Delhi, and people are most anxious to see him. The latest rumour is that the Prince of Wales is coming out with His Highness.

ABSTRACT OF POLITICAL INTELLIGENCE, PUNJAB POLICE No 11, 20TH MARCH 1886

Wild rumours are current regarding the powers that will be conferred on him. Sardar Thakur Singh Sandhanwalia is said to have sent letters announcing that the Maharajah has re-embraced the Sikh religion in England, and has betrothed his daughters to the Buriya Sardars in the Ambala district.

The Sikhs are elated and declare that they will pay their respects to His Highness, if permitted to do so by Government. The Hindus, on the other hand pray that Duleep Singh and the Sikhs may never come into power again, but are of opinion that the Nihangs* and Kukas may be foolish enough to join any demonstration got up in his favour.

## ABSTRACT OF POLITICAL INTELLIGENCE, PUNJAB POLICE NO 12, 27TH MARCH 1886

Pohlo Mal, agent of Sardar Thakur Singh Sandhanwalia, stated that the latter has received a telegram announcing that the Maharajah Duleep Singh will start for India on the 16th March. Since the departure of the Maharajah has been reported, Karah Parshad to the value of Rs. 5 is offered daily in his name at the Golden Temple in Amritsar.

This was becoming serious. The Viceroy and Secretary of State agreed to buy the Maharajah off. Sir Owen Burne was authorized to make a final offer: £50,000 in return for a promise never to return to India. There was a brusque meeting in London at the Carlton Club on 21 March. The Maharajah waited with his lawyer, Mr Lawrence of Farrer's and Co. Sir Owen turned up and objected to the lawyer's presence. Mr Lawrence withdrew. The cash was offered and rejected. Sir Owen pointedly referred to 'the Viceroy's powers to imprison and stop the pension of the Maharajah but did not want his observations to be constituted as a threat'.

Bamba must have begged her husband to accept. There was yet another interview in the India Office on the 24th. The Maharajah again dismissed the offer as 'paltry'.

'He was not to be a fakir and cared nothing for his position in England.' Sir Owen duly recorded the Maharajah's words. 'Imprisonment by the British would exactly fulfil the prophet's words. He would escape then be supernaturally raised as a prophet himself, there would

---

* Nihangs: militant Sikh sect who adhered strictly to the symbolism propounded by Guru Gobind Singh. All personal accoutrements must be of steel, and life lived as ascetic warriors.

be a great war between England and Russia in which he would play a part – on which side he did not know.'

## 53 Holland Park, London, 24 March 1886

There was worse to come. That night the Maharajah returned to Holland Park and drafted a proclamation to the Punjab, imperiously dispatching a copy to Fleet Street. Baffled readers of the *Standard* read it the next day.

MAHARAJAH DULEEP SINGH'S APPEAL TO HIS
COUNTRYMEN, LONDON, 25 MARCH 1886.

My beloved Countrymen. It was not my intention ever to return to reside in India, but Sut-gooroo, [The True Guru – God] who governs all destiny, and is more powerful than I his erring creature, has caused circumstances to be so brought that against my will I am compelled to quit England ...

I now, therefore, beg forgiveness of you, Khalsa-Ji, or The Pure, for having forsaken the faith of my ancestors for a foreign religion; but I was very young when I embraced Christianity.

It is my fond desire on reaching Bombay to take the Pahul again. But in returning to the faith of my ancestors I have no intention of conforming to the errors introduced into Sikhism by those who were not true Sikhs such as wretched caste observances or abstinence from meats and drinks, which Sut-goroo has ordained should be received with thankfulness by all mankind, but to worship the pure and beautiful tenets of Baba Nanak and obey the commands of Gooroo Gobind Singh.

Sut-gooroo's Will be done.

With Wah Gooroo Jee ki Futteh,* I remain, My beloved countrymen, your own flesh and blood,
Duleep Singh

* 'All victories belong to God' – a common Sikh salutation.

Lord Kimberley was furious. He had heard this guru nonsense all before but here it was in a London newspaper, never mind a Tory penny-sheet. He ordered Sir Owen Burne to find out if it was genuine, whether Duleep Singh would repudiate it. The dangerous game of *chantage* seemed lost. Did the Maharajah really mean to go through with it?

He was already on the starting block. The entire family had decamped to Holland Park from Suffolk the week before, Bamba, the six children grumbling but excited, their nanny, their ayah (Indian nurse), the valet Arur Singh, plus a baggage-train of trunks, cases, hatboxes, caskets of jewellery, books, tin boxes of documents, umbrellas and parasols. More impedimenta, including the Maharajah's shotguns, had been consigned to Messrs Grindlay's, the colonial shipping agents. There were also several dogs.

On the eve of departure, the Maharajah cabled Sir Owen about the *Standard* letter: 'It is perfectly genuine, and therefore I do not desire to repudiate it. We leave here about ten this evening, and sleep at the Great Eastern Hotel in Liverpool Street, so as to be ready to quit England tomorrow morning.'

The Scotland Yard man, watching the house from the shadows between pools of gaslight on Campden Hill, saw the regal procession of the last King of Lahore clatter across darkened London in hired carriages on the night of 30 March 1886. The fractious caravan was heading to the red-brick gothic railway hotel in the east of the city, ready for next morning's tide on the Thames.

That the party was being watched is clear from what happened next. The Maharajah had some last-minute business. That night at the Great Eastern Hotel he drafted four telegrams bearing a single codeword addressed to India. He probably tipped the porter to send them twenty-four hours after his departure. It is easy to conceive of a detective asking to see them on the day before they were sent. The Political and Secret Department knew their contents, to whom they were addressed and, where they lived, before the *Verona* had cleared the Nore Light.

Lord Kimberley sent the Viceroy a telegram the next day, the 31st: 'Duleep Singh's communications should be carefully watched. He is now in a state of mind which seems to border on monomania.' The minister's secret servants meanwhile were busy relaying complete details to India of the Great Eastern telegrams. The Lieutenant-Governor of the Punjab was to be informed: 'Maharajah Duleep Singh wired from London on the 1st instant [i.e. the day after the *Verona* sailed as scheduled; the Delhi wire-tap was not authorized until the following month] to the following persons resident in the Punjab: Sardar Jamiat Ray, Mullah, Gurdaspur, Prohit Harkishan Das, Shah-almi Durwaza, Lahore, Hira Singh, Sialkot, and Sardar Thakur Singh, Amritsar – the single word "Started".'

On the morning of that last day in England the party rose early to catch the boat-train from Fenchurch Street station. The *Verona* weighed anchor, chugging across the Thames to pick up more passengers at Gravesend. The Maharajah had a last letter to consign, to Queen Victoria. It read:

S.S. VERONA 31ST MARCH 1886

My Sovereign: Before quitting England I humbly venture to address your Majesty in order to convey to your Majesty the inexpressible gratitude I feel for all your Majesty's graciousness both to me and mine during my stay in this country now extending over some 30 years.

I could not face the pain that such a event would cause me if I ventured to take my leave of your Majesty in person and therefore I humbly implore your Majesty's forgiveness for not paying any last homage before starting for India.

Your Majesty's heart broken subject – Duleep Singh.

There was a last drama at Gravesend. According to the Maharajah's own account (given later to Lady Login), an anonymous member of the India Council appeared to offer once again £50,000 should he give up. Duleep declined. The tide was running. He thought he was going home.

# 12

# Casey

❦

*Reynold's Irish-American Bar, 23 rue Royale, Paris, March 1886*

How DID IT happen that the Maharajah, born to be King of the Sikhs in a palace in Lahore, exchanged identities with an Irish rebel born above an ironmonger's shop in Parliament Street, Kilkenny? The switch, effected on the platform of a Paris railway station, would, for a time at least, throw Her Britannic Majesty's diplomats into the utmost confusion. It looks so improbable, such a pantomimic plot twist, as to be incomprehensible.

To understand how the Maharajah Duleep Singh became Mr Patrick Casey in order to make a wild journey into imperial Russia with a nineteen-year-old girl at his side, it is necessary to follow a trail leading to a Parisian bar and to the revelation of what brought him there – a piece of black propaganda crafted by the more secret servants of the British empire. It is almost as if they wanted him to succeed.

The toast in the Irish-American Bar was 'dynamite', drunk in the absinthe-based cocktail of landlord Jim Reynold's invention. It was called a 'BSY', which stood for 'Bloody Scotland Yard'. The saloon in the street of hump-backed houses that ran south from the church of La Madeleine was notorious. It was a place for conspiracy and prodigious drinking; anyone with tale to tell, a grudge against England, would find a ready listener in the rue Royale.*

There was more to celebrate that 17 March than the feast of St Patrick. As he drank beneath the green-and-gold harps of the Irish

---

* The bar was demolished in 1904. In 1998 the site was Gucci's main Paris handbag emporium.

flag and the stars-and-stripes festoons of the United States of America, one of Mr Reynold's regular customers had just been named as one of the most dangerous men in Europe. It was an honour. Patrick Casey was the 'apostle of dynamite'.

A bizarre pamphlet had just been published in London. Called 'The Repeal of the Union Conspiracy', it linked Patrick Casey, his brother Joseph and their drinking companion Eugene Davis, a Cork-born poet with a talent to tell tales, to a conspiracy embracing Irish Nationalist MPs, the Mad Mahdi, the Boers, French Canadians and American dynamite-fiends. Mr Casey would have read it with a wry smile. In Paris in exile for fifteen years, he had handled nothing more dangerous than the typesetting machines at the *Morning News* and the *Galignani Messenger*, English-language newspapers where he worked as a compositor.

Casey was already a card-carrying Irish rebel hero. He had been involved in the huge explosion set against the walls of the Clerkenwell House of Detention in 1867 intended to free his brother Joseph. Instead it had demolished half the London working-class distract, killed 8 and injured 160.

The four Casey brothers (and their mother Mary Anne, née Corcoran) had fled to Paris, in time for the crushing of the Second Empire by the Prussian Army. They served in the French Army, and two were wounded in the defence of Paris in 1871. Still, it was safer than London. They settled down to a life of journalism, boozing and revolutionary barroom blatherskite.

Reynold's Bar was where to do it. Bragging Americans would arrive straight from the le Havre–Paris train to walk up the latest scheme to slip Ireland from the lion's paw. Grizzled military men, tanned from distant colonial wars, came to discuss the latest developments in destructive weaponry.

The bar was patronized by other raffish souls. It was quite the place for adventurous cross-Channel visitors to do a spot of slumming. It had opened as the 'English and American Bar' until Mr Reynold had sensed a shrewd business-boosting opportunity. The goings-on within would later be the subject of a sensational libel trial in London. In evidence it was stated: 'English racing gentlemen go there, and I have seen ambassadors go in there for a glass of good whiskey and water.' It was perhaps such a prospect that would later draw the Maharajah to the rue Royale.

It was also the place to gather information. Moustachioed Scotland Yard detectives brooded on its benches, talking in cod-Irish accents. Home Office secret agents posed as ferocious dynamiters, watching each other in the mirror-glass advertising Dublin-imported porter and Dunville's VR whiskey. Paris correspondents of London newspapers willingly flashed white five-pound notes in search of a story. As the boozing and fantastical talk went on late into the night, it was imposs-ible to tell who was the enemy of England and who was the spy.

According to a contemporary account by the Irish nationalist and historian Michael Davitt, an agent from 'the secret-service department of the Home Office in London' turned up in Paris, early in 1884, to seek out Casey and Eugene Davis, armed with a letter of introduction from a London Fenian.* Davitt called him 'Major Yellow'.

Yellow claimed to have been a British officer, a native Irishman, who burned with revolutionary desire to avenge the wrongs of his country. 'They plotted at a small hotel in the rue Volney. Yellow paid for all the drinks. The other two "conspired" according to order,' according to Davitt. Dynamite outrages were planned, and reported on, at regular intervals. Mysterious conventions of Irish-American bombers skulking into town on transatlantic liners with sticks of 'Atlas A' quarry dynamite and cases of 'Peep o' Day' alarm clocks (favoured American-made timing devices) were diligently reported. It was all fantasy.

But things could get complicated in the spy business. 'There also appeared on the scene three other secret-service agents in British pay who, however, were unknown as such to each other, and neither of whom knew or was known by Yellow,' recorded Davitt.

One of these was a Scotland Yard detective whom Davitt codenamed 'Brown'. Another was a spy operating in New York and Philadelphia whose real name was Hayes; while another was a young woman who 'gave herself out to be the illegitimate daughter of a prince who had been the consort of a European queen'.

The operation descended into farce. All the agents in turn sought

---

* Fenian: from Fianna, soldiers of Irish mythology. The Indian Mutiny of 1857 and the Fenian rising a decade later were the two greatest internal challenges the British Empire faced in the nineteenth century. The IRB was founded in 1858 and its American shadow, the Fenian Brotherhood, the same year. When it came, the rising in rural Ireland and Dublin was crushed with ease, and an attempted invasion of Canada from US soil ended in fiasco.

out Casey and Davis's revolutionary drinking firm who talked up bloodcurdling plots over ever more drinks. Hayes relayed to London his suspicions about Yellow's scarifying, while 'Brown' searched the hotel rooms of his mysterious companions in order to discover who they really were. Eventually, Yellow was sacked by the Home Office when his apparently well-informed reports of dynamite plots being cooked up in Paris failed to predict the real Irish-American mission that exploded two bombs in the chamber of the House of Commons in January 1885.

Yellow's reports meanwhile had served another purpose. They were assiduously leaked to the Conservative-supporting London evening papers to supply material for anti-Irish editorials. The Paris correspondents of London papers soon found their way to the hotel in the rue Volney, in particular the legendary *Times* foreign correspondent, the bull-headed Moravian-born Henri Adolphe de Blowitz, who achieved a notable scoop, an interview with the 'apostles of dynamite'. He told his excitable readers in April 1884: 'Last evening, I had a long conversation with Mr Patrick Casey, who said: "If Ireland had an independent Parliament, and a volunteer force, she would win her independence in ten years. But that cannot be secured by constitutional agitation. I have fallen back upon using the powers of science, even as far as dynamite . . . it will probably come to blowing up the passenger steamers belonging to the English Atlantic lines; and then the dynamiters will attack the merchantmen. Dynamite is a terrible power . . . one cake of it would blow this restaurant into the air. As for detectives, they are simply boobies. I have the most supreme contempt for either English or French detectives."'

De Blowitz next turned to James Stephens, Casey's cousin, founder in 1858 of the Irish Revolutionary Brotherhood (IRB), now long in Parisian exile. '"The various dynamite factions in New York," said Mr Stephens, "are inspired and directed either by fools or by miscreants. What will be the results of the dynamite policy if continued? The certain death of revolutionary action in Ireland during the present generation, if not for ever."'

John O'Leary, the third interviewee, had a more dramatic solution to Ireland's ills: '"The only way to convince Englishmen would be to meet them out in the open field by force, or the fear of force. I believe in that kind of persuasion. We would have a chance in the event of a war with Russia, because Russia is the great enemy of England. If a war broke out and the Emperor wanted a foreign legion he could get one from among the Irish."' Or, he might have added, from the disgruntled and dispossessed in another corner of the empire: the Sikhs of the Punjab.

These statements reflected the comprehensive splits in the Irish nationalist movement that had followed the failure of the Fenian rising of almost twenty years earlier. They parallel those in Irish republican politics of the late twentieth century: a choice between parliamentary legitimism and armed force.

The 'moral force' faction was represented by the Irish Nationalist MPs led by Charles Stewart Parnell, fighting from within in Parliament, and their allies in Ireland itself, the Land Leaguers led by Michael Davitt, who sought reform of the pernicious landlord system by rent-strikes and boycotts.* An armed rebellion in Ireland was all but impossible, held in check by a draconian Coercion Bill and a level of armed policing per head of the population six times that of India.

The armed struggle wing had rancorously broken up. One group had fled to Paris, there to keep a purist flame of the 1867 rising alive with the noble but hopeless agenda of meeting British force in the open field. The IRB in Ireland and England went underground. Its American offshoot, now styled the Clan-na-Gael (family of the Gaels), could operate openly and had grown dramatically to 20,000 members by 1884, drawing recruits from the post-famine Irish diaspora in East Coast cities. The Clan, seen originally by the IRB as mere auxiliary fund-raisers, was full of passion, militarily strengthened by ex-civil war veterans and politically animated by a bunch of hard-line prisoners released from English gaols in 1871. These included Jeremiah O'Donovan Rossa and John Devoy, whose speciality had been secretly recruiting Irishmen in the British Army. 'Contaminated' regiments were sent safely out of the way to India.

The Clan, headed by a Revolutionary Directory, saw itself as a government-in-exile. In 1879 they opened negotiations with the Russian ambassador to Washington when it looked, not for the last time, as if war with England was imminent over the Balkans.

---

* Lord Dufferin, a substantial Irish landlord, complained to the Secretary of State for India in 1886 that his tenants – having 'paid up like lambs' the year before – were now demanding a thirty per cent rent reduction.

The old maxim held true: Ireland's friend was England's foe. It did not matter who – the Sudanese Mahdi, the King of the Zulus, the Czar of Russia, the German Kaiser, even the last King of Lahore.

But some could not wait. In 1881 O'Donovan Rossa split with the Clan and launched a 'skirmishing fund' to take the war to the heart of the enemy. The skirmishers' chosen weapon was gunpowder – barrels of it, and detonated to considerable effect in a four-year bombing campaign that began with a failed attempt to blow up the Mansion House in London. Three days earlier Czar Alexander II had been assassinated in St Petersburg. It began to look like an international conspiracy. The Queen's private secretary, General Sir Henry Ponsonby, urgently attended the Home Office to express Her Majesty's fears that Buckingham Palace would be blown up.

The next blow came in Ireland itself: on a May morning in 1882, in Phoenix Park on the western fringe of Dublin, a black cab drew up as Sir Frederick Cavendish, the Chief Secretary for Ireland, took a morning stroll outside the viceregal lodge. Four men jumped out and slashed him and Thomas Henry Burke, the permanent under-secretary, to pieces with surgical knives. The assassins left a black-edged calling card bearing a previously unheard-of name, 'The Invincibles'.

The British government received a profound shock. An ex-Bengal civil servant called Edward Jenkinson, assistant secretary for police and crime at Dublin Castle, was installed in London as 'spymaster-general'. He was supposed to work with Sir Robert Anderson, veteran Fenian affairs adviser at the Home Office since the Clerkenwell explosion. The two men hated each other. At the same time and quite separately the Special (Irish) Branch was formed within the Metropolitan Police, supposedly the prime anti-Fenian agency outside Ireland.

Jenkinson was scathing about his London colleagues. He regarded the Metropolitan Police's anti-Fenian branch as hopelessly inefficient. 'There is not a man there with a head on his shoulders,' he wrote after the explosion in May 1884 that demolished a lavatory in Scotland Yard itself: 'They have no information and if anything happens they all lose their heads, and everything is confusion.'

Intelligence-gathering in America was coordinated meanwhile through the consulate in New York, which hired Pinkerton's detective agency to do its spying. The British Foreign Office was ever eager to place itself at one remove from dirty business against troublesome individuals on foreign soil, while simultaneously scorning the plodding methods of Scotland Yard.

Each overlapping agency – the Foreign Office, Dublin Castle, Home Office special adviser, the Metropolitan Police's Special (Irish) Branch – had its own, jealously guarded, agents. Anderson at the Home Office, for example, had a prime asset, a spy at the heart of the Clan-na-Gael called Henri Le Caron.* His true identity was not revealed until he gave evidence at a sensational Irish political court case (the 'Parnell Commission') involving *The Times* newspaper in 1888–89.

This was the nexus of revolutionary feuds and Whitehall intelligence service turf-fights into which the Maharajah Duleep Singh was sailing. There were spoofers and posturers, informers and double-agents everywhere. In one of them, the Maharajah would put his utmost trust.

The American-inspired bombing campaign against England intensified. In great secrecy the Clan itself resolved to launch attacks. There were bombs at barracks, gas works, *The Times* newspaper office, and three explosions on the London underground railway. The Albert Memorial and the Bank of England were guarded by armed police, the railway to Windsor was lined with soldiers, and a special pilot locomotive ran ahead of the royal train to Balmoral for fear of Fenian fire. There was a new factor, Mr Nobel's invention, nitroglycerine fused with china-clay – 'dynamite' – stable, portable and easily to smuggle. The Americans claimed that 'just twelve men could blow up a city the size of London'. The so-called 'dynamite press' foamed with blood-curdling plots, to the fury of the British government.

The Clan leadership, embarrassed by O'Donovan Rossa's messy freelance gunpowder operations, sent a bombing mission to England to run the 'skirmishers' out of the country and to leave calling cards of their own. In 1883 a Clan-financed bomb factory was discovered in Birmingham. In December 1884 a three-man bombing team atomized themselves beneath London Bridge when a massive charge of lignine

---

* Le Caron, real name Thomas Willis Beach, operated within the FB–Clan-na-Gael undiscovered from 1867. He wrote a best-selling autobiography, 25 *Years in the Secret Service*, which contains these tantalizing lines: 'On the other plots and schemes I can only touch in the lightest possible way. They included the assassination of Queen Victoria, the kidnapping of the Prince of Wales or Prince Arthur and a hundred and one odd schemes in which Duleep Singh, General Carroll-Thevis [sic], Alfred Aylward, and other soldiers of fortune or discontent all figured.' No more is revealed.

dynamite detonated. A second team was more effective; on 5 January 1885, the Tower of London was bombed and two explosions ripped through the chamber of the House of Commons. This was clear and present danger. The Queen's jubilee was eighteen months away; it was time to take off the gloves.

There was a conviction among the more zealous intelligence operatives in London that the Parnellite MPs, the Irish-American dynamiters, the murderous Invincibles of Phoenix Park and the IRB exiles in Paris were all part of a seamless conspiracy. Paris held the key; the transit point for American bombers using the soft route via New York–Le Havre–Paris–the Channel ports–London. The Casey-Davis drinking firm would come up with the proof. If they did not, it could always be invented.

Thus the mysterious propaganda sheet, 'The Repeal of the Union Conspiracy', published by a Mr Ridgway of Piccadilly, appeared in March 1886, just as the Maharajah was taking ship for India. No author was named for the wild allegations which claimed to prove: 'The remarkable manner in which the Irish revolutionary movement has dovetailed into the so-called constitutional movement of Mr Parnell.' The names of Patrick Casey and Eugene Davis came up repeatedly as did that of James O'Kelly,* a Parnellite MP: 'Why were cheers so continually given for the Mahdi in Ireland at public meetings during the past Soudan expeditions? Simply because it was well known that Mr O'Kelly was actually engaged in endeavouring to reach that inspired prophet for the purpose of giving him information and active support in his crusade against the British invader. Those who know are aware, from his private correspondence with the dynamite section of the Irish Revolutionary Party in Paris, that he was deep in intrigue with the violent French party in Egypt, and with the agent of the Mahdi in Cairo.'

Furthermore, the pamphlet alleged, O'Kelly was a member of the 'Military Council of the Irish Revolutionary Brotherhood', a fire-breathing body in Paris planning the destruction of the empire. The council evidently included Alfred Aylward, an eccentric English-born champion of the Boers, and four exotic military men. These were named as:

---

* James O'Kelly MP was indeed a former Fenian. In 1877 he had tried to put together a Spanish–American–Irish expedition to capture Gibraltar.

'General Carroll-Teviss, an American soldier of fortune who has served in the Franco-Prussian War, and in almost every other European and South American struggle of the past fifteen years.

'General Macadaras, a Frenchman of Irish extraction, who organized the Foreign Legion [the Irish Brigade] in the Franco-Prussian War, was another person selected for his warlike propensities.

'An ex-British officer and a dashing war correspondent who survived the Egyptian campaigns has also been deep in the military councils of the I.R.B.'

The last rebel-soldier to be named was Captain John McCafferty, an ex-officer of the Confederate Army, who was evidently the dreaded 'Number One' of the Fenian Directory of Seven in New York and who had recently arrived in Paris to reconstitute the fearsome-sounding 'Committee of Public Safety'.

'All this time McCafferty lived in the most confidential relations with a small body of Fenians who lived in Paris, viz., Eugene Davis, Patrick Casey and his brother Joseph Casey, the hero of Clerkenwell,' the pamphlet stated.

'At the time they were thus engaged, Davis was acting as correspondent to O'Donovan Rossa's paper in New York, dating his letters from 338 rue St Honoré, and Patrick Casey was the vice-president of the Committee of Public Safety which planned the Phoenix Park murders and some of the most daring dynamite explosions.' Two Parnellite MPs had been on 'terms of the closest intimacy' and had 'indulged their gastronomic tastes in company with many an Irish conspirator at the well known bar of Mr Reynolds in the Rue Royale'.

'But Mr Casey was not a man merely to talk. He had sent a confederate to London charged with a terrible mission, nothing less indeed than the throwing bombs from the strangers' gallery of the House of Commons upon the table between the treasury bench and the opposition.'

The anonymous publication, immediately dubbed the 'Black Pamphlet', had unlooked-for effects. On 3 April 1886, a copy was found in his pigeon-hole at the Savage Club in London by a Mr Edward St John Brenon, an Irish journalist and poet.* He had visited Paris

---

* Edward St John Brenon (real name Brennan) was an habitué of the Alhambra music-hall. He later sought out the Maharajah on his Paris death-bed.

two years earlier and had sought out Casey and Davis. *The Echo* newspaper ran the story on 22 April 1884 as: 'The Dynamitards in Paris – By One Who Knows Them'.

'One Who Knows Them' seemed to know a lot about the movements of British agents. 'The departure of Scotland-yard detectives for Paris was in due course made known to the leader of the Irish Revolutionary party. From the moment of their arrival until that of their departure their movements were carefully watched,' he had written.

> When Detective Moser, accompanied by his wife, took up his lodgings in a small hotel in the rue St Lazare, in which he had heard some of the Invincibles resided . . . they were immediately familiar with his alias and the military prefix with which he adorned it was a subject of hilarious comment.
>
> When he went to Le Havre, his departure was signalled to a favoured correspondent of a Liberal London daily newspaper, who followed him. The scene at Havre was ludicrous in the extreme. The police in our service, disguised as sailors, expected to make extraordinary discoveries; but instead of doing so they were duped, and finally became the laughing-stock of the Invincibles and the French mouchards.
>
> Another detective sent over to make discoveries was a Captain Stephens (a gentleman who was the secret representative of the Irish police). He went to Mr Pat Casey with a letter of introduction from an Irish Member of Parliament. This gentleman was supposed to come to Paris to enlist the sympathies of Frenchmen in the Congo Question – whatever that may mean.
>
> Captain Stephens may have succeeded in hoodwinking the Member whose introduction he bore; but he in his turn was hoodwinked with amazing ability by the wary Mr Casey, who, while humouring the pseudo-mission of the Irish detective, laughed in his sleeve at his credulity.

The author of the 'Black Pamphlet' disapproved of this guying of Irish detectives for, it would turn out, very personal reasons – and the way *The Echo* article went on to acquit the Stephens–O'Leary axis, the old IRB purists, from the universal dynamite conspiracy. Two years after writing this article, Edward St John Brenon was named in the 'Black Pamphlet' as being part of the conspiracy. Immediately he sued the publisher, the hapless Mr Ridgway, for libel.

The case came to the High Court in London in May 1887. The plaintiff had to make a painful admission: he had scarcely met a 'dynamiter', he had snitched all the bloodcurdling information from a colleague, J. C. Millage of the rival *Daily Chronicle*. When it came to the defendant's turn to give evidence, he refused to be called. His barrister, Mr Kemp, rose to proclaim: 'There never was a case of this kind brought into a court of law in which the position of the defendant was so difficult as was that of Mr Ridgway. He was only the publisher of the pamphlet, which was written by one who was said to have given his personal experience. It was Mr Ridgway's position that the only evidence that it was possible to give would be that of men who could not appear before them except at the possible sacrifice of their lives.'

The defence could not call 'the man who wrote this pamphlet, for the oath which he had taken would render him liable to destruction if his name were mentioned. (Sensation in court.)'

Mr Kemp's theatrics failed to convince. The jury swiftly found for the plaintiff. 'If a libel, what damages?' asked the judge. Cheering greeted the announcement of the huge sum of £500.

The author of the 'Black Pamphlet' was never revealed. Who would risk such wild multiple libels? Who might profit from it? According to Michael Davitt, it came back to Major Yellow. He had returned from Paris in 1885 in semi-disgrace and was relieved of his secret Home Office commission. Yellow set up headquarters above an Irish pub in Wardour Street, Soho, and brooded over revolutionary tracts such as *The History of the Carbonari*, James Stephens's *Autobiography* and *The History of Secret Societies in Europe*.

'The next year, 1886, he and others produced a pamphlet called "The Repeal of the Union Conspiracy; or Mr Parnell, MP and the Irish Revolutionary Brotherhood", the whole argument being that the Irish party and the National Land League were but parts of a treasonable organisation engaged in dynamite and other outrages,' Michael Davitt wrote. 'It was compiled chiefly from the drunken ravings of

Casey and other Paris self-styled dynamiters, the "revelations" of the spy Hayes – and Piggot's pamphlet "Parnellism Exposed".* For this work a sum of £1000 was received (it is alleged) from the secret-service fund, under the control of the Unionist government [Lord Salisbury's administration] which came into power in the summer of that year.'

The 'Black Pamphlet' was a freelance operation, Davitt implied, paid for retrospectively by the new Conservative government which tacitly approved of its black propaganda.†

'The Repeal of the Union Conspiracy' was high fantasy, later to be thrown out of court as a hoax, but nobody outside a very secret knot in Whitehall knew this yet. It had an immense influence on a nascent conspiracy that had nothing to do with Ireland and everything to do with the fertile plains of the Punjab. First it presented Patrick Casey and Eugene Davis as the most dangerous dynamite men in Paris. Second it provided a cast-list of ferocious-sounding military men who bristled with the means to make war on England – Carrol-Teviss, Macadaras, McCafferty, and the mysterious Fenian ex-British officer. It even gave clues where to find them – the poste restante at 338 rue St Honoré, and Mr Reynold's bar in the rue Royale.

When the Maharajah Duleep Singh came to read the 'Black Pamphlet', it must have looked like an invitation to a revolution.

---

* An Irish journalist called Richard Piggot acted as chief 'dynamite-revelationist' for several London newspapers from 1881 onwards. He was also a blackmailer and forger employed by the anti-Home Rule 'Irish Loyal and Patriotic Union' to denigrate Parnell by linking him with the Phoenix Park murders. A pamphlet to that effect called 'Parnellism Exposed' was published in November 1885. To propel the propaganda campaign, a mysterious 'black bag' containing incriminating letters left in Paris by a 'fugitive Invincible' was 'found' in early 1886. Piggot claimed he was led to it by Casey and Davis. The letters were the basis of the block-busting 'Parnellism and Crime' articles run in *The Times* from 7 March 1887 onwards. The allegations engendered the Parnell Commission at the High Court in 1888–89 in which *The Times* (backed by the secret-service resources of the government) sought to prove the charges. Piggot sensationally confessed he had forged the letters before fleeing to Madrid and committing suicide on 1 March 1889.

† The author was Captain Stuart Stephens named by 'one who knows them', a 'colonial adventurer' late Gold Coast Hussars. Sacked for heavy drinking, he appealed to Sir Stafford Northcote (later Lord Iddesleigh, the short-lived Conservative Foreign Secretary) for help. 'Colonel Yellow' then embarked on his clandestinely funded black-propaganda career.

# 13

# Jindan

SS Verona *(Peninsular and Orient Steam Navigation Company), at sea, April 1886*

'MAHARAJAH WISH – I wish.' Bamba could never have persuaded her husband to stay. Who was she in the face of prophecy? He strode the promenade deck of the rakish P & O steamer like a commodore. The princes were boisterous, clattering up the companion-ways, seeking out Captain de Horne and his smartly uniformed officers on the navigation bridge. The boys proved 'very popular' aboard the ship, even laden as it was with loyal servants of the empire returning to their duties. Nineteen-year-old Victor evidently disapproved of his father's antics. He called him 'my idiotic parent'.

The princesses clung to their governess. Bamba stayed in her day cabin as the ship transited the stormy Bay of Biscay, praying for divine guidance. From Gibraltar she wrote to her friend Mrs Lansing in Cairo: 'The Verona, 15 April, 1886. All the dear ones are in good health. We were very poorly one day, we have enjoyed the voyage so far. The Lord has been very merciful, I know he will not leave us at any time.'

The Maharajah hogged the first-class saloon, telling bemused passengers of England's injustices. His story fell on receptive ears. A Mr Drew was aboard, apparently a political agent of the Maharajah of Kashmir, the biggest 'native state' in India, sundered from the Sikh Empire in 1849. The mysterious Mr Drew promised to carry a seditious letter to Srinagar. This was to have extraordinary consequences two years later.

As the *Verona* nosed into the rising heat of the eastern Mediterranean, unknown to the Maharani, warrants were being urgently prepared for her and her children's arrests. Her husband expected nothing less.

The telegraphs had been flying since the moment they left the Thames quayside. The Maharajah was blithely steaming out of the home government's jurisdiction; to apprehend him at Gravesend would have meant a scandal. London kept up the pressure but it was now for the Viceroy in India to decide what to do. Lord Dufferin had the legal powers to deal with uppity natives. From Simla, the summer capital, Sir Henry Mortimer Durand, the Indian government's Foreign Secretary, sent out India-wide alerts the day after the family sailed. For example:

### TELEGRAPH TO BOMBAY GOVERNMENT

Duleep Singh left with wife and six children. A warrant will be prepared and sent to you. Viceroy hopes Maharajah's removal may be so managed as to cause no excitement. We ought to include wife and three sons and three daughters in arrest warrants if possible.

In Simla a frantic hunt began through old colonial legislation to find a legal basis for the detentions. Mr Macpherson, a lawyer in the legislative department, unearthed it like a Golconda-mine gem: Bengal Regulation III of 1818 and its modification by Bombay Regulation XXV (State Prisoners) of 1827. They allowed restraint of persons under the governor of Bombay's signature 'for the security of British dominions from internal commotion'. Not only were these pre-Government of India Act regulations still in force, the Bombay rule applied to a sweltering way-station under its administration: Aden, the British colony at the tip of the Arabian peninsula where the *Verona* was due to make landfall. On 8 April the warrants were sent to Bombay for signature and for onward transmission to Brigadier-General Adam George Forbes Hogg, the Aden resident, much decorated veteran of the Indian Mutiny and the Afghan wars. The affair was to be kept as secret as possible. In communications the Maharajah's family were to be referred to as the 'Burmese Party'.

The legislation, though, applied only to 'natives'. Was it legal to arrest the wife and children? The Punjab government telegraphed Simla with what they knew. 'Bamba' appeared to be an 'English lady'

– that would make her and the children European British subjects. Case law had shown doubt whether Bengal Regulation III of 1818 applied if the persons to be detained were 'European'. The files were searched for finer details: Bamba appeared to be 'Egyptian' or 'Abyssinian', not European, so that was all right.

'There is nothing I have seen in the papers to show that Duleep Singh has undergone the process of naturalization in the United Kingdom – but it would be wise to consult the Advocate General,' an official noted.

Sir Courtenay Peregrine Ilbert, secretary to the Bombay government, minuted back: 'Not worthwhile. If it is necessary for *reasons of state*, that Duleep Singh and his party should be detained, then we must run the risk the legality of our own proceedings being questioned. We have done our best to conform to the law.' The Viceroy told the Aden resident on 17 April: 'You will understand it is not desirable to bring warrants into unnecessary prominence, particularly those for the Maharani and girls.' The warrants were drafted.

The 'Burmese Party' sailed on, oblivious to the rising alarms in the Viceroy's camp. At first Lord Dufferin seemed minded to let the Maharajah get to India, then spirit him away to some hill station to live out his life, should he wish, as monarch of a bungalow in an Indian simulacrum of Sussex. But as the *Verona* bunkered at Valetta, the Maharajah's 'Proclamation to His Countrymen' had arrived in the Punjab. It appeared in the Lahore newspapers on 16 April. The *Tribune* allowed the Maharajah his grievances, saying: 'The Sikhs fondly cherish the memory of the "Lion of the Punjab" and the heartless treatment that his son and heir has received at the hands of the Government has deeply wounded their feelings – an unworthy slur upon the loyalty of the brave Sikhs.'

The chances of a revolt in the Punjab were nil, the *Tribune* editorialized: 'The Sikhs would never desert their English masters, and a little consideration beforehand to the feelings of those who have fought in China, Africa, Burma, Afghanistan, and who reconquered India for the white people during the Sepoy Mutiny, would not have been wasted. Poor Duleep! your countrymen can weep only for you.'

The Viceroy cabled Kimberley that day: 'In consideration of the fact that Duleep Singh has issued an address to Sikhs in which he announces intention of assuming authority over Sikh nation, and in view of communications of a menacing character in reference to troubles in India and war with Russia, we have thought it desirable to issue warrants for detention of Maharajah and party at Aden. Order to this effect has been sent by telegraph to Aden authorities.'

The doughty General Hogg was told to make the party as comfortable as possible. It was vital that their health should not suffer, but it was even more important that the 'Maharajah should not be permitted to communicate with outside world. In the event of his not returning to England, agent from hence will arrive before end of month, but Maharajah should not be made acquainted with this circumstance.'

Sir Henry Durand in Simla was aware of the political complications. He messaged his legal officials on 17 April: 'I have asked before the ages of the children ... we cannot risk ridicule by serving warrants on babies.'

The Queen must be told. There must be no way out, no soft-hearted intervention by Duleep's royal patron. Lord Kimberley sent notice of the arrest warrants to Osborne. Her private secretary replied: 'The Queen was rather startled by the announcement made in the letters you enclosed on the arrest of Duleep Singh. She said that he had brought it entirely on himself and it was evidently dangerous to allow him to proceed to India.' There was no escape.

## SS Verona, *Suez Canal, 14–16 April 1886*

At Port Said the soaring, electrically lit *Pharos* beckoned the *Verona* into the Suez Canal, the engineering wonder of the age. The Maharajah had come this way before. The canal was a scratch in the desert in 1864 when he had made the second passage to India that found him his bride. On that journey, twenty-two years previously, he had transited the isthmus by train bearing his mother's remains in her lead-lined casket.

His mother. In his legalistic outpourings on the injustices of his childhood, he had never mentioned that day, so long ago, when he was led away to the Shalimar Gardens. Lady Login recorded that, in the years of his late adolescence, he 'rarely mentioned her'. He had told his quasi-adoptive English mother that 'the Rani Jindan had only disgraced him', and that she 'used to strike him daily'. His English mentors had expunged her. But in the 'half-cracky' letter to Queen Victoria which seemed to have started the whole mad business, it was Rani Jindan who had revealed the prophecy.

'I did not remember any of this apparent nonsense until a short time before the death of my mother,' he had told the Queen eighteen months before embarking for India. His mother had said, 'When the right moment arrives, circumstances will so shape themselves that thou will be compelled to quit England against thy will' – exactly what was happening as the SS *Verona* chugged towards his destiny.

Jindan's odyssey since her forced removal from Lahore in 1847 had been as extraordinary as his own. She had escaped from British captivity at Chunar Fort, disguised as a beggar-woman, fleeing into the Himalayas where she found a troubled sanctuary in Kathmandu, the capital of Nepal. By 1860 Duleep had reached his majority. His eyes were set on ever-more exotic sporting horizons; he had spent the summer hawking in the wilderness of Sardinia. He spoke of going to India after even more ambitious game and acquired 'an india-rubber boat and a swivel duck-gun, besides all the latest inventions in rifles, &c., for tiger shooting'. He sent his mother a message, passed on by the British resident in Kathmandu, that they might meet again. The Governor-General agreed; the Rani could do no harm now, news had come from the high mountains: 'She is much changed – she is blind and takes but little interest in what is going on.' He must not, however, go anywhere near the Punjab.

Mother and son met in Spence's Hotel, Calcutta, on 16 January 1861, for the first time in thirteen and a half years. Jindan was overcome with emotion. Duleep seemed embarrassed: 'My mother has determined she will not separate from me any more, I suppose we shall return to England together as soon as I can get passage,' he wrote to Sir John Login.

He found his homeland repellent: 'India is a beastly place. I heartily repent ever having come out. Old servants bother the life out of me with questions. The heat is dreadful. I hate the natives, they are such liars, flatterers and extremely deceitful.'

Ships in the Hooghly river were full of Sikh troops returning from the second China war. When they heard rumours of Duleep's presence in the city they flocked to shout old Khalsa war-cries outside Spence's Hotel. Lord Canning was distinctly alarmed. To the Viceroy, the Rani

Jindan was a 'she-devil'. He asked the Maharajah, 'as a favour', to leave Calcutta on the next available ship. As a further incentive the Rani was given back her jewels which had been seized on her escape from Fort Chunar. The elephants ordered for the tiger hunt were cancelled. The rubber boat and duck-guns were repacked. Mother and son sailed for England.

## *Lancaster Gate, Kensington, London, Spring 1861*

They made a strange-looking party pottering round Kensington Gardens: Duleep, now getting quite portly, and the Rani, his mother, chewing betel leaves in the Indian manner, stooped and half-blind in a London-made crinoline, 'worn over native dress and with pearls and emeralds arranged in a sort of fringe beneath her feather bonnet'. Jindan's beauty had decayed, her pale eyes were dimmed with age. Behind them trooped a retinue of elderly servants who had followed her from exile. They too were smothered in pearls and emeralds.

Duleep had taken a capacious house in Bayswater, 'No 1 Round-the-Corner Lancaster Gate', to accommodate the Queen Mother and her transplanted court-in-exile. Soortoo the slave-girl, Duleep's childhood playmate in the Lahore zenana, dutifully attended her old mistress who passed her days in a 'stifling, darkened room behind heavy curtains'. They talked about the old days, the lost glories of the Lahore durbar. Jindan told her son of his estates, the palaces, the *jagirs*, the salt-mines with their stupendous income. It was Duleep's private property. She spoke of the Koh-i-Noor. The glittering genie was out of the bottle.

The Maharajah took his mother to blustery Mulgrave Castle, seat of Lord Normandy, near Whitby in Yorkshire in July 1861. There she remained with him, 'resisting all efforts of his friends to make her arrange a separate establishment in another house on the estate', until a year later when he returned her to a new Kensington establishment, Abingdon House, under the charge of an English housekeeper. Sometimes she would wrap herself in a 'dirty old sheet'; sometimes appear in dazzling gold embroidery.

Perhaps the son was wearying of his mother's grumbles, perhaps the recollections of his blood-spattered childhood were too painful.

There was no doubt in his English mentors' minds what she was up to. Sir John Lawrence thought 'she would be the evil genius of the Maharajah'. Login wrote to Colonel C. B. Phipps, the Queen's private secretary: 'I am afraid the Maharajah is getting thoroughly under his mother's influence . . . our only hope of saving him from discredit is to get him to live apart.'

Duleep Singh was returning to his 'native habits' under her worrisome tutelage; worse, his Christian soul seemed in peril. One minute he was planning to return to India as a mendicant missionary, the next he was declaring: 'I feel it very difficult to lead a Christian life – I am constantly erring before God.'

It was a sorrowful time. The Queen, the court, it seemed the whole country, had been plunged into the deepest mourning when the Maharajah's old patron, Albert, Prince Consort, had died in December 1861. But from Osborne, Colonel Phipps kept up a storm of invective, no doubt reflecting the grief-stricken Queen's own opinions: 'The arrival of the Maharani in England is a misfortune though it is impossible to oppose his filial wish,' he wrote. 'Nothing could be more destructive to the Maharajah than that he should succumb to his mother's or any other native influence. I fear that as long as he remains under her influence, he will retrograde in his moral character, instead of advancing to become an English gentleman.'

The Maharajah meanwhile wrote cheerfully to Login from Mulgrave Castle: 'I wish to have a conversation with you about my private property in the Punjab and the Koh-i-Noor diamond – and will you kindly procure a copy of the Punjab Blue Book?' This would not do at all. The Maharajah was prying into some very delicate territory. Officials strove to bundle the Rani Jindan back to India where 'she would do less harm'. She would avoid such indignity. The Messalina of the Punjab was dying.

The Maharajah was in Scotland, hunting at Loch Kennard Lodge, the day the message came. He arrived at his mother's London bedside and thought she was 'getting better'. She died the next morning. The house was seized with wailing and lamentation enough to rouse the whole of Bayswater. Sir John Login arrived once again to bring some organizing zeal into his former charge's affairs. What to do with the Rani's remains? She was a Sikh, a queen, she must be cremated, which was quite impossible under English law.

A strange letter appeared in *The Times* a week later, on 8 August 1863, under the headline 'A Case of Conscience'. It read:

> Sir. Her Highness the Maharanee, Jindan Kaur, of Lahore, mother of his Highness the Maharajah Duleep Singh, died on the 1st current at Abingdon House, Kensington, in the Hindoo faith, and we understand it is proposed to bury her. The practice is contrary to the religion of the Sikhs, and, as his Highness the Maharajah denies our right to dispose of the body according to customs, we are constrained, as a matter of conscience, to appeal to the country for protection.
>
> Agreeably to our rules, the body ought to be burnt and the ashes given to the Ganges. The thing is simple enough in itself, and, as it infringes no moral or physical law, we certainly cannot believe the wisdom and intelligence of the land would oppose our acting as our religion directs.
>
> Her Highness was particularly careful about everything relating to caste; indeed, so much so, that up to her demise she refused to eat when his Highness the Maharajah happened to be on the same carpet with herself, and so that she might not be compromised, had a separate establishment of Indians, who attended to her table and everything connected with it.*
>
> In asking to dispose of her Highness's remains according to our religion, then, we feel we are fulfilling her Highness's wishes, and are satisfied, had she known her dissolution was at hand, she would have left definite instructions for the disposal of her body after the forms of the Sikh religion.

Lieutenant-Colonel James Oliphant, Comptroller of the Maharajah's household, replied indignantly:

> My attention has been directed to a letter written by Utchell Singh and Kishan Singh (two discharged servants), in which they would have it believed that it was the intention of his Highness the Maharajah Duleep Singh that his mother should

---

* A Hindu rather than a Sikh religious practice – but members of the old Punjabi ruling class adhered to it.

receive the rites of Christian burial. His Highness never had any such intention.

Yesterday, at 10 o'clock, the remains of the late Maharanee were removed from Abingdon House to be deposited temporarily in a vault at Kensal Green Cemetery, following the course which was adopted in the case of his Highness the late Rajah of Coorg [Princess Gouramma's father].

The remains of the Maharanee were attended by his Highness, myself, several of his personal friends, and by all the retinue of Her late Highness.

No Christian rite was attempted, His Highness, when the coffin was placed in the mausoleum, merely addressing his people in their own language with affectionate earnestness on the uncertainty of human life.*

Two months later, on 18 October 1863, his surrogate father, Sir John Login, died. His grief 'was most sincere and unaffected'. He was entirely an orphan. It was time to find a wife.

Thus it was that the Maharajah had last made this India-bound journey twenty-two years earlier, his mother's remains in the ship's hold, his head full of her entreaties. Her body was burned according to Sikh rites at Bombay. He scattered her ashes on the waters of the Godavari and erected a small *Samadh* at Nasik on the left bank. The Maharajah returned to Cairo to marry Bamba and thence to Elveden to 'advance to be an English gentleman'. And, so his mentors must have earnestly prayed, to forget all about the Rani Jindan.

---

* Lady Login's memoirs give a very different account: 'A large number of Indian notables attended the interment. The Maharajah addressed the native attendants in their own language, comparing the Christian religion with that of the Hindoo, and assuring them, that in the blood of Christ alone, was their safety from condemnation in a future state.'

# 14

# Steamer Point

❦

THE INDIAN GOVERNMENT had strung its snare at Aden as cleverly as a Suffolk gamekeeper, but the Maharajah would not fall into it quite yet – the *Verona* was delayed docking for a day by headwinds. On the morning of 21 April the ship came alongside the jetty at Steamer Point.

The colony was a place to transit hurriedly, not to stay. The P & O 'Traveller's Pocket Book' warned: 'The climate of Aden is not unhealthy, but the heat is intense, not only from the sun's rays, but from the radiation produced by the colour of the rock. Strangers should, therefore, take every precaution against unnecessary exposure.' The temperature was 105 degrees Fahrenheit. The Maharajah would be stuck in this broiling crater of an extinct volcano for five weeks.

When the resident, Brigadier-General Hogg, strode in his ostrich-plumed hat up the companion-way, the Maharajah seemed quite prepared. He had told his fellow-passengers he expected to be arrested. It was all perfectly civil. There were no rough soldiery with bayonets fixed, no mention of warrants or the catch-all of Bengal Regulation III. Bamba's Mayfair-made dress and the collars of the children's sailor outfits went unfelt. He was even to be allowed a telegram to his London lawyer. But the Maharajah wanted his martyrdom; the guru had prophesied it thus. Wearing his cashmere jacket and turban donned at Suez, he declared to the bemused voyagers: 'I leave this ship unwillingly – my case will be the subject of a great state trial – before the House of Lords!' There was clapping and cheering.

'His Highness refused to leave the ship unless arrested, so in presence of the captain I told him he must come with me, and touched him on the shoulder. He complied at once and the rest of the party came voluntarily. All are staying in Resident's house. More immediately,' General Hogg cabled Simla.

The Morse-keys were tapping busily again within an hour: 'As far as I can gather, Maharajah wishes to send two sons back to England, Maharani and girls to Cairo, and to go himself to Egypt. He does not wish to return to England. Seeks permission to telegraph his solicitor in London.'

The Maharajah seemed anything but outraged at his 'arrest'. Beneath the residency's sluggishly turning fans he embarked on a languid round of telegrams couched in the utmost gentility. He cabled his fashionable Lincoln's Inn lawyer, Mr Lawrence of Farrer's and Co., who assured him his address to the Sikhs contained no treasonable content. The Maharajah telegraphed the Viceroy: 'I desire Your Excellency clearly to understand that whatever instructions you give, provided the word "disloyal" is not employed with them, or I am requested not to return to India, will be loyally carried out by me. I request that I may be permitted to correspond with friends in England, and also that my seventeen servants awaiting my arrival at Bombay be sent on here, the Government paying all their expenses.' The Maharajah seemed back on form. To deny him would be ungracious. The Viceroy would consider it.

Lord Dufferin replied from Simla soothingly: 'It is my desire that Your Highness should be treated with every possible respect and consideration. I deeply regret the unhappy circumstances which have occasioned Your Highness's detention at Aden, especially as I had taken some pains to arrange for Your Highness's comfortable establishment in this country.'

The Viceroy was using gruffer language in his communications to London: 'Clear the line to Bombay. We have told Maharajah that he may send his wife and girls to Cairo, and we propose to tell him that his two sons may go to England and himself to Egypt on his giving a written promise that neither he nor any member of his family will attempt to come to India.'

The sticking point was the *Standard* manifesto. Did his profession of a desire to re-embrace the Sikh religion count as a declaration of disloyalty? 'The address to my co-religionists has been published from no disloyal motives whatever, but to lay before my countrymen my bitter complaint against restrictions put upon my movements in India,' the Maharajah told the Viceroy. On the same day, the exhaustive 'Punjab Paper' letter to Lord Salisbury he had composed the month before departing was published in the *Observer* newspaper in London. 'No fault had been found,' the Maharajah insisted.

'I have made the whole party as comfortable as possible in this climate,' General Hogg telegraphed. The Maharajah was allowed to cable Messrs Grindlay's, his shipping agents, and his lawyer in Bombay, a certain Mr Kittey.

Lord Dufferin was softening his line. He now agreed the Maharajah could go to Cairo on giving his word as a 'prince and a gentleman' that he would not pursue his ambitions to return to India (although a signed protocol should follow). And there was another thumping concession: 'I shall have great pleasure in accordance with his private telegram addressed to me by His Highness in sending his servants now at Bombay either to Aden or Cairo at Government expense.'

The Maharajah seemed delighted at this last. There was a new glint in his eye. He told General Hogg that he must consult his lawyers before signing anything, that he would now send the Maharani and the princesses to Germany, and that he himself would go to 'Europe' rather than Cairo.

The Aden–Simla telegraph traffic for that last week of April 1886 was drenched in politesse. The Viceroy thanked 'His Highness the Maharajah for his honourable and gentlemanlike communications'. He asked him to look on him as 'a friend who would give him the best advice', while 'exposing His Highness and His Highnesses's family to inconvenience was a matter of deep personal regret'. Perhaps he really would give up and slouch back to England.

The sticky days were passing, the Maharajah began to brood in the enervating heat. Bamba and the children flopped listlessly in the scant shade of the residency garden. Then on 1 May the stately telegraphic dance suddenly changed. Duleep cabled Lord Dufferin: 'On further reflection, determined on sending family to England. I remain here a *prisoner* at Your Excellency's pleasure. Request that Government send 17 servants from Bombay.'

General Hogg 'reasoned with him without effect', reporting: 'The Maharajah says his expectations are shattered.'

It was just the opposite. The Viceroy had made a mistake in allowing his '*détenu*' to communicate with the outside world, then permitting his servants to seek out their master. He was even paying their fares. If the Maharajah could not become a Sikh in the Punjab, his Punjab partisans would come to him.

The intelligence failure seemed general. Before the arrest the Viceroy had cabled: 'Maharajah should not be permitted to communicate with outside world.' This restriction was lifted almost immediately. Messages were clearly getting through from Aden to India. Thakur Singh in Delhi was reported to be 'receiving English letters'. The Delhi telegraph office wire-tap was authorized on 15 May but 'produced no results'.

The resident continued his interminable conversations with his reluctant guest. The Maharajah's mental turmoil was deepening. On 5 May, he told General Hogg variously that he could not return to England because of 'the ridicule'. Then that he would return if promised a judicial investigation by the House of Lords, the great state trial his martyr-ego craved. Then, just as suddenly, the Maharajah became graspingly venal, declaring that he would return for an immediate cash payment on reaching London of no less than 'a quarter of a million pounds'. The Indian government exploded with anger: 'His terms are preposterous – there is no need to comment,' Durand cabled Hogg.

The family had to be removed from Aden's heat. Bamba's reactions are not recorded, but this time she must have obeyed her husband with relief. The children, their nanny and the Maharani boarded the mail-steamer for England the next day. She would never see Duleep Singh again.

The Viceroy told Queen Victoria of the latest tumble in her favourite's fall from grace, writing from Simla:

> After, however, the Maharajah had actually sailed, we received a telegram from the English government informing us that His Highness had issued a very mischievous and improper address to the Sikhs of the Punjab and had held very menacing language at the India Office.
>
> As India is not a country where tricks and experiments of the kind can be played with impunity, Lord Dufferin and his government felt themselves compelled to instruct the

Commander at Aden to request the Maharajah to land on arriving and become that officer's guest.

His visit here would be productive of nothing but embarrassment and inconvenience . . . He might be tempted to acts of imprudence which would compel us to resort to very severe measures against him . . .

PS. Lord Dufferin is sorry to say that since writing the above, he has received a most provoking telegram from the Maharajah saying that he has changed his mind and that he intends constituting himself a prisoner at Aden; while sending back his wife and children to England.

The Queen absolved her Viceroy in a letter from Balmoral:

The Queen Empress thanks the Viceroy for his last kind letter about the poor Maharajah Duleep Singh. He was so charming and good for so many years that she feels deeply grieved at the bad hands he has fallen into, and the way in which he has been led astray & away.

The Queen thinks it will have a very bad effect in India if he is ill used and rather severely punished, especially if the Maharanee (an excellent and pious woman) and their children especially the two boys, quite Englishmen, are in poverty or discomfort.

In the Maharajah's present state of excitement, nothing can be done but he is sure to quiet down and then the Queen is ready herself to speak to him.

Some money should be settled on his wife and children and a good man of business be placed about him and enough given him to live as a nobleman in England. The Queen wishes he or his son could be made a Peer, and then they could live as any other nobleman's family.

It is most important that his Indian advisers and relations should be kept from him for they are those who have brought him to this pass.

There it was again; the Queen still blamed those rascally Indians. She could return him to the fold, but by the time she gave her advice to Lord Dufferin it was already far too late. Things were working out as planned in the library at Elveden. The Maharajah must take Pahul and reclaim his kingdom. Emissaries from Thakur Singh had already taken ship, coming to make him a Sikh again.

The British had made an intelligence blunder. There was no excuse. They had been reading the Maharajah's telegrams since that last night at the Great Eastern Hotel when the 'started' messages were sent. The Punjab Special Branch had intercepted another message sent when the *Verona* docked at Alexandria. The political intelligence report for 1 May, the day the Maharajah declared himself a 'prisoner', read: 'Sardar Thakur Singh Sandhanwalia has received a telegram from Maharajah Duleep Singh from Cairo announcing his arrival there. He expects another message from Aden, and will then start for Bombay with other friends to meet Duleep Singh.'

The Punjab swarmed with spies and informers. The political intelligence report for 8 May read: 'Ram Singh, a mounted constable of the Gurdaspur District Police, who is in service with Sardar Thakur Singh, stated that he received a letter from the Maharajah announcing his arrival at Aden and requesting him to entertain 10 or 12 old and trusted Sikh retainers of his family and to make them take the Pahul again in token of fidelity to the cause. When this letter reached Thakur Singh, he was staying at Amritsar with several of his friends and adherents. The party held a secret conference at which *Karah parshad* was distributed and every Sikh present was required to take the Pahul afresh.' Their next destination was Delhi.

Thakur Singh had long ago been fingered as the key Duleep-intriguer in India. He was followed by spies and his communications intercepted. He even had to apply to the government to move around, which he did twice at the end of April asking permission to go to Bombay to meet the Maharajah on arrival. Durand ordered 'no reply'.

From the Imperial Hotel Thakur decamped to the Sikh temple at Kotwali, but was still barred from leaving Delhi. He ordered his namesake, Thakur Singh of Vagha,* and a servant named Jowand Singh to travel urgently to Bombay and there take ship for Aden. No attempt

---

* Thakur Singh of Vagha, Lahore district, had reason to be a Duleep partisan. His mother was 'a daughter of the sister of Rani Jindan's' (motherhood aged thirteen was not unusual), according to the political intelligence report on him, and he had 'shared the Rani's imprisonment, but on his escape was returned to his mother'.

was made to stop them. They arrived in the colony on 8 May.

The multiplying Thakurs threw the British into confusion. General Hogg was completely bemused. He thought 'the Thakurs' were some kind of extreme Sikh sect. 'That's his name', Durand cabled from Simla, but added to the confusion by saying he was the notorious Thakur Singh Sandhanwalia, who had stirred up the Punjab in the Maharajah's cause.

The disinformation blossomed. Officials messaged each other: 'You may have seen a report of Thakur Singh's having committed suicide by poison on his way down to Bombay. The rumour arose from the accidental death of [yet] another Thakur Singh from a fall from his horse in Port Blair (capital of the Andaman Islands)'; 'I cannot make sense about Thakur Singh Sandhanwalia. The police reports showed he went to Delhi before going to Bombay. The story of his death was a hoax. He wrote to the newspapers and contradicted it. The Punjab must I think be mistaken about his being still at Delhi. If not, then he is represented by an impostor at Aden.'

On 8 May the Maharajah cabled the Viceroy: 'My first cousin, who was adopted by my mother as her son, and another have arrived here without my knowledge. I request permission to see them, and also that they may be permitted to stay with me.' He did not mention that Thakur Singh of Vagha was secretly bearing more than 100,000 rupees in gold and jewels from the Maharajah of Kashmir to stoke Duleep's war-chest, as a Punjab police investigation later discovered.

What was the Viceroy to do? News of the Maharajah's detention was all over the Indian newspapers. One reported that 'he had been confined to a desert island in a mad act by Lord Dufferin'. A stream of alarming intelligence reports were reaching Simla from Sir Charles Aitchison, Lieutenant-Governor of the Punjab. Not only was support for Duleep being muttered by soldiers on leave trains, the word in the bazaars was that 'Sikhs would receive him back into the faith, as his conversion to Christianity was effected when he was a child'.

Two ominous words kept recurring in the intelligence summaries: 'Russians' and 'Kukas'. An informer reported that Jamiat Rai of Gurdaspur (a recipient of one of the 'started' telegrams) was on the move and spreading word: 'The Russian government are friendly with the Maharajah and have a secret understanding with him.'

The Kuka business was more troublesome. The sect was proclaiming the 'spirit of Guru Ram Singh had entered the Maharajah'. It was reported on 24 May that the Khalsa Diwan (the Sikh National Association), had expelled a member who had published a book containing heretical passages. The Lahore Special Branch had searched through it for portents. It was dangerously seditious. The police report stated:

> The book begins with genealogical trees of five Sikh Gurus, namely, from the fifth to the tenth Sikh Guru. It contains a meagre account of the Sikh conquests after the death of Gobind Singh up to deportation of Maharaja Duleep Singh and of his mother Jindan.
>
> On the genealogical trees, the author gives the names of the four sons of the tenth Guru, and of the different sects of the Sikhs. Amongst the latter, he mentions the Kukas, and styles their leader as Guru Ram Singh.
>
> This is objectionable from the Sikh point of view, as, according the Sikh religion, no spiritual leader can be recognised as Guru subsequent to the death of Guru Gobind Singh. The book concludes with a very objectionable passage. 'The British Government held Rand Chand Kaur (Rani Jindan) guilty for being concerned in the conspiracy to kill the English residents at Lahore by administering poison in their food, and, in consequence, deported Maharajah Duleep Singh and his mother with the concurrence of the councillors.
>
> 'Kashmir was then made over to Gulab Singh for a consideration of 50 lakhs of rupees. Croesus died although he possessed 40 coffers.'
>
> The people are now in hopes that by the royal and imperial favours of the Empress of India, the throne of Lahore will be restored to Maharajah Duleep Singh. Sardar Thakur Singh Sandhanwalia, who has, by his perfect belief in the Sikh faith and by his excellent undertaking, exonerated himself from the disgrace attached to his family [the murder of Sher Singh] is expecting to be made a Wazir.

The Viceroy agonized. Perhaps assenting to the Maharajah's conversion would calm him and the Punjab down. There was a suggestion of exiling him to Burma to shut him up. Dufferin cabled Hogg on 8 May: 'His Highness Duleep Singh can see the two persons who have arrived from India in the presence of an English officer who understands the language. You had better be present also. Nothing of an objectionable nature ought to be allowed to pass.'

The Maharajah cabled: 'I desire to take advantage of my cousin's presence here to be reinitiated into Sikhism. Kindly telegraph Resident, saying I may go through the ceremony in his presence.'

Dufferin concurred. There was no regulation that could be dusted off to enforce a British subject's religion. He cabled General Hogg on 15 May: 'You can allow the ceremony to be performed, but you yourself should not be present, nor should any of our officials, having the look of countenancing the proceedings. It would be well to prevent any private communication between the Maharajah and the Punjabi gentlemen. I dare say your tact and skill will enable you to arrange the business in a desirable manner. I have myself witnessed it.'

The eve of the day set for the baptismal ceremony was Queen Victoria's birthday. Brigadier-General Hogg hosted a grand dinner at the residency at which Duleep Singh 'Put on his diamonds and the Order of Grand Commander of the Star of India'. It was a high imperial scene, the British officers in mess jackets and stiff collars, the Maharajah decked out in the chivalric pomp that had been invented after the Royal Titles Act of 1877 that had proclaimed Queen Victoria the Empress of India. It could have been mess-night in Camberley, apart from the heat and the lizards. The Maharajah was saying goodbye to all that.

He asked the general for a king-sized retinue to attend his baptism: a Sikh Granthi (reader of the scriptures), an attendant with a copy of the *Granth*, cooks (if not Punjabi then high-caste Hindus), Hindu water-carriers, valets and attendants including a *dhobi* (washerman), *durzee* (tailor), *mehtur* (sweeper) and *burkundees* (musketeers).

It was to be not quite so grand. General Hogg did what he could, accommodating the Maharajah's visitors and scraping together whatever transiting Sikhs there were in the colony. The ceremony took place on the morning of 25 May. Present with the Maharajah were Arur Singh his servant, Thakur Singh of Vahga, Jowand Singh, Attar Singh and another soldier from a troopship transiting Aden.

The War Office later distributed a description of the baptismal ceremony for the enlightenment of Sikh regimental officers. 'The Pahul is the "gate", the oath of initiation of the Sikhs who follow

Guru Gobind Singh,' it explained. 'A true Sikh does not become a Singh until he had been initiated by drinking of the Amrit or nectar.' The Maharajah did just that, wearing the *kach*, the short trousers to the knee, holding his hands together in supplication. The Amrit, purified sugar and water, was mixed in an iron bowl stirred by the two-edged dagger (*khanda*).

The Amrit was sprinkled into the Maharajah's hands, held up like a cup, as prayers for the victory of God were said five times. The Amrit was then sprinkled on the Maharajah's head and the iron bowl drained. At last *Karah parshad* (a sweetmeat) was placed in the bowl and eaten by the Maharajah as he sat cross-legged on the ground.

He was a Sikh again.

General Hogg cabled Simla: 'After much delay, the Maharajah was remade a Sikh this morning. I was not present nor did I in any way countenance the same, but I took steps to ensure there being no objectionable conversation with the five Sikhs who were present.'

What to do with the born-again Sikh? The heat was brain-scrambling. Kimberley told the Viceroy on the baptismal day: 'You may leave him for a time to bake at Aden, but it would not do to let him die.' Two doctors examined the Maharajah and reported weakness of the heart. The hapless Hogg cabled: 'The weather is now very hot and he says that he felt very queer in the head. I think at times that he is very queer.'

He seemed a burned-out case. The Queen's private secretary wrote knowingly to the Viceroy on 23 May: 'We thought we had got rid of him. But he is coming back on our hands again.... he must take up his lodgings again in Covent Garden.' But it was not Miss Ash's embrace that the Maharajah was anticipating.

The startled Viceroy received a telegram from Hogg on 30 May: 'Maharajah wishes to telegraph to the Queen of England asking for public trial. Shall I allow?' The next day the Maharajah himself cabled: 'I return to Europe. From 1st of July next I resign stipend paid to me under Treaty of Annexation, thus laying aside that iniquitous document.'

It was not the money he was after, it was destiny. He was going to bring down the temple, if not in the Punjab then in the Palace of Westminster, with some ghastly theatrics in the House of Lords. A troublesome Conservative MP, Robert Hanbury (a Carlton Club chum) was already asking questions in the lower House. The Queen's jubilee was approaching. An imperial scandal would be appalling. Lord Kimberley, the Secretary of State, told General Ponsonby on 3 June: 'I wrote to the Queen last night explaining that the Maharajah cannot demand a trial. The very expense of proceeding under the Indian regulation of 1818 would be prohibitive. He must be quite off his head.'

That same day at Aden, Duleep Singh boarded a French mail-steamer, the SS *Natal*, bound for Marseilles. He had told General Hogg simply that he was 'going to Paris'.

Queen Victoria wrote to her minister: 'Some kind and firm person should meet him at Paris & set him straight, pacify him & prevent his ruining his children.' The Queen's godson especially should not be ruined by his poor and, she still is convinced, good hearted but utterly deluded father and his follies. The Queen is grtly grieved as she was so fond of him and for many years went on *so well*.' She memoed Sir Henry Ponsonby on 9 June: 'The Queen . . . still thinks she cd. bring him round if she saw him.' It was not going to be that simple.

## 15

# 'A Sikh Martyr Will Be Born'

❦

*Grand Hotel de St James et Bristol, 211 rue St Honoré, Paris,*
*July 1886*

WHEN THE MAHARAJAH boarded the SS *Natal* of the French Messageries Maritimes at Steamer Point, he had disappeared from English sight, and, mercifully for civil servants in Whitehall and Simla, from the groaning in-trays of the government of India. The Aden resident had cabled London simply on 3 June 1886: 'He heads for Paris.'

The French mail-boat headed through the thundery heat of the Red Sea, but the Maharajah was obviously recovering from Aden's debilitations. At Suez City, on 7 June, he felt composed enough to do what was now a compulsion: cable a long list of complaints to whatever newspaper would print it. The *Times of India* published his 'Suez manifesto' a month later.

Although I am a naturalised Englishman yet I was arrested at Aden without a warrant, one having been issued since I re-embraced Sikhism while staying at Aden.

My health having broken down through residence at Aden, I am now travelling on my way back to Europe in order to drink the German waters.

Although the India Government succeeded in preventing me from reaching Bombay, they are not able to close all the roads that there are to India; for I can land at Goa or Pondicherry [Portuguese and French coastal enclaves], or if I fancy an overland route, then I can enter the Punjab through Russia.

In that event, I suppose the whole of the British Army would be sent out, as well as the assistance of our ally, the Ameer [of

Afghanistan], invoked to resist the coming of single individual, viz, myself. What a wonderful spectacle.

As soon as I am restored to health, I hope to appeal for to the oriental liberality of both my brother princes as well as the people of India. Should, however, the Government place its veto upon their generous impulse, then I shall have no alternative but to transfer my allegiance to some other European power. I find it very difficult to collect my thoughts at present owing to bad weather.

The Maharajah had no intention of docilely taking the cure at Baden-Baden. The SS *Natal* arrived at Marseilles eleven days after leaving Aden. He boarded the connecting 7.40 p.m. sleeper to Paris and arrived at the Gare de Lyons in time for breakfast the next day.

He knew the French capital of old, from pleasure-seeking forays with his racier English friends. Paris's midsummer charms were laid out for plucking – ladies heading in carriages from assignations in the Bois to discreet hotels, the cafés crammed with well-appointed men talking politics and money. Paris was convulsed by one of its endless government crises. General Georges Boulanger at the war ministry was making ever louder noises about a war of revenge against Germany. There was big money talk of switching the Russian securities market from Berlin to the *hautes banques* of Paris to fund a colossal railway-building plan. Nothing could happen until Rothschilds Frères lifted the ban on Russian loans, imposed in protest against the empire's ever more abysmal treatment of the Jews.*

The Majarajah had clearly learned a few lessons in conspiracy. There was work to be done, a secluded residence to find, bankers to appoint, a confidential secretary to engage. He took rooms in the Grand Hotel de St James et Bristol, 211 rue St Honoré, a fine *ancien régime* mansion built round a courtyard, discreetly sealed from the street behind a massive oak door. The bank of Messrs Mallet Frères, a five-minute stroll away in the rue Anjou, would be both a mail-box and a depository for his cash and remaining jewels. They greeted the Indian milord

* The 'May Laws' of 1882 introduced by interior minister Count Ignatiev imposed brutal new restrictions on internal movements and professions open to Jews. His successor, Count Tolstoi, was no less an anti-Semite. 'Nihilism is a disease,' Tolstoi explained to the *Standard*'s St Petersburg correspondent, John Baddeley, 'you can no more stamp it out than you can the Jewish leprosy.' Both men were key backers of the Maharajah's flight to Russia.

with deferential discretion as a topaz or two went into the strong-box.* The British embassy was just around the corner – that would have amused him.

He could not resist penning another laborious whinge, this time to his old tea-party confidante Sir Robert Montgomery, long-suffering conduit to the bureaucratic jungles of the India Office. It was dated 21 June 1886: 'I have returned here from Aden a desperate man. Now I beg you to give credence to all rumours that may reach you regarding myself. I have laid aside the iniquitous Treaty of Annexation which was extorted from me by my wicked Guardian when I was a minor; thus claiming to the lawful sovereign of the Sikhs which I really am.

'I will shortly proceed to Russia and if the Emperor gives me encouragement then I will go to Merv, otherwise to reside at Pondicherry. What can the stupid Lord Dufferin do to me now? He has succeeded in driving away from his allegiance a loyal heart which would have freely bled for England and you English in spite of all the injustices received. Goodbye my kind friend. Judge me not too harshly . . . D.S.'

There was a scribbled footnote: 'PS having become a Sikh I have abandoned all my family who are Christians.'

Sir Robert did what the Maharajah must have expected him to do: he immediately sent the letter to Sir Owen Tudor Burne, the 'case-officer' at the India Office. Was the Maharajah serious or had the Aden sun turned his head completely? The Queen must be told, whatever the embarrassment. Sir Owen minuted on the Montgomery letter: 'The above has been shown to Lord Kimberley who decided that the best course would be for the present to ask Lord Lyons [the British ambassador to Paris] to be kind enough to watch matters and keep us informed.'

No one could call the Maharajah a gifted conspirator. Very soon after arriving in Paris he wrote to the Russian ambassador, Baron Arthur Pavlovich Monrenheim, requesting an interview, and immediately told his friend from shooting days, the Duke of Grafton, what he had done by letter: 'I wrote yesterday to the Russian Ambassador offering my services to the Emperor and requested a passport which, as soon as I receive, I shall go with to St Petersburg. If I am well

---

* A secret agent in India was later to intercept a Paris-posted letter from the Maharajah: 'I have deposited all my money and jewels to the value of 100,000 rupees with Mallet Frères, Paris.'

received by the Emperor I shall go to the border of India. If I not I shall go to Pondicherry and be a thorn in the side of Lord Dufferin.' His Grace passed the letter to Windsor Castle.

Sir Owen Tudor Burne got down to work. To begin with he thought it all rather amusing: 'His Highness is at present airing himself in Paris no doubt wasting his substance on what the Parisians call the fair "horizontales",' he cabled Simla. He next contacted Sir Philip Currie, under-secretary of state at the Foreign Office, relaying his own minister's advice that the Paris embassy should mount a discreet watch. Consensus was growing that the Maharajah was crazy.

Currie told Lyons: 'I send you a letter from Sir Owen Burne about Duleep Singh who seems inclined to give trouble. He is supposed to be rather off his head, but as far as I can hear the principal sign of insanity he has shown is in refusing to draw his allowances.'

It was time to tell the Queen. Lord Kimberley informed her private secretary on 30 June: 'Duleep Singh talks of going to Russia or to Pondicherry: and has resigned his pension! He is evidently going quite mad.'

Lord Rosebery, the Foreign Secretary, was not about to disagree. He minuted Ponsonby the same day: 'As to the Maharajah I believe him to be mad. We have thought it sufficient for the moment to ask Lord Lyons to keep an eye on him. I was shown a letter of his which I understood had been communicated to the Queen, which was simply insane.'

The Maharani and the children had made the debilitating journey home the way they came. They arrived on 4 June, 'delighted to be back in England', and put up at Claridge's until the money ran out. They, at least, were blameless. Lord Dufferin waded in, advising Queen Victoria in a letter: 'His Highnesses' two sons were extremely popular on board the ship on which they came to Aden and that the whole expedition was undertaken very much against their will and that of their mother.' He did not want any of them flying the coop again. 'The more completely they can be induced to regard England as their home the better, as the appearance of even a grandson of Ranjit Singh in the Punjab might have many inconvenient consequences.'

Anything that remained in the bank accounts had been cleared out. Elveden had been stripped by the brokers' men. They were now holed

up in Holland Park with 'hardly any furniture left beyond a few beds'.
The newly remade Sikh had abjured the mission-school girl because
she and their children were Christians. What was to become of her?
Sir Henry Ponsonby asked on the Queen's account. 'Who is looking
after her and can the Queen take any steps to save her?' Lord Kimberley had gloomier news; he told Sir Henry for the Queen's ears: 'That
he was sorry also to have heard an unsatisfactory account of the Maharani who whether from despair or being neglected had taken to drinking
alcohol to an injurious extent.'

Sir Robert and Lady Montgomery went to the Holland Park house
to see what could be done. Bamba wrote to her mission friend Mrs
Lansing: 'Sir Robert thought it better not to write to the Queen but
to Lord Kimberley, which I did, I sent the letter last night and Victor
is to go to the India Office at one o'clock today which he did to talk
with him there . . . Please ask Dr Lansing not to mention anything to
anyone about what Victor said the lawyers told him to say.'

She wrote despairingly to her husband. The Maharajah chose to
reply instead in another bizarre ramble to Sir Robert Montgomery.

PARIS, 2ND JULY 1886 PRIVATE.

Having received a letter, the first since we were all together
at Aden, from the Maharani, in which she says that you and
Lady Montgomery were most kind to her, I must write a line
to thank you for the goodness of your hearts towards her.

I also understand that a communication is to be made to
me from the India Office to the effect that Government will
provide for my family. Now I ask you kindly to prevent any
communication from being addressed to me.

I have closed all correspondence with the Council of India
as well as with the Government of India . . . because I would,
if I reply at all to such a despatch, it would be in anything but
a civil manner.

For I neither respect such a tyrannical and unjust administration, nor am I any longer loyal to the British Crown having
offered my services to Russia.

I seek now nothing from you gentlemen as I have been
refused justice and my loyalty insulted. I have only one prayer

now that God may, before I die, enable me to have my revenge on the India administration and humiliate that Government, and to cause the expenditure of many more millions of poor John Bull's money than the £3,000,000 I should have asked for the loss of my private property.

God bless you, my oldest and kindest of friends and your good and kind lady, although I am a rebel now in earnest.

The India Office thought the Maharajah was out of his mind. His price had suddenly leapt to £3 million. Queen Victoria had soothingly advised all along that she could save him, but first he had to be found. He was a 'British Indian Subject' on French soil – no Bombay arrest warrant would work in Paris. Control of the case was slipping to the Foreign Office. The Paris embassy's letter-book contained a clue as to the next move – a copperplate accounting entry: 'Paris July 1st 1886. To the Earl of Rosebery from Paris Ambassador. I have the honour to inform your Lordship that I have this day drawn a Bill upon you for one hundred and eleven pounds sterling in favour of Messrs Rothschild Brothers of this city payable thirty days after sight, on account of Her Majesty's Foreign Secret Service.'

Someone in the Foreign Office was running a spy. The same amount would henceforth go out every month. But things were not as simple as they seemed. Lord Lyons, the ambassador, was in fact extremely reluctant to have anything to do with the troublesome Maharajah. He wrote to Currie at the Foreign Office on 2 July:

In your letter of 26th June you ask me to keep an eye upon Duleep Singh and let you know anything I may hear of his movements.

He is still here, staying at the Grand Hotel, and holding, I am told, language very much the same as that used in his letter to Sir Robert Montgomery of the 21st ultimo, of which you have sent me a copy.

I will put myself as much as I can in the way of hearing about him and his movements; but the information I am likely to obtain in this way will probably be scanty, and tardy.

If you attach real importance to certain and timely intelligence about him, you must I suppose put a spy upon him, but this should be done entirely en dehors de l'Ambassade [outside the embassy] either through the London Police or any other channel you may have. If the Embassy is mixed up in the mater, we shall run the risk of attacks in the French newspapers, interpolations in the Chambers and what not.

Somehow the embarrassed diplomats in Paris found the Maharajah. The Grand Hotel was just down the street, after all. There was an urgent imperative to do so – the Queen had composed a letter to be delivered directly to Lyons from Windsor Castle in conditions of great secrecy. Lyons replied to Sir Henry Ponsonby: 'The letter you enclosed to me on the 6th. has been put this morning into the hand of the person to whom it was addressed.

It was the Queen's last bid, but it would not stop him.

WINDSOR JULY 6TH 1886.

Dear Maharajah, I hear extraordinary reports of your resigning your allowance . . . and of your intending to transfer your allegiance to Russia!! I cannot believe this of you who always professed such loyalty and devotion towards me – who you know have always been your true friend and who I may say took a maternal interest in you from the time, when now 32 years ago, you came to England as a beautiful and charming Boy!

I watched your life with true interest and thought your Home with your amiable wife and fine children was a pattern to all Indian princes! But after the death of your really true and devoted friend Col Oliphant bad and false friends have surrounded you and put things into your head and heart which I am sure never could under other circumstances have entered them.

Let me appeal to all that is good and noble in you to ask abandon wild ideas and plans which can only plunge you into deeper difficulties and lead to disastrous consequences.

Think of me as your best friend and the Godmother of your son who bears my name. Trusting that you may be able to give me assurances that these reports are untrue. Believe me always, Your true friend. V.R.I.

The once beautiful and charming boy replied four days later:

> Gracious Sovereign . . . It greatly pains me to have to inform your Majesty that it is no longer in my power either to contradict the current reports to give the assurance which you so graciously demand . . .
>
> I had no other course left open to me except either to turn a traitor or continue to submit to the insults repeatedly offered to me by the Administration of India . . .
>
> Unfortunately however, my nature proving too proud to follow the latter course, I offered my services to Russia but as yet have received no definite reply . . .
>
> I have, Most Gracious Sovereign, not only resigned my stipend but have also set aside and annulled that wicked treaty of the Annexation of the Punjab which was extorted from me and my ministers by the late Marquis of Dalhousie when I was of tender age and the ward of your Majesty's government.
>
> Your Majesty I implore you to pardon me when I say that I am a proud Sikh although I may and most likely will break – yet by the help of God I will never bend, however disastrous the consequences of my own acts might prove but will cheerfully lie on the bed I have made for myself.
>
> Imploring your forgiveness, Most Gracious Sovereign, for thus freely giving vent to my feelings . . . as well as for this badly written letter, but being much out of health I am not able to write any better. I most humbly implore to be permitted to subscribe myself your Majesty's most devoted humble faithful servant, Duleep Singh.

On the day the Maharajah wrote his reply, 10 July, he disappeared. Lyons messages London limply: 'The person about whom you wrote to me on 26th ult. is still at Paris, but he has left the Grand Hotel and I do not know his present address. He has his letters addressed to the care of his bankers, and he goes himself to fetch them, but he does not allow the bankers to know where he is living. If certain and timely information about him is wanted, I can only suggest the steps to be taken *en dehors de l'Ambassade* which I mentioned in my letter to you.'

The Secretary of State for India thought it all done with. He replied jauntily to Lyons: 'Nothing need be done at present as D.S. is said to have shaved his beard off with the view of turning back a Christian!'

The view from Windsor, however, was wreathed in gloom: 'The Queen got this sad & extraordinary letter from the poor, mad Maharajah yesterday. It is hopeless . . .' she noted on 15 July.

Five days later, Gladstone's Liberal government fell, defeated on Irish Home Rule. Lord Salisbury was Prime Minister again, as ruthless a political operator as any of his Elizabethan forebears, with Richard Assheton Cross (now Viscount Cross) as Secretary of State for India. The Maharajah would find scant tolerance for any further antics.

On 30 July he wrote a jauntily lighthearted letter to his boyhood friend Tommy Scott (now a major in the Indian army). 'I style myself Lawful Monarch of the Sikh Nation – doesn't that sound Grand my boy . . . the only thing I have settled on doing (as I am a Sikh now) is to fight the administration of India to the last and create all the mischief I can in India. Fancy our meeting on the battlefield! But I promise you (should it ever come to pass) the first shot.'

His reasons for changing faith were illuminating: 'I renounced Christianity first because I have been reading many books on the subject which shook my faith in the divinity of Christ,' he wrote '– and because I myself would not have given a year's purchase of my life while residing in India from the attacks of the fanatic Sikhs. For they would have said to me that it was all very fine for me to have embraced any religion I might have pleased to when young, but at my present time of life I must either return to the faith of my ancestors or die as a disgrace to Sikhism.'

His imperial surrogate mother had despaired of him. He had slipped the bounds of pious Bamba and his 'Christian family'. Paris was full of charms and portents. The Maharajah felt as unencumbered as the wandering fakir he had talked of becoming. His real journey was about to begin.

# 16

# The Dancing Mouse

❦

*257 rue St Honoré, Paris, July 1886*

HOW THE MAHARAJAH first encountered Mr Patrick Casey in the first days of his Paris sojourn is not recorded in the British foreign-secret-service archives. Whitehall had effectively lost sight of him on 10 July when Lord Lyons told London he had disappeared from the Grand Hotel in the rue St Honoré.

How and where Pat and Duleep's fates might have entwined becomes clearer with a simple walk up a Paris street. The long, narrow rue St Honoré paralleling the Tuileries has an unusual numbering system. The hotel at number 211 is virtually opposite number 257, the *imprimerie* of M. Charles Schlaeber. As far as London was concerned, the jobbing printshop was the foundry of Fenian propaganda in Europe, described dramatically to Queen Victoria as being the 'Irish secret press in Paris'.

The Maharajah was famous, an enemy of England. The Suez 'manifesto' was in the papers, although the fact of his arrival in Paris was not. It is easy to imagine the 'notorious dynamiter' of 'Black Pamphlet' fame wiping the ink from his fingers to approach the exotic figure as he crossed the street to his hotel. How about a drink with Mr Reynolds? It was 'where English gentlemen of the turf went for good glass of whiskey and water', after all. It looked like a simple coincidence – but as I dug deeper, I found a much stranger agenda.

The day the Maharajah vanished, 10 July, was a busy one for Lord Lyons. An excitable Englishman had come to the embassy that morning with details of 'a plot alleged to be hatching here by Irish Americans'. The ambassador immediately telegraphed in cipher to Sir Julian Pauncefote, permanent under-secretary at the Foreign Office: 'I think it better to send you the statements for what they may be worth. If the authorities in England think they deserve further examination, their only feasible plan will be to employ an agent of their own here and to direct him to keep quite aloof from the Embassy.'

The plot centred on that old favourite, the Irish-American Bar. The statement was recorded by Mr Francis Elliot, an embassy official: 'A man came to me this morning and said that he was convinced that some dynamite plot was being prepared by Irish Americans who frequent Reynold's Bar. An unusual number of them, about 40 he thinks, come there at the moment. He does not know any of their names but believes two of them to have been concerned in the Tower explosion. One of them left Paris a day or two ago.'

The informer's name was Smith. The file was sent on Lord Rosebery's instructions to Edward Jenkinson, the Dublin Castle 'spymaster' now uncomfortably installed at the Home Office as Fenian finder-general. He was characteristically brusque in his reply to Sir Julian, saying a week later: 'I return the letters about the man Smith. I have been over to Scotland Yard about him. If he makes a statement I am to see it. In future it could save a great deal of trouble if, in such cases, Lord Lyons were to tell any person coming to him with similar indiscretions to wait in Paris. I have an agency in Paris, and I could better instruct *my* agent there to see an agissant [sic] and take his statement – or I could reel in an agissant and after examining him, instruct my agent to make further inquiries.'

He added: 'The Scotland Yard authorities have really nothing to do with such matters outside London.'

The Special (Irish) Branch of the Metropolitan Police were not to take this latest insult of Jenkinson's lying down. Its head, James Monro, told the commissioner, Sir Charles Warren, a week later: 'Enquiry into the man Smith's antecedents had been completed, and there seems to me little doubt that he has let his imagination dupe him into the belief that he has discovered a dynamite plot. Reynold's people have evidently been playing practical jokes on him.'*

The 'Reynold's Bar plot' may have been another drunken hoax, but the Whitehall spat over the affair is very revealing. Lord Lyons, just

---

* Monro was in fact very reluctant to set Scotland Yard detectives on the Maharajah. He would tell Sir Henry Matthews, the Home Secretary, on 12 November 1886, 'an agent employed to watch [anyone in Paris] is sure to be arrested by the French police and kept in custody until he disclosed his employers'.

as in the Maharajah's case, insisted that spying activities be kept strictly 'aloof from the embassy', although £111 a month was now moving through his books drawn on behalf of 'Her Majesty's Foreign Secret Service' to an anonymous recipient.

Jenkinson had 'an agency in Paris'. 'My agent' was obviously kept well away from the Metropolitan Police and their record of comic-opera antics in the French capital. Jenkinson reminded Sir Julian Pauncefote at the Foreign Office of the fact in his letter. This was very professional, very secret spycraft. The Rothschild bank payments, authorized by the Foreign Secretary, were going somewhere. It is clear that the developing Jenkinson–Pauncefote axis in Whitehall now had an agent in Paris operating under deep cover within the Irish Revolutionary Brotherhood of whom Scotland Yard knew nothing. The embassy was the agent's cashier, nothing more.

As Duleep drank toasts to Ireland and India's liberation – bathing in Patrick Casey's excoriation of Mrs Brown and her works – neither could know that a powerful counter-conspiracy was beginning to gather round them. The Maharajah's first encounter with the Irishman was obviously very soon after his arrival in the French capital. The urge to make a public noise again as overwhelming. The Maharajah composed two 'proclamations', the first dated Paris, 15 July 1886, printed at Schlaeber's printshop in the rue St Honoré with a covering slip inviting newspaper editors to 'insert the letter in their influential journal'. Patrick Casey certainly did the typesetting; Punjabi spellings are inserted in the Maharajah's hand on the proof copy. It contained the same old stuff, but this time larded with the royal 'we' so beloved of Queen Victoria – he was a king after all – and the salutations of the Guru.

PROCLAMATION No. 1

By the grace of Sri Sat Guru Ji, We Maharajah Dalip Singh, the lawful sovereign of the Sikh nation, under the Treaty of Bhyrowal entered into without coercion between ourselves and our Darbar on the one part and Great Britain on the other, do from hereby in consequence of the insults and indignities repeatedly offered to us . . . set aside and annul that iniquitous and illegal document, the so-called 'Terms granted', which was extorted from us in 1849 by our wicked guardian, the

Christian British nation, when we were an infant of only 11
years of age, and by the above first mentioned covenant, under
the protection of England. Wah Guru ji di Fateh. Duleep
Singh. Maharajah of Sikhs under Treaty of Bhyrowal 1846.

The second proclamation, was addressed to 'Brother Princes and
Nobles and the people of beloved Hindustan' and contained an
interminable reprise of British iniquities barely concealing an appeal
for money.

By the grace of Almighty God, the Creator of the Universe,
the most merciful and gracious, and of Sri Gobind Singh Ji.

The poor old British lion is becoming so trapped as to show
the white feather at the mere buzzing of a gnat, but that is
not to be wondered at, because that Sikh is the son of the
renowned Lion of the Punjab as well as the lawful sovereign
of the Sikh nation.

We, therefore, appeal to your oriental generosity, brother
princes and nobles and the people of Hindustan, as we vastly
prefer to suffer the greatest degradation, humiliation and
shame of begging our bread from you beloved countrymen,
to being under any pecuniary obligation to such a most iniqui-
tously unjust, tyrannical and foreign Government.

The Government of India, out of spite, may indeed put its
veto upon the generous impulse of your hearts, but if you all
unite, it will be powerless to harm you as you cannot all be
deposed or sent to the Kala Panee [the black water – exile]
for not paying any heed to such a timorous administration as
it has now become. For see, that notwithstanding all its boasted
vast resources, how it dreads the return to India of a Sikh who
unlike you does not even possess a single soldier.

The proof copy was signed 'Duleep Singh – lawful Sovereign of the
Punjab' crossed out for 'Sikh Nation'. Somebody (probably Casey)
must have lent on the Maharajah to go quiet for a while. The two
proclamations were printed, bundled up and stored to be used when
the time came. They sat in their brown paper bundles like unexploded
bombs. The Maharajah could not resist hurling at least one of them
in the direction of Windsor Castle. A copy of Proclamation No. 1 was

sent in 'the strictest confidence', to his weary solicitor, Mr Lawrence, with instructions to show it to the Duke of Grafton, who felt, as the Maharajah must have predicted, compelled to inform the Queen. His Grace wrote on 20 July: 'I enclose what I suppose will be the last production from the poor Maharajah for his infatuation has blinded him to all reason . . . but the printed paper I feel you should see at once.' Sir Henry Ponsonby minuted on it: 'I think he had better be left alone till the want of friends and money compel him to reason . . .'

Someone in Paris thought the time had come to proclaim the revolution. The *Journal des Débats* dramatically reported on 7 September, 'An uprising of the people of north-eastern India against British rule and in favour of Russian invasion. Grave events are imminent in central Asia.' Reuters picked up the story and two days later it was run in the American papers. Duleep back-tracked frantically, cabling Sir Robert Montgomery two days later: 'No proclamation has either been prompted or authorised by me although I have two ready by me to be issued, but I find it hard to sever old ties.'

It became easier to break the bonds as the weeks passed. On 10 October the Maharajah wrote to his confidant Lord Henniker, a landed Norfolk neighbour, and conduit to the court. 'It is now too late. I start very shortly for the East . . . There are 45,000 Sikhs in the British army. It is true they have been loyal, but they had no leader. I am now with them.' Again the Queen was told of the letter's contents. Sir Henry Ponsonby minuted Her Majesty's reaction; she was running out of patience: 'The Maharajah's language and conduct has alienated the Queen's friendship, and that she now only feels anxious that the Maharanee should not suffer for her husband's folly.'

The proclamations were the same old tirade of whinging, cringing and insults. The British authorities could have dismissed them as more blackmailing ravings if not for a growing prickle of unease. Duleep had made overtures to more serious players than rascally cousins in the Punjab and boozy Fenians – there were the Russians to consider. He had told Queen Victoria from Paris in his letter of 10 July: 'I have offered my services to Russia . . . but have yet to receive a reply.' The conspiracy was about to get a lot darker.

The date of that 'offer' was to become important. The Maharajah claimed at Aden he done nothing 'disloyal' and he remained very sensitive on the point. The mysterious Reverend Antonius Tien was meanwhile preparing the dossier about 'intelligence agents from St Petersburg' visiting Elveden Hall that he was about to disclose to Sir Owen Tudor Burne.

The Foreign Office in London later put together what they knew in a long report based on information gleaned by Sir Robert Morier, the British ambassador to St Petersburg. The Maharajah's first formal overture had apparently been made in London, in March 1886, just before the flight to the Great Eastern Hotel, when he had written to Baron de Staal, imperial Russian ambassador to London, offering his services to the Czar.

The baron was obviously shown the 'I proceed to Russia' letter which had caused such a flutter. Lord Kimberley told Sir Owen Burne in London on 4 July: 'The Russian Ambassador asked me last night who Duleep Singh was as he had seen his letter saying he was going to Russia. I told him briefly.'

Kimberley's stated views on the Maharajah would indeed have been brief, and probably unprintable. They were relayed in diplomatic language by Baron de Staal from the London embassy to his political master, Nicholas de Giers, the Russian foreign minister. Morier was to record a later conversation in the Russian capital which explained much. 'The Minister told me that a year ago, M. de Staal had a letter from Duleep Singh proposing this visit. The ambassador immediately reported on the subject giving a very unfavourable account of the intended tourist and was instructed to do everything to prevent his carrying out this project.'

Whatever supplications the Maharajah may have made to Russian diplomats in London, the British had already effectively nobbled the key figure in the imperial government, the Lutheran, Swedish-born foreign minister Nikolai Girs (his name was gallicized to Nicholas de Giers in the fashionable manner of the St Petersburg court; as a Baltic noble he had adopted the 'de' form), a staunch defender of the Bismarckian peace. Duleep did not know the British were dripping discreet poison. His next move was to roll up at the Russian embassy in Paris some time in the first week of July.

The embassy on the rue de Grenelle was in a sensitive condition. The ambassador, Baron Mohrenheim, had been huffily recalled in March 1886 (he took up residence on the Italian riviera) when the Russian anarchist-aristocrat Prince Peter Alexandreevich Kropotkin was released from prison by French presidential amnesty (he fled to the safety of Harrow-on-the-Hill, north of London). There had been a similar incident a few years earlier when a bomb plotter named Leon Hartman* had been released and had also fled to English exile. The imperial government fumed; harbourers of assassins and terrorists were to be reviled.

Thus the trouble-making Maharajah was received by the *conseiller d'ambassade*, Prince Ernest Kotzebue, in prickly circumstances. The first interview was brief and is undocumented, but Duleep turned up again on 17 July clutching Queen Victoria's 'let me appeal to all that is noble and good in you' letter. He would not let his Russian host make a copy of it for transmission to St Petersburg. Kotzebue asked: 'From where does the Queen know that you came to the Embassy?' The Maharajah 'did not seem to know' (he was dissembling – it had been in the 21 June letter to Montgomery that had first set all the alarm-bells ringing in Whitehall).

What did he expect to get out of Russia? The Maharajah's replies convinced the diplomat of one thing. 'A large sum of money . . . he hopes to extract up to three million pounds sterling from the English government,' Kotzebue informed de Giers in a secret dispatch to St Petersburg. 'It is to be feared that the offers which the oriental Prince makes us are only a means of blackmail. He thinks he will be able to frighten the English and make them pay by threatening them with the prestige that he would gain by placing himself under our protection.' The Maharajah gave him 'an unsealed letter addressed to our former ambassador to London, Count Shuvalov [1875–80]. On my observing that the English would not be so simple as to give him money without making sure of his loyalty, he said that they are so afraid of the difficulties he could raise for them in India, that they would make any sacrifice in return for the hope of preventing him from it.'

The answer was no. No insurrection, no vengeance, there would be no multi-million-pound game of *chantage* with England courtesy of the Russian Army. Against the word 'blackmail' in the original dispatch, de Giers minuted: 'It was clear to us from the beginning and that is why we said no.'

---

* Real name Lev Nikolayevich Gartman who in 1879 had attempted to blow up the Czar's train.

For now, the foreign minister chose to keep the overture secret from his sovereign, authorizing Kotzebue to reply to the Maharajah on 28 July: 'Highness, The Imperial Government protects peace – which it desires and sustains within its own vast possessions. Far be it from the Russian Government to encourage or foment trouble in India. She has no reason so to do, and Your Highness must not think that the means to promote plans of insurrection or vengeance will be found in Russia.' The revolution was postponed.

The Maharajah tried his luck with Prince Kotzebue again in another visit to the rue de Grenelle on 17 September. The counsellor reported everything to de Giers:

> Maharajah Duleep Singh has come again to see me. He tells me that proclamations have been published in the Punjab calling upon the people to revolt in his name and with the assurance that it would be supported by Russia. He affirms that this has come about without his giving the order, even without his knowledge. But he thinks that a rising in the Punjab would perhaps be opportune today in view of the political events which are brewing. He has again offered his services to the Imperial government, in spite of our reply which had rejected his first overtures.
>
> Moreover, he thanks us for having clearly declared that he cannot count on us. If he continues to have hopes, it is because he is convinced that a war between Russia and England is imminent.
>
> I have told him that he should not have illusions, that the reply he had received was final.
>
> 'Then so as not to expose my poor people, I shall send the order to my adherents to suspend all action.'
>
> 'That is what is best for you to do.'
>
> He wished to remain in Paris for about two months more and then will try to go to Pondicherry to settle down there, he said.
>
> While leaving me, he again repeated to me that the war with England is inevitable and that notwithstanding our present refusals, we shall see him serving our cause because of his hatred against the power which had despoiled him and because

of his thirst for vengeance. He congratulates himself that he shall find in his people a very useful ally, considering that it lives at the borders of the frontiers of Afghanistan and its warlike qualities surpass those of the other Indian peoples.

This time de Giers showed the Maharajah correspondence to the Czar. Alexander III minuted on the Kotzebue report: 'maybe some time it will be useful'.

For now the Maharajah was stuck. He wrote on 12 October to another potential patriarchal patron, the French President Jules Grévy, wanting French nationality and permission to reside at Pondicherry: 'Should you, M. le President, condescend to afford me the protection I seek . . . I will in return cheerfully spill my last drop of blood in the service of France.* I give my word of honour not to cause any trouble to the British government as long as France is on amicable relations with England.'

M. Grévy memoed his foreign minister: 'not advisable to give protection to a man whose presence in our territory in India would certainly offend the British government.'

The Elysée stayed silent and the door to Russia seemed shut tight. But Patrick Casey could help. He knew a Russian gentleman, a doctor and journalist, no friend of England. He had influential connections in Moscow and St Petersburg. Perhaps the Maharajah would like to meet him . . .

The Maharajah was lying low, but other visitors to Paris sought him out in that autumn of 1886. His father-in-law, Ludwig Müller, turned up from Alexandria on his way to see Bamba in London and again on the way home. Müller must have marched his wayward son-in-law to the bank and made him sign a paper to the India Office giving Bamba and the children a glimmer of charity. 'Having already informed you that I have renounced my stipend,' the Maharajah wrote on 13 August, 'you are at liberty to apply any sum you think fit for the maintenance of my wife and children.'

---

* The German foreign ministry opened a file on the Maharajah on 25 October 1886 with a report sent for the attention of the Kaiser himself from the London embassy: 'Your Majesty will remember the rebellion of the sepoys . . . against the British masters. The latest of these rebellious movements is of the Indian nobleman the Mahrajah Duleep Singh the son of the ruler of the Sikhs.'

Nuggets of more sensitive information from these familial visits reached Sir Owen Burne via a letter from Arthur Oliphant: 'With regard to Pondicherry, I recollect Müller said here in October that when in Paris, the Maharajah stated he contemplated obtaining the permission of the French government to reside there – and that Müller replied by digging the Maharajah in the ribs and while looking him straight in the face said "you don't think I am such a fool as to believe you would do that." The Maharajah burst into a hearty laugh and answered, "Well it is part of my plan", or "trick" or "game". Whether Müller said the word used by the Maharajah was plan or trick or game I cannot recollect, but the impression left on my mind and the impression then on Müller's mind was the Maharajah was endeavouring to frighten the British government into acceding to his terms.'

The Maharajah insisted on meeting Bamba's father at his hotel, his own address must remain secret. Müller wrote to Oliphant in November: 'The Maharajah called on me every day and had long conversations, but I am sorry to say that I have not discovered any sign of his getting his ideas into better favour. He was callous even to the dangers I expressed to him of the heavy insurances he might be liable to were he to expose his life to any extra risk.'

The Paris correspondent of the *Advocate of India* newspaper managed to seek him out, reporting in early October: 'Duleep Singh is in Paris engaged in writing his memoirs and those of his family. He avoids English society and English bankers and lives in seclusion. His Highness is said to have made no impression on the Parisians.'

Sir Charles Dilke, the Liberal politician (who had been forced into semi-exile by a marital scandal), was staying in the Grand Hotel and observant enough to do a bit of freelance spying. He informed a Whitehall friend on 26 November: 'You may tell the India Office people from me if you like that Duleep Singh, whose address is care of Mallet Frères, the great bankers here, seems to be trying to get up a Russian party in North-West India. I dare say they know it.'

An anonymous 'Punjabi gentleman' bumped into him in the Hotel de Londres et New York in December and told the *Lahore Tribune*:

> He looked stout and strong. His manly and handsome countenance bore the impression of thoughtful anxiety. He talked with me in Punjabi, which he speaks very fluently and much

better than I. My first question was, what induced him to turn against the British Government. He replied: 'I was loyal to the backbone, I was a staunch Conservative. I never cared for India, nor for her people. I never dreamt of the Punjab throne. I was compelled to turn against the Government by the dishonest and shabby treatment I received from their hands . . . I had no political object in view in coming to India but had a mind to pass the remaining days of my life in a very quiet and secluded way in Madras.'

My second question was why he had changed his religion. He told me that he had no political object; he thoroughly studied his ancestral religion and found it far superior to the Christian religion. Besides Christians as a class were Christians only in name, but not in practice. They were the most dishonest people on the face of the earth and always ready to crush the weak and poor. The Government had no right to interfere with the religion of anybody.

While the Maharajah skulked around Paris hotels, his partisans in India were on the move. They were obviously in telegraphic contact; the Punjab police reported instructions from Paris to Thakur Singh in October that he should seek refuge from imminent arrest by going to Pondicherry.

Duleep's cousin arrived in the palmy French colonial enclave on 6 November 1886 with a sprawling retinue: three sons, their wives, children and eight servants. 'The real object of their journey was kept a profound secret,' according to the police report. 'With the exception of his two eldest sons, was known to no one else. It was only on the pretext of pilgrimage to Nander [a Sikh shrine in central India where Guru Gobind Singh died] that he managed to take his daughters-in-law and servants away from their homes and friends. Their horror can be well imagined when on arrival at Pondicherry they were informed that they would have to remain with him until Duleep Singh's arrival.'

Thakur Singh sought an interview with the French governor, M. Menist, who took down his statement and submitted it to the Foreign Office in Paris. The reaction was sympathetic – an allowance of 1,000 francs was granted (Duleep telegraphed saying 'take no money' in a typically grandiose gesture) and an offer of protection as long as they cared to stay on French territory. Someone in the French government was on Duleep's case. A young lieutenant of Chasseurs à Pied named Félix Volpert made contact with the Maharajah in Paris around this time, and promptly headed off for French India – a gentleman in whom the British Secret Service were later to take an abiding interest.

The Pondicherry sanctuary was burgled a year later by a police agent. Documents and letters sent from Paris in the autumn of 1886 were recovered and summarized in a Special Branch report, including a pathetic scrap which said: 'All my English friends have written to me and also the Queen herself to return to my allegiance, but my answer is that it is too late to do so now, be the consequences what they may.'

One document retrieved by the spy provides a tantalizing clue to the identity of the Maharajah's most pivotal encounter in Paris, with Patrick Casey's Russian confidante, the man who would spirit him east. It was addressed to the editor of an obscure newspaper published in the tiny French enclave of Chandernagore in Bengal.

'The Maharajah Duleep Singh presents his compliments to the editor of The Beaver and requests him kindly to insert the letter printed below in the above influential journal,' the flimsy scrap of paper stolen in Pondicherry read.

The spy had found the pro-forma slip printed at Schlaeber's *imprimerie* in July 1886, accompanied by the 'Brother Princes and Nobles' plea for money. The agent who stole it from Pondicherry added a gloss:

> There is also a centre of Duleep Singh's intrigues in Bengal, and the headman is Shashi Bhushan Mukerji, editor and proprietor of the extinct paper Beaver; at present residing at Kalighat, Calcutta.
>
> In September 1886 [other documentary evidence points to a date of 7 January 1887] Duleep Singh opened communications with him through a Frenchman, the Beaver's agent at Paris, and by paying £1,000 induced him to publish his letters in the Beaver and also to influence the editors of the Bengali papers to further his cause. The Frenchman used to print papers etc, for Duleep Singh.

*155*

This man Mukerji after carrying on a lengthy correspondence with Duleep Singh managed to get another £1,000 from him. With this and the money he swindled out of 'The Beaver' lottery, he has now retired from business and has invested Rs. 60,000 in Government Promissory notes.

In February 1887 the Punjab police Special Branch turned to the matter of Mr Mukerji's troublesome little newspaper. The doughty Mr McCracken wished to 'draw the attention of the government of India to an issue of a paper styled "The Beaver" dated Chandernagore, Wednesday, January 19th, 1887, containing some correspondence between Maharajah Duleep Singh and an anonymous person under the initials 'E.C.' at the address of Messrs. Mallet Frères et Cie, Paris.' The mysterious 'E.C.' and the 'Frenchman at Paris' were obviously the same person, although the detectives in India had no means of identifying him.

Monsieur 'E.C.' was no mere jobbing printer. He was one of the 'most strange and devious personalities of the time', according to the American diplomat George F. Kennan* who, in a masterly history, placed him at the conspiratorial heart of a strategic revolution in the power politics of late nineteenth-century Europe.

'E.C.' was Elie de Cyon, born in Lithuania as Ilya Fadeevich Tsion, a Jewish doctor who had sought a career in Paris in 1874 when his students at the St Petersburg Surgical-Medical Academy thought him 'too reactionary'. He was a doctor of medicine, physiologist, neurologist, journalist,† conspirator, forger (according to one account) and spy. He was also the Paris correspondent of *Moskovskie Vyedmosti (Moscow Gazette)*, the newspaper edited by Mikhail Nikoforovich Katkov, one of the most powerful men in Russia. The Maharajah had found his ticket east.

---

* George F. Kennan: b. 1904 US Ambassador to Moscow, architect of the Cold War doctrine of 'containment' of the Soviet Union. A diplomatic historian, he became fascinated by the origins of the Franco-Russian alliance forged from 1886 to 1893 and Cyon's role in it; he regarded the alliance as the wellspring of the European catastrophe of August 1914.
† Cyon's literary output was prodigious. As well as journalism he produced over forty books on politics, medicine and the life-sciences. A cardiac nerve is named after him. Among his stranger medical texts was *Spatial Perception in the Japanese Dancing Mouse* (a congenitally deaf fancy oriental breed).

# 17

# Revenge

❦

*Rue Juliette Lamber, Paris, 17me, 27 February 1887*

THERE WERE PLOTS being cooked up in Paris during the war-scare winter of 1886–87 in grander surroundings than Mr Reynold's Bar. Just off the Boulevard Malesherbes was the new house of Juliette Lamber – 'Madame Adam', as everyone called her – beauty, intellectual, patriot, revanchist, distruster of all things English and soon-to-be patron of the Maharajah Duleep Singh. She was so famous the Paris authorities named the newly built street after her.

She was the owner and publisher of the political journal *La Nouvelle Revue*, which thumped out a staunch chauvinist-republican line, with the habit of taking up wild causes in its columns, like that of Captain Achinov who was to lead a Russian expedition to Abyssinia seeking to found an Orthodox colony in the realms of the Negus. In mid-1886 she had scandalized her Parisian journalist peers by appointing a right-wing Russian crank, one Elie de Cyon, as the magazine's director.

Clever, ambitious women in late-Victorian London may have revelled in the 'salon' as a vehicle to advance a husband's career, but the widowed forty-five-year-old Juliette Lamber was at the heart of affairs. '*Tout le gouvernement*' came to her house or to weekends at the old Abbaye de Gif, her country house near Versailles. She had two consuming passions. The first was vengeance on Germany for the defeat of 1871; the second was Russia – the means to exact that revenge – with a conjoined, victorious war. Her salon was the centre of constantly shifting plots and intrigues to make the dream a reality. The *Daily Telegraph* correspondent, Campbell Clarke, was a frequent visitor. *The Times*, with its pro-German line, was excluded.

A Parisian gossip columnist described a *bal masqué* at the splendid new house with room for 500 revellers transformed for the night into a 'temple of pleasure'. The guest list was enlightening.

Madame Adam is delightful in her pink striped white silk dress and coquettish bonnet and welcomes each guest with a smile and gracious word.

The whole hôtel is *en fête*. A host of surprises are awaiting the guests. It starts at the stairs where a guard of honour is stationed and two clowns announce each guest under their assumed name. A buffet is served in the first floor apartment where there is a crowd waiting for the supper which will be served a half past two in the morning.'

[A *tableau vivant* is described, an allegory of the martyred lost provinces of Alsace-Lorraine, performed by two scantily clad young actresses.] But time passes and the crowds press in. Madame Adam's charming daughter arrives in black lace dressed as Charlotte Corday. Not too far away is a handsome Duc de Guise – it's General Tevis.

There's Monsieur Ney as the chamberlain of Napoleon I. Cardinal Richelieu enters, followed by the Empress Anne of Austria, a flamboyant Clytemnestra, the goddess Diana, the opera diva Elena Sanz in character as Carmen, a Van Dyck Spaniard, half a dozen Hamlets, Robert Vallier *à la grecque*, Benito Juarez, an abundance of Chinese and Japanese.

Finally supper arrives. The guests only leave at daybreak from the pretty hôtel. An undisputed success is Madame Robert de Bonnière, delightful in her sky-blue bodice, her beautiful blonde hair cascading down, her complexion fresh as a rose-bud, and her lithe figure arched, slim without being skinny. She has the charms of a lively primitive with all the grace of the most exquisite modernity.

Around her more guests flock admiringly – there's General de Castex, Prince Karageorgevich, Edmond Dollfus ... M. Elie de Cyon.

Tevis, Vallier, de Cyon. The society columnist provided a list of names that were about to entangle the Maharajah. Doubtless had he strode into Madame Adam's salon dressed '*à la Sicque*', the revellers would have simply assumed it to be another triumph for the Parisian costumier's art.

The very conspiratorial knot into which the Maharajah was blithely heading had little to do with the 'great game' for the Oxus and the Sutlej and everything to do with the Rhine and the Vistula. Bismarck, the German Chancellor, had seemingly congealed the European continent into an immovable armed peace with the League of the Three Emperors (Dreikaiserbund), Russia, Austria and Germany linked in a monarchical bond. The pact was sealed in secret in 1881, renewed in 1884 and was due to expire on 18 June 1887. But two powerful forces were moving to bring the old order down: the pan-Slavists in Russia and the 'revanchists' of Madame Adam's Paris salon. Elie de Cyon was the busy go-between.

Moscow was the other end of the line, stronghold of the militant wing of pan-Slavism, the beneficent-sounding 'Slavonic Benevolent Society'. It was anything but. Founded in 1867, it was a vehicle for both reactionary Russian nationalism and for a geo-political vision with very radical implications. Mikhail Nikoforovich Katkov, the editor of the *Moscow Gazette*, was an early adherent.

Another key mover was Count Pavel Nikolayevich Ignatiev, former Russian minister at Constantinople, a nationalist-imperialist with a driving vision of just how powerful a modernized Russia could be. Russia faced an historic choice: push out into the Balkans and beyond, even to subsume Constantinople itself, to unite the Slav peoples from the 'Adriatic Sea to Arkhangelsk'; or retreat into its Asiatic fastness and consolidate its new-won barbarous empire of the steppes. Pan-Slavism unleashed meant war.

The war with the Ottoman Empire had come in 1877, propelled by a Slav rising in Bosnia-Herzegovina which spread east across the Balkans to be suppressed by the Turks with great cruelty. The Russian Army seized the crossings of the Danube, conducted a four-month siege of Plevna, and by January 1878 were at the walls of Constantinople. The British urgently sent a fleet to protect the Turkish capital. War with England was very close, but the Russian Army was exhausted.

The Treaty of San Stefano which ended the war was the pan-Slavish pinnacle: Turkey conceded the independence of Montenegro, Serbia, Romania and Bulgaria. The European powers would not have it. The Congress of Berlin, convened the following year, reassembled most of the old order in the Balkans and Czar Alexander II meekly submitted, to the fury of the Moscow propagandists. A truncated semi-independent Bulgaria was proclaimed with a conveniently-produced German prince, Alexander of Battenberg, as ruler.

Germany emerged as the broker of the new balance of power in Europe. In Russia the pan-Slavists fumed, the revolutionaries hoarded explosives. A strange, dispossessed alliance of far-right and far-left was forged. The reforming Czar was assassinated by a bomb detonated by the revolutionaries of Narodnaia Volia (the 'People's Will') as he travelled in his carriage to sign a manifesto granting Russia a constitution. The pan-Slavist ultras did not mourn.

The new Czar, Alexander III – 'sluggish, unambitious, unmilitary', according to the British ambassador, Sir Robert Morier – had no inherent sympathy for Germany. Nevertheless he settled down to the dynastic certainties of the Dreikaiserbund: Habsburg, Hohenzollern and Romanov. The League was a high secret of state, but the alliance informed domestic Russian politics. After the pact was sealed, the pan-Slavists were pushed down. General Skobolev, the hero of Plevna, made a rabble-rousing speech in Paris (on Madame Juliette Adam's invitation) and was dismissed in disgrace. He died in mysterious circumstances soon afterwards. The ambitious Count Ignatiev, now minister of the interior, brought about his own temporary eclipse by suddenly proposing a kind of constitutional monarchy. The Czar, he suggested, should be crowned in the new Cathedral of Christ the Saviour in the old capital, Moscow, on Easter Day 1883. It would be a 'unique Russian kind of constitution which would silence our pseudo-liberals and nihilists', Ignatiev declared.

Constantin Petrovich Pobedonostsev, the powerful Ober-Prokuror of the Russian Orthodox Holy Synod (a political position established by Peter the Great), the Czar's childhood tutor and most trusted adviser, warned his former pupil: 'If decision-making is transferred from the government to any kind of popular assembly, that will be a revolution, the downfall of the government and the downfall of Russia.' Katkov called the proposal 'a triumph of subversion'. Ignatiev was sacked and replaced by the arch-conservative Count Dmitri Petrovich Tolstoi.

The status quo at St Petersburg was sealed when the German-leaning Nicholas de Giers took up the seals of office at Singer's Bridge, the foreign ministry on the banks of the Moika, the Neva's tributary.

The 'German party' had won. Nothing, it seemed, was going to change. But two fractious little conflicts a thousand miles apart were to prise open the cracks. One was in the mountains of Central Asia, the other in the primitive appendix of Christian Europe, Bulgaria.

The Russian Empire had been expanding southwards into the Caucasus for five decades. Unlike the colonial collisions embroiling the other European powers, the Russians were punching into air – until they occupied Merv in 1884. On 30 March the following year, General Alikhanov, a Mohammedan, wiped out an Afghan force at Pendjeh, an obscure oasis on the line of march towards Herat. The Russian Empire had bumped up against the ramparts of British India.

In the spring of 1885 it looked to London as if the dread crisis in Central Asia had arrived. Gladstone's government had just been deeply humiliated by the death of General Gordon at Khartoum. The Pendjeh crisis gave it a last chance to restore its crumbling prestige. The expeditionary force designed to rescue Gordon was withdrawn from the Sudan and mobilized for India.

Where could the British strike a decisive blow? The admirals suggested a raid on Vladivostok in the far east, mounted from a fleet base in Korea.

Russian cruisers nosed into the North Atlantic. But an Anglo-Russian war could not be fought at the fringes. It would have to be an expedition to the Black Sea again, to confront the main body of the enemy, reviving the horrors of the Crimea, but this time without allies. A battle of containment must be fought meanwhile in the mountains of the north-west frontier of India. It was for this disastrous-sounding venture that Duleep Singh had volunteered his services and roused the suspicions of the Duke of Cambridge after the dinner at Euston Hall.

A telegram of early August 1885 from the Secretary of State for India to the Viceroy speaks of the deeper strategic agenda: 'Private and most secret. Lord Salisbury communicated with Bismarck as to whether he would arbitrate the Afghan frontier question. He sent friendly reply but declines on grounds he would be thought to be putting pressure on Russia. He adds his belief that Russia will not arbitrate but wishes to protract negotiations and desires a distraction to her army on account of Nihilism in it.'

The crisis was not really over Pendjeh at all. It was all about what modern strategists would call 'leverage'. Even shadow-boxing for fly-blown Afghan villages, Russia now had a foot in the door of British power. Should London get difficult over the Balkans, by sending another fleet to prop up Constantinople, the Russian Army could kick in the door to India. The Punjab was the key.

In London there was an explosion of Russian-peril pamphleteering with titles like the 'The Russians at the Gates of Herat' and the 'Coming Struggle for India'. Eager officers of the Indian Army were in ecstasies of excitement at the prospect of war in the Hindu Kush. In London the mood was different. The recently formed intelligence branch of the War Office, with the pragmatists of the India Council as political allies, preferred 'masterly inactivity', to a 'forward policy'. This split, akin to that over anti-Fenian operations, explains White-hall's at first diffident reaction to the Duleep Singh affair. Was it just another 'Russian scare'? Which agency could best deal with it?

From Indian Army intelligence in Simla, meanwhile, flowed a stream of excitable reports on Russian intentions derived from agents slipping through Turcoman bazaars with tousle-haired enthusiasm. The game would go on like this for years.

One of the players was not a pink-checked adventurer. He was a British agent, a Mohammeden – a former Calcutta railway ticket-inspector, it would turn out – who styled himself 'Mr Lambert's Man'. On 11 May 1885 he reported from Bokhara, deep in Russian Turkes-tan, to General Sir Peter Lumsden at his forward headquarters on the Russo-Afghan border. It read:

> Care of British signaller at Meshed. I send you this intelligence to you at risk of my life with a view that it may be of some use to the Government whose servant I am. After perusal please send it to Mr J. Lambert C.I.E. in India, and to *no one else* otherwise my life is over.'
>
> ... Six hundred Akhal Tekes have been enlisted by the Russians, they are armed with Berdan rifles. Twelve Teke boys are being trained as trumpeters ... there are two nine-pounder B.L.R. steel guns, 300 cossacks and a battalion of infantry at Merv ... Camels are so exhausted they are unable to work ... England's name is heard with great respect in every tent and

they say in the case of Russia waging war with England or Afghanistan, they will rise up in her rear ... the people of Bokhara and Samarkand are against Russia, but they can do nothing ... God helping, I will try to communicate with you again. I have &c Mr Lambert's Man.

The Bokhara report, breathing imminent personal danger, was fascinating enough, but this was just the start of Mr Lambert's Man's undercover career. I would come to know him as agent 'L.M.'. He would travel from Bokhara, to the Punjab, to Pondicherry, to Cairo, to Constantinople, to a house in Clapham Park, south London, on the trail of Duleep's partisans.

It was Turkey which extracted the Gladstone government from the crisis of 1885. The Sultan's ministers conveniently refused to allow the Royal Navy to pass the Dardanelles. The Russians lost interest in being able to threaten the British from Afghanistan. They agreed to arbitration; broad agreement on a Russo-Afghan frontier line was reached on 10 September 1885. Negotiations would grind on in St Petersburg for two years. Meanwhile the building of the strategic trans-Caspian railway continued, its spurs reaching ever further into Russian central Asia. If war came, it would be when the railway was complete.

There were new troubles in the Balkans. In September 1885 the province of Eastern Roumelia, kept under Turkish rule by the Congress of Berlin, rose in revolt. Prince Alexander of Battenberg, his sentiments now very anti-Russian, behaved as an absolute dictator. He spurned the nationalist politicians who were backed by the Russian military, appealing to the hated Turks for help when a border spat with Serbia turned into a vicious little Balkan war.

A personal union of Bulgaria and Roumelia was declared under Prince Alexander with the Turkish Sultan as suzerain. The Russians were furious, the prince was kidnapped from his palace by his own officers (aided by pan-Slavist secret agents, according to Lord Salisbury). He escaped, returned in triumph and just as suddenly abdicated. The Russian General Kaulbars arrived in the capital, Sofia, in November 1886 to restore order, backed by a landing of imperial marines. In a fit of metaphor-mangling the British ambassador at St Petersburg privately cabled Lord Salisbury: 'We cannot have the Russian mammoth rampaging around the aquarium of Europe.'*

In December another German princeling, Ferdinand of Saxe-Coburg-Gotha, was elected by the council of regency as Bulgarian ruler over St Petersburg's candidate, an obscure Caucasian prince. The imperial kommissar departed Sofia in a sulk. The Germans were blamed for rubbing Russia's nose in another Balkan humiliation as England smirked from the sidelines.

A British document about the crisis was kept secret for over a hundred years. It was the statement of a Russian spy in Whitehall's (reluctant) pay, released by the Secret Intelligence Service (SIS) only in 1993. It links the Balkans, central Asia and the Suez Canal in a strategic continuum, just as the conspirators around the Maharajah sought to.

STATEMENT OF PIERRE GEORGEVICH
MADE NOVEMBER 11TH 1886 REGARDING RUSSIAN
DESIGNS IN BALKAN PENINSULA AND PLANS IN EVENT
OF WAR WITH ENGLAND.

About four months ago while in the Russian embassy at Constantinople (in which I was employed as military agent) I was made fully acquainted with the plans of Russia.

Her scheme is not to annexe Bulgaria, but to avail herself of the disorders there, then to occupy the country with about 150,000 troops and to concentrate at Varna and Bourgas a large quantity of munitions of war with the object of distributing them among the Slavs in the Balkan peninsula for the purpose of effecting a general rising.

A large Russian stationnaire [a blockship disguised as a merchantman] is intended to be sent to Constantinople laden with mines and torpedoes in order to close the passage to ships.

It is calculated that it would take as long for the British fleet

---

* Queen Victoria deeply distrusted Morier, accusing him of supporting the Russians in Bulgaria against her beloved 'Sandro' (Prince Alexander of Battenberg) – and wanted him sacked. Lord Salisbury told her impassively in September 1886 that 'we have nothing against him except secret reports, which passing through Prince Bismarck, may have been distorted'. German intelligence was spying on HM Ambassador to Russia and reporting to London.

to get through the Dardanelles to the Black Sea as for the Russian fleet to get from Varna, or Bourgas, or Trebizond, or Sebastopol to the Bosphorus.

This plan is quite material and ready for execution. I don't know whether the stationnaire has arrived, but I think so. I was employed in working out the plans which I have detailed both at St Petersburg and at Constantinople.

If war should break out between England and Russia, the plan would be put at once into execution, and the Bulgarian army would march on Constantinople, backed by the Russian troops of occupation, which would be at first massed on the frontier of Servia in order to confront Austria if she should move.

Greece would attack at the same time. The Turkish troops are concentrated in old Servia and Macedonia. A rising would take place simultaneously in Bosnia and Herzogovina. They are all Slavs.

Central Asia: General Doudourkov Koursakov [Corps commander at Pendjeh; later to be an enthusiastic backer of the Maharajah in Russia] was summoned three months ago to St Petersburg from Tiflis and received secret instructions with the object of bringing about a rupture between Persia and Afghanistan, with a view to Russia joining Persia against the Afghans. A large number of Kurds have taken service in the Persian cavalry and are paid by Russia 5 roubles a month, Persian soldiers get no pay.

Suez Canal: Hirovo, the late Russian Agent at Cairo, has bribed some of the pilots of the Suez Canal and has obtained valuable information with regard to the facilities for destroying the Canal, or stopping the navigation.

Pierre Georgevich, it turned out, was a Paris-based Montenegrin with an agenda of his own. He wanted £200 for his report which Major-General Henry Brackenbury, director of military intelligence judged to be 'absurd, the gossip of the Turkish capital'. When Georgevich wrote again at the end of 1886 with news that '60,000 Russians were heading for the Afghan frontier', Sir Julian Pauncefote, the Foreign Office spymaster, told him 'the information you gave is of no value at all'. He was offered £50 to go away.

The Prisoner of Zenda antics in the Balkans none the less had major consequences. The League of the Three Emperors was irreparably shaken, Russia would have to go to war with Austria to get its way and – as the Georgevich report, however doubtful, indicated – was preparing to do so with 'England' as well. In November 1886, as the Maharajah sat on his Patrick Casey-printed parcels of seditious proclamations in Paris, the plan was 'ready for execution'.

What interest did the revanchist intriguers in Paris have in an Anglo-Russian fight? They had a great deal to gain. Anything that would shake Bismarck's league of peace was to be embraced; the British Empire was its uncovenanted underwriter. Anything that could winkle the pro-German peace-party out of the St Petersburg foreign ministry was to be connived at; a war in Central Asia would do just that. A colossal opportunity beckoned.

That opportunity was already being whispered of as 'L'Alliance Franco-Russe', a military compact between France and Russia. A curious little publication with that title appeared in Paris in January 1887. Its author was anonymous; he was a 'Russian General Officer' who argued the benefits of such a strategic revolution. France could challenge Germany – Russia could do the same. But like the 'Black Pamphlet', it was not quite what it seemed. It was scathing in its attacks on figures at the Russian court – when a copy reached St Petersburg there was uproar and a hunt ordered for its author, a search that would soon embroil the Maharajah.

The pamphlet and its mysterious originator were a fevered topic in the rue Juliette Lamber. An alliance between obscurantist autocracy and the republican, atheist heirs of 1789 seemed impossible. To ambitious generals in Paris and St Petersburg it made military sense. How to keep England with its hateful navy from joining Germany's side? The Irish-Americans were promising to dynamite Atlantic shipping. There was a strange Maharajah wandering around Paris plotting some sort of rising in India. Elie de Cyon had good reports of him. Juliette Adam took up the runaway King of Lahore as her latest exotic cause.

# 18

# The Editor

❦

## Moscow Gazette *offices, Strastnyi Boulevard, Moscow, Winter 1886–87*

THE RUSSIAN JOURNALIST into whose hands the Maharajah's fate was now falling could usually be found, after a day of energetic editing, in the family apartment adjoining the Moscow newspaper office. Each night he would preside over an enormous dinner table. Within a few months Duleep Singh would be sitting at it.

Sixty-eight years old, portly, grey-whiskered and patriarchal, Mikhail Nikoforovich Katkov would treat Madame Sophie Petrovna Katkova, his eleven children and a troop of adulatory hangers-on to tub-thumping discourses on what was wrong with Russia (a great deal) and what was wrong with the world beyond its enormous borders (a great deal more). The loyal buyers of the *Moscow Gazette* would read all about it the next day.

The post-Soviet view of Russian history makes the figure of an imperial press baron problematic. But, from the 1870s onwards, Mikhail Katkov was there with the other great international press figures of the age – Hearst, Pulitzer, Gordon Bennett, Northcliffe – exploiting the new power of popular print, their newspapers informed by telegraphy, distributed by railway and consumed by the newly-literate of the cities.* The irony was that in imperial Russia getting to the heart and mind of the Czar was what mattered. Alexander III listened to the editor, not the readers, of the *Moscow Gazette*.

---

* Katkov remained editor-publisher of the magazine *Russian Messenger* and published, in instalments, Dostoevskii's *Crime and Punishment, The Brothers Karamazov* and Leo Tolstoi's *Anna Karenina* (which he censored in parts for not being sufficiently pro-Serb). He was not the *Gazette's* proprietor, but leased the title from Moscow University.

As Russian civil society congealed in a sour repression of enemies within, especially the Jews, Katkov devoted his energies to lashing enemies without. When Russia's humiliations in the Balkans mounted, England and its rulers entered the same demonology as Bismarck. Paris, Katkov had decided, was the portal to Russia's destiny, and his agent there, Elie de Cyon, was its keeper. Aged forty-five, slim and dandyish in imperial beard and pince-nez, the doctor looked more like a Romantic composer than a conspirator.

Cyon related in his memoirs how he received a signal from Katkov in April 1886 that the time had come for a propaganda campaign for a Franco-Russian alliance. The *Moscow Gazette* ran a series of articles praising the French Army and editorials urging that Russia had no need to take heed of Germany in Balkan policy. The thesis was that Russia had been tricked by Bismarck into the war of 1877 and then hauled before the Congress of Berlin like a criminal. Then the loathsome Battenberg had mounted a Bulgarian *putsch* on German instigation, but Russia, through misplaced loyalty to 'the concert of powers', had done nothing and became the laughing-stock of Europe.

On 30 July 1886 an astonishing editorial appeared in the Moscow Gazette over the signature 'K' (Cyon in fact wrote a big chunk of it) urging the abandonment of the Dreikaiserbund.* It was a secret treaty but Katkov evidently knew a great deal about it. 'Without Bismarck's agreement one is given to understand one may neither lie down nor stand up; he runs the whole world,' 'K' fumed.

It was at this point that Madame Adam appointed Cyon editor of the *Nouvelle Revue*, in his words to 'possess in Paris a publicity organ with which to support in France the campaign being waged in Russia by the *Moskovskie Vyedmosti*'. Rival Parisian editors were thunderstruck. *Le Siècle* commented: 'The *diffamateur* Cyon was too reactionary even for a minister of the Czar – just the man to direct one of the great republican magazines of France.'

The conservative doctor now had a radical and very hidden agenda. He was that strange thing in history, a journalist who becomes the story. He relayed some of it in his own memoirs published in 1895.

---

* Soon after the editorial's appearance, a German foreign office official suggested buying off Katkov with a secret bribe of 50,000 Roubles a year. Bismarck turned down the plan, but the incident shows the awakening imperial German intelligence interest in Katkov and his intrigues. Berlin also began to take a close interest in Elie de Cyon.

They are full of half-truths and obfuscation but give fascinating clues as to the depths of the conspiracy in which the Maharajah became engulfed.

First, there is an account of how the doctor and the Maharajah met: 'In 1885, at a time when events in Central Asia had put great strain on Anglo-Russian relations [the Pendjeh crisis] many Irish fugitives had made themselves known to me, as a close associate of Katkov's,' Cyon wrote. 'They were offering Russia the services of Irish nationalists, particularly of the group established in America. I have no need here to specify the nature of their proposals which I relayed purely and simply to Katkov.' So it was the revolutionary drinking firm of Patrick Casey and Eugene Davis who made the first overture, with a line apparently open to the dynamite hard-men of New York.

'On 8th March 1887, one of these émigrés, who had a very important position in the group, asked permission to introduce the Maharajah Duleep Singh to me, whose moving life history he had recounted,' de Cyon continued. He was very specific about the date. He was lying. The Punjabi Special Branch had picked up correspondence with an 'E.C.' of Paris in February that year. There were other indications that the doctor and the Sikh were in contact months before that.

It is clear that Elie de Cyon met Duleep in Paris in the late autumn of 1886 with the Irish as the intermediaries. Cyon was dissembling to distance himself from an individual who had journeyed from Russia to meet Duleep in the depths of that Parisian winter. Even when he wrote his impassioned memoirs in 1894, the true facts were still too dangerous to reveal.

The tensions in the great war-scare winter of 1886–87 were being ramped up as much by Berlin as by General Boulanger. Bismarck had his own agenda – to get a seven-year military spending bill (the Septennat) through the Reichstag. A stream of 'imminent French attack' alarms was conjured up in intelligence reports from Paris, aided seamlessly by General Boulanger's revanchist posturings. The realists in the French military were alarmed. A gaping hole was becoming apparent in the war minister's revised mobilization timetable.

Cyon had high-level connections with such men. An old confidante was General Saussier, military governor of Paris and vice-president of the *Conseil de Guerre*, a tough old soldier who had been pushed aside from the top job by Boulanger.

In October 1886 Cyon made an urgent journey to St Petersburg, summoned by Katkov. The rumour was that Russia was about to normalize relations at ambassador level after the Kropotkin affair and a new French envoy was to be admitted to the Russian capital. It was vital to the intriguers that this individual should be a partisan of 'L'Alliance Franco-Russe', even a clandestine one. A soldier would be better than a diplomat, able to broker contacts with the Russian Army. Cyon, it was intended, would fix it with an open line to Paris.

From 21 to 24 October 1886, Cyon sent a string of telegrams to Madame Adam from St Petersburg as the appointment was being decided. This time the plotters tripped up; the man chosen was Antoine Laboulaye, a career diplomat. The circumstantial evidence around this episode is that Elie de Cyon had a deeper purpose. He was working for the General Saussier section of the French general staff which was desperate to bring the Boulangist tightrope-walk down to earth but equally anxious to make the most urgent contacts with the Russian military. Cyon was their emissary.

The French military realists knew that if war came now it would be a disaster. If the Germans attacked, a cobbled-up Russian threat in the rear would be the only chance of salvation. Standing like a boulder in the path at the Singer's Bridge was the foreign minister, Nicholas de Giers. On 3 December 1886 the Freycinet government fell (for domestic reasons). The new French Prime Minister was René Goblet; the new foreign minister was Emile-Leopold Flourens, a provincial lawyer and volatile diplomatic amateur.

On 12 December, Lord Iddesleigh,* the British foreign minister, dropped dead in the ante-room at no. 10 Downing Street. Lord Salisbury assumed his office as well as that of Prime Minister, in the words of a Conservative historian, to 'conduct foreign affairs by personal correspondence from his vast and venerable mansion at Hatfield, almost as if they the private business of his own estate'.

At this most dangerous time, with Europe on a hair-trigger for war, a wild, parallel, freelance diplomacy was in play with Elie de Cyon as its conduit.

---

* Sir Stafford Northcote, a former Secretary of State for India.

Maharajah Ranjit Singh (1780–1839) and his ministers. With Lahore as his capital the 'Lion of the Punjab' built an independent state of conspicuous wealth and power. Squabbles for succession would tear it apart.

'The Court of Lahore', the epic painting by the Hungarian itinerant artist August Schoefft (1809–88). Completed in St Petersburg around 1852 after his return from the Punjab, it depicted the kingdom of the Maharajah Ranjit Singh at its glittering zenith fifteen years earlier. The painting once hung on the grand stairway at Elveden Hall; today it is in the Lahore Fort Museum, Pakistan.

'Maharajah Ranjt Singh listening to the Granth being read near the Golden Temple, Amritsar', another reconstruction of the lost kingdom of Lahore painted by August Schoefft in Vienna around 1850. The boy playing with a hawk in the foreground is presumed by many to be the infant Duleep Singh, but the artist has changed his age or depicted a different child aged around three.

'Rani Jindan seated on a cushion'. Sketch in oils attributed to August Schoefft made in Lahore, 1841.

Maharajah Duleep Singh as a ten-year-old: an elusive but remarkable image from the dawn of photography – a calotype made in Lahore by the East India Company surgeon John McCosh on the eve of the Anglo-Sikh War (1848–49).

Maharajah Duleep Singh, the 'beautiful and charming boy' as Queen Victoria called him – photographed by Dr Ernst Becker on the lower terrace of Osborne House, Isle of Wight, 1854.

Maharajah Duleep Singh in his wedding clothes, 1864.

RIGHT The iconic painting of the Maharajah Duleep Singh made by the court portraitist Franz Xaver Winterhalter at Queen Victoria's instigation. The sittings took place at Buckingham Palace in the autumn of 1854; the background was the painter's invention.

Maharani Bamba soon after her wedding. She married Duleep Singh in Egypt in June 1864 and was brought to England speaking only Arabic. Queen Victoria warmly welcomed her at Windsor.

Ludwig Müller, German-born banker of Alexandria. He stayed in touch with his rebellious son-in-law throughout, visiting the runaway Maharajah in Paris several times to broker a settlement for his abandoned daughter – relaying information meanwhile to Whitehall.

Mulgrave Castle near Whitby in Yorkshire, leased to the Maharajah by its owner Lord Normanby, was an introduction to the life of an English landed gentleman. The Maharajah took his mother there in 1863.

Tennis party at Elveden, *c.* 1878.

Elveden Hall near Thetford, as completely rebuilt by the Maharajah in 1874. A solitary turbanned figure stands outside. In 1894 the house was sold by the British Government to Lord Iveagh, who added a domed central block and repeated the 'Duleep Singh wing' alongside to the east.

OPPOSITE Elveden's 'eastern' interior as created by the English architect John Norton in mock-Agra style. In 1998 the Hall doubled as a Manhattan mansion for the orgy scene in Stanley Kubrick's last film *Eyes Wide Shut*.

Prince Victor aged around ten, with unshorn hair and cradling a fowling piece. His father introduced him to shooting at a tender age, writing to him at Eton: 'Cheer up, old chap. I am looking forward to your coming home for the holidays and our going out together to shoot the "long tails".'

Pony girls – Princesses Bamba and Catherine at Elveden, *c.* 1878.

Royal hunting party at Elveden, 8 December 1876; the Prince of Wales is seated centre, the Maharajah (in Tyrolean hat) on the ground flanked by his two sons.

Elveden gamekeepers, *c.* 1883, at the time the Maharajah maintained one of the finest shooting estates in Europe.

## *India Office, St James's Park, London, September 1886*

London had been untroubled by the Maharajah for months, Thakur Singh Sandhanwalia was bottled up in Pondicherry. The fix had gone in at Singer's Bridge against the 'intended tourist'. The Punjab police were on the alert, picking up nothing more than down-country rumours. There had been a flurry of Foreign Office intelligence about Fenians in Russia, but otherwise all was quiet. The most sinister news from the Punjab was the report of a proclamation found in September 1886 at the police barracks at Multan – scene of the last revolt which triggered the fall of the Sikh kingdom. Printed in Punjabi, it was crude and boastful, but in the context of the diplomatic drama unfolding in Paris its contents were highly significant.

### SPY OF THE RUSSIAN MONARCH

I, a spy of the Russian monarch, left Russian territory three months ago, having been appointed on a salary of Rs. 140 per mensem, and have come to the Punjab for the purpose of viewing the administration of the army and giving notice.

Another spy arrived today in my stead and has brought this information that Italy and Turkey have allied themselves with the Russian monarch. The Khedive of Egypt has given notice that he will rule the country by himself. The ill-fortune of the Government is known to everyone.

Maharajah Duleep Singh has for some time past been with the Russian monarch, and has now been placed in command of 75,000 troops at Paina. In Burma thousands of Government servants have been killed in battle.

The Mahdi too has established himself in the Soudan. No Government ships can pass through that country. In Bokhara lakhs of mounds of food for soldiers and animals have been collected. Englishmen in high positions are sending their families home.

The Russian monarch, having the welfare of the inhabitants of the Punjab and Hindustan at heart, warns them to recover at once all monies they may have in the hands of Government, or else they will regret it. The Amir of Kabul too has allied himself with the Russian monarch.

A message has been sent to the Mahdi to come to the Punjab at once, as the Mohammedans are yearning for him. Whoever has a wish to enter Russian employ can get it at Bokhara according to his abilities. The Russian language is more prized than the English. It is now spoken in Bokhara.

[signed] Spy of the Russian monarch.


## Hotel de Londres et New York, rue St Honoré, Paris, December–January 1887

The Maharajah, of course, could get nowhere near the Russian monarch. Without a fully visa-ed passport, no one could cross the border. Duleep could do little more than cruise the hotels around the rue St Honoré, but something was buoying him up. As Parisians prepared to celebrate either Christmas or the imminent return of the Prussians, the Maharajah was bursting into propagandizing life. Mr Robert Watson, an old retainer from Mulgrave Castle days, got a message through to his 'dear old master' via Mallets Bank saying that the sympathetic MP Robert Hanbury was going to raise his case in parliament. Duleep's reply showed a cynical new grasp of European *Realpolitik*. No such debate would be allowed, he said, because:

> My tale would reveal to the British public that Russia is not the only unjust, unscrupulous, and immoral nation in the world. England appears at this moment to be much interested about the liberties of Bulgaria, because Russia is meddling with their freedom, yet Great Britain herself hesitated not to depose me, her ward, from the throne.
>
> No. Watson I have done with the British Government for ever and by the help of the God of my fathers, I will for once at least overthrow the tyrannical, immoral and unscrupulous administration of India.
>
> Let Russia give me only 10,000 men to appear with on the north-west frontier of India, and the thing is done. For there are some 45,000 of the Punjabis, my former subjects, in the

British army at this moment, who would come over to me at once, and when other British troops would be sent to oppose me then the whole of the Punjab would rise in their rear. Also all native princes would make common cause with me, for they have suffered injustice like myself from our present rulers.

I enclose copies of two proclamations which will shortly be issued. Hitherto no proclamation has been issued either by my knowledge or sanction in the Punjab. Good bye Watson! May God bless you.

There they were again, the two propaganda sheets waiting for the coming day of glory.

Mr Watson wrote two letters from his suburban fastness at 'Loftus', Altburn-by-the-Sea, south Yorkshire. The first was to his 'dear old master' begging him 'to hesitate before precipitating such a catastrophe'; the second was to Queen Victoria copying the Maharajah's letter and its contents.

'My first duty as a loyal subject is to Your Majesty, and secondly to do my utmost to try and avert the utter ruin of one to whom I am deeply attached,' he wrote. 'With this object I enclose the copy of a letter I have just received from the prince, bearing date December 7th, and I beg most humbly to implore Your Majesty to bring pressure to bear on Your Ministers to at once do justice and avert a calamity.'

The unfortunate Mr Watson's cosy Yorkshire home had become the post-box for ever-more bizarre communications from Paris for the Queen's attention. On 30 December 1886 he passed the latest on to Balmoral, received by him two days earlier. 'My Dear Watson, I will not return to my allegiance on any other conditions than the payment of three million sterling to me by the British Government, let them make what other proposals they please,' the Maharajah proclaimed, adding an ambitious new request. He would abandon his rebellion if his Punjab estates were restored, and if he was both raised to the peerage and given a seat on the Council of India both in London and Calcutta in order to 'Assure justice in India. No-one (though I say it of myself) knows so well as I do both the English and the Indians by the peculiar circumstances of my life.'

There was an interesting postscript: 'I am assured of pecuniary aid up to one million pounds sterling and therefore, I am not likely to accept any proposal that the British Government are likely to make. As I only at present require £10,000, this sum will be placed in my hands within six weeks by which time the political events in Europe will have developed themselves more decidedly.'

He got the money (or the promise of it) from somewhere, and quickly. On 1 January 1887, Mr Watson told Sir Henry Ponsonby: 'I beg to say that I had a short note from Prince Duleep Singh by the last evening's post, wherein he informs me that he is not in want of money and that God has raised him other true friends, meaning I suppose that he is now in possession of £10,000. PPS: I also hold a third intended proclamation.'

The letters were copied to Lord Cross, the Secretary of State for India. 'Who is Watson?' he gruffly minuted on the file. An official scribbled dryly: 'This shows how these things are worked.'

Sir Owen Tudor Burne was a lot tougher. He told the Queen's private secretary on 3 January: 'If Duleep Singh goes to Central Asia he will do so to die.'*

The idea of blackmail threats to the Empress of India passing through a Yorkshire seaside villa was as implausible as the doctor-journalist Elie de Cyon, expert on Japanese dancing mice, heading for St Petersburg with the French mobilization plan in his pocket. Both were true.

Things were also beginning to move fast for the Maharajah. Somebody had arrived to pledge £10,000 to stoke the war-chest at Mallet Frères between 28 and 30 December. The 'third proclamation' referred to in Mr Watson's postscript was also significant. Dated 7 January 1887 on the original, it aired the old rants, but with a certain new political sophistication.

---

* Sir Owen added to this letter of 3 January 1887: 'He is mad enough to do anything and I feel sure his brain is affected. He has now sent home a settlement bid to his lawyers settling, I am told, the bulk of what private property he has at his disposal on an illegitimate child and giving the Maharani and his children some lesser shares.' In 1907 a 'Ranjit Singh' of Portland, California, wrote to the British Consul in San Francisco insisting he was the legitimate son of the Maharajah and Queen Bamba – 'born in England after my brother and three sisters', and brought to America by a mysterious 'Mrs Beveridge' in 1893. The India Office ignored the claim. In June 2000 a retired Scottish-born surgeon, Dr W. D. Forbes of Vancouver, claimed that he was the Maharajah's great-grandson via a liaison with a Scottish chambermaid in 1871. No evidence was offered.

PROCLAMATION No 3

Courage! Courage! Courage!

We your own flesh and blood, tell you, lift up your bowed down heads and drooping hearts for your redemption draweth near and by the help of the Almighty, Aryavarta shall once more be free and the rising 'Young India' shall enjoy both liberty and self-government.

Yes, beloved countrymen, an avenger of our common great wrongs is indeed about to appear, and the just God of the Universe will shortly cause your wicked rulers to be crushed under his feet. But you must have a little more patience yet, so as to allow us to work out your salvation most effectually.

Therefore, believe our word when we tell you that you sit on your thrones only until a convenient opportunity presents itself to your so called just rulers for your deposition. For look at what has lately taken place in Burma. In spite of the declarations of the Queen's proclamation of 1858 to the contrary, does it appear to you that the days of annexation have come to end as yet?

Therefore, friends, if you have not yet entirely degenerated into cowards and become effeminates, nor turned into mere puppets in the hands of your deadly enemies, then rise up and make common cause with us and share with us also in the glory of liberating our Mother Country. But although we thus invite you to take part in this grand and glorious both work and duty, do not for a moment suppose that we shall seek any aid from you, for God has otherwise made us strong who were once so feeble.

Sri Khalsa ji, you by your far renowned great valour saved the British Empire in India in 1857 and you did well then to act, so for we ourselves at that time were most loyal to England. Besides owing to our absence from India at that period, you had no leader appointed by Sri Sat Guru Ji of your own nation to instruct you as to the part that you should have taken in the warfare that was then going on, but now in the coming struggle we your Lawful Sovereign, commanding you to prepare for our advent into the Punjab.

We command also such as of our loyal subjects as may then be serving in the British army, and who may be left behind, to attack the British forces sent against us in their rear and those who may be in the troops opposing us to come over to our side. But let our enemies and disloyal subjects beware for we intend to annihilate them utterly.

Sri Khalsa ji, we exhort you to study the Sakheean and learn therein your glorious destiny as predicted by Dusswan Padshah Sri Guru Gobind Singh Ji.

Wah! Guroo ji di Fateh. Duleep Singh Sovereign of the Sikh nation. (7 February, 1887)

The proclamation was designed, as a note on the handwritten draft reveals, 'to be issued after our arrival' (the original is in the India Office Records in London). By the first week of January 1887 the Maharajah was moving on to a war-footing, and advancing with the confidence of a sleepwalker. Just where he was heading was being decided by events far away in ice-bound St Petersburg.

# 19

# Winter

❦

## Moscow, January 1887

RUSSIA'S TWO great cities of the north were gripped by ice and the midwinter daylight lasted for only four hours. Mikhail Katkov was completing his polemical masterpiece beneath faltering gaslight, pouring his journalistic energies into an editorial 'leader' (Russian newspapermen used the English expression) destined to have a readership of one, the Czar himself.

It was 10 January 1887 (new style). The Orthodox Christmas had just been celebrated. The solemnities of Epiphany and New Year were about to be intoned with incense and the chanting of monks. (The Russian calendar was twelve days behind that of the West.)

Katkov was consumed with rage. On 15 December, under pressure from Berlin, de Giers had published a communiqué on imperial foreign relations full of praise for Germany and criticism for 'certain [Russian] press organs'. Soon afterwards Bismarck had sent the Czar a personal resumé on why the eagle-crowned empires were entwined by history and dynastic principle. The Czar's reaction was 'short and ill-humoured' but, according to de Giers, 'he thought it stupid to suppose that by flirting with France, we should make Germany disposed to make concessions to us – as Katkov and his friends argued'.

The Russian journalist toiled late into the night on a monster memorandum. Its contents were revealed nearly a half-century later by the Soviet regime. It was to have a profound effect on the Czar and inform the mood in the St Petersburg court for three months and more. It opened a *Polniya* in the political ice through which the Maharajah would slip to get to the East.

The contents were highly personalized; K judged the Czar's

ministers against his own views of patriotic correctness. General Peter Semiovich Vannovski, the war minister, was 'a true servant of the Czar' and 'Russian in feeling', K said, but he was suspicious of certain higher officers. General Nikolai Nikolaeivich Obruchev, the army chief of staff who had an aristocratic French wife with a château in the Dordogne, seemed sound enough. But Nicholas de Giers at the foreign ministry was the obstacle.

Germany was Russia's bane, Bismarck was the puppet-master and de Giers was his creature – this was the document's thrust. The imperial Foreign Office had blocked conspiratorial action against the Bulgarian regency on German orders, the memorandum stated. Katkov could not believe that the Czar had willingly agreed in 1884 to the renewal of the Dreikaiserbund, a treaty agreed before he assumed the throne. The diplomats must have pushed him into its renewal 'to please our friends'. In his exhaustive analysis Katkov showed an intimate knowledge of the very-secret exchanges in train at the Russian embassy in Berlin, where discussions had turned, should the Dreikaiserbund die unrenewed in six months time, to the prospects of a separate bilateral neutrality pact.

The Czar received the memorandum at Gatchina, the imperial country estate, by special messenger on 11 January. He pored over it for two days. The first effects were felt at a New Year's reception for the St Petersburg diplomatic corps. Representatives from the hated Bulgarian regency had been touring European capitals and had found some mild encouragement in London. They had been frostily received in Paris. Sir Robert Morier stood sheepishly in the presentation line at the Winter Palace. The white-gloved imperial hand passed by. The Frenchman Antoine Laboulaye was bathed in a glowing encomium.

Unaware of the Katkov memorandum, de Giers seemed relaxed and confident after the New Year festivities. On the afternoon of 17 January the telephone rang at Singer's Bridge.* He lifted the brass and ebonite earpiece to hear the reedy voice of an imperial aide-de-camp demanding urgent attendance for an audience at the Winter Palace.

The foreign minister emerged an hour later 'crushed and depressed'. His loyal private secretary, Count Lamsdorf, confided to his diary:

---

* The Czar was a keen advocate of the telephone as an instrument of state control. By 1885 the royal palaces in St Petersburg were linked on the Bell system to 'all the major government departments, barracks and prisons'.

'The intrigues of Katkov or other nefarious influences have knocked our ruler off course.' The Czar was done with the German and Austrian alliance; the secret new bilateral pact was a mistake; the negotiations in Berlin must be suspended. He was even threatening an all-out invasion of Bulgaria should the treacherous Prince Battenberg return. The Katkov press foamed with war frenzy. De Giers must go. The cataclysm was a whisker away.

London, meanwhile, had fears closer to home. Lord Lyons sent Lord Salisbury a dispatch on 25 January drafted by the military attaché in Paris. It said: 'It has more than once been dreaded that General Boulanger would attempt some kind of coup d'etat and proclaim himself military dictator . . . but General Saussier, a hard-swearing *sabreur* of the old school is still Governor of Paris, and has taken pretty good precautions against being caught asleep by a handful of men.'

Emile-Leopold Flourens, the French foreign minister, meanwhile was close to panic: 'The most precious interests of France are at stake,' Flourens telegraphed Laboulaye at St Petersburg. A second cable a day later (15 February 1887) said: 'The fate of France is in your hands. It is evident today that if Russia falls into the trap that is being prepared for her – we shall immediately be attacked on our eastern frontier. The soul of the Emperor of Russia, so great and so loyal, cannot permit France to be wiped out. So long as they [the Germans] have not succeeded in paralysing his action they will dare not carry out the Machiavellian plot which has been hatched with a view to simultaneous complications in East and West.' By the 'Machiavellian plot' he meant a rumour he had picked up from a mysterious source that Bismarck was urging the Russians to attack Austria in a con-jured-up war over the Balkans, while the German Army would smash France. We would be *écrasé* (crushed), said Laboulaye, 'without even having a chance to go on the defensive'. He seems to have been convinced an attack was imminent by code-breaking intercepts made by the French military intelligence service under General Boulanger's control.

Where had the idea of a 'Machiavellian plot' come from? It sounded pure Katkov. An editorial by K had appeared in the *Moskovskie Vyedmo-sti* on 3 February 1887: 'Berlin is just now in the process of stirring up things in Southeastern Europe with a view to involving Russia there and thus distracting her attention. But none of these plans will succeed

... anything is possible.' It caused a sensation when reported in Paris, but to a government minister this was still just newspaper ranting, unless someone had travelled from the east to reinforce the message.

The wild, freelance diplomacy initiated by Cyon's October mission to Russia with General Saussier's plea to the Russian Army in his pocket had prompted a visitor in return. A 'highly-placed Russian' was in Paris that midwinter. He was General Evgenii Vasilyevich Bogdanovich, nominally of the interior ministry, with a responsibility (which would soon turn out to be very useful to the Maharajah) as an inspector of railways. It was whispered that he was the mysterious author of 'L'Alliance Franco-Russe', the pamphlet which had caused such a stir among Madame Adam's *salonnières* and such scandal in St Petersburg.

The general's appearance must have been unusual. Swaddled in a heavy military greatcoat and fur-hatted he was, so he claimed, suffering from a *maladie des yeux* and would emerge from his shuttered hotel room into the winter Parisian light only with his eyes bandaged like H. G. Wells's invisible man. In this curious condition he apparently sought out Elie de Cyon at his apartment at 44 rue de la Bienfaisance. He recalled in his memoirs: 'A visiting card was sent up to me. Mikhail Nikiforovitch [Katkov] had traced in crayon on it: "Dear Illich Faddeievich, General Bogdanovich has come to France 'pour soigner ses yeux', he wants to make your acquaintance, *that is why I give you this card*." [Cyon's italics].'

The emphasis is interesting. Cyon devoted two pages of his memoirs to denying Bogdanovich met anyone in Paris on Katkov's behalf, and especially General Georges Boulanger. 'It was all completely untrue. The great editor had no need for a second intermediary to myself . . . only I was initiated into his intimate hopes and fears,' the doctor wrote. 'The General was an inspector of railways, completely ignorant of French politics. He had come to France for a cure for an eye ailment, he only crossed Paris on his way to Nice and it was only on his return to this city that he passed several weeks here. Indeed, it was only towards the end of this second *séjour* that he approached me.

'During his stay in Paris he gave General Saussier a gift, an elaborate bowl, from the merchants of Moscow in recognition of his russophile toast on the occasion of the anniversary of Sebastopol. He was in Paris to promote a French translation of his book the *Battle of Navarino*.*

Cyon insisted that Bogdanovich never met Boulanger: 'When the General summoned him to the War Ministry on the rue Saint Dominique to congratulate him personally on the *Bataille de Navarin*, Bogdanovich refused him saying "his malady of the eyes could not let him leave his hotel room".

'It took all the ingenuity of Bismarck, backed by the compliance of our own diplomats in Paris and Berlin, to transform these innocent encounters into crimes against the state – and especially to attach Katkov's name to the journey,' Cyon wrote.

Cyon was dissembling. Just as he was so precise about the date when a 'senior Irish émigré introduced the Maharajah to me', his denials went on for too long. The general had not come to France simply to cure his eyes; he was there as Katkov's emissary. It is also clear that Cyon introduced him some time in late January 1887 to a very interesting gentleman – the Maharajah Duleep Singh.

Bogdanovich certainly had discussions with General Saussier and he met Flourens, the foreign minister, as subsequent diplomatic documents proved. Whether or not he met Boulanger would become more much problematic – it became an episode in which Her Majesty's Foreign Secret Service were to take a great interest. But just then the ambitious French general had problems of his own. His bungled recasting of the railway mobilization timetables had opened up a black hole. The rolling-stock calculations were wrong. The French Army could not get to the frontier in time to fend off an attack. Even Boulanger saw it and appealed to Saussier for help. It would take three months to sort out. France would be at Germany's mercy.

General Saussier approached Cyon, urging him to leave for Russia with a message of much importance for the 'proper persons' – a letter from President Grévy himself. The letter does not survive. There is no evidence other than Cyon's own memoirs and a few other scraps, but he certainly made a journey full of high political incident.

When he boarded the train for St Petersburg at the Gare du Nord on 6 February 1887, the journalist had once again become the story, but this time he had a message to the Czar of Russia from the President

---

* The foreword to this history of the Anglo-French-Russian victory over the Turkish and Egyptian fleets in 1827 contains the dedication: 'To the glorious French army'. The publisher said 'it would cause a sensation – expressed by someone so close to the person of the Czar'.

of France burning a hole in his pocket. He had been told the survival of France depended on his mission.

In Paris the Maharajah had more visitors. Arur Singh, his faithful servant, had been dispatched from Aden to go to India and wander the Punjab 'like a fakir'. He had returned in January to seek out his master in Paris and had then been ordered to go to London on some urgent housekeeping business.

Victor, the Maharajah's eldest son, now a Sandhurst cadet, arrived in Paris in the last week of January, having received similar instructions. The prince reported everything to Arthur Oliphant, son of Duleep's old 'Comptroler', in London who, in turn, told Sir Owen Tudor Burne at the India Office in a long letter dated 13 February. The Maharajah was 'bent on revenge', according to Victor. He had 'received assurances of support from India, and had received large sums of money, but whether the money was from India or Russia he did not know'. Sir Owen's intelligence antennae must have twitched. He already knew from the Watson correspondence that £10,000 had arrived or had at least been promised from somewhere.

'The Maharajah has cleared out of Coutt's custody all the jewels he means to use for his own purpose,' Oliphant continued. 'Victor, accompanied by young Farrer of Farrer's & Co, 66 Lincoln's Inn Fields, took to Paris the last lot of jewels. Victor told me his father refused to take him to his apartment, and old Müller never succeeded in finding it out.

'Farrer's & Co. heard from the Maharajah as lately as Friday last (11th) and I believe the letter had reference to some money the India Office had paid to his account at Coutts – some £1,400 for his expenses to and from Aden – and I suggested to Farrer's to ask for the Maharajah's sanction to their paying the only two claims which I know of which are outstanding against the Maharajah – some £1,050 for the ladies' apparel and outfit, for which the Maharani is being dunned.'

The Maharajah was as keen as ever to be reunited with his Purdey shotguns. Arthur Oliphant reported: 'I have not heard if Grindlay's [the shipping agents] have yet supplied his guns and rifles to Batoum; but they received orders many weeks ago to have them in readiness to ship at a moment's notice.

'I think the man Arur Singh should be watched. If his story is true, the detective police in India made it so hot for him that he couldn't remain and he got out of India in disguise,' Oliphant told Sir Owen. 'He was here last week waiting to take some clothes over to the Maharajah from Holland Park.'

Oliphant, who had recently been charged with looking after the Duleep Singh children, had no doubts about what to do with their errant father: 'From the letters I have had from the Maharajah, all of which you have seen and are at your disposal, and from all the circumstances which have come to my knowledge about him, I have long since arrived at the conclusion that he is a traitorous and dangerous lunatic,' he wrote.

The India Office was coming to the same conclusion. At first the Maharajah's travails had all seemed rather amusing. Now Oliphant's amateur intelligence report added to the new hard-line already set in London. The 'dangerous lunatic' had opened correspondence again with Sir Robert Montgomery. On 28 January he asked him to: 'Cause a receipt to be sent to my solicitors, Messrs Farrer's & Co., for the Star of India which they forwarded at my request to the India Office some time ago, and which I am anxious to possess before my departure (which may now take place any day) from Paris.

'Doubtless you will be surprised to hear that I have received promise of pecuniary aid up to £1,000,000, on certain conditions, and, from India, assurance of loyalty of the entire Punjab and allegiance of some 45,000 Punjabis in the British army,' the Maharajah added. '... The trodden-down worm at last has been enabled through the mercy of God to lift up his bowed down heart and head in order to avenge the injustice and the insults (as the only reward for his loyalty) showered down upon him for the last 36 years.' The proclamations were again enclosed, including the 'Courage! Courage! Courage!' war-cry.

Within hours the documents, as the Maharajah must have intended, were circulating in the corridors of Whitehall. On 1 February Sir Owen Tudor Burne had an urgent meeting with Sir Julian Pauncefote at the Foreign Office. The Viceroy was flashed that evening; Lord Lyons, the ambassador in Paris, was telegrammed; Lord Salisbury was informed. The Queen had to be appraised of the latest disagreeable developments.

In a cipher telegram timed at 9.30 p.m., 1 February 1887, Lord Dufferin in Calcutta was warned: 'Secret. Duleep Singh wrote to

Montgomery on the 28th January stating promise of pecuniary aid up to a million sterling and assurances of loyalty from entire Punjab. He encloses three very seditious proclamations . . . Copies go to you next mail. He states two first proclamations will be published at once in France and that he leaves Paris shortly. His destination is probably Russia. We have asked Lyons to keep watch over proceedings.

'As Lahore newspapers report mendicants going about Punjab foretelling restoration of Khalsa power you may like to impress on Aitchison [Lieutenant-Governor of the Punjab] necessity of vigilance.'

On 10 February Lord Dufferin was urgently warned again in a cable from Lord Cross: 'Information reaches me that Duleep Singh starts at once for St Petersburg, not as a supplicant but as a Prince in pomp and jewels and offering alliance, instigated by Sirdar Thakur Singh Sandhanwalia. This man should be watched – where is he . . . ?'

Lord Lyons had already received instructions. Sir Julian Pauncefote had told him on the 2nd: 'Sir Owen Burne of the India Office called here yesterday, on the subject of Duleep Singh's "agissements" in Paris. Lord Cross is anxious to obtain your assistance so far as you may be able to give it for the purpose of watching the Maharajah's proceedings and movements. I have shown the memorandum to Lord Salisbury who desires me to inform you of Lord Cross's wishes to request you to do what may be in your power to meet them.'

Lord Lyons, who had been so reluctant to get his embassy entangled with 'spying', was now at a complete loss. He sent Lord Salisbury a cipher telegram on 11 February: 'Can you give me any further clue to finding Duleep Singh at Paris? No. 37 Rue d'Anjou is a first-class bank; he has his letters directed there but they will not or cannot give his address. It would be very inadvisable for me to apply to the French Police for information.'

The Queen Empress had her own views. The next day she sent a cipher telegram from Osborne to her embattled Prime Minister. 'Ought not the Russian Govt be warned [not] to accept offer of one who is alas! a rebel?'

Where was the Maharajah? Could British intelligence really be so incompetent? Others had sought him out in Paris – Punjabis, Russians, Irish-Americans. As far as Whitehall was concerned, any news had come direct from Duleep Singh himself, in the stream of letters to Sir

Robert Montgomery and though the seaside letter-box of Mr Watson. The best intelligence so far was that in Arthur Oliphant's letter of 13 February with its debrief of old Müller, Prince Victor and Arur Singh. The letter had an extraordinary last line: 'I heard from my cousin in Paris last week that the Maharajah goes, generally accompanied by a *demoiselle* for his letters to 37 rue d'Anjou and that his address where he lives is only known to one of the partners in the Bank.' The Maharajah had a girl with him.

The conference in Whitehall between Sir Julian Pauncefote and Sir Owen Tudor Burne on 1 February had obviously got down to some very secret business. Lord Lyons was proving useless. Pressure to do something was now being applied at the highest level. How could Lord Salisbury tell the Queen they had lost the Maharajah? The Oliphant and Müller letters were being passed on by the India Office to the senior civil servant – in effect the executive head of Her Majesty's Foreign Secret Service. He already had an agent (the Fenian mole) in place in Paris. It was time for direct action.

In the India Office records in London there exists an exceptional account of the Duleep Singh affair. Uniquely, it runs sequentially from mid-February 1887 until the year before the Maharajah's death, as a single volume of over 500 pages. I read it over two days in the summer of 1998 with heart-pounding excitement. No academic historian of the period seemed to know of its existence, and nor did the Foreign and Commonwealth Office's own historian.

Handwritten on embossed India Office letterhead paper it is the complete transcript of the Paris spy's communications with his Whitehall masters. The originals, passed from the FO to the India Office, were copied and destroyed on receipt. It breathes the cleverest spycraft, names are obscured, there are multiple cut-outs and diversions. The intimate watch would continue for five years. The spy's identity is revealed only as 'Our Correspondent'.

The file proper begins with a short note. Dated 15 February 1887, it is from Francis Hyde Villiers, private secretary to Sir Julian Pauncefote at the Foreign Office, to Sir Owen Tudor Burne, the Maharajah's long-suffering case-officer at the India Office. It said simply: 'Dear Sir Owen. Sir Julian Pauncefote desires to inform you that he has taken steps with a view to obtaining, if possible, the information you want.

As soon as we hear anything I will let you know. I return the papers which you sent me yesterday.'

Burne scribbled an equally revealing minute on the letter in red ink for his India Office colleagues: 'I suggest that we should wait for a few days and not disturb F.O. action. The F.O. have some doubts as to the efficiency of English detectives in such cases as I myself have.'

There it was – the bungling sleuths of Scotland Yard were to be kept out; it was to be a strictly Foreign Office operation. Only a handful of people in Whitehall would know (or ever know) the secret. From the moment the Russia-bound Maharajah looked like a real threat, there was a spy at the heart of the matter. Our Correspondent functioned as the Maharajah's clandestine chief of staff in Paris; almost every letter, every telegram, would pass through the agent's hands (there was another route of communication to India via Constantinople which took the intelligence services longer to break into) and be on Lord Salisbury's desk the next day. Within three days of the Villiers 'taken steps to provide the information you want' note, the Paris mole would go live with this scrap on 18 February: 'I believe Duleep Singh is over in London for a few days but is expected back in Paris shortly.'*

It was as if history had been bugged and I had the transcripts in my hand. The Maharajah had no conception of the depths of the conspiracy into which he was so blindly striding. It was as deep as the snow on the Strastnyi Boulevard.


*Anichkov Palace, St Petersburg, February 1887*

As the spymasters in London were spinning their webs in that first week of February, de Giers, the apostle of peace, was still clinging to office in St Petersburg by his fingernails. He admitted that he planned nothing now but 'the most dignified way of departing' and a placid retirement at his country estate near Vyborg in the Finnish birch forests of his childhood. He must have hoped his imminent fall would

---

* He had confused Duleep with Arur Singh who had gone to get clothes from Holland Park.

not imperil the career of his son, also called Nicholas, a junior official at the Paris embassy.

On 6 February there was an imperial ball at the Anichkov Palace on Ostrovsky Square. Fans fluttered and heads turned in uniform collars as M. and Mme de Giers entered the chandeliered salon. Conversations hushed as they passed – the foreign minister was already regarded as 'politically dead'.

Cyon arrived in St Petersburg on the 9th; he said in his memoirs he crossed the capital heading for the Nikolayevsk station and the Moscow train 'without stopping'. But he had plenty of time to transmit General Saussier's information on France's military peril and entrust President Grévy's letter to the Czar to the 'right people'.

The doctor arrived in Moscow on the morning of Thursday 10 February, and rushed straight to the Strastnyi Boulevard where he lunched alone with Katkov. Cyon brought news from Paris. He outlined in great secrecy the exotic potential of the Maharajah. Katkov told him in return that the Czar was ready to break with Germany. Cyon next sent telegrams to the editors of the *Journals des Débats* and *Le Figaro* with the news, and more messages to Madame Adam and 'several other persons' in Paris. News leaked from the telegraph office and there was frantic speculation on the Moscow Bourse.

The two men huddled in conversation late into the night and on into the weekend of 11–12 February. The import of Katkov's memo to the Czar had become known through a calculated indiscretion of Count Tolstoi. Both men were convinced that an anti-Bismarck majority in the looming German elections would mean immediate war. Their reasoning was pragmatic. Bismarck needed parliamentary approval for money but only the Kaiser could sack him. Without a favourable Reichstag to vote through a seven-year military programme, the Septennat, he would have launched a war against rearming France. General Boulanger's posturing would provide the excuse.

There was a lot of talk about money – the equally strategic prize of shifting Russian borrowing from Berlin to Paris. Cyon had talked to the '*hautes banques*', including the 'Jewish Rothschilds', he revealed. Katkov resolved to send Cyon back to St Petersburg with a letter for Ivan Alekseivich Vyshnegradski, the imperial finance minister.

On Monday 14 February, Cyon arrived back in the capital primed for the most momentous business.* He had to spend a week waiting for an interview with Vyshnegradski, but used the time profitably: he had interviews with Constantin Pobedonostsev and Count Dmitrii Tolstoi, the two most important men in Russia after the Czar. Tolstoi exuded bonhomie, praising Cyon for his editorials attacking the follies of liberalism. Cyon saw Count Pavel Ignatiev and 'held talks for three hours with the former statesman'. Ignatiev made clear his ambitions: he intended 'taking de Giers place' and 'was a firm supporter of Katkov's policy'. Everything seemed set: the hard-men would very quietly seize the levers of power.

On 21 February the German Chancellor got his majority in the Reichstag, assuring the passage of the Septennat. Cyon read about it in the papers on the 23rd. The war for now seemed postponed.

The next day Cyon had another meeting with a someone he refers to in his memoirs as 'General X'. The mysterious officer was already a confidante, he was probably the man to whom he had relayed General Saussier's message on France's military peril on his first transit of the frozen capital. General X was going to a party at the German embassy that night. Cyon asked him to keep his ears open.

When they met the next morning, 25 February, General X had dramatic news. Berlin would now insist that the Czar give a clear message that in the case of a war between Germany and France, Russia would do nothing if France was seen to be the aggressor. But what if an unendurable provocation was made? (It nearly was in April 1887 over the Schnaeble affair.)† France would be crushed without an ally and Russia bottled up, no doubt to be turned on next. The general urged Cyon to return to Moscow immediately 'to warn Katkov of the danger'. He rushed by carriage through the snowbound, silent streets just in time to catch the night train from the Nikolayevsk station.

\*　　\*　　\*

* Elie de Cyon, 'one of the most fascinating figures in the underworld of European politics' as the German historian Fritz Stern called him, had multiple motives for the mission, including, it seems, self-enrichment. He was working all along with Gerson Bleichroder, Bismarck's private banker, whom he sought out in Berlin on his way back to France to report on the highly secret financial moves.

† On 22 April 1887 the so-called 'Schnaeble affair' nearly precipitated war. M. Schnaeble, a police official, was arrested by the Germans at Pagny-sur-Moselle on the disputed frontier and charged with treason. The Boulangists erupted, the French government back-pedalled, believing Bismarck was provoking them to war. M. Schnaeble was released with a scant apology after a week.

In London meanwhile, Lord Salisbury was cabling his ambassador in the Russian capital to get a grip on the Maharajah's wild schemes to fly into the arms of the Czar. The Queen was becoming very agitated about the one who was, 'alas, a rebel'. Salisbury urged a meeting with the foreign minister before, as every diplomatic indicator had it, de Giers' grip on power was prised loose.

Sir Robert Morier reported back on 24 February: 'With reference to Your Lordship's telegram, I have the honour to state that I had today an opportunity of referring in conversation with M. de Giers to the case of Maharajah Duleep Singh. I said that a rumour had reached me that he was proposing to come to St Petersburg and I, therefore, thought it right to tell His Excellency that he was in a state of open rebellion to the Empress of India.'

The foreign minister told Sir Robert that he had learned of the Maharajah's initial intentions a year ago, 'but that he had heard nothing lately of any such plans, nor did he think it likely that he would carry out his intentions'. He reprised the approaches to de Staal in London and to Kotzebue in Paris and their brisk rebuttal on his own orders, 'to do everything to prevent him carrying out his project'. Sir Robert reported:

> 'De l'econduire'* was his Excellency's expression. 'In fact,' observed M. de Giers laughing – 'C'est un monsieur dont nous ne pourrions faire la connaissance á moins que nous ne soyons en guerre.' [If we were to make this gentleman's acquaintance, at the very least we would be at war.]
>
> Even in that case, I observed, I could hardly recommend him to Your Excellency, because by twice changing his religion and other outrageous acts he has so discredited himself as to have lost all value and importance in his own country.
>
> Before leaving, I said, 'I may then inform Her Majesty's Government that Duleep Singh was duly *econduit* (dismissed) when he made his advances at London and Paris?' After reflecting a moment His Excellency replied that 'this would perhaps be too strong a term, because after all there was noth-ing in his letters which would have justified such a drastic

---

* Sir Robert wrote his own translation for Lord Salisbury in the margin of the original letter: 'to warn off, also to refuse, deny, not comply with'.

treatment. He made no proposal which could be taken up, and only expressed his extreme desire to study the beauties of St Petersburg and pass his respects to the Russian Government and he was told in quite unmistakable language his visit was not desired.'

I may mention that M. de Giers referred casually in the course of our conversation to the numerous letters which he was in the habit of receiving and not answering from Fenians in America.

Why would de Giers casually drop 'Fenians' into the conversation?

A morsel of intelligence had meanwhile simultaneously reached London from Calcutta. Dated 22 February, it was from a mysterious agent, 'J', who had penetrated the Calcutta end of Duleep's line of communication, *The Beaver* newspaper in French Chandernagore, a tiny enclave upstream on the Hooghly river from the winter capital of British India. J reported:

I beg now to report that Maharajah Duleep Singh is carrying on correspondence with the editor of The Beaver, Shashi Bhushan Mukerji – I saw one of these letters which was dated Paris the 7th January. I need hardly say that it was in the language of sedition and was nearly three pages long.

In this Duleep said that for good or evil, he had left his case entirely in the hands of Russia and he hoped at no distant date to lead an invading army to India and become the King of the Punjab.

With this letter he sent two proclamations, both of which were printed in English, one dated 15th July 1886, the other was simply 1886. The following mail brought another letter from the Maharajah, where Duleep said that he had nothing to lose by his Russian alliance; his sole object now was to be avenged, and he would be satisfied if he could strike one blow; in another part he says that some of the Punjabi sardars and 45,000 Khalsa are ready to fight for his cause.

The Maharajah and the Babu [Mr Mukerji] are not corresponding direct, but are playing the 'old confidential dodge' of double envelopes. The letters to the Babu are sent in a mail bag of the French Government and are delivered to peons of the chef-de-securité. Those for the Maharajah have the outer cover addressed as: Mallet Frères et Cie. 37 Rue d'Anjou Paris.

The Punjabi Special Branch had picked up intelligence in mid-January that the Paris terminus of *The Beaver* link was a Frenchman in Paris, a Monsieur 'E.C.'. French government mailbags, double-envelope dodges – someone was obviously initiating the Maharajah, the world's worst conspirator, into the ways of spycraft.

Elie de Cyon meanwhile was a long way from Paris; he was on his way once again from St Petersburg to Moscow, desperate to impart General X's warning to Katkov. He arrived on the morning of 26 February to plunge back into four days of interminable talks with his mentor. It was the Russian Lent, the seven-week great fast, and Katkov was looking gaunt, subsisting on a curious diet of stale mushrooms. He poured out his thoughts, pacing the room, raving and ranting till late into the night. Cyon sensed he was desperately ill. This was Katkov's political testament: Russia must conclude a defensive alliance with France, wait for the Austrian–German treaty of alliance to expire, then proceed to an 'active policy'. It would be war.

Cyon was ordered to write a leader for the *Moscow Gazette*, which he did in two hours before catching the St Petersburg train just as it was pulling out of the station.

There were to be two more shadowy encounters in the Russian capital before Cyon caught the night train back to Paris. The first was a lunch date with General Bogdanovich, who vehemently denied the whispering campaign that he was the author of 'L'Alliance Franco-Russe'. The second was a meeting on the platform of the Warsawa Station with an emissary from General X.

There was the highest military intelligence to take back to Paris – the Austrians were mobilizing in Galicia, the staff officer had said, German divisions were concentrating in East Prussia and Silesia, their agents already scouring Polish villages for billets and horse fodder. Russia would be invaded no later than the end of March . . . then it would be France's turn.

# 20

# Our Correspondent

Moscow Gazette, *Paris bureau, 63 rue de Rennes,*
7 *March 1887*

ELIE DE CYON returned to Paris with the most dramatic news possible; according to the highest authorities in the Russian Army, a general
war in Europe was less than a month away. The Germans would surely
crush France. The Maharajah must be mobilized with the utmost
dispatch. In Paris he was just another exile; only in Russia would he
have any influence against England.

Events were already moving fast. First, someone in the French capital had got to the Maharajah and learned his confidences for clandestine
transmission to London. A one-line report (the one confusing Arur
Singh with Duleep Singh) had been sent to Francis Villiers at the
Foreign Office on 18 February. But the spy's first full dispatch was
dated 8 March 1887. It was very detailed:

> Maharajah Duleep Singh is in Paris and has been interviewed.
> The following is the substance of what he said:
> 'I am England's foe. I was her loyal subject. My people
> wished to remain her allies but I have been insulted by her
> government and my just claims have been disavowed: I was
> imprisoned at Aden when I was on my road to India after an
> absence of 30 years, and I swear I had no disloyal intentions.
> Now I am preparing a rebellion, and if I can obtain Russian
> help I shall succeed in driving out the British.
> 'Brought up a Christian I have again become a Sikh' (adding
> in a very excited manner), 'I shall be damned, I know, but I
> shall have vengeance! Lord Salisbury has refused to submit to

an arbitration my claims to certain private property in the Punjab which belonged to my family. But I shall agitate the question in public and my counsel has sent out a confidential agent to India to obtain full information of the value of my property.

'Previous to my departure from England, where I shall never return, I settled all my fortune on my wife and children so that they may not be reduced to want when I am proclaimed a rebel which must be shortly, but now I am a free man, and I refuse to touch any subsidy from the British Government.'

He says that he receives remittances from India. He produced a letter from one of his cousins in Pondicherry wherein he is styled 'Your Majesty.' In this letter money is promised when he is in Russia – 'the delay in Paris does not please us,' they say – and there are assurances 'from conversations with Sikhs that the whole country will join the Russians if they are accompanied by your Majesty and the Punjabis are sure that it is so, but they will fight against the Russians should your Majesty not be with them.' 45,000 is the number of disaffected sepoys of Sikh origin mentioned in the letter.

Duleep Singh was to have left Paris but did not, for want of a passport, on the 17th February [precisely when Cyon was frantically cabling Paris from St Petersburg]. He has an agent in Constantinople where, if matters can be arranged he will go in person and thence to Russia. But the passport difficulty stops him. He tried for French naturalization but was refused it in consequence he says of the interference of Lord Lyons.

He was also unsuccessful at the Russian Embassy. He wants to offer his services to Katkov. He keeps his address secret as he is afraid of the English and wishes to avoid notice. He wore the same coat as in the photograph. [London must have supplied the spy with one.] He now wears a short beard.

If what Duleep Singh says is true, it is evidence that he is not yet in touch with Russia and that he is not at present engaged in any dangerous conspiracy.

Anything he may do in the future I shall know of – meanwhile I hope that what I have written may be kept quite secret and that at present no action of any kind may be taken on it.

The spy knew a great deal but not everything. He was aware of the Pondicherry connection and of an 'agent in Constantinople', but the rebuff from the Russian embassy seemed to convince him Duleep was blustering. At this stage he was unaware of E.C.'s parallel diplomacy and the Bogdanovich mission.

The Maharajah was anxious to unburden himself to the mysterious individual he would later describe as 'my only one true private friend in Paris'. The next day, 10 March, he showed the spy his tabernacle of documents; the 'beautiful and charming boy' letter from the Queen, the voluminous memorandum of his woes sent to Lord Salisbury, the Carlton Club letter from the sympathetic MP, Mr Hanbury, and of course the three proclamations. But there were two new dramatic developments transmitted in copy to London that night: a letter to the Czar of Russia and one to Mikhail Katkov, both dated that same day.

The Maharajah wrote to Katov:

> Monsieur. By the advice of friends I write to ask you to have the goodness to place before H.I.M. [His Imperial Majesty the Czar] the accompanying letter which I have ventured to address to him and also another from Queen Victoria for H.I.M.'s perusal.
>
> I further request you Monsieur kindly to use your great influence in obtaining my Russian naturalization, as I desire from my heart to become a loyal subject of H.I.M.
>
> But if that be not possible then be so good as to procure me a letter of authority to pass my baggage and sporting guns and ammunition both at Batoum and Baku on the way to Teheran in Persia.
>
> Perhaps it might not be out of place to state here for your information that I am an unfortunate Indian Prince, one of the monuments of British injustice, but am in no want of pecuniary aid as my loyal subjects have already placed sufficient means at my disposal and are further largely providing for my future maintenance so that I am quite independent of everybody in this respect. Requesting an early reply, I have the honour to remain Monsieur . . .

The editor must have been baffled by the ex-King of Lahore who seemed as interested in a hunting trip as in overthrowing the British

Empire. Czar Alexander III must have been equally perplexed at his own communication. It read:

> May it please Your Imperial Majesty. I venture to address you, Sire, in the ardent hope that Y.I.M. may be graciously pleased to grant my prayer.
>
> It is useless for me to endeavour to bring myself to Y.I.M.'s recollection, for doubtless Sire, you cannot but have forgotten so humble an individual as myself, though I had the honour of being presented to Y.I.M. by the Prince of Wales when Y.I.M. visited England now many years ago.
>
> I earnestly implore you, Sire, to find a safe asylum in Y.I.M.'s dominions as one of your most loyal subjects.
>
> In offering my loyal allegiance to Y.I.M. I do not ask any pecuniary gain whatsoever, as my loyal subjects have already furnished me with sufficient means and are further largely providing for my future maintenance, so that I am entirely independent of everybody in this respect.
>
> I also venture to forward with this letter in another envelope a note addressed to me by H.M. Queen Victoria some months since for Y.I.M.'s perusal, and pray that it may be returned to me in safety . . .

'Duleep Singh has plenty of money,' Our Correspondent's report continued. 'He intends to leave Paris for Constantinople next week and there await an answer from St Petersburg. He stated that Merv or Savakhs, the latter for choice, would be the place of residence he would select. If this be impossible, he intends to pass his time shooting in the vicinity of the Caspian.'

There was a problem. The Maharajah did not have a British passport. This would have been incidental had he not been seeking the Czar Alexander III's help to start a revolution. In the European order of the 1880s, crossing frontiers was paper-free. The Gold Standard was universal. There was no quarantine. If an Englishman wanted to inspect the Parthenon he could catch the boat-train, accompanied by an elephant if he so wished, and pay his way with a handful of gold sovereigns from his waistcoat pocket. Passports had been eliminated across the continent *except* in Russia and Turkey.

The Russian passport system was as Byzantine as the state. The St Petersburg embassy sent London a long memorandum on the rules:

> All foreigners arriving in Russia are bound to show at the frontier a national passport for which he has received a visa at the Russian Embassy or consulate in his country [reported Mr Charles Eliot, the second secretary]. The embassy is bound to inquire into the character of the persons whose passports it visas and in no case visas for passports be issued for Jesuits or gypsies.*
>
> Once in Russia a foreigner is obliged to show the passport with which he has arrived to the Governor of the first capital of a province through which he passes.
>
> Those travelling direct by rail to any destination must show their passports at that place. On thus presenting his passport a foreigner must answer questions as to his name, profession, birthplace, religion, time of arrival in Russia and to whether he is married.
>
> At the expiration of a year, a foreigner must present himself at the Chancery of the Chef du Gouvernement of the province where he resides (in Moscow and St Petersburg to the Military Governor).
>
> He also has to fill up on his arrival five forms stating his profession etc which are sent to various offices. A foreigner residing at St Petersburg or Moscow is obliged to have a ticket of residence and to pay various dues in the same manner as Russian subjects.

Thus did the suspicious empire guard its borders. London could relax. Without a passport from Her Britannic Majesty on which to stamp a visa, the border remained closed.

---

* Russian Jews needed internal passports and their movements outside the 'Pale' of western Russia were rigidly controlled. In the conquered Caucasus deportations of Jews were still being brutally effected.

## Nevskii Prospekt, St Petersburg, 13 March 1887

There were reasons for the guard without, although the Czar's most dangerous enemies were within. On the morning of 13 March (1 March old style), Alexander III prepared to depart the Anichkov Palace with his wife and son to attend a memorial service at the Citadel Church for his father, assassinated exactly six years before. Six young Nihilists, members of the 'Terrorist Fraction of the People's Will', were waiting, one with a dynamite shrapnel-bomb doused in strychnine concealed in a hollowed-out volume of the Russian Criminal Code.

General P. V. Orzhevskii, deputy interior minister and head of the secret police, had reported to de Giers two weeks before the attack: 'St Petersburg is completely free of Nihilistic danger.' But his bitter rival, General P. A. Gresser, chief of police in the capital, had evidently penetrated the conspiracy, shadowing the bomber, a twenty-three-year-old student named Andreyushkin.

The iron gates swung open, the imperial coach clattered through, heading under the soaring arch into Great Admiralty Street. At the very last minute the bombers were bundled off by Gresser's men, 'a cloud of detectives in various disguises', as Sir Robert Morier described them to Lord Salisbury. The ambassador continued: 'It was only later when the Prefect arrived after luncheon at the Winter Palace, that the emperor was informed of the arrests. He observed: "I am in God's hands – I trust to Him to protect me." '*

Rumours of the attack swept the imperial capital. The police tried to hush it up but Reuters got hold of the story. On the 15th it appeared in the London and Paris papers. Russia seemed to be on the edge of a precipice but Duleep Singh seemed as determined as ever to get there. Intelligence activity in Whitehall was frantic – Sir Robert Morier had reported a rumour that assassination attempts on the Czar were being planned 'from England'.

At the Foreign Office Sir Julian Pauncefote also had time to consider the latest news from Our Correspondent: 'Paris, 15th March. I have

---

* Five of the conspirators were hanged in the Schlusselburg Fortress on 8 May 1887, including a young zoology graduate called Alexander Ulyanov whose younger brother, Vladimir, is better known to history as Lenin.

found out where Duleep Singh is living. He has a young English girl with him . . .'

## Paris, 15–17 March 1887

There were, so Our Correspondent reported, to be three Russia-bound travellers, the Maharajah, the 'young English girl' and Arur Singh; plus, it would turn out, 'several dogs'.* Cyon, who slipped silently across frontiers with the highest secrets of state in his pocket, must have despaired. What kind of circus was he sending to his master in Moscow? Our Correspondent recorded Duleep's intentions in his secret dispatch of 15 March: 'Before leaving Paris he is to receive letters for Katkov and Achinov [the eccentric captain with his dreams of a Russian Orthodox colony in Abyssinia, taken up by Madame Adam]. He starts for Marseilles on Thursday evening next intending to embark on the French steamer via Naples on Saturday. He has some difficulty in obtaining a passport but is trying to get one in the name of Mr. and Mrs. Lorraine which name is at present on all his luggage. Should he fail in this, he will apply to the British Consul by whom his difficulty with the British Government, is, he thinks, most probably unknown, for a passport in his own name, or will use one in the name of his agent in Constantinople whom he speaks of as Rasool, an Indian Mussulman.'

'Mr. and Mrs. Lorraine' – Duleep and Ada sounded like a music-hall act.

The Viceroy was cabled by Lord Cross the next morning: 'Duleep Singh said to be making start tomorrow night for Constantinople and Russia via Marseilles. Have warned White.† Giers disavows knowledge of such movement.'

Sir Julian Pauncefote telegraphed Lord Lyons: 'We have reason to believe Maharajah Duleep Singh will leave Paris tomorrow evening for Marseilles. He will perhaps try to obtain from the Embassy a

---

* I have been unable to discover the names of these rebellious dogs, only that they were spaniels. I suspect they came from Elveden, then Holland Park, to be brought to Paris by Arur Singh. They made it all the way to Moscow and back to France but their fate thereafter is unrecorded.
† Sir William White, British ambassador to Constantinople.

passport for himself and for a young English girl who is with him under the name of Mr and Mrs Lorraine. Lord Salisbury begs that if application is made to the Embassy it may be refused. He will also be much obliged if you will instruct Mr Perceval [the British consul] in Marseilles to do the same, and, if possible, ascertain privately if Duleep Singh actually embarks on Saturday, taking however most special care not to let the Maharajah discover that any enquiry of that sort is being made.'

The bumbling Lord Lyons was soon in trouble again. He telegraphed back: 'Paris. Secret. The day before yesterday (that is to say the day before your letter reached me) an Indian named Arur Singh obtained at the Consulate here a passport, saying he was going to India via Constantinople. I mentioned this in my telegram to the consul at Marseilles. There was nothing apparently suspicious in the language or appearance of the man.'

Arur Singh was described as a 'handsome man of about six feet in height and 40 years of age'. He was accompanied by a Frenchman, who called himself J. J. Genet, 'Ex-Chef d'Institution, 43 Boulevard St Michel, who offered to vouch for the Indian's identity and nationality'. They turned up at the consular section on the morning of 16 March. Mr Falconer Atlee, the vice-consul, messaged upstairs to his chief.

Lord Lyons received the party in his private rooms on the first floor of the embassy and asked Arur some mild questions. Why was he going to India? 'To visit my birthplace in the Punjab,' the supplicant said.

'Perhaps the only question I put to the Indian of any real importance was whether he knew no one else in Paris beside M. Genet, who could give him a certificate of his nationality, for instance, I suggested, Duleep Singh,' Lord Lyons explained to London. 'The Indian answered without hesitation and with every appearance of veracity, that he of course knew Duleep Singh by name, but not personally, and therefore could not venture to apply to him for a certificate.'

Arur Singh had his passport. One down, two to go.

Duleep's activity was evidently frantic over the next few days. Cyon, Casey and Our Correspondent went into a huddle around him. The account at Mallet Frères was heavily drawn on. On 17 March, the day after Arur Singh went to the British embassy, the spy sent this portentous message to London:

I can surely manage to obtain all the threads of an intrigue which may become very serious if the Russians become convinced of Duleep Singh's power to help them, or to create trouble in India, should take him up even so far as to comply only with his request to reside at Sarakhs or Meshed, whence he pretends he can keep up his communications with the three princes, who, he asserts, positively are disposed to join forces or furnish funds in the event of a Russian advance which will be the signal for another insurrection.

The princes whom he has designated are, the Rajah of Kashmir, the Nizam [of Hyderabad] and the Prime Minister, or whatever his title may be, of Gwalior. Not being up in Indian titles, I may have given these wrong but the places are accurate. He is also anxious to communicate with Ayub Khan [the exiled ruler of Afghanistan] who is, I believe at Herat.

So far his communications with the future rebels have been conducted through a cousin, or cousins (he speaks of numbers) now at Pondicherry, and as he announced yesterday that he should ask leave of Russia for the residence with him of these people and their families 'who can pass through India without any trouble'.

It might be well to have their movements watched without going so far as to stop their journey. It seems to me that with proper vigilance, intelligent local agents might pick up some valuable information and ascertain with whom they are in relations.

Duleep Singh was to have left for Marseilles tonight. Some indiscreet questions as to his proposed movements and whether he meant to 'visit Russia' have convinced him that he is being watched and will be accompanied by a detective.

This he told just to me and then to others by whom he was thus advised 'Stop over at Marseilles until the next Messageries steamer, 9th April, for Odessa via Constantinople not leaving the ship at the latter place.'

But in the meantime, should his friends there and at Moscow so advise, he is to return to Paris and go by rail to St Petersburg where the Minister of the Interior Bogdanovich [in fact a minor official], Katkov and Ignatiev, to all of whom he is specially recommended, will take him in hand.

He is to travel under an assumed name, probably that of Reginald Lorraine, if a passport so worded can be obtained for him, if not with another name which will be communicated to the Russian Government 'as a Prince he may travel incognito'.

All his books and papers are to be forwarded directly to Mr Katkov in Moscow, and should he sail by the Messageries he will be specially recommended to the Captain by an administrator of the company, and by someone else to the French Manager of the Ottoman Bank at Constantinople to whom he is to apply if he encounters any difficulties there.

Some of his friends objected, however, very strongly to his journey via Turkey predicting his possible assassination through British intrigue, and this has so worked upon him that he has postponed his departure until Monday the 21st instant at earliest hoping in the interim to have some news expected by telegraph from Katkov of the nature of the reception that he may expect at St Petersburg, and so the matter now stands.

Yesterday his servant Arur Singh obtained a passport from the British Embassy which is visé for Turkey. Arur Singh was questioned as to his knowledge of Duleep 'whom he swore he does not know personally and was told that Duleep was dead'. He was warned he says, 'that he would not be permitted as a British subject to enter Russia'.

He takes the girl with him as his wife.

Armed with Our Correspondent's very detailed account, Lord Cross informed the Viceroy within hours: 'Whatever might have been done with Duleep Singh in past times – it is impossible to treat with him now ... We keep through the F.O. the strictest watch on Duleep Singh's movements at Paris. As we are informed – he is to leave in company with a young girl for Constantinople this morning.' The Secretary of State's cable ended: 'Meanwhile look after his friends and relations at Pondicherry.' They would be.

Duleep had gained an improbable new name: Reginald.* But Mr and Mrs Reginald Lorraine were still going nowhere. He needed a British passport (a folding parchment document, without a photograph) on which to get the precious Russian visa stamps; Ada could travel '*comme sa femme*'. Which of Queen Victoria's subjects in Paris would willingly give up such a thing? Patrick Casey of Kilkenny, Duleep's junior by only two years.

So Patrick Casey went to the British embassy's consular section in the former mansion of Princess Borghese at the smarter end of rue St Honoré and declared himself through gritted teeth to be a loyal British subject. According to his own account: 'I had been in France for seventeen years without ever claiming a passport. I paid 6 francs and 50 centimes for it, and I therefore considered that it was my property, duly paid for, which I could dispose of as I liked. Yes: they handed me this piece of paper, on the 17th March . . . and I considered that I had a perfect right to do what I liked with it.' The consular staff apparently found the episode 'ironical'.

Casey then went to the rue de Grenelle, stated he was not a Jew, Jesuit or Gypsy, paid his 50 kopecks and received two double-headed-eagle visa stamps for Monsieur and Madame Casey.

On St Patrick's Day 1887, the King of the Sikhs and the bold Fenian rebel traded places.

## Paris, 20–21 March 1887

Our Correspondent burst into life again three days later. He now viewed Duleep's mission with the utmost seriousness. 'The passport business has been settled,' he messaged the Foreign Office. 'The passport has been handed to a friend by whom the Russian visa will be obtained – I earnestly plead that no action may be taken here about the passport and that the man be allowed to get to his destination.' The spy had his own agenda. He failed (or rather chose not) to tell London directly about the Casey switch, merely mentioning 'a friend'. This was to cause a month of mind-boggling confusion. He continued:

---

* Probably Madame Adam's punning. 'Reginald': old Norman – 'belonging to the Queen'; or old French, Reynaud – 'a ruler'.

He will hang himself if you give him rope enough, and only by letting him alone temporarily can you get at the bottom of what I am convinced is a formidable conspiracy.

I feel sure that I can help to defeat it, all I ask is leave to work it out subject to your approval in my own way. Duleep Singh will leave on Monday night for St Petersburg via the Nord railway. Don't have him followed; he will certainly communicate with me after his arrival unless frightened off by the presence of detectives on the journey . . .

If detectives have been watching Duleep Singh in Paris, I hope they have been taken off. It was suspicion that he was being watched, and indiscreet questions put by someone to his servant that made him change his mind about going to Constantinople via Marseilles last week.

When he actually leaves Paris I will communicate again, and then the Ambassador at St Petersburg might be warned. But as we are in the way of hearing of Duleep Singh's future plans and movements, the wisest thing in my opinion is to leave him alone.

The spy enclosed a copy of Duleep's eve-of-departure message to Thakur Singh Sandhanwalia in Pondicherry:

My dear Cousin,

I have the happiness to inform you that long before you receive this letter I shall have reached St Petersburg. In future I shall not sign letters in my own name, but in another, and in my next will give you my new address.

I leave here tomorrow Monday 21st March. Now the Princes of India must subscribe money to enable us to raise an army on the frontier, in order to get them rid of the English yoke.

The great difficulty was not being able to go to St Petersburg. But Guroo has enabled me at last to overcome it. I have already found a gentleman who hates the English as much as we do and will be able to help us. It is he who has helped me to leave Paris for St Petersburg and I hope to bring him with me as soon as things are settled with the Russian authorities.

You must renew agitation both in the Punjab and in India with great vigour for I think things will come to a crisis very soon, for troubles are appearing in Afghanistan and I trust we shall be able also to create some trouble for the British Government.'

This was 'a formidable conspiracy', the spy messaged. He wanted, like a good counter-espionage agent, to collar the lot; let the Maharajah proceed and see who else might be implicated. He ended his dispatch: 'Let us see how his advances are received by Russia and let him do more to compromise himself and others.' Duleep and 'the girl' were on their way, the Guru had predicted it thus.

# 21

# The Magician and the Fortune-teller

❦

*Gare du Nord, Paris, 21 March 1887*

THE GREAT PARISIAN TERMINUS of the north was itself an emblem of longed-for revenge. This was where the imperial armies of 1870 had confidently entrained for the German frontier and had returned, broken and bleeding, from Sedan. The female allegorical statue of the conqueror's capital 'Berlin' which adorned the frontage of the Gare des Chemins de Fer du Nord, remained as it had been since the great humiliation crowned by a chamber-pot. The late-afternoon spring sun stole through the glass-roofed train-shed, stirring the smoke and steam into a sulphurous yellow light. Porters toiled with the baggage, smartly-kepied conductors shouted the imminent departures of the *grandes lignes*. Knots of bored soldiers stood around, rifles piled, waiting for movement orders.

The Maharajah's party swept on to the platform, Ada pouting and truculent, Duleep stern and imperious, Arur Singh bustling over the cases. This was not a clandestine defection to the East; there was a baggage-train of valises, trunks, wicker baskets, hatboxes, japanned tins of papers, emeralds and pearls. More of the Maharajah's boxes had to be left behind. Duleep Singh clung to a satchel containing a fortune in gold francs, a sheaf of highly compromising letters of introduction from Cyon to the Katkov cabal, and Mr Casey's precious passport. The dogs barked loudly. A year ago he had embarked on his failed flight to India with Bamba and six children on a Bombay-bound steamer. Now the passenger-list had changed. Casey bid them well. Cyon preferred not to come. Nothing could go wrong now.

That morning the Paris papers were full of momentous news. *Le Voltaire* led on an astounding revelation run three days earlier in the pages of the 'Gazette de Moscou, organe de M. Katkov'. The editor had proclaimed: 'A secret treaty known as the triple alliance [the Drei-kaiserbund] is due to expire this month – an arrangement so pernicious for Russia into which she was lured at the time of her national humili-ation.' There was more to excite the Maharajah: a report that it was the Berlin police who had tipped off their St Petersburg counterparts about the Nihilist plot to assassinate the Czar on 13 March.

The *Moscow Gazette* asked: 'Who is the person most directly inter-ested in seeing the foreign policy of the French and Russian govern-ments simultaneously paralysed by internal revolution?' Bismarck, the German Chancellor himself, Katkov implied, was priming the revolu-tionaries' bombs. The German newspapers had countered, even more hysterically, that it was the pan-Slavs – with Katkov and Pobedonostsev at their head – who were behind the plot to kill the Czar. Duleep must have been baffled.

There was also a more festive note in the Paris newspaper: a detailed preview of the celebrations in Berlin to mark Kaiser Wilhelm I's nineti-eth birthday, due the next day. An old friend, the Prince of Wales, would be in the German capital just as the Maharajah would be rum-bling through on his journey of revenge. How exquisite.

At 4.45, the Nord Express was called. Its route was via Charleroi, Liège, Cologne, Berlin, Konigsberg, the frontier at Edytkouhnen on the East Prussian side, Verjbolovo on the Russian frontier, thence on to Wilna, Dunaburg, Pskov, Gatchina and St Petersburg – a distance of 2,719 kilometres over three days.* Fifteen minutes later the train steamed ponderously out of the Paris station.

Our Correspondent, obviously intimately acquainted with Cyon's intricately-laid plans for the journey, flashed London the next day: 'Duleep Singh left Paris on Monday for St Petersburg. He will be met at Egatkahum by one Greenberg, Russian agent there – a banker at Weidballen, the Russian frontier station, and will be told by him if he is to stop at St Petersburg, Hotel d'Europe, or go on to Moscow, Hotel Dussaux.

---

* I have used the spellings given in Galignani's *Guide de Voyager en Russie* (1887) edited by M. Tastevin. Casey would doubtless have given Duleep a copy; his newspaper published it. Edytkouhnen variously appears as Egatkahum or Eydkuhnen, Verjbolovo as Weidballen, Vierzhbolovo, Wierzbolow or Werzebolow. The border crossing was where Prussia, Poland, Lithuania, Byelorussia, Russia and their tongues met.

'If he has any difficulty in Russia he is to telegraph General Bogdano-vich, Minister of the Interior. He will preserve his incognito until naturalized as a Russian which is to be his first step. All his books and papers are left with [blank] by whom they will be forwarded to Katkov.

'He has with him one Englishwoman, two spaniels, 13 trunks and his servant Arur.'

Cyon was working frantically in the background. He says in his memoirs that he met the Maharajah first on 8 March – the dateline on Our Correspondent's first full-length (and accurate) dispatch. I question this statement for reasons stated previously, but find no argument with his account of the farrago of bizarre incidents that surrounded the Maharajah on his journey east.

The doctor had assembled a 'dossier' on the Maharajah, an outline of his doleful history, evidence of the support of Indian princes for the planned overthrow of the British Empire (the three mentioned in Our Correspondent's report of 17 March), also the letters to Katkov and to Czar Alexander III dated 10 March. It was intended to reach Moscow before the Maharajah, but was delayed in transit for reasons the Doctor was to record later in his memoirs:

'The dossier, posted as a registered letter, was opened and examined at Berlin (luckily it only contained copies), which led to a delay in transmission. I had only taken the chance of sending this packet with the formal assurance of the inspector, M. de Selves, given after my complaints about numerous losses of registered letters, that letters for Russia were put into special bags carefully hidden and addressed to the foreign bureau "Kibarty", at Werzebolow.

'There must have been some defect in this method of transmission, as my letter was opened on the pretext that the envelope had torn, after which they had sent it on to Moscow with several German seals on. These seals carry the inscription: "Geld Decantir" round a crown beneath which is the roman numeral "IX" with a trumpet. An employee at Berlin had taken the trouble to put the postal weight on the envelope.'

So the Maharajah was travelling unheralded, except by Cyon's discreet reports on his February mission to Russia. But this account holds deeper significance. There had been 'numerous losses of letters', he said. Now the Maharajah's file had been opened in a Berlin post office.

It looked as if someone in German intelligence was taking a deep interest in Doctor de Cyon and his friends.

Cyon recorded the last days in Paris. 'Duleep Singh left furnished with a passport in the name of the fugitive Irishman Patrick Casey, which he had legalised at the Russian consulate. His journey was not made alone. I was highly put out, on learning too late to prevent it, that besides a Hindu attendant who was responsible for his safety, the Maharajah was accompanied by a young English female. *This was to become dangerous . . .*'

## Friedrichstrasse Bahnhof, Berlin, 22 March 1887

By mid-afternoon on Tuesday the 22nd, the Nord Express was nosing into Berlin. The string of wagons-lits clanked through the Zoo station, transited the north of the snow-covered Tiergarten and swung southwards across the Spree into the heart of the city, where the practical Berliners had placed their railway stations. They were not termini, trains went in one end and came out the other. Berlin was always a city on the way to somewhere else. The German capital was *en fête*, celebrating the ninetieth (and last) birthday of Kaiser Wilhelm I. Enormous red-white-and-black flags fluttered in the spring breeze. Oak leaves garlanded portraits of the venerable Kaiser, his son the Crown Prince Friedrich Wilhelm and his wife Princess Victoria, daughter of the Queen of England. There would be Wagner at the opera that night: *Lohengrin*.

At the Friedrichstrasse station there was an irksome hiatus as the train was rearranged. German Schlafwagen were coupled to the French sleeping-cars, a brisk locomotive of the Prussian state railways set at their head. Conductors fussed up and down the carriages dressed in uniforms like admirals. The passengers alighted to seek coffee, pastries and newspapers.

It could have happened to any traveller. About to climb back on the train, the Maharajah clutched his precious valise. Next second he looked down – it had been filleted by a deft butcher's cut. The money, the passport, the letters – everything had gone.

Why the robbery was effected remains a mystery. Cyon thought the reason 'To a greater or lesser extent political. Luckily for the

Maharajah, he had several thousand more francs, and his precious jewels escaped the thieves, of whom one was apprehended a year later at Budapest. He was associated with a group of international pick-pockets, but we never found out what happened to him afterwards.'

Patrick Casey later thought the robbery was the work of English agents. Perhaps it was the German Secret Service – both would have a reason to hobble the Maharajah. Just as probable is that the Hungarian master pickpocket chose the Emperor's birthday as a good day to go dipping at a crowded Berlin railway station.*

The police were summoned and statements taken. The Berlin detective must have been baffled: why was Herr Casey an Indian gentleman? Ada sulked. Duleep evidently telegraphed Cyon in Paris who told him to abandon the mission. What was the Maharajah to do? He had once got as far as Aden; now he was adrift in the heart of another hostile empire. But the Guru had predicted it thus: 'Deep Singh, after becoming dispossessed of all he had inherited, residing in a foreign land, will return but that before the latter comes to pass Deep Singh will suffer much persecution and will be reduced to absolute poverty.

'The Gooroo further predicts that Deep Singh will marry a Christian wife, and his children by her the Gooroo calls "Englishmen" in the prophecy.

'The Gooroo foretells that there will be a war between the two dogs Boochoo and Dultoo.'

The Maharajah had been robbed of a fortune. The Christian 'wife' was at his side. The dogs of war were snarling across Europe.

It was his destiny. They caught the next train east.


## Gatchina, 22 March 1887

The Czar was at the imperial country estate outside St Petersburg on the evening of the 22nd, gloomily hosting a family dinner in honour of the Kaiser's birthday. He was unaware, of course, that Mr and Mrs

---

* The thief was caught. The *Standard* reported from Vienna on 14 May 1887: 'The St Petersburg Correspondent mentioned some time ago that when the Maharajah Duleep Singh was travelling between Paris and St Petersburg, his bag, containing five hundred pounds in notes, four hundred and ninety-eight sovereigns, and three thousand francs, was stolen. I learn from Pesth that the thief has been arrested today in the person of one Wilhelm Belics.'

Casey were clanking up the line from Berlin towards them. De Giers had been invited; protocol demanded it. Conversation was stilted. The Russian foreign minister knew something extraordinary the Czar did not. He told Sir Robert Morier about it the next day. The latter reported the conversation to Lord Salisbury in a long dispatch. 'M. de Giers was evidently deeply depressed. He feared that there was grave evil looming,' said the ambassador. 'He had received notices from the various European capitals, and London among them, to the effect that great activity existed among the nihilist leaders there. A very distinct warning had reached him that the attempt on the 13th of March was merely "an affair of *tirailleurs*" which would shortly be followed by more serious operations and that the Czar was doomed.'

De Giers reportedly had sat at the imperial dinner table with 'the telegrams containing this intelligence in his pocket; but that seeing the perfect tranquillity and cheerfulness prevailing in the august domestic circle, he had not been able to bring himself to communicate the news to His Majesty'. The Czar was doomed and did not know it, but De Giers, the British ambassador and Lord Salisbury did.

## *Verjbolovo, German–Russian frontier, 23 March 1887*

The Nord Express steamed on across darkening East Prussia with its red-brick farms, gaslit towns and Lutheran spires. There was a short break at Edytkouhnen on the German side. The little station was heavily fortified. Troop trains laden with spike-helmeted soldiers waited in specially-built sidings. The martial sight must have been inspiring. Just as he had done to make landfall at Aden, Mr Casey evidently decided to don his Maharajah's finery. Russia was just one mile away. He would enter in style.

The Czarist empire guarded its frontiers as resolutely as did its Soviet inheritors. The bureaucratic rigours of the crossing at Verjbolovo were a legend among seasoned travellers. M. Tastevin's guide for voyagers advised: 'A properly visaed passport is essential to enter Russia, all baggage will be inspected at the frontier. The traveller may import three livres of gold or silver objects, a dozen gloves, 100 cigars, articles necessary for an art or trade, atlases and guides but all other publications will be sent to the state censor and forwarded if permitted later. It is unadvisable to change money at the border, better to send letters of credit to the banks of Moscow or St Petersburg.'

The train hissed to a halt. An officer of the frontier gendarmerie shouted 'passe-ports'. The whole trainload decamped into a huge gaslit shed, shepherded by gendarmes in their grey-and-red uniforms, booted and spurred, sabres and Smith & Wesson (Russian-Pattern) pistols at their sides. All baggage was strewn on a ramp for intimate inspection. Security was tight after the March 1/13 *attentat* – and there were plenty of rumours of another.

A senior frontier policeman sat at a raised desk, his rubber stamp sniffing the air for enemies of the state. The Maharajah, Ada and Arur shuffled forward. The dogs, fashionably dressed in embroidered winter coats, growled. 'My name is Monsieur Casey, I have important friends in Moscow – unfortunately I have lost my passport.'

I discovered two separate but interweaving accounts of what happened next. The first was from a Captain B. M. Kays of the Northumberland Fusiliers, a soldier-spy reporting a conversation he had a year later with the Russian General Lessar. Lt-Gen. Henry Brackenbury, the director of military intelligence, thought it important enough to send to Lord Salisbury: 'Referring to Duleep Singh, M. Lessar told me that he arrived at the Russian frontier with no passport but accompanied by a native and a lot of dogs. He had £20,000 with him,' the captain reported. 'Those on the frontier took him for a strolling acrobat, and it was not till after detaining him, that permission was received allowing him to go on to Moscow where the proprietor of a newspaper took him up. Lessar says he should be of no use to the Russians as he is not clever enough, in fact they think him an ass.'

The second account was from Cyon: 'On 23 March, I was informed in a telegram from Werzbolowo [by "the banker Greenberg" presumably] that M. Casey who was travelling with a retinue had arrived at the Russian frontier without a ticket, money, passport or papers; he said that his wallet had been stolen on Berlin station when he was boarding the train! The authorities wanted to send him back to the German frontier, but he made reference to me, assuring them that he had possessed letters of introduction from me to Katkov and many dignitaries in St Petersburg; the Chief of Police had therefore allowed him to stay at the station for twenty-four hours to wait for my reply.'

The strolling acrobats would have been quite comfortable. The frontier station had a commodious restaurant which was 'cool and airy – with chairs of clean white wood – the display of viands is perfection and the tea is as fragrant and refreshing as nectar,' wrote a contemporary British traveller. His only complaint was that the bookstall, 'in charge of a very pretty young girl', stocked only Russian publications 'apart from one novel by Zola'.

Ada moaned and whined at the Maharajah as their fate was being decided over thousands of miles of telegraph wire. Cyon in Paris was very busy: he cabled Katkov in Moscow telling him Casey was Duleep Singh and sent another cable to General Gresser, St Petersburg chief of police, riding a tide of imperial favour after his last-minute confounding of the 13 March *attentat*.

'Prince Dolgorouki, Governor-General of Moscow, promptly telegraphed an order to the frontier to allow Patrick Casey and his suite to freely enter Russia,' Cyon recorded. 'Great was the amazement of Werzebolowo's authorities because no such order had ever been given before.' Not once in his account of Duleep's journey does the doctor mention General Evgenii Bogdanovich.

'At Werzebolowo station, with the strange allure of a Hindu Prince, he was taken to be a magician,' Cyon continued, 'travelling with a fortune-teller [*une somnambule*]\* and a professional strong man; two finely dressed-up dogs seemed to confirm this idea, and it became a certainty when discovered within the prince's suitcases were his rich oriental costumes of which the gems were thought to be imitation.

'How could Katkov and I take such a lively interest in a troupe of English mountebanks? The station employees didn't understand at all.'

As Duleep faced down the Russian frontier police, Lord Cross was in the India Office telegraph room cabling the Viceroy. '7.25 pm: Private and strictly confidential. Duleep Singh has left Paris for St Petersburg. F.O. have means of information and wish us to take no steps here or in India to watch him. You shall be kept informed. His son is at Sandhurst and quite loyal.'

Patrick Casey's Travelling Circus was through the wire. As evening darkened into night, a bell rang in the waiting room. From a siding

---

\* Cyon's reference picked up on the fashion among Frenchmen of the late 1880s to embark on affairs with circus-girls. In Huysmans' novel *À rebours*, the hero, Des Esseintes, falls in love with a muscular female acrobat.

clanked a spark-spewing monster, a wood-burning Russian locomotive. With its soup tureen smokestack and outsize cow-catcher it would have been as at home on the Chesapeake and Ohio railroad as in the Grand Duchy of Lithuania. At the frontier the calendar went back twelve days and the track gauge widened by 89 millimetres, a precaution ordered by Czar Nicholas I against invasion.

The magician and the fortune-teller settled into a strange new universe. In the dark beyond steamed-up windows, the brick farms of Prussia gave way to wooden huts. The mahogany-lined Russian sleeping-car with its duck-down mattresses was warm and comfortable. The charcoal-fuelled samovar perfumed the air. Linen-bloused waiters served vodka and tea beneath candlelight. Late snowfall muffled the clanking progress of the wheels. They made love.* Duleep and Ada spent another night in the capacious, broad-gauged train (other Western travellers reported an absence of plugs in the wash-basins, a persistent Russian phenomenon) rolling north-east at twenty miles an hour towards the great city on the Neva. Dawn broke pink and grey over a landscape of birch, conifer and frosted heather. It might have been Thetford Chase in winter. They rumbled through Gatchina, with its ornate station like a miniature imperial palace, guards blinking into wakeful duty. An hour later they could see the gilded spires of St Petersburg.

---

* Ada bore a daughter nine months later.

# Part Two

'DO NOT travel in Russia without having your passport in perfect order.
   Do not talk politics'

*Advice to continental travellers:*
London, Chatham and Dover Railway Co. Timetable, 1887

# 22

# A Beautiful Friendship

*Hotel de l'Europe, St Petersburg, 26 March 1887*

THE NORD EXPRESS arrived in the imperial capital after its journey from the frontier and expired in a final fiery exhalation of woodsparks. When Mr and Mrs Casey stepped on to the platform of the Warsawa station, this time there was no tap on the shoulder from a servant of the English Crown. Instead M. Shatoukin, a minder from the *Moscow Gazette*, welcomed them to St Petersburg and steered them towards waiting winter-stained droshkies with friendly words. He spoke English well; his wife came from England, where they went on holiday every year.

Duleep and Ada settled into the luxuriously modern Hotel de l'Europe on the Nevskii Prospekt with its French chef, hydraulic lifts and hot baths. The Maharajah telegraphed de Cyon in Paris with the triumphant news of his arrival.

Slush enveloped the city, blinking into sub-Arctic spring. The Neva's thawing ice heaved and cracked, pushing out towards the Gulf of Finland. De Giers brooded at the foreign ministry, sensing his own imminent departure from the river's banks as Katkov prepared to sweep into the capital to meet 'the traveller'. But this was Russia, where events proceeded on their own glacial course. A message arrived at the Hotel de l'Europe that the Maharajah should proceed at once to Moscow. There was renewed upheaval. Monsieur and Madame Casey plus Arur Singh boarded yet another train to transit overnight the 400-mile Nikolai line aiming famously arrow-straight for Moscow, so it was said, because the railway-enthusiast Czar, Nicholas I, had drawn it that way on a surveyor's map.

The Foreign Office spymasters were baffled as they read Our

Correspondent's dispatch of 30 March. The Paris mole was obviously standing by Cyon's shoulder as he received Duleep's news. Mr Francis Villiers informed Mr William J. Maitland, private secretary to the Secretary of State for India, of its contents: 'A telegram was received on the 26th instant from Duleep Singh announcing his arrival at St Petersburg. He was staying at the Hotel de l'Europe, and Katkov was expected from Moscow. I see that Katkov's arrival at St Petersburg was announced in yesterday's papers. Another telegram [the one sent to Cyon] dated the 27th Sunday, announces Duleep Singh's arrival at Moscow, so he must have received orders to leave St Petersburg very soon after his arrival there.'

Plans had changed. Rather than storming the imperial palace with Duleep at his side, Katkov had decided to get the Maharajah to the safety of Moscow to await the moment of triumph. He had already unsuccessfully tried to hold him at the border.

Our Correspondent found the move 'logical'. 'Katkov has gone to finish up with the dismissal of de Giers,' he reported, 'and the presence of Duleep Singh might be used by the German party, the anti-Katkovs, to prevent a change of foreign policy, and holding out encouragement to a pretender would be synonymous with a renewal of the era of foreign complications.* I am furthermore inclined to this view by the contents of a telegram from Katkov to Gruneberg at Wirdballen [the border station] received too late to be acted upon in which I read: "Stop the traveller for a time: the moment unfavourable".'†

The moment was certainly sensitive. Katkov had been pushing his feud with de Giers with a gambler's recklessness. Morier described the situation in St Petersburg to Lord Salisbury in a cable of 26 March as a 'journalistic coup d'etat ... by one consumed with vanity and ambition who has thrown down the gauntlet to the Emperor himself'.

This time Katkov had gone too far. The revelation of the existence of the Dreikaiserbund had enraged the Czar. He minuted on a copy on the *Imperial Review* (a summary of press reports prepared by the chief censor): 'If he has learned of this it was only from a traitor.

* The pan-Slavist-animated expansionist policy which led to the Russo-Turkish war, buried by the 'treacherous' Treaty of Berlin. The phrase would come back into the Soviet political lexicon.
† I have been unable to discover how Our Correspondent was reading an internal Russian telegram. It must have been copied to Cyon in Paris.

Katkov plays the role of some kind of <u>dictator</u> forgetting that foreign policy depends on me. I command you to give Katkov a warning . . . in order to subdue the madness that surrounds this matter.'

The reprimand was never given. Constantin Pobedonostsev was at Gatchina to tutor the Czarevitch, the future Nicholas II. He persuaded the Czar that a 'warning' to the errant ultra-conservative would only help the hated liberal cause. Katkov instead got a private rebuke and an invitation to the imperial country estate for a cosy *tête-à-tête* on 25 March.

Katkov again volubly expressed his opinions, the Czar 'agreed with them' but explained that, for now, de Giers was a necessary evil. Russia was not ready for war. 'Why not go and see de Giers at the Singer's Bridge,' the Emperor suggested, 'and persuade him you are right. They will receive you if I wish it.'

Katkov had another matter to discuss – one of great sensitivity. He placed a file on the imperial desk – the one that had survived its adventures at the Berlin post office. Czar Alexander III picked up a covering letter with its lion and crown crest and embossed address in gothic lettering: Elveden Hall, Thetford, Norfolk. Of course he recognized the sender – the Indian rajah, the friend of the Prince of Wales whom he had met on a visit to England in May 1874, a splendid fellow; let him come to Russia. He wrote a margin note on the letter: 'In any case, it is necessary to give him an answer.'

Cyon recorded in his memoirs: 'Katkov gave the Emperor, Maharajah Duleep Singh's dossier which I had just sent him. At Katkov's representation the Czar authorised the ex-King of Lahore to come and live in Russia. This authorisation, which the Minister of Foreign Affairs had obstinately refused for two years, marked a new victory by Katkov over his rival.'

The triumph seemed complete. The *Berlin Post* thundered on 29 March: 'Is the seat of the Russian Government now the ministerial bureaux of St Petersburg or the office of the *Moscow Gazette*?' This was a creeping coup mounted by a newspaper. The press baron was mutating into a press czar.

## Hotel Dussaux, Kitaisky Prospekt, Moscow, April 1887

The travelling circus rumbled overnight across northern Russia to the old capital, Katkov's town, the citadel of pan-Slavist ambition. Mr and Mrs Casey were hastily conveyed on the night of 27 March from the Nikolevsky station to M. Shatoukin's recommended hotel, the 'Dussaux'. It was not Moscow's grandest, according to M. Tastevin's useful guide, but '*bien tenu*' rooms could be had, from 1.5 roubles a night.

Herr Miersch, the German-born proprietor, was perplexed; there was no passport to be surrendered. Every foreigner in Moscow had to have a passport but an inspector came the next day from the prefecture of police with reassuring words – and there seemed to be plenty of jewels to go into the hotel safe.

There was no French chef at the Dussaux. The Muscovite menu was unfamiliar but princely enough: *ikra* (fresh caviare) and *outka* (wild duck). Ada toyed with the *schee* – cabbage soup with sour cream. Duleep might have enjoyed a steam bath at the next-door Tsentralya Bani, richly tiled in the eastern taste, as Mrs Casey attended to her toilette in the confines of her bedroom. Ada seems to have been ordered to lie low.

On 31 March, a source in the interior ministry first relayed to de Giers news of 'a strange group of people's arrival in Moscow'. There was no sign of them. The Caseys stayed in the hotel, waiting for instructions, with one very necessary outing by Duleep to open a bank account at Zenkers and Co. round the corner on Roshdestvenski Boulevard. He also located the telegraph office on Mjassnizkaya street, open day and night. For a year it would function as the command headquarters of his rebellion. Cables to France cost 18 kopecks a word. He had plenty of money. On 3 April the Maharajah sent a one-line message to Cyon in Paris: 'We return to St Petersburg tomorrow. Letter of credit safe. All progressing so far satisfactorily.' Cyon told Our Correspondent who told London.

Francis Villiers commented on the intelligence: 'It appears therefore that Duleep Singh has been recalled by the authorities, or by Katkov who is still at St Petersburg. The letter of credit mentioned is made out in his own name. [He had obviously made a transfer from Mallet

Frères.] We do not recommend any action at present. We shall learn what happens at St Petersburg and be able to follow his movements. It will be best to let the matter develop further.'

Lord Salisbury meanwhile was receiving very secret intelligence on another matter. The rumour of another attempt on the Czar's life was 'devoid of all foundation', Morier cabled on 1 April. It had indeed emanated from Berlin – an apparent attempt by someone to make a killing on the stock market.

The consultations in Whitehall on the Maharajah meanwhile became more fevered – had they taken a huge risk in not 'recommending any action'? 'De Giers' influence is waning and though his resignation has not been accepted his elimination is merely a question of opportunity,' noted Mr Villiers on 8 April. The Paris correspondent agreed, messaging on the 15th: 'The Katkov versus de Giers quarrel, is I know, not settled. Katkov is not out of favour as is supposed from the reports of ignorant journalists. It is probable that, not being ready to unmask, the Russians will not at once give the pretender that effective aid which he hopes for, but he will be allowed at least to locate himself in a neighbourhood where he can be used if and when wanted.'

There was a parallel development. Colonel Boutourline, military attaché at the Russian embassy in Chesham Place had lately crossed the Channel 'to confer respecting Duleep Singh', it was noted in the spy's dispatch of 8 April. The colonel would later be mentioned by HM Foreign Secret Service as demanding that 'all communications concerning Irish matters be addressed through him as they were the responsibility of the Minister of War'.

The colonel obviously sought out Elie de Cyon in Paris. The spy reported on 23 April: 'Colonel Boutourline has again been over in Paris on orders received from Russia making a report of the status of the Maharajah orally. "He stated to [blank]: The Prince has left many debts in London and been involved in all sorts of *frasques* [escapades], but he is a power that could be utilised."'

The Foreign Office evidently had someone in the Russian capital primed to pick up the Maharajah's trail. But Duleep, unwittingly, outfoxed them. He did not leave Moscow as he had told his Paris confidantes he would. M. Shatoukin, the emissary from the *Moscow Gazette*, turned up again at the Hotel Dussaux on the afternoon of

3 April with instructions to wait for Katkov's return from St Petersburg. But, even more confusingly, Our Correspondent had failed to report the Casey passport switch to his Foreign Office masters. This omission was about to cause two weeks of high diplomatic farce.

Sir Robert Morier telegraphed Lord Salisbury on 6 April that a rumour had reached him that a certain 'Paul Casey, apparently of good position accompanied by his wife, and by a native of India (of the name of Sing-a-poor or something like it) arrived on or about the 25th of March at the Hotel d'Europe in this City, but only remained one day, proceeding immediately to Moscow.' What was he to do?

The Foreign Office sent Sir Robert's message on to Lord Cross, Secretary of State for India, with an explanation: 'Not much doubt as to who Mr. Casey is! Our Correspondent did not tell us that Duleep Singh had taken that name, but it appears from the first of the two attached newspaper extracts that he did so, at any rate, when he was robbed.' (These were the reports of the apparent-Irishman's embarrassments with the Berlin detectives.)

In St Petersburg, Sir Robert was still baffled. 'Is Casey the well-known Fenian?' he telegraphed London on the morning of 14 April. 'He pretends to have lost passport, but Singh has one under name of Arur from Lord Lyons, no. 73 of March last. I think it very desirable I should be able to tell M. de Giers who these people are.'

The cipher messages flew backwards and forwards throughout the long day. St Petersburg was three hours ahead of London, where there was a crisis meeting that morning at the Foreign Office. It was judged very important that de Giers should be kept in the dark, 'as it might attract attention, perhaps arouse suspicion'. In fact, it would show Whitehall to be either involved in the conspiracy or grossly incompetent. Sir Robert was informed at midday (London time): 'Person mentioned in your despatch is Duleep Singh. We are aware that he is at St Petersburg. Do not make further enquiries or take any action without instructions . . .

'Not desirable you should have any communication whatever with M. de Giers about Duleep. If questioned, you can say you have not received reply to your despatch,' Francis Villiers messaged. 'Letter by next messenger giving you further explanation.'

It was too late. Sir Robert had already been blundering around the Russian capital like a mammoth in an aquarium. That afternoon he cabled back to London apologetically: 'I have already notified privately to M. de Giers [he had done so that morning, the 14th] that Patrick Casey and Singh, whom I did not know to be Duleep, were at Moscow, protected by and having daily intercourse with Katkov.'

The ambassador got it so wrong because he had already bumblingly embarked on some freelance intelligence-gathering of his own in the old Russian capital. Mr August Weber, the acting British vice-consul in Moscow, had been ordered five days earlier to find Mr and Mrs Casey. On Saturday the 9th he had sidled round from the consulate on Petrovsky Boulevard 'to take lunch' at the Hotel Dussaux, where he encountered Arur Singh. 'The Hindoo asked me whether I would like to see Mr. Casey,' Mr Weber reported, 'to which I replied in case any assistance were required, I should do my best to aid him. With this message Arur went upstairs and shortly returned to tell me that Mr. Casey would be glad to see me.'

The acting vice-consul scaled the Dussaux's ominous stairs. 'I was introduced to a man of some 48 years of age about 5ft 5in in stature, of a sallow, darkish and unhealthy complexion,' he reported, 'who received me amiably and spoke at length about the way he was robbed of his satchel, but upon my offer whether I could help him with regard to his lost passport, he showed me a Russian police permit according to which he was at liberty to stay or travel at his pleasure.'

Mr Weber could not tell a Punjabi from a Kilkenny man. Having met the last King of Lahore he had informed his ambassador: 'In my opinion he is the man who in 1881 or 1882 was the receiver of the funds sent from the United States to Ireland by the Irish Fenians.' That is exactly what Sir Robert had told de Giers in his 'private note' (written in French) delivered to Singer's Bridge on the morning of 14 April before London woke up – adding of Mr Casey the 'well-known revolutionary' and his mysterious companion Mr Singh: 'I am convinced we must deal with two very dangerous individuals, of which the connection with Mr. Katkov is to say the least . . . very dubious.

'How and why the protection of the great Moscow journalist was afforded is one thing, but how this protection was extended between Wiedballen [Verjbolovo] and St Petersburg, intrigues me to very high degree,' added Sir Robert. 'It's now up to M. Gresser [the police chief who was already in on the Nord Express border-dodge] to find out the truth. In any case it seems my duty, especially in matters of international mischief-making, to warn you confidentially of anything my government knows.'

'*We* must deal' with these dangerous individuals,' Sir Robert had privately confided to the Russian foreign minister. A beautiful friendship was in the making.

The runaway King of Lahore and his truculent girlfriend would have made terrific copy but the Russian press of 1887 was not interested in human-interest headlines. Katkov wanted something. In the stifled, decaying polity of imperial Russia even ultra-conservatives sought change. There were those who craved war, a victorious flexing of pan-Slav muscle. There were others who wanted war because they knew Russia would *lose*. The boy-king Duleep had lost the throne of Lahore because of such a plot. Could it really be happening again?

Sir Robert Morier thought so. He told Lord Salisbury in a dispatch sent the day the Maharajah boarded the Nord Express. 'There are two main streams making for war . . . a radical party, quite distinct from the slavophils, who believe that a war, better still, an *unfortunate* war, would necessarily be followed by a break-up of the present system. The other stream is the national one, that of the party which believes that a great crusade would not fail to be successful.'

Just whose interests was the Maharajah serving? On 12 April the Russian Secret Service intercepted and sent direct to the Czar a telegram from Berlin to the German embassy in St Petersburg. It relayed a Paris-derived report just received about Cyon. The Czar sent it to de Giers. It stated that Cyon 'was a dangerous revolutionary', supposed to have said in French parliamentary circles that he was 'working for a German war with Russia because Russia would be *defeated* and thus the Czar would be forced to grant a constitution'.

The reply next day from Von Bulow, the German chargé d'affaires in the Russian capital, was even more extraordinary. Cyon was 'a mendacious and venal Jew with revolutionary tendencies', he told Berlin, and 'close to Katkov'. But this meant that the editor was either mad or a secret revolutionary. Czar Alexander III minuted on the intercept in his own hand: 'The Germans really hate Katkov don't they . . .'

It was Saturday 16 April, Easter Eve, the spiritual climax of the Russian year. It was the custom that decorations were dispensed in the long hours before the great service which marked the end of Lent. At the foreign ministry de Giers waited for an imperial sign, the rumoured delivery of the Cross of St Vladimir. There would be a ball at Singer's Bridge on the Tuesday to celebrate the honour.

At midnight, the paschal solemnities were celebrated in the chapel of the Winter Palace. The imperial couple had arrived from Gatchina. De Giers, a Lutheran, was not invited. He and his faithful aide Count Lamsdorf stayed up all night in the deserted ministry. No honour-bearing messenger came. A diplomatic reception at the British embassy three days later brought even deeper humiliation.

'Sir Robert Morier took a rather high tone, after a dinner in which generous amounts of wine had been imbibed,' according to Cyon. 'Surrounded by diplomats and high officials, he suddenly announced his imminent departure for Moscow.' The ambassador told the glittering company that he had just written to Queen Victoria to ask for: 'Authorisation to place myself in Moscow alongside Katkov. One no longer knows here to whom one should be talking politically. M. de Giers doesn't speak either for the Russian people, or, as we have just had proof, for the Czar.'*

The remarks congealed the room. De Giers was losing allies fast. Even the British ambassador (however bibulous) seemed to be turning against him.

On Easter Sunday, General Orzhevskii, the head of the secret police who had been hugely incensed at the way the Casey stunt had been pulled at the border, suddenly 'retired' after losing the long-running internal power battle with General Gresser, chief of police in St Petersburg. What could save the apostle of peace? De Giers needed a weapon to take the fight to Katkov. It had already arrived, accompanied by an English girl and several dogs, on a train from Paris.

That same Easter Eve, as de Giers waited in vain for the imperial honour, the Maharajah Duleep Singh and Mikhail Katkov met for the first time in the editor's apartment next to the offices of the *Moscow Gazette* on the Strastnyi Boulevard. The Sikh and the Russian embraced in a hugely bearded kiss.

---

* Queen Victoria had her doubts of the Balliol-educated Sir Robert. She told her daughter: 'He is untruthful I am certain and gossips in society – he is a bad diplomatist.'

Duleep, so deferential to his imperial majesty of the moment, was enraptured by the patriarchal figure. He wrote to Cyon in high excitement:

> At last, yesterday, I had my first interview with the 'Great Man' who returned from St Petersburg the day before.
>
> K. is indeed a wonderful man – old yet young. Full of courtesy, and possessing a kind heart.
>
> He received me with interest, kindness and great courtesy, and we parted with a kiss. K. said that when he mentioned my name, the Emperor at once recollected my having been presented to him by the Prince of Wales and was much pleased and gratified with my letter, which K. himself placed in his hands.
>
> However K. added that the Foreign Office was much opposed to my wishes, but he had taken care to place my affairs in the hands of influential friends before leaving St Petersburg, whither he will return in the course of a few days. He said that a reply will come in a week or ten days.
>
> Of course it was useless to talk to him about anything further till I know the views of the Imperial Government, though he seemed sanguine about the result. I suppose when K. returns to St Petersburg I shall accompany him, and will be there introduced to his friends who take an interest in my mission if not presented at Court.
>
> So far, therefore, you will agree with me, my friend, that everything has proceeded as well (indeed far better than) one could have possibly expected. But for the incident of the loss of money, nothing one could have expected better . . .
>
> I have written to my faithful Abdul Rasul to join me at once, as it may become necessary to send him forward immediately.

The letter was signed simply, 'Casey'.

Katkov was as enamoured as Duleep. The next day, Easter Sunday, the editor swept round to the Hotel Dussaux for more wildly fantastical talks. It was going wonderfully; there was no need for incognitos, it was time to unmask. Duleep wrote to Cyon that night, 17 April: 'I am much pleased, and if you should write you can now address me in my proper name. I am also now to prepare a statement in connection with affairs of India (which I have already talked over with you) to be placed before the Emperor. No other steps at present are to be taken. I can not tell you how happy I feel now, and thank you and [blank] for getting me into Russia. The rest must remain in the hands of Providence.

'The English resident here [August Weber the vice-consul] and the Embassy think that I am Casey who was connected with affairs in Ireland some time back. It is very amusing. Monsieur K. said it was not at all necessary to hide my name. But I told him that I could not have obtained the passport at all otherwise.

'Please ask [blank = Cyon] to forward my Box containing papers as soon as possible as I can not prepare a satisfactory statement without these.'

The letter took six days to reach France. It was not for Elie de Cyon to bear the Maharajah's Box to Moscow – the doctor had already once again taken the train east. The climax of the Katkov–de Giers struggle was very close. Cyon wanted to be there to see the German alliance buried.


At the end of April, Fleet Street began to wake up to a sensational story: Runaway Rebel King in Russia. They found Duleep and they found Arur – but no one as yet had found Ada. At first all was fantastic confusion. 'The Mysterious Strangers in St Petersburg', ran the *Daily Chronicle* headline on 26 April. 'The Irishman spoken of as having seen M. Katkov, and as having obtained a safe conduct to penetrate to Afghanistan, is a Mr Patrick Casey. He is the same individual who was recently robbed of 30,000 francs under somewhat extraordinary circumstances, at a railway station in Berlin. The Hindu companion is simply Mr. Casey's valet, and is a coloured man, who has been passing in Paris as a dispossessed Indian Prince.'

The *Standard*'s peppery St Petersburg correspondent, John Baddeley, worked out who one of the party was, explaining to the London paper's readers on 28 April: 'With Duleep Singh and his friend Patrick Casey in Russia, a distinction must be made between the attitude of the Emperor and M. de Giers on the one side and M. Katkov and the

Muscovites on the other. If the Moscow journalist who unseats ministers just as easily as Warwick uncrowned Kings sets the constituted authorities at defiance, the latter must answer for the results and bear the blame.

'Duleep is an enemy to the British Government, but he travels with a genuine passport issued in Paris. If M. Katkov likes to interview him, as he has done repeatedly, no open objection can be raised, but the same cannot be said about Patrick Casey [the *Standard*'s favourite Fenian bogey-man]. Why was this person allowed to enter Russia without a passport contrary to the stringent regulations that Russian ministers themselves declare must not be relaxed on any pretence whatever?'

Why indeed. A very serious incident was brewing. Who was running Russian foreign policy? The 'Fenian–Afghan–Katkov' conspiracy was the only diplomatic talking point in town. Why were Irish dynamiters and rebellious Maharajahs apparently wandering freely around Moscow?

On 27 April Lord Salisbury ordered no more dissembling. Morier should tell de Giers it was Duleep Singh who was in Moscow, and express the 'very serious view Her Majesty's Government would take should the Maharajah be allowed to make any move towards Central Asia'.

The Russian foreign minister seemed as confused as the ambassador when they met in St Petersburg on 30 April. De Giers was 'annoyed and perplexed at the anomalous position in which this extraordinary, I might almost say grotesque, incident had placed him,' Sir Robert reported. 'He had entirely failed to ascertain by whose assistance Duleep Singh has crossed the frontier.'

Sir Robert told him: 'I had heard that the culprit was General Bogdanovich.' He knew because Our Correspondent had told Her Majesty's Foreign Secret Service of the fact on Tuesday, 22 March, as the Maharajah and Ada were trundling on the Nord Express towards Berlin.

Sir Robert asked whether the general 'would have sufficient authority to enable a friend patronized by him to enter Russia without a passport'.

'He might; strange to say,' de Giers replied. 'He [Bogdanovich] had succeeded in getting himself attached to the ministry of the interior as some sort of inspector of railways and as such he would be known to the police, both on the frontier and elsewhere.'*

Sir Robert's scrap of information – 'the culprit was Bogdanovich' – would turn out to be intelligence gold.

---

* The railway gendarmerie was controlled by the interior ministry not the ministry of war.

# 23

# The Ambassador

THE MAHARAJAH HAD unmasked and was strutting round Moscow in oriental pomp. It was May Day – not yet an auspicious date in the Russian revolutionary's calendar. In Paris, Madame Adam's circle was triumphant; Duleep's very presence in the empire was a symbol of the hated German party's humiliation. In St Petersburg, Sir Robert Morier and the foreign minister were now working in concert, the British ambassador to stop Duleep reaching India, the Russian to stop Katkov's creeping coup. Maybe, maybe, de Giers clung to the thought, the conspirators had gone too far with the magician and the fortune-teller, Monsieur and Madame Dynamitard.

Mr August Weber meanwhile was still snooping round the Hotel Dussaux, talking to chambermaids and trying to buttonhole Duleep's servant. He reported on 3 May: 'The Maharajah went last night to Mr Katkov's house in full Indian dress with the Star of India on his breast and adorned with precious stones – this took place at 9.00 p.m. He was accompanied by the Sardar Aroor Singh in a black dress with turban, driving in a carriage. The Sardar told me their further stay at Moscow would depend on the movement of the Russians in Central Asia – especially their movements towards Herat. Future events may justify any precautions that may be taken in consequence to counterbalance that sort of game.'

Ada seemed to be emerging from her hotel room purdah. There were little shopping trips to 'The English Magazine' on Kouanetsky Bridge to buy marmalade and Twinings tea, and a visit to the portrait studio of M. Daziaro, the fashionable photographer. A sharp-eyed reporter noted: 'The Maharajah is accompanied by a young lady of about twenty years of age with an unmistakable London accent – for whom he has bought a sewing machine.'

Sir Robert Morier and de Giers met the next day, 4 May, at the foreign ministry. There was a big agenda to get through. The ambassador informed Salisbury about the meeting in the first of two dispatches sent that same day: 'My Lord. I asked M. de Giers today what was the truth as to the reported intention of the Emperor to visit the Don Cossack country. He replied that His Majesty intended to go there, but that for obvious reasons it was necessary to keep the matter absolutely secret till he left.

'In the course of conversation His Excellency referred to the continued threats of attempts on the Emperor's life, and he has shown me a very secret report which he has recently received from the Minister of the Interior. This report averted specially to a conspiracy being prepared in London, the persons engaged in which had declared that the next attempt on the Emperor would be made with the certainty of success in about two months time.'*

The ambassador's second dispatch on 4 May concerned both bomb-plots and the Maharajah. He told Lord Salisbury:

> I saw M. de Giers again today and asked him what answer I was to return to your Lordship's telegram [that of 27 April about stopping Duleep reaching Central Asia]. He had seen the Emperor and would therefore, he said, be in a position to give me a reply.
>
> His Majesty appears to have been very angry at his police not having been aware of what had happened and observed

---

* For once Scotland Yard was brought into the affair. Sir James Monro, the assistant commissioner, was sent highly selective information by Sir Julian Pauncefote on the 'London bomb-plot' reported by de Giers and asked to investigate. Monro produced a report for the Home Secretary a week later, on 14 May, which concluded. 'I am *not* aware of any plot being carried out in London concerning the life of the Czar.' There was no London bomb.

The Monro report was confided to de Giers on Lord Salisbury's sanction. 'I am in the sad position of being unable to see you before your trip to the country because of an attack of gout,' the ambassador wrote on 31 May. 'I received yesterday the enclosed report from the chief of the [British] secret police. I beg to you to regard this communication as extremely confidential. You will see there is no evidence of a conspiracy against the life of the Czar . . .'

The rest of the letter is missing. A Foreign Office historian noted that the St Petersburg embassy letter-books were left in a waterlogged cupboard after the Bolshevik revolution of 1917, brought to Moscow, then evacuated to the Urals to escape the advancing German Army in 1941.

that it was odd that the British Ambassador should have a better police than he himself in his own capital, an occasion which M. de Giers improved by remarking that a nihilist might easily come in by similar means.

Where I am strongly inclined to believe, M. de Giers met with opposition was from the Ministry of the Interior, not that I believe that Count Tolstoi is for one moment aiding and abetting M. Katkov in his intrigue with Duleep Singh because he is an obstinate sort of man who never loses sight of the great grievance he considers Russia has against England, the harbouring of nihilist refugees such as Hartman.

His Excellency declared that the expulsion of the Maharajah from Russia would create a great scandal, but that he could assure me he would be watched, and that the necessary precautions would be taken to render him harmless.

He was however extremely anxious that I should not represent him as having entered into any engagement with H.M.'s Government to guarantee the innocuousness of Duleep Singh, for he said, 'With the experience we have had, who can tell what might chance to happen.'

This was the beginning of de Giers's counterstroke against Katkov and it was very clever. A plot was brewing in London, he had been informed, to assassinate the Czar in 'about two months time'. A whisper was reaching London about an Irish-American conspiracy to celebrate the Queen's approaching jubilee 'with a fireworks display' in Westminster Abbey. Two empires were in peril – they should work together.

Who had spirited 'Mr Casey', the apostle of dynamite, into Russia? The Jew Cyon. Who had pulled the switches at Verjobolo? The inspector of railways, General Evgenii Bogdanovich. Who had seen the Maharajah file? Tolstoi, Pobedonostsev, Ignatiev – the Katkov cabal. Let Duleep's tinpot conspiracy mature, was the unspoken agreement, it would flush out a much bigger one.

Sir Robert Morier's second report of 4 May was circulated at the India Office and drew some revealing comments. Lord Cross, the Secretary of State, minuted: 'This letter affords a singular illustration of the political condition of Russia. A panslavist General can ensure the crossing into Russia of Maharajah Duleep Singh without a passport and this is done without the knowledge of the Minister of Foreign Affairs or of the Chief of the Gendarmerie. The remarks made by M. de Giers look very much like an admission of his powerlessness.'

The choleric Major-General Sir Henry Rawlinson, chairman of the political committee, added: 'I do not share Sir R. Morier's implicit faith in M. de Gier's explanations. This supposed antagonism of the civil and military elements in the Russian administration are sometimes very convenient. All I venture to say is Crednet Judeus.'*

The Maharajah meanwhile had the little matter of an invasion of India to consider. On 1 May he sent the first in a cycle of seditious letters to his 'only private friend' in Paris. The correspondence took place over several weeks, the Russian-received component of which would later fall into the hands of the government of India in an extraordinary way. Because they reveal so much, I have repeated the letters here in sequence.

'My dear [blank],' Duleep wrote to his mysterious Parisian partisan (it could not have been to Cyon, he was in Russia):

I have not written to you sooner because there was no news to communicate. I wrote to Katkov regarding your desire to communicate to him but he was leaving for St Petersburg where he would see [blank].

He (K) will send you an answer through him on the subject. About your writing in the American newspapers he said that he had no objection but of course he said 'I do not know what the subject is', and unfortunately I could not give him the copies of my proclamation which are all in that wretched box left in Paris.

My own idea is that no steps should be taken just at this moment as it appears that the British Government and the Royal Family of England are trying very hard to get me out of Russia and any publication published by me at present would give them an excuse for saying that I was endeavouring to raise a rebellion in India.

The great thing after all was to get to Russia, and Katkov – the rest will doubtless follow in time.

* 'Don't believe the Jews' – it is not clear whom Sir Henry had in mind.

[blank] wrote to me to say that he had forwarded testimonials to the minister of war about me. They might produce a good result. Please forward the letter addressed to Abdul Rassoul as I have twice written to him from here, and he does not appear to have received any communication from me as yet.

Also get some friend of your's to post the other from England otherwise the continental postage stamp might lead the authorities in India to detain the letter which is rather an important one.*

I much regret to put you to the expense of postage stamps – and must therefore remain in your debt until we meet which I trust will not be very long hence, if Russia means to move towards India.

While Duleep worried about the cost of stamps, 'Blank' in Paris was about to drop some whopping clues as to his true identity. First he sent a copy of Duleep's 1 May letter to London – he was 'Our Correspondent'. Second, he wrote for American newspapers. He was also about to reveal a one-letter codename.

The Maharajah's May Day letter took twelve days to reach Paris. 'Blank' replied on the 15th:

Mon Prince. I had almost thought myself forgotten when your letter arrived, I posted the enclosure [to Abdul Rasul] to Constantinople and through one of my Irishmen had the other mailed in England, where you will see from the enclosed cuttings that your Russian journey had made a sensation. [This was the *Standard*'s 'Warwick the king-maker' article.]

I am quite of your opinion about the article at least so far as it regards you. The hour has not yet sounded, but is not distant. I know that in England the Government is convinced

---

* This message dated 1 May was to Lala Jhinda Ram, chasing the non-existent money offered four months before in the Paris Hotel. 'Yes my beloved countrymen, by forgetting me your faces are blackened indeed,' thundered Duleep. 'Tell my well-wishers not to get discouraged, for it will most probably be some time before I appear on the frontier of the Punjab, as the railway to Herat is not finished yet, though progressing rapidly.' Mr Ram, in fact an impecunious barrister from Multan, felt 'duty bound' to send the seditious letter to the British government.

of the inevitability of an Anglo-Russian War and fears that France may take sides with the Muscovites.

The two military parties of the Irish nationalists have drawn up a proposal for the establishment of an Irish military colony near the Indian frontier – 600 to 1,000 men engaging to attract to it 11,000 to 13,000 Irish deserters from the British army.

The colony is probably to be commanded by one of our most devoted friends, who will act as the Imperial Government of Russia may dictate, and it is suggested that, if necessary and expedient, it will be ready to march in the service of any deposed sovereign and place him on the throne.

I am waiting for M. de C. to send document, but you might refer to the matter with Katkov, for no time is to be lost. Pray write me a line on the subject.

The signature was simply 'C'.

I pored over this letter for a long time. It revealed an intimate knowledge of Irish revolutionary politics; the 'two military parties' were the Clan-na-Gael in America and the Irish Republican Brotherhood in Paris. But who was the 'devoted friend' who would command an Irish Legion 14,000 strong? Who was the 'Irishman' who could pop over to London to post seditious messages to India? 'C' could not be Cyon as he was referred to separately in the letter. Nor could he be Casey, who was also to be spoken of in the third person in the cycle of seditious correspondence, in a postscript to the Maharajah's reply.

The 'C letter' reached the Hotel Dussaux on 18 May. The Maharajah replied joyfully:

My dear [blank].

I received your letter yesterday and am greatly cheered by it. It would be really a great thing if what you say about the establishment of an Irish colony on the Indian frontier could be brought about.

For then you and I alone without the aid of the Imperial Government would throw the English out of India, as all the Indian Princes would join us with their armies in the enterprise.

Mr. K is still at St Petersburg and consequently I have been delaying from day to day writing to you, having no news to communicate. It is not easy to see him, even when he is here, and I find it a better plan to write to him so he then has the matter before him in writing to consider, than to converse with him on the subject.

I do not think that anything will be immediately taken in hand by the Imperial Govt. It appears to be quite impossible to hurry matters in this country. Besides Russia seems to be almost entirely preoccupied with Germany.

I see by the newspapers that England is trying to form an alliance with France. I pray God that she may not succeed in doing so, for were she to be successful in this matter it would greatly strengthen her and we wish her to remain isolated and weak. But what would be most disastrous, would be a political union between her and Russia and the probability of this is talked of.

Therefore you will understand how insecure my position is here, and why matters do not proceed so rapidly as you and I could wish.

I am just sending my Sikh to India with letters to the Princes. I much wish that my proclamations were published in America and copies of the journal containing them to be reproduced in the newspapers in India, as their circulation would shake to the foundation the British Empire of Hindoostan. But I think it prudent to wait until I have obtained naturalization and am certain of not being turned out of the country by the interest of the British Court.

I will write again as soon as K. returns and I have any news to communicate.

PS: A thousand thanks for the interesting cutting from the journal: How surprised and amused Mr Casey must have been when he read himself discussed in the newspapers in that manner.

PPS: The Emperor has left St Petersburg for some time therefore I do not suppose that now I shall be presented to him, but I still live in hope. I hope I have not done wrong in asking my friends in India to send replies to me under cover to you . . .

C would now be reading all the correspondence coming from Thakur Singh Sandhanwalia in Pondicherry. He sent it straight to London. He was a prince of spies.

It now seemed just a matter of time before Duleep would enter the Russian capital in Katkov's triumphal chariot. On 10 May the Maharajah addressed an exhaustive memorandum to Czar Alexander III. It was translated into Russian, and it seems that it was first taken by Katkov to the emperor in person. The whining supplicant had been transformed; this was a detailed blueprint for war.

It was informed by the detailed arguments of a political economist, a military grand strategist and an expert on guerrilla warfare. The Paris cabal had evidently worked very hard on its drafting. Turn away from the Balkans and crush the British Empire, Duleep advised. He even knew the size of the artillery train required: 2,000 cannon. Once in Russia's thrall, India would prove 'a gold-mine'. It was breath-takingly cynical in its profit and loss account. But Duleep could not resist a more mystical reference to the words of the Guru. The letter is reproduced here in full.

From Maharajah Duleep Singh to the Emperor of Russia, 10 May 1887.

Before proceeding to lay before the Imperial Government the humble prayer both of the Princes and People of India for deliverance from their oppression, I think it necessary to state here that for myself I seek no gain whatsoever, for I am a patriot and only seek to deliver some 250,000,000 of my countrymen from the cruel yoke of the British Rule and to benefit the deliverer at the same time and will serve the Imperial Government (should it think proper to employ me) without any remuneration whatsoever.

Through my cousin Sardar Thakur Singh (a man well known both in the Punjab and mostly all over India) I have been deputed by most of the powerful princes of India to come to Russia and to pray the Imperial Government to take their cause in hand.

These Princes with altogether some 300,000 soldiers in their

service are prepared to rise should the Imperial Government think proper to make an advance against the British
provided that I, their representative, be permitted to accompany the Imperial Army so as to assure them of the generous
and gracious intentions entertained towards them by the
Emperor.

For the English have taken good care to fill the minds of
the people of India (who are extremely ignorant) with false
reports as to the oppressive nature of the Russian rule, though
the British Government itself has broken solemn engagements
whenever it suited its own purposes to do so – having broken
two treaties with myself alone.

Among the many advantages that would accrue to the
Imperial Government by invasion of India are the following:

The Princes of India, when freed and if allowed to manage
their affairs in their own way, would join together and pay a
large tribute annually into the Russian Treasury. Although I
am authorised to name only £3,000,000 per annum yet in my
opinion after the settling down of the country they would
easily pay between £8,000,000 and £10,000,000. The British
raise an annual revenue from the country of some £50,000,000
and £60,000,000 sterling, out of which an army of 100,000
Europeans and Officers and English civilians (who receive very
high salaries) absorb at least £25,000,000.

The rest is employed in the administration of the country
and in the payment of interest upon capital advanced by England for the construction of railroad and upon the Public debt
of India and pensions to retired officials in England. Also the
import and export trade between England and India
amounting to some £50,000,000 per annum each way would
be secured to Russia. India is indeed a gold-mine to England
and most of her wealth has been and is derived from that
source.

I have been much struck already during my very short stay
in Russia with the low value of things in this country from
want (in my opinion) of suitable markets for their disposal.
But could the same commodities be taken to India I feel
persuaded that from 100 to 300 per cent over the prices

they fetch here would be realized for them out there. The markets of Central Asia are not to be compared with that of India.

I guarantee an easy conquest of India. For besides the promised assistance of the Princes of India with their armies, it is in my power to raise the entire Punjab in revolt and cause the inhabitants to attack in their rear, the British forces sent to oppose the Imperial army.

My loyal subjects would also destroy all railway, telegraphic, and other communication and blow up bridges and cut off all supplies while the Princes revolting would harass the British troops left behind as a reserve. England is only strong at sea but she has no army. She has only some 100,000 Europeans and about the same number of native soldiers in her service in India. Out of the latter some 45,000 men are Punjabees and who are the best soldiers that England possesses in India.

All these are loyal to me and will come over at once to the side of Russia (provided that I be permitted to accompany the Imperial Army of invasion) should they be sent to confront the Russian troops, or they will attack the opposing British forces in their rear, should these Sikhs be left behind.

Under these circumstances no British army could hold its own, however powerful it might be (which it is not), being attacked both in front and behind. It may not, perhaps, be out of place with due modesty to state here why I have some power over my countrymen and can render such invaluable services to the Imperial Government in the way described above. In the first place I am the acknowledged head and sovereign of some 20,000,000 (of which about 8,000,000 are Sikhs) people of the entire Punjab, a country inhabited by the most warlike races of India and are all loyal to me.

Secondly the last teacher of the Sikhs prophesied somewhere about 1725 regarding myself and has mentioned me by name in his Prophecy.*

He has besides other matters predicted also that a man

* Guru Gobind Singh died in 1708. It was a tenet of Namdhari (Kuka) belief that he miraculously did not die but wandered the Punjabi forests for a further hundred years to pass on the Guruship to Baba Balak Singh.

bearing my name would after becoming deposed [dispossessed] of all he had inherited and after residing alone in a foreign country for a long time, return and with aid of a European power free the Sikhs from the cruel bondage that they would be then suffering under for their sins.

Therefore, a great deal can be made out of the Prophecy if properly worked, as the predicted time of its fulfilment is near at hand and the people of the country are extremely ignorant as already stated.

At this moment the whole of India is with me and as soon as the People of Hindoostan are assured of my arrival in Russia their joy will know no bounds at their coming deliverance.

With all humility I would endeavour to dissuade the Imperial Government from regarding complications in the South East Europe for the present, because many powers are sited to oppose the realization of its wishes in that quarter but to turn its entire attention upon the conquest of India and upon crushing England. For by wrenching India out of the hands of England, the Imperial Government will acquire a source of Great Wealth, whereas I greatly doubt that so much will be gained by taking Constantinople.

Furthermore, if, I may be permitted, I would venture to state that, should the invasion of India be entertained in the Imperial councils, an army not less than 200,000 men and 2000 cannons be provided for that purpose. Not that this force is at all necessary for the conquest of India.

We will impress wavering Princes and people of that country of the greatness of the resources of Russia and thus half the battle would be gained.

In having thus freely expressed my views, I pray that I may not be considered disrespectful towards the Imperial Government but as a loyal subject of the Emperor (which I already consider myself to be, though I have not received the right of naturalization), I feel it my duty to say what I have to say without reserve.

The Imperial Government, whether it thinks proper to invade India or not or to employ me or not, can please itself in the matter for it is no concern of mine.

I have been deputed simply to make an appeal on behalf of 250,000,000 of my countrymen for deliverance from the cruel yoke of the British Rule and having done so my duty is ended and, if graciously permitted by the Emperor to enjoy both liberty and safety in his Majesty's dominions, I shall occupy myself in sport leaving the Almighty to bring about the deliverance of my unfortunate people in His own good time.

Should the Imperial Government, however, think proper to turn its attention towards the conquest of India and desire my services for that purpose, I would suggest that two or three gentlemen speaking English well should be appointed both to further discuss the matter with me and to enquire into the truth of the assertions I have made with regard to India. May 10, 1887. Duleep Singh, Maharajah.

The Czar made handwritten observations on the Russian translation. On Duleep's supplication to become his subject, Alexander III wrote: 'It is desirable.' On the apparent readiness of the princes of India to rise in revolt: 'it would be desirable to verify this.' Of sending English-speaking emissaries to test the ground, he minuted: 'it could be done.' He was wary, but he was hooked; the Czar left his fingerprints all over the conspiracy.

Katkov kept up the pressure by sending letters to the Czar's confidant, Constantin Petrovich Pobedonostsev, who wrote to his imperial master: 'I learn that the Hindu Prince is now in Moscow where he awaits your reply to his letter, and M. Katkov has written to me today [13 May] asking me to intervene.'

Alexander III replied: 'The prince will receive an official response in a few days' time. I see no inconvenience to his staying in Russia. I have read with interest his memoir and I believe he could one day be of use to us in India where we have no shortage of questions to debate with the English.'

N. M. Dournovo, who had been appointed police president in the capital on General Orzhevkii's disgrace, weighed in with his own pro-Duleep intelligence: 'After inquiry with one who knows India well, M. Haas the former French consul in Burma, I am told the name of Maharajah Duleep Singh carries extraordinary prestige in India. His presence alone near India would be worth an army. M. Haas confirms that the Mahdi of Sudan has less authority than the one they call "The Lion of Lahore".'

*The Times*, terribly behind the news, reported on the day Duleep drafted his letter to the Czar: 'The Maharajah Duleep Singh will, it is expected, return to St Petersburg shortly and Russian fashionable society is now deeply pondering whether it shall give him the cold shoulder or offer him a brilliant reception.'

He was already a star in Moscow. Like any newspaper editor, Katkov wanted to show off his celebrity signing. On the eve of his departure for St Petersburg, 18 May, there was a glittering party in the Maharajah's honour at the Strastnyi Boulevard. The city's grandees might meet the Sikh prince who was to lay the crown of India at the emperor's feet. There was more: 'Queen' Ada was evidently now at Duleep's richly-embroidered side.

Intelligence of extraordinary detail meanwhile was flowing from Moscow to Paris and thence to the secret crevices of Whitehall. On 19 May Our Correspondent burst into life again, telling the Foreign Office: '[blank] entered into full details of Duleep's situation. He has been taken up openly by Katkov who gave a great fête at which he appeared in full war-paint with all his jewels.'

There was another source of news: Ada was blabbing to someone. 'The information given in the papers was obtained from the *girl* by whom he is accompanied, by the wife of one of Katkov's employees, in turn, as gossip of interest, gave it to the wife of someone attached to the British Consulate at Moscow.' Our Correspondent's 19 May dispatch continued:

> It is the intention of the Russian Government to send the Maharajah to some point near the Indian frontier where he will be strictly watched to keep him out of mischief, and where he may be used as circumstances shall dictate.
>
> This will be after consultation with Russian members of the Afghan Frontier Commission by whom, it is considered, he may be made very useful at a given moment.
>
> In this connection, permit me to say every effort and every pretext will be put forward to adjourn a solution of the boundary question which if settled would destroy all possible pretext

for Russian advance and aggression for which England should be prepared.

Very little comparatively remains unfinished on the trans-Caspian railways and if necessary their completion will not be awaited for the inevitable conflict.

Everything depends upon the solution of the Bulgarian and Franco-German dispute – if such a modus vivendi can be inaugurated in both cases as will allay Russia's fears of a European conflict – she will *attack in Asia*.

This was information of critical importance, whether or not it had been spun up for maximum effect. It was presented to London as the imperial government's own hidden agenda, not Katkov's unofficial warmongering. The Russians were going to wreck the Afghan boundary talks to maintain a pretext for war. When the moment was right, Duleep would be produced like a rabbit out of a hat. It did not matter when the railway reaching out across the steppes was completed; if a fix could be found in the Balkans, Russia 'would attack in Asia'. It was a formidable conspiracy. Ada seemed to be very gossipy with the English wife of one of Katkov's confidantes. This could prove useful.

The Maharajah's son, Prince Victor, received a letter in London from his errant father posted in early May which brought more information. He dutifully passed it to the India Office. It was typical Duleep – full of triumphal boasting but equally concerned about getting his sporting gear to Russia so he could hunt snipe or go fishing on the frozen river Ob.

As I am going to make Moscow my headquarters for some time, and not return to Petersburg, my address will be as above [Zenker's Bank] and I shall be glad to receive a line from you saying that you are quite well.

I cannot tell you how happy I am to find myself in Russia. There is plenty of grouse shooting and fine salmon fishing in the north of Russia, and if not better employed I mean to indulge myself in some first-rate sport. The woodcock shooting on the coast of Black Sea is very good and so is snipe and wild fowl shooting in the Crimea.

So you see, my dear old man, I have reached the sportsman's

paradise. Besides, money from India, in spite of the stupid British Government's forbidding, will flow to me like water now that I am in Russia.

To once reach Russia was all that was necessary, and my loyal subjects required me to break off all relations with the British, and give them as a proof of my sincerity my entering the dominions of the Czar before they would undertake to send me large sums of money.

I can imagine the rage that the India officials will be in at my success, though they will pretend to suppress me altogether, but which they will find impossible to do nevertheless.

Yes! they have made a blunder the cost of which will be enormous to the British nation, though it may bring no good to me. But revenge for all the insults I have suffered will quite compensate me for all the inconvenience that I have to undergo.

Write me a line, childie, about your health, though do not in it, or otherwise, mix yourself up in my affairs.

Send the two knives you and Fred have made for me to Purdey to pack up with my other things.

Send my love to Fred and blessing of the Guru of the Sikhs and with the same to yourself, my childie.

PS. The joy of your cousin will know no bounds now! I telegraphed my arrival to them, so all India will know.

Victor's reply gently suggested the spurned £25,000 a year stipend be turned back on for the family's benefit. The Maharajah replied in high dudgeon. His son was a 'fool'. How dare he 'write and ask for the money said to belong to me at the India Office':

Whether the 'Tschar' helps me or not, I am quite independent of everybody, and perfectly happy and mean shortly to overthrow the British rule in India to which end I have dedicated the rest of my life. But take my advice, my child, and do not believe anything the newspapers write either in my favour or against me.

You will soon be of age and will consequently be able to settle your debts.

Let the Trustees sell the pictures or the jewels if they please, for I cannot be bothered afresh with matters connected with England. All that is over as a dream and I have awakened to new life and the destruction of the British power.

But if you wish to retain my affection for you, childie, do not mention again to me such matters, nor ask me to humble myself to my bitterest enemy. Look upon me as dead.

But I will never swerve from my purpose or I would not be the son of the Lion of the Punjab whose name I dare not disgrace.

You will see, my childie, by and by. Let the English brag and boast; they will cease their high talk. They are utterly undone, believe me, my son.

PS. I could see you starve and even would take your life to put an end to your misery, but will never return to England. I am entirely changed since you last saw me. I will freely shed my blood for the Emperor of Russia.

On 23 May, Katkov was back in St Petersburg to await an audience with the Czar. One more heave and de Giers would be toppled. The waiting was unbearable but all seemed to be going so well. The Maharajah's comprehensive blueprint for an invasion of India had been delivered to the Emperor. The 'traveller' was tucked up in the Hotel Dussaux against the moment he might be spirited to the Afghan frontier.

The *Moscow Gazette* now openly raged against England. Sir Robert Morier sent a portentous K editorial printed that day to Lord Salisbury. It read: 'All now knew how our closest allies [Germany and Austria] were on the side of the English intrigue, and had acted at one with that country. Had we been left face to face with Lord Salisbury and not been compelled to act in concert with Germany, we should long ago have broken the nets in which English intrigue has involved Bulgaria.

'The late change of government in England was over the Irish question,' continued Katkov. 'For that Germany cares less than for the influence of the change over the Bulgarian question. Gladstone fell in July last and in August we saw the consequences in Bulgaria of this entente with Bismarckian Germany, which some naive publicists in the Journal de St Petersbourg reckon the eternal ally of Russia.'

'The rest of the article is devoted to showing that Russia need have no fear of Old England,' Sir Robert commented, 'when members of the House of Commons cry: "Down with the speaker" and the whole country is hopelessly divided and disorganized about Home Rule.'

The Maharajah paced up and up and down waiting for the victory telegram. Ada was tiring of Frau Miersch's cabbage soup. The Czar must respond; any day now Duleep would be summoned to Gatchina to meet his Imperial Majesty to plan together the conquest of India . . .

The stuffy days passed. No message came to the Hotel Dussaux. Duleep told Our Correspondent on 25 May: 'Mr K. is still at St Petersburg. I addressed him a letter a few days ago asking whether I might take a villa in the country as it is getting extremely hot here in the city, besides I am not so comfortable living at an hotel as one would be in one's own house, but have received no reply as yet.'

He was still desperate to be reunited with his box. 'Please send off my box by luggage train as soon as you can but insure it for £50,' he wrote.

The London newspapers were in a lather of excitement but the Maharajah played it uncharacteristically coy. 'The Times correspondent at St Petersburg asked to see me the other day,' he wrote to Paris. 'But I, of course, refused to do so. You may rest assured that I will be interviewed by no one without direct permission of K. The business which we have in hand is too important to be lightly talked of with anyone of that class.'

Mr Dobson of *The Times* was not easily dissuaded. 'Passing through this city on my way south-eastward, I put up for the night at the Hotel Dussaux, where the mysterious Indian Maharajah and his still more mysterious Irish companion are at present residing,' he reported in a dispatch sent on 26 May. 'To make the coincidence complete, my room chanced to be next door to the apartments of these two interesting persons.' He claimed that Katkovites in the imperial capital had warned Moscow by telegraph of his own intended journey, and that he was tailed by shadowy figures from the moment he got off the train. 'If M. Katkov's power has lately become so great that the newspaper correspondents whom he sends abroad are now called his ambassadors,' he wrote, 'I presume that by the same scale of elevation we may designate the members of his journalistic staff who now hover round Duleep Singh and all persons likely to approach His Highness, as in some part extra members of the Russian State police.'

Sir West Ridgeway and his secretary, Captain A. J. Borrow, members of the Afghan Boundary Commission, were on the same Moscow-bound train, so Mr Dobson reported. They too seemed to sense Katkov's imminent victory. Frustrated at Russian stalling in the St Petersburg talks they had 'come to see this semi-oriental city from whence the Russian government of today is undoubtedly controlled'.

Printing House Square's finest had tracked Duleep down – apparently. But in the lobby of the Dussaux, there was renewed pantomime.

> When I entered the hotel I encountered a stout, bearded and chocolate-visaged man, lounging on the landing of the staircase, gazing into vacancy with true oriental listlessness, and dressed as a British tourist in all but a huge, dark-coloured turban.
>
> I at once put him down as the Indian Prince who had told Katkov and company that 40,000 Sikhs were ready to rush to his aid on the Indian frontier, but I was mistaken.
>
> This Indian was the Maharajah's aide-de-camp, as he calls himself, Arur Singh. As to the reputed Irishman, Patrick Casey, it was the Maharajah himself who travelled into Russia under this Irish name.
>
> He was passed over the Russian frontier by telegrams to and from M. Katkov. M. Bogdanovich I must mention, author of the French pamphlet 'L'Alliance Franco-Russe', who, it is said, enabled Duleep Singh to enter Russia, is M. Katkov's ambassador, as I have heard him called in St Petersburg.*
>
> This much is positively certain, that the Maharajah has already been in telegraphic communication from Moscow over the Russian wires with an important and well-known point on the Afghan frontier. This may give an idea of what he and the Katkovites may be hatching at Moscow, and it will be interesting to follow the further developments of this Indo-Muscovite intrigue.

* Dobson knew about Bogdanovich because of a briefing from the British embassy. The authorship of the 'French pamphlet' was a clever extra twist.

Mr Dobson sent up a note to Duleep. Arur Singh brought the reply: no interviews, certainly not with *The Times*.

## Hotel Dussaux, Moscow, 29 May 1887

At last the waiting seemed to be over. On the morning of 29 May a telegram for the Maharajah came to the Hotel Dussaux from Katkov in St Petersburg. 'Your Highness, your business is in good way. Your memoir [the war-plan] was read with much interest. You can consider yourself in safety and at liberty to reside and travel everywhere in Russia. In some days (very soon) you will receive official advertisement thereof.'

Duleep was jubilant. He sent a copy of the cable to Paris in triumph on 30 May: 'My kind friend, this is a great piece of news and I hasten to send it to you. The rest now can follow whenever it suits the convenience of the Imperial Government. What I dreaded most was that the court interest from England would have had me turned out of Russia.

'Had that wretched box (which contains my papers) reached me, I could have written a more perfect statement, but it does not now matter very much – but please send it on as soon as you can. My spirits are at this moment in the seventh Heaven. God bless you and Madame [blank] and [blank] for getting me into Russia. Your most grateful Duleep Singh Maharajah. P.S. Do you still desire that I address my letters to Madame [blank]?'

The Maharajah's spirits were in 'seventh Heaven'. He did not know that, the day before, as Katkov was sending his cable, the conspiracy had begun to go disastrously wrong. In London, Paris, St Petersburg, Moscow and the Punjab, some subtle strings were being pulled.

# 24

# King Over the Water

❦

*The Punjab, April–June 1887*

THE MAHARAJAH believed he was unstoppable. It was time to send an emissary to India to prepare for the great rising and, even more important, to rattle the money-box. There had been plentiful promises, but precious little cash. Where was the 'oriental generosity' of the brother princes of India?

The editor of *The Beaver* in French Chandernagore, Mr Shashi Bhushan Mukerji, was supposed to be raising a monster subscription from a legion of hidden partisans; instead he had received £2,000 of Duleep's money as the price of printing his 'proclamation'. The former King of Oudh had promised a lakh of rupees; it was still no more than a promise. But there was good news: a letter had arrived from Calcutta from an 'unknown friend', an Indian official who was eager to betray his British masters. He must be sought out.

The Maharajah had told Our Correspondent in the reply to the C letter: 'I am just sending my Sikh with letters to the Princes.' The faithful Arur Singh was to bear them from Moscow on a journey of the utmost sensitivity.

London knew about it from the start. The Paris spy had messaged on 31 May: 'Would it not be well to have his Sikh Arur Singh watched carefully to ascertain with whom he is working, yet not to take him yet awhile? I offer the suggestion respectfully, adding that, if Arur be arrested, Duleep Singh may distrust his present intermediary [i.e. Our Correspondent himself] and obtain another. I am convinced that after they find no return in this business, the Russians will send *me* on an errand which it may be useful for you to know.

'Arur will probably go to the "Princes" mentioned in my earlier memos, but I have not a description of him nor do I know by what route he is going to India – so it will be difficult to get on his track there.'

Thus, around 26 May, the faithful Arur Singh departed Moscow, heading by train for Odessa on the Black Sea, clutching several bulging portmanteaux, a wad of cash and a box of precious papers. He would travel by French Messageries steamer via Constantinople, Suez, Madras and Pondicherry to consult Thakur Singh, and on to the French enclave of Chandernagore near Calcutta in Bengal to squeeze Mr Mukerji for the promised money. His journey would take two months.

The Indian police were primed to go into action. So far the Maharajah file had been the concern of the Punjab Special Branch and Mr Donald McCracken. From the end of 1886 it began to cross the desk of Colonel Philip Durham Henderson, general superintendent of the Thugee and Dacoity department. From Simla, the summer capital, he would now mount an India-wide operation and work intimately with his ministerial master, Sir Henry Mortimer Durand, Foreign Secretary to the government of India, who was equally eager to enmesh the conspirators.

There were two immediate focuses of concern, the mood in the Punjab and seditious activities in French Pondicherry, seat of Thakur Singh's 'government-in-exile'. The British intelligence loop was as elegant as one of Duleep's pearl necklaces. Our Correspondent was now reading most communications between the Maharajah and his 'rascally cousin' (they were routed Moscow–Paris–French India; there was another route via Constantinople). Each missive was opened, copied and transmitted to London. The Foreign Office told the India Office who told Simla. The conspiracy seemed to be completely penetrated.

The immediate concern was the mood in Sikh regiments of the Indian Army. General Sir Frederick Roberts, Commander-in-Chief, India, wrote to the Viceroy on 12 February: 'I do not believe that there is any general dissatisfaction in the Punjab, but I have always thought that the return, or even threatened return, of Duleep Singh to India would raise hopes of a return to power among certain sections of the Sikhs, and that his presence with a Russian force in Afghanistan might cause some trouble.'

Colonel Hennessy of the 15th Sikhs said it more forcefully: 'With regard to Duleep Singh's influence it would indeed be a bold man who said he had no fear of it in his own regiment. The spirit of the Sikhs is not dead and they are full of national fire. I should tremble in my shoes should that gentleman arrive at our borders with the Russians! The Government should hold him fast and secure in England.'

Sir Charles Aitchison, the Lieutenant-Governor, wrote on 17 February: 'I do not think the intrigues of Maharajah Duleep Singh need cause immediate anxiety. What might happen if he were to appear on our frontier with a Russian army is matter of pure speculation, though we may assume it would put the loyalty of many under a very severe strain.

'There can be no doubt however that Duleep Singh is deeply intriguing and great vigilance is necessary. Orders have been issued which will have the effect of making it very difficult for him to do anything really dangerous without Government being forewarned . . . For the present at least we must be vigilant, very vigilant that is all.'

On 10 March the Punjab government instructed all commissioners to keep a special watch on all known Duleep sympathizers. In sweltering police compounds, long lists of suspects were hammered out on primitive typewriters.

Another agent was about to get on the Maharajah's trail. He was entirely different in origin and spycraft to Our Correspondent in Paris, yet his part in Duleep's destruction was to be as great. He was young, clever and utterly zealous in his pursuit of intriguers. He could flit through a bazaar or a police cell passing as the most conspiratorial Sikh partisan. He was a 'Punjabi Mussalman himself'.

Colonel Henderson ran him under the codename 'L.M.'. Throughout January to March he wandered in disguise through the Punjab, putting together a very well-informed report which was delivered to the general superintendent on 9 April 1887. It began by reprising Thakur Singh's overtures to the Maharajah at Elveden. It revealed an intimate knowledge of discussions on the Bombay-bound *Verona* and the intervention of Mr Drew, agent of the Maharajah of Kashmir.

It described in full the Pahul ceremony at Aden and who was there. The mysterious L.M. further reported that the Maharajah's war-chest had apparently been massively boosted under General Hogg's nose: 'Rs. 60,000 in gold and about Rs. 60,000-worth of jewellery were sent to Duleep Singh by the present Maharajah of Kashmir, through Thakur Singh, 2nd. The gold and jewellery were made over to Thakur Singh, 2nd, by Diwan Gobind Sahai at Lahore who delivered them to Duleep Singh, through Arur Singh, his servant at Aden.'

The spy picked up the trail of Thakur Singh Sandhanwalia who, 'being disappointed with the turn which things had taken and, being ashamed to return to the Punjab, went over to Patna. There through the priests of the Sikh temple he advanced small sums of money to the Akali Sikhs,* and sent them to the Punjab to preach to the Sikhs that Duleep Singh has gone over to Russia, and that in a very short time he will advance on India at the head of the Russian troops.'

He also told them: 'That the time for the fulfilment of Guru Gobind Singh's prophecies, in which it is written that Duleep Singh will be great, good, and just, and will be the restorer of Sikhism is near at hand, and that every true Sikh should be prepared for his reception.'

Thakur Singh then returned to the Punjab, according to the spy, and there intrigued with 'Sardar Man Singh of the Amritsar Golden Temple, Bawa Khem Singh, spiritual leader of the Sikhs, the Granthis of Amritsar, and many other old Sikh families' to forward the Maharajah's cause. 'The Sikhs are under the impression that they are a part of the machinery of the Government of India, and that without their assistance the British cannot rule India.'

The Kukas could pose particular problems the spy reported: 'They openly say that the prophecy of Ram Singh about the appearance of a just and great king from the west, who will emancipate them from the tyranny of the English, will be fulfilled through Duleep Singh under whom they will be all powerful and will suppress kine-killing in India.

'Besides this, they believe that Ram Singh (spiritual leader of the Kukas) has miraculously gone over to Russia from the prison at Mergui, and will lead Russia and Duleep Singh's advance on India. As regards Ram Singh's having died a natural death, they say it is a story concocted by the British Government.

---

* Akalis: the 'crocodiles' or 'immortal ones' – a militant Sikh sect distinguished by the wearing of razor-edged quoits in tall conical turbans.

'The Mohammedans of the Punjab have no sympathy whatever with the Sikhs and their would-be leader. If they see anything wrong either with the Hindus or the Sikhs, they will be the first who will get them into trouble by giving information to the Government,' the agent concluded. This was significant.

The Viceroy sent an updated version of the report to Lord Cross in London on 14 July:

> The enclosed memorandum on Duleep Singh, by a native detective of our own, may interest you. In every village Duleep Singh's affairs are freely and constantly discussed. The persons who have suffered through the fall of Sikh dynasty, and who will gain by Duleep Singh's success, are busy in inciting the people to support Duleep Singh's cause. Most prominent among them are the relatives of Sardar Thakur Singh Sandhanwalia.
>
> About 20 days ago, a fakir was noticed travelling about in the Lahore district quietly making inquiries as to the feeling of the people and at the same time informing them that Russia will gladly receive any Sikh going over to their country. Two carpenters of Bhadana recognised him as the one whom they noticed at Quetta.
>
> Nothing can positively be ascertained as to where this agitation and interest will eventually lead, and the opinion of the oldest Sikhs and Mohammedans is that it depends on the spur of the moment. If on Duleep Singh's arrival on the frontier, only a few of the Sikhs rise up, their brethren will follow them; but, on the other hand, if they stand fast, they will fight to the last against him.

For now, the Sikh regiments seemed loyal enough. 'The native troops, either the Sikhs or the Mohammedans, take no interest in Duleep Singh,' said the Viceroy. 'I have heard one officer of the 31st P. N. I. [Punjab Native Infantry] Regiment remarking that if the Government will offer something for Duleep Singh's head, he will be the first to shoot him down.'

You did not need to be a spy to feel the rumblings of revolt in the Punjab. The Lieutenant-Governor's 'be vigilant' order had produced a flood of police reports on pro-Duleep suspects. In early June Mr

Warburton, the Amritsar police superintendent, reported with alarm: 'The behaviour of the Sikhs has quite changed in the villages. They are defiant and insolent now to mission ladies and order them out of their houses saying "We do not want you. In a short time you will see what will happen". I have already frequently reported in my confidential diaries the hostile feeling of the people against us. It is impossible to say when the volcano we are sitting on may break out.'

Colonel Henderson now had a new concern: it was not only Kukas who might give trouble to American mission ladies, there were also Europeans in British India who might be part of Duleep's Moscow intrigue. Henderson suddenly became obsessed with something called the 'Aryan League of Honour', convinced he had found a nest of secret adepts of the Maharajah.

'Some curious information has been received on excellent authority from Calcutta,' he wrote to the Police Commissioner of Madras on 15 June:

> When Colonel Olcott was in India in 1882–83, he founded a secret society among the Theosophists in Calcutta called 'The Aryan League of Honour,' to which only a few selected men were admitted. The purpose of this secret society is said to be to send information to Russia, and the headquarters are now said to be in Madras.
>
> An agent of the society was sent to England and is supposed to be the medium, or one of the mediums, of transmitting information. This man is one Mohini Mohun Chatterji, who worked for some time in an attorney's office at Calcutta.
>
> About four years ago he went to England on the plea of being called to the Bar. He is known to have made frequent visits to the continent, and is now in America ostensibly engaged on a translation of the Vedas, a task for which I understand he possesses no qualifications whatever.
>
> I heard from England myself that Mohini Mohun was in the habit of seeing a great deal of Duleep Singh. Taken in conjunction with the possibility of Duleep Singh's name being used as a means of agitation in the Punjab, it is important to know whether there is any foundation for the idea that an organization exists in India for the purpose of communicating with Russia.

There is a prevailing impression, whether right or wrong, that the members of the inner circle at any rate of that society have aims and objects other than those ordinarily expressed. The information on this subject, though for the most part vague, comes from so many sources that it is difficult to disregard it. And at the present time the necessity for vigilance to intrigues going on in India has been impressed on the Government of India.

The deputy police commissioner of Calcutta, Mr Andrew Barnard, also got in on the hunt, writing three days later: 'When Colonel Olcott was in Calcutta in 1882–83, he founded a secret society amongst the Theosophists called "the Aryan League of Honour" to which only a few selected were admitted, amongst these were Narendro Nath Sen, the Editor of *The India Mirror*.

'Mohini Mohun was very thick with Colonel Olcott and Madame Blavataksy* when here, and whilst in England was, I hear, in the habit of making frequent trips to the continent. 'If these people have anything to do with Russia, it is most probable that Mohini is one of their means of transmitting information, and that his brother, Romoni, also sends him news. The only way of getting proof of this would be by stopping their letters whilst going through the Post Office.'

The Aryan League's letters were to be opened. Prominent journalists were allegedly part of the conspiracy. The next countermove would be to bring clandestine pressure on the 'vernacular press', the plethora of small-circulation Punjabi-language newspapers that had lately become very excited about the Maharajah. They were translated and a summary sent each week to the Political and Secret Department.

Mr William Mackworth Young, secretary to the Punjab government, knew whom to blame. 'But for the native press we should never had any trouble with Duleep Singh,' he wrote on 16 June. 'His cause had been taken up by the down-country papers not because of general interest in the subject but as an excuse to abuse the authorities and further sales. Very few of the editors of the Punjab newspapers have a real interest in the Maharajah's case.'

Young had a jaundiced view of journalists. 'Measures should be

---

* The Russian-born mystic, founder of Theosophy, was accused of being a spy when she started writing for Mikhail Katkov in 1886.

taken to prevent this despicable body of men from playing on the sympathies of the people. One or two prosecutions conducted to conviction would produce an excellent effect,' he wrote. The Russian state censorship system had lost control of Katkov and look what had happened. It was the same in British India. On 4 June Inspector Barnard recommended placing a 'strict private watch over Sardar Dyal Singh, proprietor of the *Lahore Tribune*'.

Henderson minuted: 'It might be a good thing to hint to the vernacular papers to keep out any mention of Duleep Singh, telling them that disregard of the wishes of Government in this respect would be considered as an indication of disloyal feeling.' The suggestion went to the Viceroy who concurred but minuted back: 'His Excellency wishes it clearly understood that there should be no indication of Government action or interference in the matter which may be laid hold of by the press or public.'

It was not just the 'vernacular' newspapers who were making mutinous noises. On 11 July the *Lahore Tribune* ran an extraordinary letter by a Captain Andrew Hearsey, which seemed to threaten a rising in the Maharajah's favour by disgruntled 'Anglo-Indians', hailing Duleep as some kind of Jacobite king over the water.

The captain ran through the old money grumbles, commenting:

> These £3 million sterling, due to the Maharajah by the Treaty of Lahore, may some day cause us expenditure of £30 millions or even more, for fools are those statesmen who wilfully shut their eyes, and like the ostrich thrust their heads into a hole in hopes to escape whilst the danger is daily and hourly approaching. Russia has a trump card in her hand in having Maharajah Duleep Singh on her Afghan frontier, and Russia knows how to play her cards.
>
> Those who do not believe in the influence that the Maharajah possesses in the Punjab are fools. Let them for only once go to the gate of the Forest of Lahore and visit the tomb of the old Lion of the Punjab, and see for themselves the way his memory is kept up and venerated.
>
> Such being the case, who can have the effrontery to assert that the acknowledged son of such a man will have no hold

whatsoever on the hearts feelings and reverence for Duleep Singh in the Punjab now as there was for Prince Charles Edward in Scotland and the north of England one hundred and fifty years ago.

There are numerous young gentlemen in India, Anglo-Indians and Eurasians, to whom the Government will give no employment whatsoever, and who would therefore willingly join the Russian army and carve their fortunes with their swords as their fathers did before.

Then an army of 25,000 Sikhs and Punjabis in Russian pay on the Afghan frontier would be nothing more or less than a checkmate to Great Britain on the Eastern Question, because it would be a standing menace to the Indian Government, especially if this force was officered by Anglo-Indian and Eurasian gentlemen, descendants, in most instances of India's conquerors.

Captain Hearsey's diatribe could have been read as a shrewd warning but it won him no friends in the Indian government. If Englishmen could think like this, things were getting really dangerous. Mr Young saw it as an ideal opportunity to bring a prosecution under Section 124A of the Press Act for 'exciting disaffection'. He added with maximum political subtlety: 'It would have this advantage, that the arm of the law would be brought to bear in a case in which the primary offender is not a native.'

Sir James Lyall, Lieutenant-Governor of the Punjab since February 1887, was not so sure. The captain had had a legal dispute with his brother, so he was 'very reluctant to move against him as this might be misunderstood'. Besides, 'the idea of a Sikh force organised against the British government and officered by Eurasians and disaffected domiciled Anglo-Indians was absurd'. Sir James was much more interested in prosecuting a Lahore newspaper for reporting that the English 'were a race of habitual drunkards', and that 'the Government was about to make prostitution a state monopoly'.

The stories in the ebullient Punjab press became wilder throughout the summer. Constrained from whipping up Duleep rumours, the *Lahore Tribune*'s excellent military correspondent brought two astonishing news items from the mysterious Russian Empire.

'An aerial car, two hundred feet long, guided by a Russian discoverer, will navigate the air some time this month. If a Russian be the first possessor of the secret of aerial navigation, woe be to India,' he reported. 'We may any day expect to hear of the advent of a Russian aerial fleet on the Banks of the Indus. Our gods fought with the giants of old in aerial cars; the secret has been lost in India, and is it to come back to us in such an unpleasant shape in the land of the five waters, which probably first witnessed the fight of gods and demons?'

There was more. Mr Hiram Maxim, 'a well known American inventor', had lately been in St Petersburg to see the Czar. 'He has latterly caused a sensation by his claim to have made one of the most remarkable weapons of war ever heard of. This is nothing less than an automaton of a gun. It is not pleasant to think of the bare possibility of such a handy mechanical Shiva – the Destroyer.'

'Would that the man from Maine might be persuaded to give us a portable Vishnu – the Preserver,' the *Tribune* reported. 'But Mr Maxim thinks he will make more money by dealing in destructives, and probably he has taken a true measure of mankind. Thus he has already been invited by perhaps the greatest sovereign in the world.

'Mr. Maxim gives a most favourable account of the Emperor. Notwithstanding all that the great British newspaper editors have said or may wish, the Czar is in no hurry to go mad. As for his supposed new sport of shooting men with a gun,* the War Minister's daughter said to him: "Only the other day I returned from a ball where I had been dancing with a certain Prince. I picked up an English newspaper when I came back and found to my amusement that the Czar had shot the Prince with whom I had been dancing some hours before."'

The Czar of Russia was not mad. No more so, in spite of what Queen Victoria and her ministers were saying, was the Maharajah. The Indian government was looking down the barrel of a gun. In great secrecy its chief executives got down to the lowest common denominator. If, through some appalling intelligence failure, Duleep Singh *did* turn up on the Afghan frontier with the Czar's divisions and the Sikhs *did* rise in revolt, could British India be held? Sir Henry

---

* Alexander III regularly carried a pistol for fear of assassination attempts. He once shot and seriously wounded an ADC who surprised him from behind.

Mortimer Durand, the Foreign Secretary, sent Lord Cross in London a memorandum of brutal practicality on 22 July.

> In the first place it seems to me that the extremely small number of the Sikh nation, as compared with other, Indian, nations, is not generally realised. The number of Sikhs in India is less in total than the number of Christians. The latter amount to 1,862,634, the former to 1,853,426.
>
> Of course the importance of the Sikhs must not be measured solely by numbers. For obvious reasons such would be very erroneous. But still worth remembering when we talk of the possibility of trouble among the Sikhs, is that there are not two millions of them altogether.
>
> In the Punjab they are less than one in twelve of the population, and elsewhere they hardly exist. It is to be remembered that the Punjabi Mohammedans are of necessity the enemies of the Sikhs, whom they outnumber by five to one.
>
> Nevertheless it cannot be denied that Duleep Singh may succeed in gaining the sympathies of the Sikhs in general, and that if so the danger to India will be *very formidable*.
>
> We can easily crush the unaided revolt of a nationality like theirs, living in a flat and open country, and unprovided with arms; but disaffection among our Sikh troops in the face of a Russian advance would paralyse our options and make our position a very critical one.

The Sikhs could be crushed with ease, the Secretary of State for India was informed. This was how the empire was won and this, if necessary, was how it would be held. It would be Sobraon all over again but this time the Khalsa would be cowed with quick-firing artillery and Nordenfelt machine-guns. But if they had the Russians behind them ... This was no comic-opera revolution. If the *Tribune* was to be believed, Duleep Singh might soon descend god-like on the Punjab in a Russian aerial chariot spouting fire.

# 25

# The Snare

❦

*Russian Embassy, 79 rue de Grenelle, Paris, June 1887*

IN MOSCOW, the Maharajah sensed triumph. In Simla, the government of India sensed disaster – a fateful 'crash' in the Punjab. But in Paris, new intriguers, and not just Duleep's duplicitous chief of staff, were subtly working to bring down the turbulent Sikh.

There were three ways to do it: money, intrigue and sex. Sex would be the last resort. First, money. Drain the Maharajah's cash-box and he would be powerless in Russia. Someone from the Russian embassy in Paris had clearly been snooping around Mallet Frères. Our Correspondent told London on 30 May: 'I hear that it is on the cards for Duleep Singh to lose the favour which he has enjoyed until now. Enquiries are being made as to his financial situation – the results are not satisfactory. He had represented that he left £20,000 deposited, but it is ascertained that he drew out all his funds on leaving Paris and although ostensibly desirous to conceal his destination, made no secret at the Bank that Russia was his objective point.

'Endeavours are being made to discover how much he really had with him, and it is hinted that possibly the robbery at Berlin may be turned to account by the robbed one to cover his impecuniosity. If this be proved, Duleep's prestige is at an end.'

Lord Cross was delighted at the intelligence. He cabled the Viceroy: 'I hear privately that Duleep Singh is in some difficulty, inquiries have been made about his financial resources, so far so good.'

The Secretary of State for India followed with a letter sent from Balmoral: 'I am told that inquiries have been made in Russia as to his means – with very unsatisfactory results – great disappointment had been caused. De Giers, I am sure, will not lend himself to any unworthy cause but Katkoff, if he had the power, would go to any lengths.' The letter to the Viceroy ended with a line laden with significance: 'You ask about a Franco-Russian alliance. Bismarck has done all in his power to help us . . . Russia is furious.'*

The second line of attack was intrigue. Our Correspondent was startled to receive an urgent summons to the rue Juliette Lamber. On 10 May he messaged London: 'Madame Adam, who has just returned to Paris, sent for me yesterday to make the following singular communication: "The Maharajah is a *traitor in English pay*. I have a copy of his letter to the Governor-General of India [the Viceroy, Lord Dufferin] offering to pump Katkov and divulge the secrets of Russia's Asian policy. This copy was given me by a lady relative of the Governor-General to whom it was confided to be shown to me."'

The industrious Mr Villiers told Mr Maitland: 'We have received the enclosed with an insinuation from our correspondents that neither of them believe the statement made.'†

Duleep was a double-agent. Things were getting very mixed in the conspiracy business. The 'real' double-agent, Our Correspondent, wrote to the Maharajah in Moscow on 12 June:

> I am sincerely and seriously grieved by a communication made to me by a lady friend recently returned from India who affirms that a letter dated in 1886 and addressed by you to the Viceroy of India was seen by her.

* The German Chancellor was also being briefed directly by the imperial German embassy in London. Berlin, it seems, was way behind with the true facts. On 30 April Count von Plessen, the first secretary at Carlton House Terrace, communicated to Bismarck: 'Duleep Singh appeared in St Petersburg accompanied by an Irishman and has been in contact with Katkov and other leaders of the opposition party. This news is derived from a telegram which was not completely legible – but I could get from it that Singh did not have a passport but was allowed to enter Russia through the offices of General Bogdanovich, author of the pamphlet 'L'Alliance Franco-Russe'. Von Plessen was probably reading the intercept of a British diplomatic telegram. Sir Julian Pauncefote would soon start feeding information direct to the embassy.
† The 'second' correspondent seems to be the Viceroy himself. Lord Dufferin thought the accusation 'very amusing'. 'If only we could persuade the Russians of its truth, it would prove useful,' he wrote to Lord Cross on 3 June 1887, thus exonerating the Maharajah from being a double-agent.
'I conclude that when Madame Adam refers to a copy of letter given to her by a lady relative of the "Governor-General" she means the Governor-General of Moscow, though, now I think of it, Lady Dufferin has a relative, a certain Madame Blumer, married to a Russian and who is as likely as not to be a friend of Madame Adam's.'

In the letter you offered to go to Russia in order to obtain precise information respecting Russian intrigues in Asia which you would communicate in exchange for the restitution of certain private estates which you claim in the Punjab as personal property.

Among other phrases is the following: 'I will spy upon Katkov.' Your Highness may rest assured that I neither believe nor ever have believed a word of this story which I firmly believe to be merely an invention of your enemies for your ruin and which I have always stigmatized as a vile calumny from the moment, more than a month ago, when it was brought to my knowledge.

But it is urgent that a more authorized voice than mine should give it the lie and I therefore beg you, as an act of simple justice to yourself as well as to your friends, to do so in such a manner that the whole world may learn its falsehood.

Be as precise as you can, and if you have a reply from the Viceroy produce it and remember that the moment is critical and that your silence before a charge of such gravity would be your irredeemable ruin.

The Maharajah replied immediately: 'My dear [blank]. I am aware of no treasonable correspondence against Russia between the Viceroy of India and myself whatever, but when there was a rumour started some years ago of this country's intended advance upon Hindoostan I did offer my services to the Home Government to be sent against that power. Yes, it is the fact and I do not care who knows it, that beside myself England did not possess another loyal subject in India. Owing to my loyalty to the Queen I was hated by my countrymen.

'You have alluded to this subject but I must beg of you to disabuse your mind entirely of it, namely that I seek personally any advantage, or desire to be a Sovereign again. No, I am too old and have no ambition whatever, and were I not persuaded fully in my mind that Russian rule would benefit my countrymen I would not for a moment seek to be avenged on the English but would bury myself in utter oblivion to brood over my wrongs.'

Duleep's denials seemed plausible enough and Madame Juliette Adam was appeased for now. The 'I will spy on Katkov' letter looked like a piece of freelance black propaganda cosily cooked up in Lord Dufferin's family counsels.

The Maharajah's reply from Moscow pleading innocence ended on a bleaker note, however. 'Mr K. returned here a day or two ago and has again left for his country seat without me seeing him, but his Secretary has been twice here,' he wrote on 12 June. 'I am invited next week to go to the home of a nobleman where I am to have some conversation with one of the great Russian Generals. I will write you the details if they are not to be considered as confidential.

'I will write to K. on the subject of your letter but you must not expect an answer for some time, if any at all, as he has not always replied to my letters. His secretary informed me that he is much pulled down and appears much worried.'

## St Petersburg, 29 May 1887

Mikhail Katkov was indeed pulled down. In that last week of May, victory over de Giers seemed a whisker away. He had sent Duleep Singh a telegram on the morning of the 29th: 'Your Highness, your business is in good way.'

Then, catastrophe: a midday summons to the dacha outside St Petersburg of the interior minister Count Dmitrii Andreevich Tolstoi, sputnik of Katkov's planet, fellow-traveller in the creeping coup.[*]

The Count was very agitated, pacing and sweating; something terrible had happened. The Czar that morning had received a telegram from Baron Mohrenheim, Russian envoy to Paris. The French government was going through another crisis, trying to disencumber itself of the increasingly volatile General Boulanger. The ambassador's cable had read: 'Freycinet eliminated. Floquet[†] trying to get premiership. Floquet has shown letter to President Grévy from Katkov, in which Katkov says a Floquet ministry would be seen with approval by Russia.

---

[*] For fear of assassination Tolstoi lived in a heavily guarded 'damp little cottage' on his country estate and, like the Czar, carried a pistol at all times.

[†] The radical leader Charles-Thomas Floquet was a particular hate figure at Gatchina. In 1867, during the state visit of Alexander II to Paris, he approached the visiting monarch, lifted his hat and said, 'Vive le Pologne, Monsieur'.

These facts are certain. The intermediary between Katkov and Floquet is Cyon.'

The Czar was furious, said Tolstoi. Katkov was behaving like a dictator. Not only was he aspiring to run Russian foreign policy, he was trying to install a government of his choosing in France. Count Ignatiev was in on this – this was tantamount to a coup. The interior minister must stamp it out. Tolstoi had his own reasons to be worried. He himself was compromised; he had seen the Maharajah file.

There was more and it was just as bad. Czar Alexander III had 'simultaneously received very compromising information' from the foreign ministry about a certain General Bogdanovich, the Jew Cyon, mysterious overtures to General Georges Boulanger in Paris, and the unusual activities of a troupe of Irish acrobats at Verjbolovo railway station. If they could so easily stroll across the empire's borders so might Nihilist assassins, as de Giers had helpfully reminded his sovereign.

'How can Katkov surround himself with such scoundrels?' the Czar had thundered. Bogdanovich must be punished.

Katkov could only mouth denials to Tolstoi. It was 'a conspiracy ... the letter was a forgery ... why had the Czar cast this shadow over him?'

Katkov begged an audience of the Czar and was received at Gatchina the next day, 30 May. Katkov fell on his knees pleading his and the general's innocence: 'That he and he alone should be visited with the Imperial anger – but his Majesty was implacable.' Bogdanovich, the Czar had also now learned, was the author of the scandalous pamphlet 'L'Alliance Franco-Russe', with its calumnies of the imperial family. He had irrefutable evidence. The Czar telephoned General Vannovksi at the war ministry and told him to break Bogdanovich.

The premonition of utter disaster became public knowledge on 8 June with a notice in the *Official Messenger*. Morier informed Lord Salisbury: 'It is reported today that General Bogdanovich, Monsieur Katkov's right-hand man, his *faiseur* in Paris, the reputed author of the pamphlet on the alliance between Russia and France, and the person I have every reason to suspect of smuggling Duleep Singh across the frontier, has been suddenly disgraced and forced to leave the army.' A week later, on 15 June, the ambassador sent Salisbury a 'Very Secret' dispatch on the Bogdanovich matter which spoke of a different agenda. It referred to events in Paris in January 1887. I have chosen to relate its significance to the Maharajah affair later in this narrative.

The threads of Duleep's and Katkov's intrigues were closely inter-woven but they had begun to unravel disastrously in the Russian embassy in Paris. The rue de Grenelle housed more than diplomats. Since 1884 it had been the operating centre of the Zagranichnaia Agentura, the foreign agency of the Ohkrana,* the secret police. Housed in two small rooms on the ground floor, it was run with zealous efficiency by Peter I. Rachkovski who employed a network of *agents provocateurs* and stooges to penetrate émigré revolutionary groups in France and across western Europe.

Rachkovski was no shadowy spymaster. He kept a luxurious villa in St Cloud and hosted lavish banquets for politicians and journalists. He was also a partisan of the Franco-Russian alliance – for good, pragmatic reasons. The revolutionaries worked against the development of closer ties with imperial Russia. The foreign agency by default worked to push French public opinion in the opposite direction.

The foreign agency employed an informer called Katakazi, at one time Russian minister to Washington, recalled in 1872 by request of the US government. He was now ekeing out a living as an Ohkrana stooge in Paris. On 3 June Katkov cabled Cyon (who had returned to France on 26 May) with the utmost urgency. The Floquet letter was a forgery. Who had supplied it to Mohrenheim? Find the conspirators. It must have come from within the rue de Grenelle. Katkov mentioned Katakazi, 'a man who would sell out anything or anyone'.

Cyon staked out the imperial embassy in Paris, citadel of foreign ministry orthodoxy, and not a place where he was welcome. He used every shady contact in the city to find out the truth. There were three conspirators, he was to report later. It was indeed Katakazi, aided by a Paris journalist named A. M. de Civiny, and the second secretary in the embassy – Nicholas de Giers, the foreign minister's son. Like Lord Dufferin's mysterious lady relative and her 'double-agent' allegations, the forged Floquet letter looked like a family affair cooked up by de Giers *fils* with the connivance of the Ohkrana bag-man. De Civiny

* From '*Ohkrannoye Otdelenie*' – Security Detachments.

confessed to the black-propaganda campaign, and that it was Katakazi who put the 'note' revealing the secret alliance in *Le Voltaire* newspaper that had so excited the Maharajah as he set off on his epic railway journey.

The journalist's confession was later sent to Cyon to Constantin Pobedonostsev for the Czar's attention, but the doctor's detective work came far too late. Katkov was already fatally damaged.

As he pleaded his innocence on his knees before the Czar on 30 May, Katkov could claim the letter was a forgery as much as he liked. He could not deny the fact of Mr and Mrs Casey's remarkable railway journey, details of which had reached the imperial ear courtesy of Her Majesty's Foreign Secret Service. The coup-by-newspaper had been spiked.

De Giers *père* and the British ambassador met again in a mood of mutual congratulation after the apparent political destruction of their mutual enemy. Sir Robert Morier reported it all to Lord Salisbury in a cable of 6 July full of cryptic cuteness.

> In the course of conversation the other day, the subject of Maharajah Duleep Singh's visit to Moscow having been touched on, M. de Giers incidently made a remarkable admission.
>
> I had all along been firmly convinced, though without positive data, that it must have been through General Bogdanovich that the Maharajah had been smuggled into Russia, and I had assumed the fact in speaking to His Excellency, as not requiring any proof.
>
> Upon which His Excellency observed 'as you know the truth I will not now conceal from you, in the utmost confidence, that it was owing to the discovery of his having been the instrument by which the Maharajah had effected his entrance into Russia that I finally persuaded the emperor to make an example of the intriguing General.'
>
> The Emperor, as I reported to Your Lordship in a former despatch, had been much incensed at the surreptitious manner in which the Maharajah had succeeded in baffling the vigilance of the regular Imperial Police officials, and therefore that of the officers appointed by H.M. to look to his own safety as well as that of the public.

De Giers, of course, who at supper at Gatchina on 22 March had kept 'the Czar is doomed' intelligence in his pocket, had been ramping up a new assassination scare with rumours of 'a plot being hatched in London'. He did not mention that Scotland Yard, having scoured the metropolis from Stoke Newington to Soho, could find no such plot. Sir Robert's long dispatch continued:

> Accordingly, the Emperor's first exclamation, when M. de Giers reported to him that I had informed His Excellency of the presence of the Maharajah in Russia – and that in reply the Czar had denied the possibility of such an arrival unknown to himself – and that, nevertheless, it had turned out to be true, was: 'It was passing strange that the British Ambassador should have at his disposal at St. Petersburg a better police than I have.'
>
> It is clear that M. de Giers had utilized this current of Imperial indignation to submerge his adversary. As he related the story to me, he only pointed out to H.M. to what an impossible position he was reduced, if as Foreign Minister he led, through ignorance of [the activities of] M. Katkov and his staff, a Foreign Ambassador into error and that in so glaring a manner as to destroy for the future all confidence in his most solemn assurances.
>
> But I think he placed the case before H.M. so as necessarily to make his Imperial listener feel *de te fabule narratur* 'the story is about you' – Horace.
>
> In a word General Bogdanovich, whose position was already undermined, had been caught in flagrante delecto doing a piece of executive business behind the back of the Emperor, of H.M.'s Ministers and of H.M.'s Police officials and his fate was sealed. But this is not all.

The British ambassador had kept the best till last. 'M. de Giers dropped the expression: "C'etait un acte de trahison".' Sir Robert thought the phrase 'very strong'. In Russia traitors went smartly to Siberia or the Schlusselburg Fortress gallows.

'M. de Giers was proceeding to make some observation when he stopped himself and changed the conversation,' Sir Robert continued. 'From what he did say, however, I gathered clearly that the Maharajah's unlawful crossing of the frontier was only a link in the intrigue which, there is no doubt, M. Katkov was carrying on through General Bog-danovich last winter at Paris and that his invitation to the Maharajah to come to Moscow was somehow or other connected with this intrigue.' It was a courtly dance. The ambassador already knew the reason for the general's midwinter journey, the agenda that Cyon in his memoirs was so keen to deny.

It was all working out beautifully. The Purdey-wielding Maharajah would understand if he had the faintest clue what was really going on. He was the tethered goat; it was a newspaper tiger the English and the Russian diplomats had been hunting. They could seemingly turn bomb-plots on and off to order. When Katkov had spirited Patrick Casey, 'the apostle of dynamite', across the frontier, it was not the Czar who was doomed; the editor had doomed himself.

## *Hotel Dussaux, Moscow, 30 June 1887*

Duleep was oblivious to the intrigues around him. Nevertheless, some-thing seemed to be wrong. The stifling days of June passed in bored frustration. Ada remained in hotel-room seclusion, growing pasty on Moscow food, while he dreamt of hunting snipe in the Crimea. Mr Nicholas William Hornstedt, the Moscow vice-consul reported: 'He is still at the Dussaux, leads a quiet unostentatious life, sees hardly anyone, is very economical, and has made special terms for his apart-ments and simple board at the hotel.'

The Maharajah wrote to his Paris confidante on 30 June:

My dear [blank].

Things move here at the rate of an inch a day, consequently 36 days are necessary to travel a yard and God only knows how long it would take for the authorities to accomplish a mile.

K. appears to be very much occupied always and to see him when here is almost impossible.

He has not yet returned from St Petersburg and I cannot help thinking that he is there occupying himself with our business and feel a sort of presentiment that he will carry it all through successfully in the end.

M. Giers is a great nuisance – should he cease to be at the head of the Foreign Affairs things would move very rapidly.

I think it would be best if you were to write me a short note only asking me in it on your behalf to ask 'K' if he has received the 'proposal' [for the Irish Legion] which was sent some time ago. I think a reply would then come.

The weather after being very hot for some days has suddenly turned cold.

# 26

# Fenian Fire

*Reynold's Irish-American Bar, 23 rue Royale, Paris,*
*28 May 1887*

THAT THE MAHARAJAH was in Moscow, the London newspapers had no doubt; that he was not Mr Patrick Casey at last seemed clear. But what was he up to? Go and find the real Casey in Paris, Fleet Street news-editors barked. If anyone knows he will. Thus Reynold's Bar once more heaved with well-funded reporters ordered to find Fenians. Bloody Scotland Yard cocktails flowed. There were repeated rumours in London of a bomb attack on the Queen's jubilee celebrations, set for 21 June, to which Casey's name was linked. This could be a huge story.

The Paris correspondent of the *Daily Chronicle* got in first. 'The Maharajah has gone to Russia for the purpose of organizing a conference of all the enemies of England,' he reported on 26 May after talking to a 'reticent' Mr Casey. 'This will consist in an endeavour to rally all the disaffected Indians and Canadians* with a sprinkling of Irish volunteers. An effort will then be made to stir up an insurrection on the Afghan frontier so as to bring the active interference of Russia.'

Mr Michael Flannery, supposedly 'one of the most energetic Fenian conspirators in France', gave the *Morning Advertiser* a riveting account two days later of the state of Irish revolutionary politics and of the Maharajah's unlikely role as Ireland's liberator. 'I don't mind telling you,' said Mr Flannery, 'that there was a division in our ranks here a year and a half ago which paralysed our efforts for a time. One party

---

* Louis Riel, a Franco-Irish-Amerindian had led a rebellion of 'Metis' (half-breeds) in Canada, seizing Fort Garry, Winnipeg. He was executed in 1884.

was for the most vigorous action possible, but the other thought it would be better to remain quiet for a time, and the less energetic counsels prevailed.'

The dynamiters had gone quiet, he explained, to give Charles Stewart Parnell a chance to fight for Home Rule in parliament, but this had ended in 'complete failure'. The Clan-na-Gael split with O'Donovan Rossa's skirmishers had been another cause of the 'extreme party's inaction', said Mr Flannery. But, 'three weeks ago a general understanding was arrived at between both wings on the Continent'.

This is exactly what Our Correspondent had reported to Duleep in the C letter of 15 May: 'The two military parties of the Irish nationalists have drawn up a proposal for the establishment of an Irish military colony near the Indian frontier,' he had written, 'to be commanded by one of our most devoted friends, who will act as the Imperial Government of Russia may dictate.'

There had evidently been a secret Fenian war congress in Paris around early May. It had united the squabbling revolutionary wings in a policy to make war on the 'national power of England'. The Maharajah was on the agenda.

'Were any practical steps resolved upon?' asked the reporter.

'Practical steps' included the use of dynamite: 'the English navy, arsenals, and docks will be struck at, but private residences, clubs, and civil departments will be let alone. It has been felt that to make war upon men, women, and children in the streets of London was not to make war upon England.'

The new militancy was made in America, Mr Flannery explained: 'the Irish out there are more extreme than their fellow-countrymen. The majority of them were expelled from their homes, and have borne across the Atlantic the hate – the intense hate – which they conceived for the English Government.'

'What is your programme?' the reporter asked.

'One section of the advanced party will operate against the naval and military power of England – while another section, working under the same leaders and under the same constitution, will be directing its attention to the Afghan frontier,' Mr Flannery replied.

'The Maharajah Duleep Singh has come to an understanding with the leading members of the Irish advanced party to work in parallel lines with them on the Afghan frontier.

'Duleep Singh is a man of vast wealth. He is still in Russia, but in a week or more will probably be in Russian Asia. It is well known now at the British embassies in both Paris and St Petersburg that he actually used Casey's passport. The passport was only obtained after a good deal of difficulty. When the application was made for it, the officials at the Paris embassy appeared to regard the proceeding as ironical.

'So far as the Russians are concerned they are willing to accept the alliance of any party, whether they are Sheikhs of India or Fenians of Ireland, in their antagonism to England. Singh does not intend to cross the Indian frontier at the present moment. He is going to make his preparations on the Russian side, where he will meet with a certain number of disaffected Sheikhs.'

'Will there be any Fenians on the spot to meet him?'

'Yes, a couple of Fenian delegates have been appointed to meet Singh on the frontier.'

When asked whether dynamite explosions could be expected in England on or about the date of Her Majesty's jubilee, Flannery said: 'I cannot answer a question like that.'

This was a fantastic conspiracy. Duleep was to inspire a rising in India. An Irish legion would march beneath the harp banner of the Republic, the saltire of imperial Russia and the war-flags of the Khalsa. Irish-Americans would wage dynamite war against the symbols of English national power. The jubilee of the Queen Empress was three weeks away. The detonation of a war craved by dark forces in Europe would be triggered in the most spectacular way possible – the assassination of Queen Victoria in Westminster Abbey.


## British Embassy, rue St Honoré, Paris, June 1887

France was the source of immediate danger. The bombers must be found – not the posturers of Reynold's Bar, but 'sleepers', quiet professional fanatics. On 1 June the Foreign Office sent Lord Lyons, who had been so reluctant to spy on either Duleep or the Fenians the year before, a most secret telegram: 'I transmit a confidential letter from Secretary of State for the Home Department with enclosures urging that good offices of the French government should be obtained to watch the proceedings of General F. F. Millen and General Macadaras, the Fenian emissaries at present residing severally in Boulogne and Paris,' it read. 'Your Excellency will observe that Mr. Matthews [Henry Matthews, the Home Secretary] considers it of the utmost importance to obtain every possible information on the plans of these two conspirators.'

The Home Office at least had woken up to the seriousness of the threat. They had the names of two apparent danger-men, the 'generals' Millen and Macadaras. Things, however, were not what they seemed.

Departmental secrecy in London surrounding anti-Fenian operations still existed and led to one of the murkiest episodes in the whole Maharajah affair. The secret bureaucratic chessboard had been rearranged. Edward Jenkinson had been sacked in January 1887, after a last bruising row with his 'bone-headed' colleagues, to be replaced as the government 'secret agent' by a senior Metropolitan Police detective, James Monro. Jenkinson's rival, Sir Robert Anderson, who had been sent into a backwater as a prison commissioner, was rehabilitated into the secret fold.

Monro was given a staff of four high-ranking police officers intended as substitutes for the 'private anti-Fenian agents previously employed by Mr Jenkinson'. The department, answerable directly to the Home Secretary, was known under various titles including the 'Special (Irish) Branch' and 'Special (Secret) Branch' with a remit to sniff out continental anarchists as well as Irish revolutionaries. This was the bureau that had reported on 14 May that there was no plot being cooked up by Nihilists in London. But Irish-American dynamiters were a different matter.

James Monro told the Home Secretary on 16 June: 'As you are aware, I have for some time past been watching the operation of General Francis F. Millen, an emissary from the dynamite faction in America.' He was 'an accredited agent of the Fenian Brotherhood united for the occasion with some of the leaders of the Clan-na-Gael. Of this I have undoubted proof,' the detective reported. 'He came to Havre under a false name, proceeded to Paris and thence to Boulogne, where he has been under observation.' Millen was evidently the master-bomber.

'His correspondence should be noted, and if the addresses of the letters which he posts are given to me, I shall be able soon to ascertain who the people are in this country whom he is tempting to commit outrage at the time of the jubilee of Her Majesty,' Monro's letter continued. 'It is also reported that a General Macadaras who lives in Paris in some style and who is intimate with Patrick Casey and his associates is sending emissaries to this country to commit outrage now . . . He is a freelance, not connected with either the Fenian Brotherhood or the Clan-na-Gael – but he has some money and his associates are undoubtedly suspects. The well-known Eugene Davis, who was expelled from Paris, has returned here, unknown I believe to the French Police – Macadaras is one of his associates.'*

The Home Secretary sent Monro's Scotland Yard report to Sir Julian Pauncefote, Our Correspondent's secret master at the Foreign Office. 'I enclose a memorandum which will supply the reasons why I think it urgent that immediate instructions should be sent to the British Consul at Boulogne to request the French police to watch General Millen,' he wrote. Lord Lyons in Paris was to tell the French government.

'The information about General Macadaras gives me more uneasiness than the others,' said the Home Secretary. 'His intimacy with Casey and E. Davis stamp him; and his independence of the known Fenian organisations takes him out of the reach of my ordinary sources of information. In view of the 21st June [the impending focal day of the jubilee celebrations] this is most urgent.'

Lord Lyons, for once, became involved with the spy business, telegraphing even more dramatic news of the jubilee-eve: '[French] Minister of the Interior informs me that strict watch is being kept on Millen at Boulogne. He is informed that several persons suspected of connection with Nihilism have left Paris, for London, within the last few days for the purpose of making an attempt on the members of the Russian Imperial family representing the Czar at the Jubilee festivities.'

Scenting the story of a lifetime, the *Morning Advertiser*'s Paris corre-

---

* An extraordinary story appeared in *The Republican* newspaper of St Louis, Missouri on 2 June 1887. It was a letter from 'a British agent' called Brodie to Scotland Yard, addressed 'Dear Sir Charles' [Warren, Commissioner, Metropolitan Police], which had somehow been obtained by a prominent Irish nationalist. It read: 'Your information that Duleep Singh had been taken off by the Irish is, I believe, true, it is confirmed here but the villains lie so much . . . it is said that General Macadaras, as he is called, is the father of that brilliant scheme.

'Macadaras went to Paris last year and thence to Russia where he was received by de Giers. On his return he opened up a correspondence with Duleep Singh, which *resulted in his leaving England*. When in Paris the latter was seen with Macadaras several times, and he has gone to Russia with a man named Casey who is Macadaras's private secretary.'

spondent had meanwhile got close to the heart of the matter. He had supped with the apostle of dynamite, Patrick Casey himself. The Maharajah, imminent explosions and war with Russia made a tremendous tale. The story ran on the morning of Friday, 17 June and copies were circulating in Whitehall by lunchtime.

'I have just had an opportunity of talking over the situation with Patrick Casey, a member of the Fenian Council,' the correspondent reported. 'The circumstances of our meeting need not be particularised here ... From the descriptions of Patrick Casey which the British public encountered in the pages of a certain notorious pamphlet [the 'Black Pamphlet' of libel trial fame] it would be impossible to recognise the Patrick Casey of active Fenianism and real life.'

'Are you not intimately acquainted with Duleep Singh, Mr Casey?' The reporter asked.

'Yes, I know him intimately, ... He came to Paris, and stayed here for about a year. It was while he was here that a person occupying a position of influence introduced him to several Russian conspirators.'

Casey had dropped a thumping clue as to the Maharajah's movements in the weeks before his flight to Moscow. The 'person of influence' was clearly Cyon, but who were the 'several Russian conspirators'?

> 'Duleep Singh very soon produced a favourable impression upon his Russian friends, and he then determined to go on to headquarters. He went to Russia direct from Paris,' [Patrick Casey continued].
>
> 'With companions?'
>
> 'They were three. One of them was a Hindoo attendant of the Maharajah's, the other I prefer not to name. When he left Paris, he was advised by his friends, who knew that he might be overtaken by the telegraph, to keep the closest watch upon his passport and his money. At Berlin station his satchel was cut and the passport, which it contained, together with a sum of 30,000 francs, was abstracted.'
>
> 'In whose name was the passport?'
>
> 'In my own.'
>
> 'And the Maharajah Duleep Singh got through the Russian frontier without any passport at all?'

'He got right through without a passport. But it was a special privilege, and he owed it to the influence of a friend in Paris. I believe myself that the robbery was the work, not of thieves, but of detectives.

'Duleep Singh placed himself in communication with M. Katkov and other prominent Russians of the same school, as soon as he arrived at St. Petersburg. He was, of course, received with open arms.'

'What is Duleep Singh now doing?'

'He is still in Russia, organising the movement against British supremacy in India. He intends to remain in Russia for some time.'

'Have you any special information which leads you to believe that there may soon be grave trouble on the Afghan frontier?'

'Soon, I won't say; but these troubles are coming, and any trouble there will be backed up by Irishmen of known ability, both as soldiers and organisers.

'I will go on to the death for liberty in Ireland. In the course of twenty-five years I have escaped about six times. I shall probably finish upon the scaffold, but that matters less to me now than ever it did, for I am getting to an age at which a man sees little in life. [He was by now aged forty-four.]

'We shall seek all the support we can possibly secure, no matter in what direction we have to turn for it. We want the Russians to give us a helping hand, in the event of our bringing about a rising; for the same cause I would accept the assistance of the devil!' . . .

'Suppose that, in a revolutionary struggle, you brought the Russians into Ireland, would you, if with their aid your efforts proved successful, wish to see them stay there?'

'We are certainly not disposed to see a single Russian stay in the country. We should recompense our ally, and then take up our independence.

'We certainly do not want to be associated at all with Russia. In Russia they are hanging all the best men at the present time. We sympathise immensely with the nihilists who lost their lives recently, and we hate the Russian autocrat as we hate the Evil One.'

'May we touch upon the question of dynamite, Mr Casey?'

'Yes, certainly.'

'Is there anything coming off?'

'In all probability there will be something coming off, and very soon, but I am not going to tell you when. When it is done, however, the usual precautions will be observed against taking human life. We don't want to hurt a man, woman, or child in England, but we intend to make a demonstration against what I may call the symbols of British Government.'

## *Westminster Abbey, London, 21 June 1887*

These symbols of British government were gathering in London arrayed in gorgeous display as never before, to celebrate the great and glorious fiftieth anniversary of Queen Victoria's accession. The night before the thanksgiving service, Westminster Abbey was searched and re-searched by teams of police. Detectives scoured the crypt for barrels of Fenian fire. Nerves were on edge. There was huge row when a cleric was discovered to have advertised his tickets for sale. The Home Secretary was incandescent. 'This clergyman must be stopped . . . this is constructive high treason! What a chance for a dynamiter to get a quiet pot-shot at Her Majesty all for the ridiculously low figure of 80 guineas,' Sir Henry Matthews thundered. Bamba, the Maharani Duleep Singh, was allotted a ticket – but her seat at the service was observed 'to go unoccupied'. The Metropolitan Police commissioner and the Home Secretary held their breath. The procession passed in high imperial pomp – the Indian contingents were especially cheered.*
There was no Fenian fireworks display.

The story that filtered out soon afterwards was that the Special Branch had been tipped off by an undercover agent two months before, watched the conspirators closely, and frightened them off. Two of them were tried in February 1888 and sentenced to fifteen years' imprisonment. But some Irish Nationalist MPs, much later, suggested

* The Queen was enamoured of the Indian tributes, although there were plentiful rows about precedence and some of the 'Native Princes were affronted by their carriages being drawn by Hackneys.' She noted in her journal: 'The handsome, young Rao of Kutch, most beautifully dressed; really he and his brother were like a dream.'

that the whole thing had been cooked up as an act of provocation. It was.

The suspicion was fed by Sir Robert Anderson's own revelation in his 1909 memoirs that: 'One of the principal agents in the plot was taken into pay on behalf of our Government, but the scheme was thwarted by Mr Monro who most fortunately had been placed in charge of the secret service work.

'The arrangement had been made during a disastrous interval before his appointment [Anderson clearly meant Jenkinson's term as spymaster] and a prominent Fenian arrived at Boulogne, I will here call him "Jinks", to carry out his twofold mission on behalf of Clan-na-Gael and the British government.'

A contemporary report by Monro, preserved among Anderson's papers, reveals more. Filed to the Home Secretary in November 1887, it rewards careful analysis. Nowhere is the Maharajah mentioned, but someone with secret influence over his life is.

> The Fenian agent F. F. Millen, whose name has lately been before the public in connection with plots of outrage in England, is a press man on the staff of the 'New York Herald' and claims the title of 'General' in virtue of military service in Mexico.
>
> He has been prominent as a Fenian for more than 20 years, and has held office in the Clan-na-Gael ever since that organization was established.
>
> This man was in the U.K. at the close of last year and sailed for New York in January '87 to promote new schemes of outrage . . .
>
> [A]s the outcome of negotiations it was arranged that two leading C-n-G men should meet with two of the Council of the rival organization called the F.B. (Fenian Brotherhood) with a view to joint action in promoting what they described as a display of fireworks on the Queen's Jubilee or in plain language a number of explosions and incendiary fires in London on 21st June.
>
> These meetings took place last March; and as the result Millen started for Europe. He went at once to Paris where he remained till 12th May, corresponding freely with various

persons in the U.K. He also put himself in communication with well known Fenians in Paris, and notably with a man named Tevis who is the principal agent of the Fenian Brotherhood in Europe.

On 12th May he left for Boulogne in order to be nearer the scene of his intended operations.

During the whole period of Millen's stay in Europe I was kept fully informed of his plans and movements,* and no precautions were neglected to prevent his crossing the channel unobserved.

Monro hit a major political problem. It emerged that London knew about the bomb plot all along. *Someone* had been telling the now-departed Jenkinson everything. 'Millen's mission was nevertheless a cause of unceasing anxiety as the date of the Jubilee approached,' reported Monro. 'This anxiety was greatly intensified by discovering accidentally that before his schemes of outrage were proposed to his confederates in New York, they had been communicated to the gentleman who preceded me in charge of the Secret Service Department [Jenkinson] and that in the event of his [Millen's] arrest and conviction he might have made statements on the subject, of at all events a most embarrassing kind. I therefore decided to deal with him on French soil.' Millen, indeed, might have a great deal to say.

Monro decided to break up the plot before it got any further. In Boulogne a Special Branch detective was set on Millen who openly warned him he was under suspicion. Part of the bombing team got to London but not the man ostensibly carrying the dynamite. The general skulked back to Paris.

'Millen forthwith reported by letter to the Fenian Brotherhood agent in Paris [the man named Tevis],' Monro recorded.

On 30 June, Lord Lyons sent the Foreign Office this fascinating scrap of intelligence: 'The following information was sent me quite confidentially and unofficially yesterday from the Ministère de l'Intérieure here. General Millen arrived at Paris from Boulogne-sur-Mer on Monday the 27th of June at 7.40 p.m. He is specially watched. Before his departure from Boulogne, he had addressed letters to

* Monro's informant was Henri Le Caron – Anderson's undercover agent in the Clan-na-Gael who had contacted Millen in Paris earlier in the spring.

General Carroll-Jervis, 3 rue Daru, Paris,* and to Colonel Farrer, Oriental Club, Hanover Square London.† Enquiries are being made respecting General Carroll and the relations he may have with Millen.'

I was getting very close to C. The 'Black Pamphlet' had named 'General Carrol-Teviss' as a 'member of the Irish Revolutionary Supreme Council'. It looked very much as if Edward Jenkinson did so in extreme secrecy to establish the agent's 'legend'. James Monro, Jenkinson's bitter Whitehall rival and successor, said that Millen went to see a 'man named Tevis who is the principal agent of the Fenian brotherhood in Europe'. Lord Lyons reported that Millen was in communication with a 'General Carroll-Jervis'.

They were all the same person, the spy activated in Paris by the message from H.M. legation in Japan two years earlier. Lord Lyons was unaware, so was the Home Secretary and so was Scotland Yard. Nobody outside a very secret Whitehall knot knew, nor would ever know, that Teviss–Thevis–Tevis–Jervis was the Foreign Office's deepest penetration agent in Paris.

There was more. It looked as if Tevis, whoever he was, had betrayed Millen's 'schemes of outrage'. But Foreign Office files revealed that Millen had *also* been recruited as a double. In April 1885 Millen approached the British consul in Mexico City where he was ostensibly trying to persuade President Diaz to invade the British colony of Belize. He was 'sickened by the dynamiters', he said. He would 'enter into an arrangement with H.M.G. to keep it regularly informed as to the proceedings of the extreme party of Irish nationalists'. Even more significantly he would: 'Warn the Government of outrages that are contemplated should war break out between England and Russia . . . names . . . plans . . . and the system under which they propose to work.' Sir Julian Pauncefote was delighted. 'Liberal remuneration would be given for information of kind mentioned, London cabled back.

The payment agreed was £2,500, The Millen contact was to be shared with Jenkinson at the Home Office but nobody else. In October 1885 Millen, alias agent 'X,' was sent, on Lord Salisbury's sanction, from Mexico to Paris on his undercover mission to spy on Irish-

---

* No. 3 rue Daru is just off the rue Faubourg St Honoré close to the British embassy.
† The Oriental Club Rules and List of Members 1889–90 includes a Major-General Rowland Farrer, late Madras Staff Corps, presumably Millen's Whitehall cut-out. The Maharajah was also a member.

American dynamiters, instructed to communicate by a *poste restante* at Charing Cross station.*

No wonder Tevis and Millen were in urgent contact during the early summer of 1887. One of them had urged the Maharajah be sent on his journey to Russia. The other was ostensibly plotting to blow up Queen Victoria. They were both on the payroll of H.M. Government.

---

* General Millen had a lot more to betray. He was certainly the 'devoted friend' set to command the Irish Legion mentioned in the 'C' letter, and he knew much about Fenian contacts with Russia. During the Russo-Turkish war he was a member of the Clan-na-Gael delegation who approached M. Shishkin, the Russian minister in Washington, looking for military aid for Ireland in the event of an Anglo-Russian war. The contacts continued, betrayed by Millen from 1885 onwards. In 1888 he tried to raise an Irish Legion in New York to lead a raid on gold mines in British Guiana from Venezuela – secretly offering again to betray the whole thing to HM Foreign Office. Lord Salisbury was tempted but the Home Secretary would have none of it. Millen died in New York in April 1889.

# 27

# Proud Rebel and Patriot

*The Katkov estate, Znamenskoe, Podolskii uzed, Moscow Province, July 1887*

MIKHAIL NIKOROVITCH KATKOV was dying. Gaunt and shrunken, he still penned wild tirades against his enemies. After begging the Czar's forgiveness on his knees at Gatchina for the Bogdanovich débâcle, the editor had returned to Moscow like a ghost and holed up behind drawn curtains at his Znamenskoe estate twelve miles outside the city.

On 13 July he suffered a stroke, paralysing his tongue and right arm. Physicians came: Professors Eltsinsky and Novastky from Moscow University, the eminent Dr Bertenson from St Petersburg, Dr Potain from Paris. The news was grave. It was all kept secret.

The Maharajah waited in vain for a summons to his patron's side, pacing his new kingdom, a rented, ramshackle dacha in Petrov Park in the north-west suburbs. Soldiers in white linen uniform blouses discreetly patrolled the estate's perimeter, Berdan rifles slung, bayonets fixed. Were they guarding him from British assassins or keeping him prisoner? Ada was three months pregnant.

The British vice-consul in Moscow reported with glee on 27 July: 'Alas for Duleep Singh, Mr Katkov is *hors de combat*, and is not likely ever to show fight again. He has taken a country house near Moscow, and I have therefore not the same opportunity to observe his movements. I hear the Rajah blusters a good deal; he told the German Consul that within three years there would not be an Englishman to be found in the whole of India.'

Duleep's affairs had indeed taken a momentary upturn the month before. On 12 June he had been summoned by Prince Vladimir

Dolgorouki, Governor-General of Moscow, where he appeared, according to Cyon, 'en grand costume d'apparat'. The meeting oozed cordiality. The Governor read out a letter from the Foreign Office 'written by order of the Emperor', telling Duleep he 'was now at liberty to reside or travel anywhere in Russia that he may please'. De Giers told the perplexed British ambassador, who happened to read about it in *The Times*, that the meeting had never taken place. The Maharajah 'only met the Governor-General casually at some social function at Count Cheremetov's house', he insisted.

Duleep seemed certain enough of what had happened. He told Our Correspondent, obviously alive to the attentions of German mail-openers: 'Besides he [Prince Dolgorouki] read out several important questions which I had to reply and which I would communicate to you at full length though I am informed to consider Sunday's interview a confidential one, as I mean to keep no secret from you, and were it not for the Berlin inquisitiveness you would have all particulars.* But it would never do to let out the state secrets of the empire to any other power in Europe. Therefore you must not mind my reticence on this subject. However, I have forwarded a full report of what took place at the Sunday interview to Mr. K. who is still at St Petersburg. Have you seen in Punch a supposed likeness of myself and Mr. K. piping whilst I, his puppet, am dancing to his tune? I think it is a clever production nevertheless.

'I trust my box has been forwarded ere this reaches you. As we shall take a house in the country very soon, kindly address to the care of Messrs Zenker.'

There seemed no more barriers to acceptance in the stuffy society of the old capital. The only complaints, according to *The Times* correspondent, were 'frequent explosions of riot in the streets against England when he is mistaken for an Englishman. His Highness is held to have done nothing which could properly exclude him from the highest Muscovite circles.' Sporting aristocrats took him up: Count Bobrinski invited him to some black-cock shooting, Count Cheremetov suggested a hunting trip in the Caucasus. Duleep declined. 'I cannot

---

* According to Russian foreign ministry archives, Prince Dolgorouki asked Duleep for the names of his princely supporters in India and written certificates of their allegiance. This was the substance of Arur Singh's doomed mission. The Marahajah replied he would divulge the names to the Czar only in person.

go because neither the princess [Ada] or my secretary [Arur Singh] understand a word of Russian,' he explained on 18 July, 'and I could not leave them behind nor could I take them with me as we have a good deal of baggage of some little value of which there would be no one to take charge in our absence from here.'

By now he knew enough of the *Moscow Gazette* editor's condition to be deeply worried. 'Mr Katkov's dangerous illness is causing me great uneasiness,' he told his Russian friend. 'Were he to die I would be left without anyone to protect me and might be turned out of Russia through some intrigue in high quarters.'

He added with Pinteresque obsession: 'My box containing papers has not yet come from Paris or I would have ventured to send a copy of my history for your acceptance but will do so as soon as it arrives.'

The waiting became unbearable. At the end of July he wrote to Our Correspondent: 'Although I am so near, yet I cannot obtain any reliable information as to Mr Katkov's health but fear the worst. Judging from the accounts which appeared in the St Petersburg journal of the symptoms of his illness, I cannot help thinking that he must have been poisoned, but more likely we shall soon know the opinion of the French doctor who was sent for from Paris as to what he is suffering from.'

The physicians could do nothing. Katkov was eaten with cancer. He died at 4.20 on the night of 1 August. Russia was stunned. Illiterate, provincial, peasant Russia. The national emotional outpouring matched that shown on the death of General Skobolev, and, as also in the case of the 'White General', rumours abounded that Katkov had been poisoned by his enemies.*

Peasants bore the open coffin from Znamenskoe in an eight-hour journey to the wooden-hutted fringes of Moscow; printworkers carried it to the church of the Nicholas Lycée where for it lay for two days, thousands of mourners queueing to kiss the corpse in the Russian manner. The cortège moved on for another funeral service held in the courtyard of the *Moscow Gazette* building. On 6 August the body of Mikhail Katkov was at last interred at the Alekseevskii monastery. Paul Deroulède, the French arch-revanchist firebrand of Boulangism, arrived just in time to orate passionately over the grave. A telegram

---

* An autopsy was performed which was confirmed by Cyon. Death was from natural causes, several malignant tumours were found. The Maharajah was convinced it was murder. 'It is my firm belief that K. was poisoned but I cannot say by whom,' he told Our Correspondent.

of condolence came to Madame Katkova from General Boulanger. Duleep and Ada did not attend the solemnities.

The Maharajah wrote mournfully to Paris on 2 August: 'The great and powerful Katkov is dead. This is indeed a great blow to our plans and I much fear that we shall not gain anything for our pains.' He sought solace as usual in the pursuit of small animals. 'I hope now to leave here for the Crimea in about another six weeks and will occupy myself in sport until wanted.'

For now the Katkov cabal went to ground. Pobedonostsev and Tolstoi did not want to know. Ignatiev kept his own counsels. General Bogdanovich seemed to have disappeared. Cyon, who had arrived in Moscow just in time for his master's funeral, returned to Paris, still frantically trying to undo the damage of the Floquet-letter affair. Duleep wrote ominously to Our Correspondent two weeks later: 'You cannot trust anybody here. For even the few friends I had made when K. was alive are beginning to hide their faces from me and I am told by the Governor-General to apply to the Foreign Office now instead of to him as hitherto, for anything that I may want.' He switched his broadsides to de Giers, demanding permission to travel to St Petersburg, then to Kashmir via Central Asia. From 6 August he began to sign increasingly oleaginous letters in Russian. He was met with utter silence.

There was some good news among the gloom. His box seemed to have arrived safely at last from Paris containing the Maharajah's precious codex – the Punjab Papers he had so judiciously transcribed in the British Museum. 'Yes my reply to The Times iniquitous article is a very violent attack upon that journal,' he wrote, 'and one that can not be answered or denied for I have the Blue Book at my finger's end ... I would not trouble you but the tools I have to work with here are no longer trustworthy now that K. is no more.'

There were new arrivals in Moscow to regale with his old catalogue of woes and to plot revenge. Mr Dobson, *The Times* correspondent, reported: 'His Indian Highness is now solaced in his hours of brooding discontent by a Turkish gentleman, who has recently arrived from Constantinople for the express purpose, it would seem, of conferring with the prince.' This was Abdul Rasul who had arrived on 23 July from Paris, the Muslim arch-enemy of the British Empire whom the Maharajah had so portentously summoned to his side in his 'Casey' letter. Their long revolutionary journey together henceforth was going to be a very bumpy ride.

Duleep's energy scarcely flagged. Armed at last with his boxful of Punjab Papers he sent a counterblast to *The Times*'s scoffing articles to the rival *Daily Telegraph*, confident that newspaper at least would show *Boy's Own Book*-style fair play by publishing. There was a flurry of communications from Pondicherry via Paris, including the extraordinary letter from Captain Hearsey in the *Lahore Tribune*, seemingly presaging an American Revolution-style rising of colonists by disaffected 'Eurasians and Anglo-Indians'.

The Maharajah was hugely excited – he must tell the Czar! He messaged Our Correspondent on 11 August:

> I have just received the enclosed cutting through my cousin from India and I pray you to translate it also into French for me and send 50 printed copies.
>
> I regret troubling you about the translating of these papers but it is most important that they should be placed before the Emperor without delay. Yes, my kind friend, in spite of the unfortunate death of the powerful Katkov, the victory is ours. For even without the help of the Imperial Government an end can be put to the British Empire in India now, as I am now the acknowledged head of a secret and a powerful combination in the Punjab.
>
> The only thing that is now required is to reach the frontier of India and come into contact with these men whose agents are on the look-out for me there. Yes, it is most curious, but the prophecy alluded to in the cutting is about to be literally fulfilled. Even if I am turned out of Russia it does not matter now. The fire has commenced to smoke in India, which I can very easily see ablaze with the assistance of my people.
>
> Hurra! The English have cut their own throats by their own folly. But who can avert destiny. Again I apologise for asking you kindly to translate the documents, but there is no one here whom I can really trust and I rely upon your promise to help me as far as you can.

Our Correspondent immediately sent details of the article to London with the recommendation, 'Captain A. Hearsey's letter is in the same strain, even with a resemblance of phraseology, as Duleep's letter that you saw, whence I conclude that said Hearsey is one of his agitators. Perhaps he might be worth looking after.'

The Maharajah had enjoyed basking in Katkov's now extinguished glow. If an eccentric article in the *Lahore Tribune* could so boost his ego, why wouldn't the English papers take him seriously? His *Daily Telegraph* letter stayed on the spike. He sent a copy to Our Correspondent in Paris with instructions to have it printed and posted to a list of notables (including the Prince of Wales) because, 'I know that if a copy of the journal containing it were sent to those people in England whose names are written on the envelopes I have forwarded to you they would not look at them, but seeing my name on the cover of a letter they are sure to open and read it.'

He suddenly sent one to Queen Victoria's daughter, the Crown Princess of Prussia, who was visiting Osborne, with a covering letter showing bizarrely conflicting loyalties.

Her Imperial Highness, the Crown Princess of Prussia

Madame: Thinking that it might interest your Imperial Highness to read the reply I have written to an article which "The Times" published against me some time back, but which the Editor of the "Daily Telegraph" has not produced, so much therefore for the wonted use of fair-play of the English, I do myself the honour to forward a copy. [Datelined simply 'Russia', 25 August:]

Little did I dream when shortly after my arrival in England from India, now some thirty-two years ago, I had the honour of being presented at Osborne to your Imperial Highness who was then very young and who used to admire my Oriental costume that, I should ever become the proud rebel and patriot that I am this day against the government of your illustrious Mother.

But the injustice, the cruel oppression, and the humiliation which have been inflicted upon me by England have opened my eyes as to what that Power really is, though professing a high code of Christian morality. I am convinced in my own mind that, if there be a God in the Universe, the British Empire of India, which is founded upon swindle and fraud will come to an ignominious end eventually.

The account of the manner in which I was robbed at Berlin while travelling as 'Patrick Casey' must have afforded some little amusement to your Imperial Highness. With profound respect I have the honour to remain, Your Imperial Highness's most faithful servant, Duleep Singh Maharajah.

Princess Victoria was utterly baffled. The court at Charlottenberg would hardly find Mr Casey's antics amusing (there had been an anarchist dynamite *attentat* against her father-in-law Kaiser Wilhelm I three years earlier). She wrote to her mother: 'My beloved Mama, To my great surprise, I today received the enclosed! I hope you will tell me whether I am to send an answer or not, and if so in what terms! I cannot help feeling sorry for him and regretting that he has fallen into such bad hands and became so soured and an enemy to England!

'I was told that the Maharajah was still very grateful to you for the kindness you showed him personally! Perhaps there might be some means of bringing him to his senses and back to the right road. He may have some real grievances too.

'Why he should write to me I am sure I do not know, perhaps because the German Government and Court make such professions of friendship to Russia which I may be supposed to share.'

The princess's final paragraph related to other matters: 'I am assured Dr Evans comes here to look after Fritz's tooth. His throat is less well than it was. I fear there is a tendency for the growth to reappear though it has not actually done so. He talks very little here and is very careful.* Goodbye dearest, beloved Mama. Ever your most dutiful and devoted daughter.'

The Maharajah received no reply, but he craved attention. With his Muscovite press patron dead, he clearly considered launching a propaganda offensive in America. He told Our Correspondent on 19 August: 'I think it is now too late for the publication of my proclamations but not for your article which I think ought to appear soon after the publication of my letter in the New York Times. The news that Russia and England have agreed to divide Afghanistan between them is likely to prove quite true. For it is only by making friends

---

* 'Fritz' was Princess Victoria's husband Prince Friedrich Wilhelm who had married the then seventeen-year old Princess Royal in 1858. He was German Kaiser for three months in 1888, dying of throat cancer on 15 June. Their son was crowned Kaiser Wilhelm II.

with Russia that she can save her Indian Empire for some time to come. However it will be a blow to our little plans, nevertheless there will be this one satisfaction realised viz that the poor old British Lion has shown the white feather! – and given in to Russia of which events perhaps, I have been the humble means of bringing about.'

And there was an interesting spat over an article in the Paris English-language paper, the *Morning News*, of which the Maharajah clearly disapproved. 'I do not think it desirable to take any notice of what appears in such miserable journals as the Morning News about me,' he wrote on 23 August, 'but have written a letter to its Editor for you kindly to post should you think it desirable to do so. The whole article is a fabrication of some ignorant and malicious person, as, since my arrival in Russia, I have never granted an interview to any newspaper correspondent, specially an Englishman. Nor is it my intention so to do,' he complained.

What makes this communication especially interesting is Our Correspondent's covering message to London. 'His reply to the Morning News I copy and enclose, as I shall if that paper inserts it, as I do not expect it will, in which case it shall be communicated to its rival Galignani, now as you know the property of that prince of blackguards James Gordon Bennett,' he wrote. The great American newspaper proprietor was moving into Europe. In October 1887 he would start Paris and London editions of the *New York Herald Tribune* – a move which would later prove significant for the Maharajah and much more so for Our Correspondent.

There were plenty of other intriguing snippets relayed by Our Correspondent to the Foreign Office as the summer wore on: a 100-franc draft to 'Mme V' in Paris ostensibly to cover printing costs; an indication that 'Madame Adam's denunciation [that Duleep was a double-agent] seems to have done no harm'; and that 'The permission to reside in the Crimea is, to my mind, significant. Duleep will be less exposed to inquisitive journalists there than in Moscow and can receive more easily any emissaries from India.'

A dispatch from Russia of 23 August was full of portent. The Maharajah had received 'letters from two of the friends I made here when K. was alive, so my evil forebodings as stated in my last letter are not likely now to be realised, thank God.' But the second line of the letter heralded disaster: 'I regret to say that I have had a telegram from

Pondicherry saying that my cousin is dead. His death is a very great loss to me. It is like my right arm being cut off. I do not know what I shall do without him in India now.'

Thakur Singh Sandhanwalia, plotter in Holland Park, bearer of the prophecy, prime mover of the conspiracy, Wazir of the Punjab, was dead. A British agent had penetrated Duleep's government-in-exile in Pondicherry. Arur Singh, the emissary to the princes and people of India, had walked into a trap.

# 28

# The Prisoner

⁊⁊

*Central Police Station, 18 Lall Bazaar St, Calcutta,*
*5 August 1887*

THE SIKH PRISONER would not say much. When he spoke it was in
barely accented English, asking for Vichy water, brandy and ice, perhaps some champagne might be made available. He wore fine new,
Pondicherry-made clothes and complained about the loss of his opera-
glasses. The midday heat of Calcutta in August was rising. The cell
was foetid. This was not going to be an easy interrogation.

The detainee was Arur Singh. Within hours of arriving in British
India, the Maharajah's emissary had been ensnared. It had begun with
an amateurish piece of agent provocateur-ing, a letter written to Moscow some time in May 1887 by a Calcutta immigration officer, Inspector J. C. Mitter. It got through via Zenker's Bank. 'An unknown friend'
declared he was a secret adherent in the Bengal police and that there
were many like him ready to rise. Money was being subscribed. The
jubilant Duleep had sent Arur to find him.*

Mr Andrew Barnard, deputy police commissioner in Calcutta, was
sleeping fitfully in his bungalow when, at 3.30 a.m. on 5 August 1887,
Inspector Mitter burst in with some amazing news. Arur Singh,
Duleep's 'ambassador', was sound asleep at his house. The excited Mr
Mitter had 'letters' from the Maharajah, 'entrusted to him for safe

---

* Arur Singh had wandered the Punjab disguised as a fakir in the autumn of 1886. He
went there straight from Aden. The police got on his trail, discovering nine months
later 'a whole consignment of second-hand clothing on commission sale with Messrs
Jametjee's sons of Lahore. The clothes have the name of His Highness Prince Victor Duleep
Singh and other sons of the Maharajah marked in the lining in fast fading marking ink.'
They must have been given him by the Maharajah's sons before they returned with their
mother to London from Aden.

custody'. Four were already open, one, addressed to the King of Oudh, lay plumply sealed in its envelope.

They had met the previous afternoon. Mitter had persuaded Arur he was indeed the dissident native policeman and asked for proof that the new arrival was 'not a member of the secret force'. Arur in answer had shown him letters bearing the lion and crown crest of the King of the Punjab.

The documents contained a new version of the stirring address to the 'Brother Princes of India'. Barnard reported by telegraph to Simla: 'Another is a copy of a letter written by one "C" at Paris to the Maharajah, and certified as being a true copy by Duleep Singh himself, and two other unaddressed letters to private individuals; the fifth letter was closed and addressed to the King of Oudh. This letter I opened and read. All these letters were of an inflammatory nature and treasonable to the British Government.

'Arur Singh told the Inspector that "C" is an Irishman, who is or was a Lt-Colonel in the British Army, and Sir Stuart Bayley [Lieutenant-Governor of Bengal] ventures to suggest that the English Police might be communicated with on the subject.'

Thus was the existence of 'C' introduced to the government of India. But the Calcutta policeman, like his political masters, had no idea the seditious statement with its plans for an Irish legion was in fact written by a Foreign Office spy, an habitué of Reynold's Bar. Arur had obviously met 'C' in Paris but though his statement about the military rank was close, the army he had served in was wrong, and he was not an Irishman.

'Leaving Duleep Singh at Moscow, Arur Singh came down to Odessa and thence crossed the Black Sea in a German steamer to Constantinople; he then went via Suez to Colombo in, I believe, foreign steamers, and there changed into one of the B.I.S.N. Co.'s steamers which brought him to Madras. The journey cost him about £102,' Inspector Barnard reported.

'He then went by train to Pondicherry where he stayed for some time with Sardar Thakur Singh, from Pondicherry he went to Hyderabad, and eventually came to French Chandernagore where he arrived on the 1st instant.

'On this date, the Inspector reported to me that a Sikh who lived like an European, had come to Chandernagore; having heard that Arur

Singh had left the Maharajah and suspecting that this might be the same man, I told the officer to keep his eyes open in case the man should come down to Calcutta; this he did, to such good effect that he noticed the Sikh, who subsequently turned out to be Arur Singh, arrived in Calcutta on 2nd instant and watched him visit certain houses in the town.' One of them, on Beadon Street, was the house of Mr Shashi Bhushan Mukerji, editor of *The Beaver*.

'With these facts before me at about 6 o'clock in the morning, I came to the conclusion that it would be advisable to arrest Arur Singh at once,' Barnard reported. The sting was childishly simple. The inspector rushed back to Arur Singh, told him they had to leave in a hurry, 'induced him to get into a ticca garri [a hired four-wheel carriage] with his baggage and then have him driven straight into the Detective Department thana [compound], where he could be quietly arrested.'

Arur was in a cell at the central police station half an hour later. The arrest was secret. The prisoner was made 'comfortable' and attended by the police surgeon, Dr Mackenzie. His bags were 'carefully overhauled', producing cryptic but fascinating results.

'In a pocket book which was in the hand bag,' reported Barnard, 'I found a letter from the Bank of Bengal to Duleep Singh, dated 1st April, 1887, a cheque for Rs. 500/- on the Bank of Bengal drawn by Duleep Singh, the person to whom payable being left blank, four French Bank notes for 100 Francs each, three envelopes addressed to "Mustafa Effendi, Constantinople", one enveloped addressed to Messrs Zenker & Co., Moscow, Russia, on the reverse of which was written the following address: "Madame Vallier 58, rue de la Rochefoucauld, Paris, France," and one English postage stamp.'

The letter to the 'Brother Princes' read:

> We send our faithful and trusted Arur Singh from here to announce to you our arrival in Russia and to inform you that we shall soon come to India to your assistance. Therefore, believe no reports to the contrary whether they be published by the British Government or by the newspapers.
>
> We shall give our life to free you from the English yoke, and only ask you to be prepared for your deliverance, for by the aid of the Almighty we shall succeed. But as it is necessary

that we should report to the Emperor of Russia who among you are for His Imperial Majesty and who for the continuance of the British rule, therefore, we request you to inform by word of mouth only our trusted Ambassador on which side you mean to take part in the coming struggle.

Look to the efficiency of your armies and get them in order.

The above is our address should you wish to communicate direct with us, but we advise you not to write to us for fear of your letters falling into the hands of the British Government.

The letter to the King of Oudh was a personalized version: 'With great joy I announce to you that I have reached Russia and hope through the mercy of God and with the aid of the Emperor of Russia soon to come to India and deliver your Majesty from the hands of the accursed English and to replace you on your throne. You and I though placed in similar circumstances by the same wicked hand, yet I have reached this great empire, while you are still in the hands of your enemies, therefore, I advise you to be very careful.'

It was time to sweat Arur Singh. Colonel Henderson descended by train from the Simla hills into the heat of Calcutta. On the morning of Sunday 21 August, he went to work. The morning interrogation lasted an hour, the afternoon's slightly longer: What were your instructions in Russia? What did you learn at Pondicherry? Who were you to see? Give us the names. We've read the letters. This is sedition, you know the penalty, tell us the truth and all will be well. Who is 'C'?

Arur Singh would give nothing away. The next day the frustrated colonel sought out the cooling comforts of the US Club in Calcutta and cabled Simla.

> I have this afternoon telegraphed to you in cypher telling you of my failure to extract anything from Arur Singh.
>
> His story is that he was sent for the sole object of raising money in India and was told not to show his face again unless he appeared with a large sum, that his instructions were to go to Mukerji, the editor of The Beaver at Chandernagore who would direct him as to his future movements and the persons from whom he was to collect money.*

* This was the continuation of the original intrigue with 'E.C.' in Paris.

Questioned regarding his visit to Thakur Singh at Pondicherry, he would say nothing except that no plans were settled
as a man sent into the Punjab to feel the ground for Arur
Singh had not returned.

Beyond one or two little bits of incidental information this
was all I could get out of him. As soon as I brought him back
in my cross examination to the main point of the intrigues in
India – he stopped short and took refuge in a solid assertion
of ignorance.

I was not mistaken in my fear that a Sikh would not be
easily brought to peach. Arur Singh is a dull, heavy man and
to all appearance about as bad a messenger as Duleep Singh
could have chosen, but he is faithful or obstinate.

I will try again to see whether Arur Singh can be induced
to speak, but do not feel at all sanguine. In case of failure,
I have asked for orders regarding his disposal. It is not advisable to keep him longer than can be helped in the lock-up
here, for the police office is a much frequented place, and
the fact of his being confined here is sure to get out before
long.

It was time for some more subtle interrogation methods.

On 29 August, Arur Singh was joined in his cell by another prisoner,
dishevelled, much-travelled, evidently a Punjabi. He was young, pale-
skinned, and spoke with a slight stutter. He whispered 'secret watchwords' that Arur had heard in Pondicherry. The prisoner was another
Duleep partisan under arrest. Arur told him everything. The 'prisoner'
was L.M., the Muslim detective who had worked the Punjab bazaars
in disguise that spring. This was very clever intelligence work; no
rough stuff, just another quiet deception.

The Muslim detective extracted intelligence of a far higher order
than Henderson had managed. Arur Singh's first 'object was to go to
all the Native Princes of India and prepare the ground for Duleep
Singh and Russia, obtaining, if possible, from each written assurances
of support which could be shown in Russia,' he reported.

'He was to appoint an agent in each state to be the medium of
correspondence, and he was to make arrangements for taking round
a Russian officer (who is to arrive, he said, in India in a month's time)

for the purpose of verifying the information obtained and given to the Russian authorities by Duleep Singh.'

Money was evidently needed to bribe 'high Russian officials'. Arur Singh was also to visit the Amritsar temple to communicate 'instructions for cutting the line of railway and attacking the British army in the rear when a Russian force should appear on the frontier'. There was also an agent in Constantinople called Mustafa Effendi who acted as a mail-box to Russia. 'He is said to be a friend of Djemal-ud-din, the Afghan at Moscow. He is in charge of the burying ground of Sultans, and according to Arur Singh is in Russian pay,' the interrogator reported.

'The Maharani does not help Duleep Singh from her allowance. He is said to have £10,000 lodged with Mallet Frères of Paris, and to be living in Moscow on the proceeds of the sale of his jewelry of which he has a large quantity with him.'

Squeezed of information, Arur was to be safely got out of the way. On 6 September he was sent in handcuffs on the Calcutta mail-train to the fort of Chunar in the North-West Provinces. The Foreign Secretary ordered: 'The prisoner should be securely guarded, being allowed such moderate freedom and exercise as may be necessary for his health. All communications between him and strangers outside or visiting the fort, particularly Punjabis, should be prohibited.

'The Commandant may suggest the amount necessary for the diet and clothing of the prisoner bearing in mind that the man is little more than a menial servant and that it is not necessary to show him any indulgence.'

On his arrival, Arur Singh asked Chunar's commandant, Major R. B. Burnaby, to communicate with the Maharajah: 'I have been directed by Arur Singh whom you sent to Mukerji, the editor of The Beaver at Chandernagore, to write to you. Arur Singh desired to inform you that he was given by Mukerji and his other friends in charge to the Calcutta Police.' Another betrayal.

## House of Thakur Singh Sandhanwalia, 10 rue Law de Lauristan, Pondicherry, August 1887

The arrest and subtly extracted confession of Arur Singh was a great coup for the Indian police. But it had only come about because of another, and much murkier, secret operation – the penetration of the 'government-in-exile' in Pondicherry which had furnished Arur Singh's second interrogator with so much conspiratorial information. With Duleep's emissary in the Calcutta lock-up, two spying missions were mounted by overlapping but separate authorities: deputy commissioner Barnard of the Calcutta police, and Sir Henry Mortimer Durand, Foreign Secretary of the Indian government. On the night of 1818 August, Thakur Singh Sandhanwalia suddenly died.

The family plus their retainers, all thirty of them, had been under close surveillance for months. They were in the habit of gathering on the beach every morning before sunrise and peering mournfully out to sea. The British consul, Colonel Fischer, reported: 'I cannot help thinking that some detective who knew their language would not find it difficult to make them communicative.'

It happened just like that. The industrious Inspector J. C. Mitter of the Calcutta police, 'arrived at Pondicherry on the evening of the 16th August, and after having an interview with Thakur Singh under the guise of a messenger from Arur Singh, returned to Calcutta by the morning train on 17th August, 1887', according to a long report to the Viceroy prepared by Colonel Henderson. The inspector pulled the same dodge – he claimed he was a disaffected Bengali in correspondence with the Maharajah. His haul of intelligence was very detailed; a blueprint for a Russian invasion and a momentous rising in the British rear.

The inspector's superior, deputy commissioner Andrew Barnard, summarized it.

> On the 10th August I placed my officer on special duty in connection with this case ... after visiting Sardar Thakur Singh, in whose household he gained a friendly footing, he has obtained the following information:

PLAN OF CAMPAIGN:

The following is the plan of Duleep Singh's party. As soon as the Russians have completed the railway they are making through Central Asia (which is expected to be in about a year and a half), a Russian army is to invade India, the native soldiers, who will be sent to the front with the British army on reaching the neighbourhood of the Russians, are to desert and to place themselves under the command of Duleep Singh, whilst the native soldiers on their way to the front are suddenly to mutiny, loot the stores and attack the British regiments; at the same time arrangements will be made to destroy railway and telegraph lines all over the country; and to enable the people, in certain places, to rise against the British rule; the native states are at this time to declare themselves for Duleep Singh, and to attack the British with their armies.

NATIVE ARMY:

In order to gain this end, Duleep Singh's and Thakur Singh's emissaries have been going round the lines of the native army, inducing the Sikh and the Rajput soldiers, to espouse Duleep Singh's cause; and in consequence of this, representatives from various regiments have been going to Thakur Singh at Pondicherry and have been taking the oath of allegiance.

This was news the police were dreading. Barnard's agent 'expressed his surprise that soldiers should be able to come to Pondicherry from great distances without arousing the suspicions of the railway police'. It was explained that:

These men leave their regiments on the plea of visiting the shrines of Rameshwar in the south of India, but they leave the train at Arconum and drift slowly down to Pondicherry, avoiding the railway station bordering on the French territory; two men of the Corps of Guides are said to have been with Thakur Singh at the beginning of August, and 40,000 Sikh and Rajput soldiers are said to have taken the oath of allegiance through representatives from their regiments sent to Pondicherry in this manner.

NATIVE STATES:

Various Native states have been communicated with and asked to join the movement, and several chiefs have taken the oath of allegiance. Great reliance is placed in Hira Singh of Nabha, who is said to have considerable influence in the states of Patiala and Jind, the Chiefs of which are minors. Hira Singh has taken the oath, and has agreed to lead the armies of Patiala and Jind, together with his own men, to the field of battle.

Rajah Moti Singh of Poonch, son of Dhyan Singh, who was minister to the late Maharajah Ranjit Singh, is also in the plot.

The Sikh soldiers of Hyderabad have sworn allegiance. 120,000 Kukas in the Punjab are reckoned on to rise at the critical moments; the Kukas are also said to be in direct communication with Russians in Central Asia.

BENGAL:

As Bengal has no army to put into the field, she is to get up political agitation to disturb the Government, and when the time arrives, to destroy the railways, bridges and telegraphs; in return for this Bengalis are to be given seats in the Supreme Council.

AFTER PLANS:

When the British have been turned out of India, Russia is to be recompensed by receiving double the amount incurred by her for the expenses of the war, or one and half times the amount if paid in advance, a yearly tribute is also to be paid to Russia. Duleep Singh is to be installed as ruler of India, and is to be helped by a Supreme Council, the country to be governed on liberal principles and the people to be allowed to have local self-government and freedom of speech.*

My officer read several letters written by Duleep Singh to Thakur Singh, in which he says that his affairs are progressing

---

* The Maharajah gave a glimpse of his political philosophy in a letter to Thakur Singh purloined by the burgling Inspector Mitter; he evidently envisaged a Bismarckian Raj with himself as Kaiser. 'Inform editors of Bengali papers that I differ with them on one point. They desire to have a republic and I want to have a monarchical government,' he wrote. 'After all their and my object is to drive away the English. I will rule India something like Germany by which the Native Chiefs will be independent kings. I will never allow any other nation with the exception of Indians to take part in the administration.'

as favourably as possible; He has had a satisfactory interview with the Governor of Moscow but is afraid to give particulars as he mistrusts the Germans and the Post Office officials.

He also says that matters have been slightly delayed owing to his Excellency Lord Dufferin inducing Mons. Giers to obstruct Russian progress towards India, but he says that the people want war and so war is inevitable.

CYPHER:
For correspondence, a crude and cumbersome cypher is also used, in which each letter in the alphabet is represented by a number of dots corresponding with its numerical position, thus D is represented by four dots and S by nineteen, but, in order to render it more intricate, the dots are formed into various figures at the will of the writer which have no bearing on the meaning.

A much more shadowy agent than the Bengali inspector was in Pondicherry in the second week of August. Sir Henry Mortimer Durand, the Foreign Secretary in Simla, received a stream of immediate intelligence telegrams in Simla from someone called 'Ali Mohammed' in the French enclave. There was this on the 20th: 'Sohan Lal of Dadri, blind of one eye, travelling with letters stitched under the lining of portmanteau, travelling in Sikh states since June last. Have him looked after please.'

Sir Henry told London on 9 September: 'While Henderson was at Calcutta, an agent of mine had been sent to Pondicherry where he succeeded in ingratiating himself with [the late] Sardar Thakur Singh, and obtaining from him a good deal of valuable information on intrigues in India.

'A telegram from me reached him en route informing him of Arur Singh's arrest at Calcutta and directing him to join Henderson here. By a judicious use of the detailed information obtained in Pondicherry, he managed to induce Arur Singh to give him a full account of the objects of his journey.'

Thakur Singh Sandhanwalia died on the night of 18 August. It is clear from Durand's report that 'an agent of mine' was in Pondicherry at the time. 'The news of his death came last night from a man that I sent,' Durand's report to London the next day continued. The time of death was known to the minute: 20.25. The news was important enough for the Viceroy to flash by cipher telegram to London: 'Thakur Singh Sandhanwalia died of fever last night at Pondicherry.' The message was received in the India Office on the morning of 19 August at 10.52 London time. The time elapsed was twenty hours. Someone had rushed from the Wazir of Lahore's death-bed to the Pondicherry cable office to alert Simla.

Ali Muhammed messaging from Pondicherry was clearly the same person as the Muslim detective who was later inserted in disguise into Arur Singh's Calcutta cell. Ali Muhammed and L.M. were the same. His real name was Aziz-ud-din, as formidable an enemy of the Duleep conspirators as anyone in Paris or London. He had already wandered the Punjab in disguise, sniffing out sedition. He would now track down Duleep's partisans across India and the Middle East all the way to Cairo.

The police were exultant at the agent's 'success'. Donald McCracken, the Punjab Special Branch officer, cabled Durand on the 22nd: 'I should be glad if you would ask Aziz-ud-din for some further particulars of his travels, whether he is likely to have assumed any disguise. PS: "The Civil and Military Gazette" has just come in, and I see in it a report of Sardar Thakur Singh's death. This is not unlikely to be true as he was reported to be very ill. Another of Duleep Singh's supporters gone!'

Did Aziz-ud-din murder Thakur Singh Sandhandwalia? There is no smoking gun in the surviving files, no written orders for the expedient demise of the 'rascally cousin' Queen Victoria found so disagreeable. He was 'old and ill', he 'died of fever', officials minuted. But something happened. The available evidence is contradictory. Three weeks after Thakur's death, Inspector McCracken in Lahore was hunting Sohan Lal, the emissary to the Punjab that the agent in Pondicherry had cabled to have 'looked after'. The inspector messaged Simla on 9 September: 'I have taken steps to track down Sohan Lal. If Government wants his or anyone else's things overhauled ... they should send me orders. The thing is easily done, but I am shy of acting in a manner of this kind without orders. I want orders before I will do it. I have been among the Philistines you see.' What did he mean?

There is another hint of unofficial executive action in a much later Durand cable of April 1888: 'Remember that Aziz-ud-din, though a clever detective and well meaning, is apt to jump to conclusions. I have known him very wild indeed,' he told the head of the Political and Secret Department in London. And Colonel Henderson received a police report from the Punjab around the same time. 'It is well known among all Duleep Singh's adherents that Aziz-ud-din was living in Pondicherry during Thakur Singh's lifetime and reported all he saw to Government. They also suspect that he caused Thakur Singh's death, and have sent his description to Duleep Singh to put him on his guard in case Aziz-ud-din goes to Russia, and tries to get into his confidence as he did into Thakur Singh's.'

The 'beware assassin' warning was repeated to the Maharajah much later. Thakur's son Gurbachan Singh wrote from Pondicherry in February 1890: 'One thing more and that is that a certain Mohammedan menial police official [this is clearly Aziz-ud-din] has been sent to Paris by the English wicked Govt. to kill Your Majesty.

'Please be careful of him and the man I hear is accompanied by some other Indians too. Therefore we most humbly draw your attention about that. My friend told me that he has gone to Paris since six months. I don't recollect his real name but he has been here too on a similar mission and he claims to his Government that he got our father poisoned by the French doctor but he is a liar. Nothing of the kind happened here. He is about 20 years of age and of a white complexion and has a little stuttering while speaking. He was to appear before Y.M. as a Sikh or Hindoo.' In Pondicherry he had masqueraded as a 'Hyderabad noble'.

This letter survives as a report from Our Correspondent to the Foreign Office. Unlike several other communications from Pondicherry it is a transcript copy. The crucial 'he is a liar' line could have been inserted to protect Aziz. There was no autopsy on Thakur Singh. His body was cremated the morning after his death. His servant Jowala Singh was deputed to carry his ashes to the Punjab and join Sohan Lal, the wandering emissary. Aziz-ud-din was ordered to track them down. He would do so and interrogate them with the same efficiency he had displayed in Pondicherry and the Calcutta police cell. They would reveal much more.

Queen Victoria later (8 December) received a personal intelligence report of the Pondicherry operation summarised by Sir Henry Ponsonby. He wrote:

Duleep Singh sent Aroor Singh from Moscow to India with letters to the Princes of India calling them to throw off the yoke of their repression.

There was also an agent of the Maharajah's in Pondicherry, Thakur Singh, from whom the detectives learned of the coming of Aroor Singh.

Thakur died and the detectives came at once to Calcutta and had Aroor arrested.

Blank cheques signed by the Maharajah and treasonable letters were found upon him besides arrangements for giving Russian officers notice of his movement.

Also letters from a Mr. 'C' believed to be an Irishman lately in the British Army – promising the aid of Irish soldiers. This was written from Paris.

The police are now enabled to watch several suspicious persons and the intrigue is broken up.

Still Mr Durand the Foreign Secretary is uneasy and believes that if Duleep Singh comes with a Russian Army to India the Sikh population may join him.

But he thinks most of the Sikh troops will be loyal. In many regiments there is no feeling for him. The correspondence between Moscow and India passes through the hands of Mustapha Effendi at Constantinople who is watched.

The Queen had also been reading (as had the Prince of Wales) Sir Robert Morier's dispatches through the summer about bomb-plots against the Czar. She could find no quarrel with her ministers' efforts, or anyone else's, to stamp out such wicked conspiracies.

# Princesses

᭟

*53 Holland Park, Kensington, London, Summer 1887*

THE UNPAID VICTUALLERS of Notting Hill hammered at the trades-men's entrance. At the wedding-cake house in Holland Park, Bamba hid from the butcher and the baker behind heavy drawn curtains. The dressmaker Madame Flarie's outstanding 'Indian outfit' account for the abandoned Bamba and the children was causing ill-mannered jokes in Whitehall. The princesses ran wild in the overgrown garden for all of the passing traffic on Uxbridge Road to see. Little Prince Edward was proving delicate. Bamba did what she could, trusting to God's mercy, and, so it was being said at the highest levels of government, seeking solace in drink – but her humiliations were to continue.

Her vanished husband had placed a most uncharitable notice in *The Times*'s personal columns in August the previous year: 'I, the undersigned Maharajah Duleep Singh, having resigned all the property professed to me in England for the benefit of H.H. the Maharani Duleep Singh and my children, hereby declare that I am no longer responsible for their debts or for articles ordered for them in my name.'

Under his father-in-law's pleading, the Maharajah had agreed to give her 'half the income of the Elveden estate' (which was nothing) and '£30 now and then'.

Queen Victoria had leant on her ministers sufficiently to ensure that something was done. In the autumn of 1886 the India Office had agreed £6,300 a year to Bamba and £2,000 a year to the eldest sons – £500 a year to be retained to pay off Victor's considerable existing debts. At Magdalene, Cambridge, he had evidently developed a taste for 'champagne and other delicacies'. Trustees were appointed: J. A. Godley, the permanent under-secretary for India, Sir Robert Montgomery and Lord Henniker. Arthur Oliphant (son of the Maharajah's old comptroller Jamer Oliphant) was made the Maharani's 'agent' and duly reported on the family's condition. Bamba was reported to be 'extravagant in many ways', yet saved money 'by entire neglect of the health and education of her children'.

There had been the question of what to call them. Were they 'royal' or not? Sir Owen Tudor Burne wrote after the fatherless family's sullen return to London from Aden: 'Calling the children Princes and Princesses is inconvenient. The only effect it has had on Duleep Singh's family is unbounded conceit and extravagance. It occurs to me whether we should countenance the sons of rajas or ex-rajas calling themselves princes or whether a more suitable title might not be invented?'

Freddie was at Eton, about to go to Cambridge, Victor to Sandhurst on a 'special cadetship' (this was a political move: 'men of Indian extraction are disqualified by parentage from entering the army under existing rules', it was noted at the War Office). Was he to be Lieutenant Prince Victor or Lieutenant Victor Singh? There was an intense discussion among India's administrators. 'The young men were always called Princes at Eton. Prince is a very harmless title abroad, witness the hundreds of Princes and Princesses in the Caucasus,' a civil servant minuted. The Viceroy cabled: 'No objection to suggestion the Queen give him no native title but whatever English precedence she thinks fit. But hope Queen will not make too big a man of him – it would not be at all to his benefit.'

At his baptism in Windsor Castle's private chapel the baby Victor was styled 'Shahzadah' – grandchild of a king. That would not do. The Queen felt it inappropriate for Victor to have the title 'Honourable' or be assigned any precedence at court. She personally came up with the odd title 'Maharaj Kumar', which Victor thought ridiculous. Sir Henry Ponsonby wrote from Osborne on 2 January 1887: 'If you don't call these boys princes I don't see what you can call them. When Her Majesty objected to one being articled to a commercial house she said the position was not one that a Prince could hold.' Ponsonby scrawled a minute: 'He may call himself Prince if he likes.' Thus it was agreed, they were still a royal family.

That just deepened Bamba's humiliation. She came out of Kensington purdah in June to attend the jubilee celebrations, but her 'absence' from Westminster Abbey for the great service of thanksgiving was commented on by the newspapers. It was explained she 'arrived late and her seat was taken up'. Then, 'some women insulted her by calling her husband a thief and herself a thief's wife'. She did not go out in society after that.

The young princesses had become most unlady-like. 'Regular hours and habits were quite unknown,' the Queen was later to be informed. A long letter from Arthur Oliphant to the Queen's private secretary dwelt on the Maharani's motherly failings: 'Princess Bamba possesses a Bible, but it has never been unpacked since they started for Aden in the spring of '86. Catherine has never possessed one. They are lamentably backward in everything; but are very desirous of learning. They both hold themselves very badly and don't know how to walk like young ladies.' Oliphant hired a drill sergeant from Thorncliff camp to march them up and down in the parlour.

'The Maharani was always going to give them lessons in calisthenics, and always going to take them to church, but these intentions as indeed all others were never carried out,' he wrote. The 'poor little things have had no play with other children for a long time.' They were 'too shy to touch the piano . . . they had never had books . . .'

Princess Sophia contracted typhoid. Her mother Bamba prayed, distraught, by her bedside, and on 17 September herself fell into a coma. Twelve hours later she was dead. She was aged thirty-eight.

Dr William Gull,* the royal physician, informed the Queen in a letter to Ponsonby: 'The Maharani had long been in delicate health from diabetes and lately Her Highness has been more than usually depressed from the illness of one of her daughters. Fatal nervous exhaustion is not infrequent in states in which diabetes exists though that may be long delayed.' The doctor attending recommended the 'immediate removal of the children'.

Thus it was that carriages arrived, amid soothing lawyers' talk of

---

* The Queen's 'surgeon-in-ordinary' was sensationally accused in 1973 of being 'Jack the Ripper' – head of an alleged masonic conspiracy to cover up a scandal surrounding the Duke of Clarence, the Prince of Wales's eldest son. The accuser, the elderly son of the painter Walter Sickert, later admitted it was a hoax but the story persisted enough to be made into a film.

trust-funds and appointing guardians of a 'suitably forceful character', to bear the four youngest children away to a rambling, ozone-blown house at no. 21 Clifton Crescent, Folkestone. How jolly to be at the seaside after stuffy old London. Arthur Oliphant, their *de facto* guardian, sent for their Elveden nanny, Miss Date, who had left the Maharani's service when Bamba's 'strange habits' had started to become ever stranger.*

Bamba was buried at Elveden's church on 23 September. At least this last act of her bizarre life seemed dignified. Her body was borne from London by special train to Thetford in a 'duplex funeral car', and carried to the graveside on the shoulders of estate workers. The Queen and Prince of Wales sent wreaths, her daughter and little Prince Edward placed bouquets on the coffin. Mr Clinton Dawkins, representing his political master Lord Cross, telegraphed the India Office: 'The Maharani's funeral. Everything went off very smoothly, the country people showing every mark of respect and regret.'

If there was a moment for reconciliation, it might be now. The Queen felt full of remorse. She wrote to her daughter a week after the funeral: 'The poor Maharani died of all the worries she went through and his desertion of her. The children (of whom there are 6!) – will be well cared for, have good guardians and allowance and kind people with them and I shall see them whenever I can. Would to God! I had done some more of late with the poor Maharajah! But really the family had become so large and so much to do about them that it was difficult to do and besides the extreme shyness of the Maharani made it more difficult to see much of them.'

She wrote as 'your affectionate friend and godmother' to Prince Victor: 'Under the present painful circumstances the loss must be peculiarly sad and trying and I feel deeply for you all.'

The Prince of Wales sent a letter of condolence to his old shooting chum. The Maharajah's reply was coruscating: 'Under other circumstances I should have felt most grateful for Y.R.H.'s condescension,' he wrote from Moscow, 'but in the present circumstances, while your illustrious mother proclaims herself the Sovereign of a Throne and of

---

* Miss Date, who had 'brought all the young Duleep Singhs into the world', had been engaged by Princess Gorchakov in St Petersburg. She died in Russia a few weeks after receiving Oliphant's offer.

an Empire which have been acquired by fraud and of which Y.R.H. also hopes one day to become the Emperor, these empty conventional words addressed to me amount to an insult.'

On the day of Bamba's interment, the Maharajah wrote cheerfully from Moscow to Mr Robert Drewitt, the Elveden estate manager: 'Setting aside all political affairs for some time to come, I am going to indulge in some splendid sport in the Caucasus, the sportsman's paradise.' He wanted his 'sporting apparatus' – shotguns and fishing rods – sent to Sebastopol. He especially asked for the despatch of Bamba's hunting saddle.*

* The Maharajah cabled later: 'Apologies – did not realise.'

# 30

# The Confession

❦

*General Superintendent's Offices, Thugee and Dacoity Department, Simla, August 1887*

THAKUR SINGH SANDHANWALIA was dead. The house in Pondicherry, seat of the 'Prime Minister of the King of Lahore', was in chaos – bugged, burgled and betrayed. British agents had penetrated the sanctuary on the rue Law de Lauristan and the approaches were watched. Informers stalked the Southern Indian Railway with orders to follow anyone who looked like a Sikh soldier on leave or otherwise. The British consul in the French enclave sent regular reports. The mantle of leading the rebellion had passed to the son, Gurbachan Singh, educated, intelligent, a civil servant,* 'one of the few native gentlemen considered fit by education and social position', apparently. The young man was further now distinguished in police descriptions as wearing 'blue-tinted spectacles'.

It was clear from Aziz-ud-din's intelligence from French India that two emissaries were on their way to the Punjab to herald the uprising. 'Sohan Lal of Delhi has been travelling in Sikh states since June last with letters stitched into portmanteau – have him looked after please,' the detective had clandestinely telegraphed. And that 'Jowala Singh has left Pondicherry with Thakur Singh's bones and seditious letters heading for Punjab.' Arrest warrants were drafted with instructions that the two men should be lifted 'quietly'. The eager Aziz prepared to interrogate them. He always got results.

Colonel Henderson ran the case from Simla with his usual vigour, sending and receiving a stream of cables from across India as Duleep's

---

* By the 1878 Statutory Civil Services Act, one-sixth of posts were opened to 'natives'.

partisans were tracked down and brought to confession. It was Sohan Lal's turn first. He had been sent to the Punjab in May with letters addressed to potential Duleep adherents. On 10 September, an urgent arrest order under the catch-all Bengal Regulation III of 1818 was sent to Mr William Merk, deputy police commissioner for Delhi.

He was traced to his home town, Dadri, in the Sikh state of Jind west of Delhi, where the two suspects seemed to have met on 5 September. Jowala Singh then headed straight for Lahore. Sohan Lal was collared on 11 September by a Sikh detective in the Delhi police department called Narain Singh. The suspect's portmanteau was neatly filleted. It was found, as predicted, to be lined with seditious material. Also found on the prisoner was an elaborate pedigree of Duleep Singh, printed in England,* and an Egyptian railway timetable for summer 1886. But much more ominous were torn papers in Gurmukhi script, containing the troublesome words 'Russians' and 'Nihangs', that had made the long journey from Holland Park.

William Merk messaged the Punjab Special Branch from Delhi on 18 September: 'Sohan Lal is down with fever and so is Narain Singh and everyone else in this beastly hole.' And three days later the Delhi policeman cabled: 'He is an obstinate villain. I shall interview him tonight. Narain Singh having prepared the way to some degree, he seems now to realise that the game is up. If you send the Pondicherry informer [Aziz-ud-din] to me, please let him come to my house, and on some other business ostensibly. Here in Delhi everyone's ears are cocked for anything that may be going on. We are in the midst of the Moharram Dehra† worries and I shall be glad when the business of guarding idolatrous and fanatical processions is over.'

Merk did the interrogation himself, aided by a Delhi police constable called Elihu Bux. Sohan Lal, still weak with fever, made a full confession. 'Thakur Singh and Gurbachan Singh told me Duleep Singh would come in a few months, drive out the English, and be king,' he admitted. He had been given five envelopes, 'for the chiefs of Nabha, Patiala, Jind, Faridkot and a fifth state whose name I forget'.

The courier had panicked and burned them. Why? 'Because Thakur Singh told me to give the letters secretly and not show them to any

* A copy of this pedigree was given to me by the Sandhanwalia family in Amritsar in September 1997.
† Moharram Dehra: a religious festival.

British or Native State official, but to give them very secretly to rajahs themselves. Hearing all this, I became very suspicious. He told me if these letters were discovered on me, he would suffer, but I would be hanged. All this made me very frightened.' (In fact, as later interrogations discovered, he burned them because an emissary from Pondicherry arrived after the arrest of Arur Singh to warn him he was under surveillance; the same emissary then set off urgently to warn Jowala Singh in Amritsar.)

'I picked out the Egyptian timetable from a lot of books and wastepapers which Thakur Singh brought from Europe and left at Dadri,' Sohan Lal admitted. 'The pedigree of Duleep Singh was left at Dadri by Narinder Singh, the torn papers in Gurmukhi script containing the words "Russians" and "Nihangs" etc. found with me belonged to waste papers of Thakur Singh which he left at his quarters in Dadri on return from Europe. All that Thakur Singh and Gurbachan Singh said was that in a few months Duleep Singh would be king again.'

Deputy commissioner Merk signed off the confession: 'The above statement was made to me on the condition that the life of Sohan Lal is spared if the statement is true.'*

Jowala Singh's mission was stranger; he carried the box of Thakur Singh's partially burned remains to consign to the flowing waters of the Hardwar river, as well as messages proclaiming that the struggle continued under Gurbachan Singh's leadership. The police decided to let him continue, see whom he contacted, and then: 'Arrest him without any fuss, any excitement among the Sikhs is to be avoided'. He was searched at Lahore, but the police let him go. He was lifted at Amritsar on 26 September and sent secretly to Simla for interrogation, conducted this time by Aziz-ud-din.

He had been Thakur Singh's servant for fifteen years, he stated. He had accompanied his master to England and stayed in London with the Maharajah, in Holland Park, where the conversation regularly turned to the prophecy and especially 'whether a Sikh, who has embraced Christianity, can be re-admitted into Sikhism'. The answer from the Granthis at the Golden Temple was yes.

'When they reached Pondicherry, Duleep Singh was in Paris. Letters used to pass through him and the Sardar. Two or three months after

---

* Sohan Lal died in prison in March 1888.

his arrival, the Maharajah went to Russia and on his arrival there sent the title of Prime Minister (Wazir-i-Azim) to Thakur Singh. Arur Singh's boxes, etc. were in his charge but later on, on the arrival of a Bengali [Inspector Mitter] they were forced open and some papers were taken out.'

Jowala Singh named a stream of clandestine arrivals from the Punjab, all noted down by his interrogator. Messages were carried hidden in book bindings – he named their addresses, including several priests at the Golden Temple in Amritsar. He named Bawa Budh Singh, a prominent Sikh of the holy city, as the medium of communication between Kashmir and the Pondicherry intriguers. The detective would have told the prisoner he had done well. He had served the Sandhanwalia family loyally for years and gained nothing. Aziz reported that Jowala Singh would turn informer for payment of 15 rupees a month.

Colonel Henderson was jubilant at the intelligence coup. They had an effective arrest list, enough it seemed to smash the conspiracy in the Punjab. 'It is pretty clear from this confession that the centre of all intrigues in the Punjab is Bawa Budh Singh Bedi, nominally in the employ of the Nepal State, but who has been living in the Punjab for the last two years,' he memoed on 12 October.

'Jowala Singh names him also as an intermediary in these intrigues with the Rajah of Poonch . . . If we are to strike an effectual blow at these intrigues, I think that Budh Singh should be arrested and confined under Regulation III of 1818. It is a question whether sufficient evidence can be brought against him for a formal trial.'

The Viceroy signed the papers immediately, while his Foreign Secretary added: 'Under arrest they are to be well treated, no unnecessary hardship being inflicted on them. This does not, of course, mean that such requisitions as were recently made by Arur Singh for champagne, &c. should be complied with.'

Three more Sikhs were targeted for immediate arrest: Magahar Singh (who had carried the warning to burn all the papers), Hari Singh, who was Budh Singh's servant, and Kesar Singh of Amritsar, who was 'supposed to have taken letters to Punjab and the three Paris proclamations. Jowala Singh undertakes to make him confess fully and give all names,' Colonel Henderson recorded.

'If Budh Singh is to be tried, all the four should be arraigned on one charge and the three subordinates admitted as Queen's evidence,' he added, 'but I suppose it is not likely that a public trial will be considered advisable. The steps recommended will, I believe, have the effect of putting an end to all trouble as regards Duleep Singh in the Punjab.' Henderson ordered: 'It will be well if all four men could be arrested simultaneously and at once prevented from communicating with each other and with outside people until their examination has been concluded. I venture also to suggest that no attempt should be made to examine any of the men, until the arrival of Aziz-ud-din, attaché to the Foreign Department at Amritsar.'

Aziz-ud-din went to work. The suspects were confined in Ambala gaol and interrogated through the day and night of 11 November. Budh Singh confessed first. 'I am thirty-six or thirty-seven, a Captain in the Nepal army, I am a Sikh. Thakur Singh approached me. He talked constantly of Maharajah Duleep Singh who he had seen in England as an incarnation of the deity and that he was coming soon to take his kingdom and the time of trouble for the Sikhs was over,' he admitted. 'Then I went to Amritsar. In April 1887 Hari Singh and Kesar Singh appeared. They had with them a book of arithmetic, in the boards were concealed letters. In my letter I was told to take the letters to Kashmir and Punch and to tell them to tear up the railways and break the bridges and make a mutiny when Duleep Singh arrived at a place beyond Kabul with the Russian army.

'After three days I opened the book and the four letters in it, foolscap size. I burned them. They were all open sheets with the seal on them in red ink. They were written in Persian.'

Hari Singh (Budh Singh's servant) confessed the same day. 'I was sent to Pondicherry with a letter for Thakur Singh with sugar and cloth. They used to say that they would lay the roads with silver for Duleep Singh. I followed Budh Singh to Amritsar and gave him the book and said that he had ruined himself and that he would ruin others too. He burned the letters in my presence.

'He told Thakur Singh by letter that the Kashmiri people had spurned them saying Thakur Singh was mad and they would only act on the orders of Duleep Singh himself. Thakur Singh said that in two years Duleep Singh would rule the country. I know no more.'

Kesar Singh, the third prisoner, had an identical tale.

This is how the Duleep Singh conspiracy was rolled up by the Thugee and Dacoity Department (Special Branch) and the government of India foreign department: extra-territorial action, burglary, clan-destine arrests, secret imprisonment, interrogations, the use of informers and 'native' detectives – Inspector J. C. Mitter, a Bengali; Narain Singh, a Sikh; Aziz-ud-din, a Mohammedan – to entrap other Indians. It was very effective. It is the way empires are held.

As the Maharajah passed the late summer days with Ada mooching round the shabby dacha at Petrov Park, he was unaware of how com-pletely the Indian end of the conspiracy had been penetrated. Arur Singh had vanished; he was either dead or had run off with 'the money' Duleep still believed was being piled up in tribute by the people and princes of India. The reality was different: confessions by frightened men in police interrogation cells, frauds and scams by Indian news-paper editors, a mixture of fantasy and dark despair in Pondicherry.

Gurbachan Singh Sandhanwalia was in deep mental turmoil. On 27 September he wrote two letters. The first was to the Maharajah in Moscow. It reported the wave of arrests but continued in high opti-mism: 'We have more authentic news that very great excitement is prevailing in the Punjab, specially among the Sikhs, and the people are more than ever anxiously awaiting Y. Majesty's arrival in or near Afghanistan. We can safely assure your Majesty beyond doubt that as soon as Y.M. reaches Kandahar or Cabul an open severe rebellion will take place.'

But on the very same day, the blue-spectacled rebel was writing to the Lieutenant-Governor of the Punjab begging for pardon: 'We are in a foreign land without friends or any sort of help and really in great difficulty and our case is one that requires the mercy of the Government,' he wrote. 'We trust that you will be good enough to make us succeed in re-establishing ourselves in the Punjab once more with respect and freedom.'* No wonder the Russians were insisting on evidence that India really was ripe for the Maharajah's plucking.

The intelligence haul from the arrest of Arur Singh and the Pondi-cherry sting was enormous. Colonel Henderson put it together in a

* Sir Charles Aitchinson, the Lieutenant-Governor, magnanimously minuted in reply: 'They are free to return whenever they like.' Colonel Henderson was less charitable: 'It is not considered desirable to give any such promise and, if the Sardar returns, it must be at his own risk, for he has seriously compromised himself in these intrigues,' he wrote. For now, the Sandhanwalias, broke and hungry, stayed where they were.

long memorandum for the Secretary of State for India on 22 September. He included précis of letters from the Maharajah when Thakur Singh's boxes were broken into. Our Correspondent had not spied all Duleep's letters; there was another mail-route to Russia running via the mysterious Mustafa Effendi, 'the guardian of the sultans' graves', in Constantinople. Putting them together filled tantalizing gaps into the bigger political dramas unfolding in Paris and Moscow.

There was this, for example, obviously sent after the meetings with Prince Kotzebue at the rue de Grenelle: 'Send me some money as soon as you can. Without it I can not proceed any further. The Russian Minister at Paris has asked me for £1,000,000 without which he will not allow me to do anything with his government.'

And there was this letter sent later from Moscow: 'I have offered three and a half million as tribute to Russia. You should now try and ascertain from Nizam, Baroda, Holkar, and C[ashmere] whether they will join me in paying this sum and thus driving away the English from India. But, as far as I am aware, they are puppets in the hands of the English and I cannot expect much from them. Tell them Russia cares very little for India and the Indians. She only cares for money.'

It was the same from the moment the Maharajah had walked into the Russian embassy. All anybody seemed to want was his money. 'Get some money from the native princes and have it sent to me, so that I may use it in bribing Russian officials – wicked as it may look, one can not get on in this world without it,' he wrote with hard-gained realism.

And there was this: 'A Russian officer is on his way to India. At the request of his friends I have given him a letter of introduction to you. I am told he is a good Persian scholar, so you will have no difficulty in conversing with him.'

Most tantalizing of all was a one-line message sent from Paris. It was crudely transcribed by the snooping Bengali detective and printed up in the Foreign Department's office copy thus: 'General Buzgovitch has arrived *here* and has brought letters from Constantine Bonodovostzeff and M. Katkoff asking me to come over to Russia.' The undated letter was clearly from the Maharajah and was written from Paris.

The Viceroy's private secretary, Sir Donald Mackenzie Wallace, minuted in the document's margin. 'Bogdanovitch? Pobedonostsef?

General Bogdanovitch was the man who smuggled Duleep Singh into Russia. M. Pobedonostsef is regarded as the most trusted councillor of the Tsar and was a great friend of Katkoff.' What he did not add was what he could not know: that the only times General Evgenii Bogdanovich had been in Paris were at the beginning and very end of January 1887, on what Cyon insisted was a mission to cure an eye ailment, with his face swaddled in bandages like the Invisible Man.

The burgled Pondicherry letters added much to Patrick Casey's statement in the *Morning Advertiser* interview: 'It was while he was here [Paris] that a person occupying a position of influence introduced him to several Russian conspirators.' It was clear the Maharajah had met 'General Buzgovitch', and others, in Paris in the depths of the war-scare winter.

What happened in those frantic midwinter weeks as shadowy figures shuttled thousands of miles on snowbound trains while Europe stood on the brink of war? What was the real reason that M. and Madame Casey were spirited eastwards? Duleep would never know. Katkov was dead. Duleep had been used to destroy him. Stuck in Moscow, he and Ada were beginning to become an embarrassment.

# 31

# Wretched Peace

❦

*Petrov Park, near Moscow, August–September 1887*

ADA WAS six months pregnant. The Maharajah paced up and down
the autumnal dacha with its swelling pumpkins, desperate for action.
His Queen was a 'fetter to his feet', he told those visitors from Moscow
who would still listen. He had a plan to get to India through Persia
but Ada would not let him go without her. Prince Dornadov Korsakov,
the governor of Tiflis, had invited Duleep south, once he got permission,
of course, to travel outside Moscow. Ada refused; she was not going anywhere, she was going to have a baby. Now, worse, Ada was insisting her
mother come to Moscow to help with the impending birth. How would
the Czar react to being presented with the Queen Mother, Mrs Sarah
Wetherill, late of The Phoenix Gasworks, Kennington?

Ada still craved company. She had taken up with an English woman
in the city, the wife of the journalist at the *Moscow Gazette*, M. Shatoukin,
who had first met them off the Paris train. They seemed very close. Then
news of Bamba's death reached Moscow (the British vice-consulate
eagerly circulated the fact). If Ada was not the Maharani she was something else. Polite society shut its doors. The Maharajah settled at the
cards table; baccarat à banque in the newly imported French style was
the game preferred by the flashy army officers who surreptitiously
came to visit and talk up grand schemes. Duleep was losing.

Arur Singh had vanished – the Maharajah exclaimed that had 'lost
his right hand'. On the scrubby country estate, the sovereign of the
Punjab had to do all the butlering and valeting himself. He had scarcely
ever made a cup of tea. He must see the Czar. His fate was in M. de
Giers's hands now – but the foreign ministry stayed resolutely silent.

He rowed with Abdul Rasul constantly. Ada loathed the brooding one-eyed Kashmiri with his ugly scar and brindled beard. He took Duleep's consort on suspicious sufferance. The Maharajah told his Pondicherry cousins: 'Abdul Rasul is more of a Mahommedan than loyal to me. Indeed his entire policy is different to mine and so we could not agree.'

The Muslims of Moscow had taken Abdul Rasul up, sent a carriage to take him to the city's mosque, but Duleep of course refused to go. His 'private secretary', as Rasul was described, seemed to be making his own alliances – Sikander Khan of Herat, General Alikhanov, the governor of Pendjeh, and Musa Khan, Prince of Kazan and aide-de-camp to the Czar, seemed most encouraging. They were all Muslims. Rasul was meanwhile corresponding feverishly with conspiratorial figures in Constantinople. He suggested that Duleep send his Ottoman friends 'presents' including 'photos of the Maharani'. It could do no harm.

The rows got worse. Around 20 October, Abdul Rasul left Moscow heading for the Middle East via Paris. He carried with him a very secret Russian Army plan for some sort of action in Egypt. He was getting money from a mysterious source. The Maharajah sensed the danger, telling Our Correspondent: 'My secretary's name is Abdul Rassoul and he is in Paris just now. Beware of him.'

Duleep now had a rival, hogging what little Russian limelight there was. Djemal-ud-din, the 'Afghan sheikh', was strutting about St Petersburg, the darling of society. Sir Robert Morier reported to Lord Salisbury: 'This individual is an Arab adventurer who had edited an Arabic newspaper in Paris containing the most violent attacks on H.M.G. who professed to be on intimate relations with the Mahdi and with different religious leaders of Islam, and was believed to have promoted disaffection in India.'

Mr Hornstedt, the snooping Moscow vice-consul, was switched from watching the troublesome Sikh to the flamboyant Afghan. 'Two or three years ago, Djemal-ud-din is said to have spent three months in England, staying with an English family, the name of this family, my informant could not recollect, but the lady of the house [was said to be] to be a grand-daughter of Lord Byron,' he reported.*

* Lady Anne Noel, wife of Wilfred Scawen Blunt the aristocratic traveller, poet and Arabist who in a long and controversial career championed Irish Home Rule (for which he was imprisoned), Egyptian nationalism and sundry enemies of the British Empire.

Even the bejewelled Maharajah could not compete with this high romantic novelty. *The Times* reported gloatingly from St Petersburg on 1 September: 'The death of M. Katkov seems to have completely swept the Indian Maharajah off the scene of Muscovite politics, and probably from Muscovite soil.

'His place has now been taken by another enemy of the British, who was also in Moscow on a similar errand until M. Katkov's death. This is the Afghan Sheikh Djemal-ud-din, who publishes letters in the St Petersburg press on the grave mistake made by the Russian Government in permitting England to interfere in the demarcation of the frontier between Russia and Afghanistan.'

The spy Aziz-ud-din later reported the two rebels' rivalry: 'Duleep was quite overshadowed. Out of this hot words were exchanged between them, Djemal and Duleep, and the result was irreparable separation between the two. Djemal-ud-din afterwards revealed Duleep's true colors and exposed him to the Russian authorities. When M. de Giers asked about Duleep's influence in India he told him that: "There was not a dog with him in India and that the new generation knew nothing about him".'

But Nicholas de Giers, however, suddenly became magnanimous. At the end of August he authorized a *carte de séjour* for the Maharajah – 'it was only courteous to do so' – and allowed that his 'heavy baggage' might come into the empire from England, via Sebastopol. At last Duleep would get his Purdey shotguns.

Our Correspondent gave London the news on 16 September: 'Duleep Singh is in high favour, orders have been given that he and his attendants may circulate freely and without passport throughout the empire to be handy when wanted: He is recommended the Crimea or the Caucasus as a place of residence. At first he was distrusted and principally on account of his avarice, like all pretenders it was supposed that at a given moment he would ask for money, but since then it has been officially ascertained that he has 100,000 roubles with Zenker and 50,000 francs with Mallet.'

By September 1887 the war storms of Europe's nervous spring had temporarily blown over. All was to be, in the Maharajah's words, 'wretched peace'. He wrote to Gurbachan Singh: 'The political situation is becoming more and more peaceful every day but all may be changed suddenly as the Russians hate the Germans. Pray Sri Sat Gooroo ji that a European war may break out soon and then we are sure to have all we desire.'

Prayers in the guru's name for a cataclysmic war could not reverse the political events of the summer. In Russia, Katkov's fire was extinguished. In France the Goblet ministry had fallen at the end of May on a budget vote. This was the political crisis which had engendered the 'Floquet letter' affair. A 'moderate' ministry was installed under M. Maurice Rouvier. Laboulaye continued as foreign minister. Boulanger was turfed out of the war ministry and sent to brood in a provincial military command.

Much more had happened. On the day when Duleep and Ada were eventfully changing trains in Berlin, 22 March 1887, the Czar's brother, the Grand Duke Vladimir Aleksandrovich, was in the capital enjoying intimate discussions with the German Kaiser and his Chancellor. The stalled German–Russian bilateral treaty was back on the agenda. The secret diplomacy went into high gear; the pact called for 'benevolent' neutrality by either signatory if they were attacked by a third great power. As Katkov's star flared and fell, for now the St Petersburg pro-Germans had won the battle for the Czar's soul. The *Ruchversicherungsvertrag* ('Reinsurance Treaty') was signed in Berlin on 13 June 1887. It would last three years. It was a colossal secret.

Bismarck himself cynically regarded it as a way of buying time – a way at least of preventing hostile general staffs coordinating mobilization plans for a two-front war. De Giers was anything but triumphant; he was 'unhappy and helpless' as turbulent pan-Slav generals licked their wounds. He needed reinsurance. He could afford to be magnanimous to be a dispossessed Indian prince.

The Maharajah meanwhile became even grumpier. He told Our Correspondent on 22 September: 'I have commenced to look about me for means of proceeding to the Afghan-Indo frontier ... and see what can be done with the "Old Humbug", the British Government of which there appears to exist in the whole Christendom nothing but false fear and not one European power seems to have the courage to try to dispel the wretched phantom – How disgusting!!!'

Our Correspondent obviously discussed the 'wretched peace' letters with Cyon. He told London: 'Mr [blank] whom I have seen this morning (29 September) interprets the letter as follows. In consequence of the increasing difficulties of the European situation, it is Russia's inter-est to avoid all Asian complications. Duleep, whom we do not consider very intelligent and by no means capable of initiating any movement, is, however, a flag which may become useful later, and will assuredly be used if circumstances so dictate. At present he can only prepare the ground and M. de Giers, having been able to judge during the Maharajah's five months in Russia of his honesty and of his ability to live without being a charge to Russia for his support, has finally con-sented to his journey east, via Sebastopol where English detectives can less easily watch his movements.'

Something very odd was going on in the French capital in the last week of September. The 'Irish Secret Press' at Messrs Schlaebers' *imprimerie* burst into life and another bizarre proclamation to the 'Natives of British India' appeared in the Paris newspapers under the joint names of the Maharajah and Djemal-ud-din.

BROTHERS.
The all-important and long-expected crisis is drawing near at hand. The hour is approaching when you will be called upon by your chiefs to wipe out the wrongs and injuries inflicted on you by the myrmidons of England; and to that call we are sure you will heartily respond if yours be the spirit of true men and the devotion of heroes.

We are only the precursors of men who are pre-eminently fitted to be your leaders and who at the present moment are diplomatically engaged in winning to your cause the active sympathy of more than one of the European states in order that when the tocsin shall have sounded you will not be found either friendless or defenceless.

Owing to the untiring exertions of these agents, the moral and material support of one of the great powers is already assured.

Meanwhile, we of the advanced guard, who have been com-pelled, through fraud or force, by England to leave our native land, despoiled of our possessions and deprived of everything that was lawfully our own, have constituted ourselves into an executive committee, the object of which is your speedy deliverance from the British yoke.

We will be enabled to despatch our emissaries very shortly to British India, with instructions to preach in secret a holy war against the invader and the embezzler. Our envoys, who have been promised the cooperation of several of the Sheikhs among you, will organise clubs and spread over the country as large a network of disaffected associations as possible.

When all these preliminary preparations shall have been completed and a proper provision of war material be supplied to you, your lawful chief will return, to work out your emancipation accompanied by several European officers of high rank, who have already laid their swords and services at our disposal.

Natives of British India, awake from your torpor and prove to the whole world that you shall no longer be the dupes of English merchants and the slaves of the English Governor.

Remember that he reached his present post of superiority by wading through oceans of Indian blood! Remember the artificial famine he caused, the massacres he perpetrated and the all but intolerable insolence which characterises him in his every dealing.

Awaken the ji, for the Fatherland, and may Allah defend the right!

Given under our hands at Moscow (Russia), on this the 29th day of September, 1887 (Christian Calendar).

[Signed:] The Executive of the Indian Liberation Society.

With its talk of 'Sheikhs', 'Holy War' and 'Allah', this was an Islamic call to arms. It appeared in the *Standard* on 11 October. The London paper pooh-poohed it as rambling rubbish. 'The proclamation merely states the accession to the plot of a few of the most peaceful of all the Mohammedan sects – about as alarming an event as the accession of half a dozen Presbyterians would be to a similar undertaking in England,' it editorialized.

An outraged *Standard* reader wrote to the Secretary of State for India. 'I hope you will lose no time to write or telegraph to India to get both these parties arrested for treason as promptly as possible. Possibly they have also become acquainted with the organisations of the nihilists and other European secret societies, so that it will be very dangerous to allow them to go long at large.'

There was some very interesting diplomatic footwork in London meanwhile. The German embassy in London burst into life again, sending a stream of Duleep-intelligence direct to Bismarck. The *Standard* report was enclosed in a message on 16 October with this note from the second secretary von Plessen: 'The Maharajah would have the ways and means to achieve his liberation. It is clear that he already has the support of one European great power ... and there may be other talks with other states.' More interestingly, 'Sir Owen Tudor Burne had documents proving that the Maharajah's intrigues were at heart just a blackmail attempt' the embassy messaged.

The next day Sir Julian Pauncefote turned up at 9 Carlton House Terrace in person. The *Untersekretar* of the Foreign Office 'did not take these Duleep Singh articles seriously – and the [British] government has no positive proof that he has contact with official circles in Russia – but one cannot be sure that if the appropriate moment should come, the Russian side could still use him against England.'

The Maharajah would be flattered to know his posturings were of concern to Bismarck himself, but he was furious at the outburst from the 'Executive of the Indian Liberation Society'. He had had nothing to do with it. He wrote to Our Correspondent: 'Please send me a copy of the publication which has appeared in Paris very lately and is supposed to be my work. From the short notice I saw of it in the Daily News it appears to be full of stupid errors. If you can become acquainted with the writer please do so and tell him not again to publish anything in which I am mentioned without letting me correct it, as our enemies only laugh at our stupid mistakes.'

An article appeared meanwhile in the *New York Star* newspaper linking the Maharajah with revolutionaries in Paris – this time naming the 'dynamite fiend' Eugene Davis as a prime plotter. News reached the Russian authorities courtesy of the British Foreign Office. De Giers put it down to Duleep's 'oriental cunning' and he told Dolgouruki: 'It would be absolutely pointless to start negotiation with Duleep Singh on the above said venture.'

The 'Executive of the Indian Liberation Society' was evidently a fantasy of Casey's made propagandizing flesh when Abdul Rasul arrived back in Paris to inject some Islamic militancy into the proceedings. When he had learned the truth, the Maharajah wrote petulantly to Our Correspondent: 'It is all very fine for Mr Casey to request that I should not contradict what has been published. It would simply ruin me in India when the word "Allah" appears in a proclamation coupled with my name. God Almighty, why do not these would-be friends consult you and me before they publish any matter of this kind? After all I am the person most concerned and instead of helping, their stupidity hinders me most effectually. I got very nearly compromised with the authorities here as well.'

Prince Dolgorouki, the governor of Moscow, had tersely summoned Duleep to explain his connections with 'unknown confederates' and 'secret societies'. Such institutions 'were illegal and not permitted to be formed in Russia'. The Maharajah knew nothing; he had no connection with Djemal; he had never heard of the Indian Liberation Executive, whatever that was; it was all lies.

His ego had been bruised. Djemal was moving in on 'his' revolution. He seemed utterly cast down, though he displayed a flash of realism when he told Our Correspondent on 2 December: 'I do not see how the Emperor could give me an audience after all that has been said about me and I have published myself . . . It was a great mistake to make a noise in the journals as I have been doing.'

And he had a new hate figure to blame. 'No doubt the Prince and Princess of Wales had a good deal to say to the Emperor regarding me when they met him in Denmark this autumn,' he wrote. (Prince Albert Edward and the Csarevich Alexander had both married daughters of King Christian IX – Alexandra and Dagmar.) 'Depend upon it my dear [blank], they will not let a single stone remain unturned in order to poison the mind of the Emperor against me. For he does not know my value in India, but the Prince of Wales does. Alas! there is no Katkov now to undo all the machinations of my foes.'

The Maharajah could not resist doing what he always did: drafting another proclamation. This time it was batted back and forth to Our Correspondent for approval of its pantheist appeals. He made the frank admission: 'Yes, the ball indeed has been set a-rolling but I greatly fear it will produce no substantial results. Still it is a very great satisfaction to frighten the enemy.' It was eventually published in the New York *Sunday Mercury* with all the free-booting swagger of American journalism.

## INDIA'S DELIVERANCE

Maharajah Duleep Singh sends greetings to his people! Still directing affairs from his headquarters at Moscow. Russia aiding him against England.

A stirring appeal. Special correspondent, *Sunday Mercury*. Moscow, December 15th, 1887.

The Maharajah Duleep Singh is still actively on the war-path, and is putting forth extraordinary efforts to fire the hearts of the Punjabis to rebellion and the adoption of his cause.

From his headquarters in this old capital of the Russian empire he is directing an active propaganda in India, preparatory to a contemplated uprising against English authority.

The following is his latest manifesto, and it is said that millions of copies of his documents are smuggled into India and distributed among the people.

MOSCOW, 10 DECEMBER 1887
Courage! Beloved Countrymen Courage! We, who are of your own flesh and blood, bid you lift up your bowed-down heads and crushed hearts, for the dawn of your deliverance is at hand, and by God's help Aryasthan will soon be free from the accursed British rule, and the rising young India shall enjoy to its heart's content the blessings of both liberty and self-government.

Sri Khalsa ji! we exhort you to study the book of Sakhians [prophecies], herein a glorious destiny is predicted, and to praise Sri Sat Guru ji in the holy temple of Amritsar in anticipation of your coming deliverance.

Beloved countrymen! put no faith in aught that is told to you by official Englishmen for as a class they are most egregious liars. We are most deeply grieved, pained and surprised at the ignorance of those who have ventured to proclaim that Russia has always been the foe of the Mohammedans.

Beloved Mohammedan countrymen do not be led astray by ignorance. Russia has ever been most considerate towards populations which have been brought up under her sway in Central Asia, and that she has frequently appointed them officers of high rank, Generals in her armies, and Governors of provinces, which have been annexed to her empire. And can one single instance of the kind be pointed to in British India?*

Hindoos, Moslems, Eurasians and native Christians, all creatures, like ourselves, of the only one true fold, we love you all equally, beloved countrymen, in accordance with the tenets of Baba Nanak. Our quarrel, beloved countrymen, is not with the inhabitants of Hindustan nor with our own race; it is with our hundred times accursed enemy, the British Government.

We command all our subjects who may be serving in that portion of the British army which shall be sent to oppose our advance in the north-western frontier of India to join us immediately, and we enjoin upon those who may be left behind to rise with the entire Punjab in the rear of the British forces and to harass them by cutting off all their railway and telegraphic communications, by the interception of their supplies, and by the blowing up of all bridges.

But we positively forbid the shedding of innocent blood. The lives of women, of children, of all non-combatants must be respected, and we swear by the living God that those of you who shall dare to disobey our orders in this respect will have their heads cut off without mercy. Let our friends rejoice, but our enemies tremble, for we have sworn their utter extermination!

Wah! Guruji! oi Fatheh!

(Sd.) Duleep Singh, Sovereign of the Sikh Nation and, though a humble patriot, the proud implacable foe of England.

## *Hotel Billo, Bolshoi Lubyanka, Moscow, October–December 1887*

The humble patriot was becoming humbler. The return to the city was to the Hotel Billo on the Lubyanka (rooms one rouble a night; dinner 75 kopecks). He told Our Correspondent on 17 October: 'We came to live in Moscow on last Sunday week from the country. This

---

* The Maharajah, unusually, had made a shrewd political point. The Russian Empire turned conquered Mohammedan Khans into imperial officers; 'natives' were not commissioned in the Indian or British armies until 1902. By 1914 there were just twelve young Indian officers.

hotel is about 50 per cent cheaper than the other we were at in last spring.'

The spy saw it as a grand strategic move, telling London that night: 'The man is economizing for future action which he will attempt if encouraged by the Czar. This I am assured he will not be, unless political complications shall render an "Indian diversion" necessary in order to prevent England's active participation in the action of the triple alliance [i.e. Germany, Austria-Hungary and Italy] against Russia. Russia expects to fight in the spring.'

High-powered politics were back on the agenda, but in London there was concern about more intimate matters. On Christmas Eve an extract was circulated in the India Office of Sir Robert Morier's dispatch no. 402 sent on 11 December 1887 for the urgent attention of the Prime Minister: 'My Lord. I may mention, that my last news from Moscow establishes the fact that the lady who is living at Hotel Billo with Dalip Singh is not the Maharani. She is English, good looking, aged 20 and enceinte.'

On 26 December 1887, Ada Wetherill was delivered of a baby girl, Her Highness Princess Pauline Alexandra Duleep Singh. It was a difficult birth.

# 32

# The Mohammedan Detective

*British Agency (HM Consul-General's Residency), Cairo,*
*28 March 1888*

CAIRO WAS the world capital of intrigue. Khedive Tewfik may have sat in faded pharaonic pomp in the Abdin Palace but real power lay with the British resident. Agents of France, Russia and Turkey snapped round the Egyptian capital for scraps.

On the morning of 28 March 1888, a confident young man, a Muslim, strode into the office of Colonel Sir Evelyn Baring, Her Majesty's Consul-General in Egypt. He was an attaché of the government of India Foreign Office, on six months' special leave, so he said, engaged in tracking down a dangerous conspiracy against the British Empire. The centre of the intrigue had now moved to Cairo. It was nothing less than a Russian-inspired rising with the aim of seizing the Suez Canal. The plot reached down the Nile to equatorial Sudan. 'I am known as L.M. – Lambert's Man,' the visitor said with a slight stutter. 'You may check all I say with Lord Dufferin.'

Sir Evelyn was astonished. His own agents had picked up only the usual Cairene underswell of rumours. Who was this native in a crisp linen European suit who appeared to be on some sort of spying holiday? He ushered the visitor outside to wait and cabled Simla for confirmation of the 'quasi-mission'. The reply came several hours later from the Viceroy himself: 'Aziz-ud-din is rather talkative and indiscreet but a clever detective and exceptionally well meaning. You may rely on his loyalty but not on his judgement.' But what agent L.M. had to say was true.

Aziz-ud-din was back on the Maharajah's case. He had, he explained, come to Cairo in pursuit of an agent of Duleep Singh – one Abdul

Rasul, presently staying at the Hotel d'Alexandrie, Room 17. For the past fifteen days Aziz had been 'risking death', so he said, by attending secret meetings at the house near the main railway station of the notorious Sudanese nationalist Zobair Pasha. Abdul Rasul and Zobair Pasha had been wildly plotting. Penetration of the conspiracy had been simple. Aziz had used the secret watchwords learned from Arur Singh while 'a fellow-prisoner' of the Maharajah's duped emissary in the Calcutta police station. He planted some exquisite misinformation meanwhile, telling Abdul Rasul that Duleep's Pondicherry cousins had turned traitor.

The so-clever detective wrote everything he had learned in a long memorandum for the Consul-General: 'Abdul Rasul is the right-hand man of Duleep Singh and in November last was conspiring against British rule with the Fenians at Paris; he was summoned to Moscow by the Russian Military Party through Duleep.

'The heads of this party in Russia are at present General Ignatiev, Count Tolstoi and Leberzev(?).* During Abdul Rasul's absence in Paris they learnt from Duleep that he knew the Sudanese and more especially Zobair Pasha. They therefore employed him to go and stir up the Sudanese so that the British must send another expeditionary force. In the case of there being a rising in India, he should instruct the Sudanese to blockade the Suez Canal.'

M. Ivanov, the Russian consul in Cairo, was in on the plot, Sir Evelyn's visitor reported, and well funded with war ministry gold. M. de Giers the Russian foreign minister, 'the friend of England', knew nothing of the intrigues on the Nile, so the detective had been assured.

If that was not enough, 'as a loyal servant of Her Imperial Majesty', L.M. felt he must tell the Consul-General of 'another danger that is being hatched'. It was nothing less than a general rising in Egypt involving 'officers in every department and every place'. The former slaver Zobair Pasha's intrigue reached into central Africa where the explorer Henry Morton Stanley was leading a volunteer expedition to relieve the eccentric Austrian doctor Emin Pasha, the 'Governor of Equatoria', whose strange dominion had been cut off by the Mahdist

---

* The (?) is in the original. 'Leberzev' seems yet another mistranscription of Pobedonostsev, the Czar's spiritual adviser.

rebellion. Zobair planned the extinction of the 'governor' and his would-be rescuer.

The Duleep Singh conspiracy had a London end, L.M. could reveal. Among his supporters was: 'A Bengali Mohammedan who is studying law in England and will be called to the bar this month. This young Bengali by associating with the Irish Fenians has become just like them. He is in Duleep's confidence and rendered every assistance to him.'

Sir Evelyn Baring was convinced. He sent the L.M. report to Lord Salisbury, asking for instructions. It fitted what London already suspected. The Maharajah may have been neutralized for now, but the Russian 'military party' were still pushing for war. Count Pavel Niko-layevich Ignatiev and his Caucasian friends were playing the Islamic card.

Abdul Rasul was a Kahsmiri Muslim from Srinagar, a former agent of the Ottoman Empire, educated, multi-lingual and driven by hatred of the British Empire. He had lived in London as secretary to a Mohammedan lawyer of Russell Square, Bloomsbury, published a wildly anti-British newspaper, and – in that diffident make-it-up-as-you-go-along way in which the affairs of the empire were (sometimes) conducted – had been recruited to go to Egypt with General Sir Garnet Wolseley's 1884 Nile expeditionary force as an interpreter. He was discovered intriguing with the Mahdi's agents and bundled back to London accused of treason. The case collapsed for lack of evidence.

'His only occupation is to serve as go-between to further intrigues of one government against the other,' Aziz reported. 'He had been used by the French in bribing the Turkish Court – sent by an express train to Constantinople from Paris with money and letters.' The French, so Aziz said, were up to their ears in anti-British conspiracies in the Middle East, flooding the Nile with gold via an Alexandria bank. This came as no surprise at all to London.

There was an extraordinary paragraph in the report: 'A French gentleman at Paris, who is the right-hand man of General Boulanger, is at the bottom of French intrigues with the Sudan. Abdul Rasul has never seen him – but deals with him through Asad Pasha [Turkish ambassador to Paris]. He says that in November last, Muhammad Ali Rogay of Bombay, while in Paris had an interview with the Frenchman, and volunteered to carry out his policy against the British government, but he suspected him to be a British spy and had nothing to do with him.'

The 'French gentleman/British spy' was Our Correspondent. He had referred to news of the Maharajah 'from Bombay' in November in a secret dispatch to London. That he was involved with General Georges Boulanger also fitted, although 'right-hand man' was an exaggeration. But he also evidently had connections with another centre of mischief-making – the corrupt, decaying court in Constantinople.

The Consul-General wanted more information. The Cairo police chief, Captain Martyn Fenwick, crept round to the Hotel d'Alexrandrie and 'retrieved' a document written in Turkish from Room 17. The translator thought it was 'some kind of proposal to the Sultan, a memorandum of the Maharajah's history, written around six months previously'. It was to be kept safe and clandestinely returned to its owner.

The stolen document added much to L.M.'s discoveries. It covered events in Paris during the winter of 1886–87. Duleep had evidently received a very secret message of support from Diwan Lachman Dass, the governor of Kashmir, offering 100,000 'well armed and organized' men. In addition, 45,000 Sikh regular troops in Kashmir, at Wadi Pichin on the North-West Frontier, could be readily subverted. 'These men await the coming of the Maharajah impatiently at Bocess and they are the best soldiers in India for bravery and courage,' according to Lachman Dass.

Kashmir was the biggest native state of British India, ruled by a compliant Dogra (Hindu) dynasty since the break-up of Ranjit's empire, but it was effectively controlled by the British resident. To the north, across the Hindu Kush mountains via the Gilgit passes, was Russian Turkestan. Kashmir was 90 per cent Muslim. Here was an offer of a Mohammedan–Sikh alliance, dismissed as impossible by Sir Henry Durand in his 'we can easily crush the unaided revolt of the Sikhs' memorandum of July 1887. British intelligence did not know it at the time, but Abdul Rasul had been summoned from London to Paris by the Maharajah to discuss precisely such a coalition around eight months earlier.

Duleep's guest had proposed a truly Byzantine scheme:

> The day England should lose India, its power would be brought to an end. If then Turkey considered allying herself ostensibly with Russia but secretly with the Maharajah, not

only perhaps would great benefits result with regard to the Egyptian and Bulgarian questions, but increased bonds of union would result between the Musselmans of India and Central Asia [Abdul Rasul's memorandum stated].

My feeling of devotion to Islam did not allow me to remain silent while such reflections passed through my mind, and I replied to the Maharajah that I regarded it as a duty of conscience of the utmost necessity to submit this case to H.I.M. the Sultan Khalifa of the Faithful.

The Maharajah having approved my proposal, we went together the following day to seek an interview with Asad Pasha, the Ambassador of Turkey in Paris, to whom I exposed the matter and who totally approved of my ideas. Finally we three decided that the case should be communicated to Constantinople. The Ambassador gave me a letter to the Private Secretary to His Majesty the Sultan confirming my mission and I left for Constantinople.

This was very compromising information. In Paris the Maharajah had dallied variously with Irish dynamitards, French revanchists, Boulangist zealots, the St Petersburg foreign ministry and Russian ultra-nationalists. Now, it was made apparent, he had also made overtures to the Ottoman Empire to engender an Islamic resurgence from the Balkans to east Bengal.

Everything the Maharajah touched was contradictory; each conspiratorial pot was a powder-keg. One of them was going to blow up in his face.

It was also clear from L.M.'s report that, in his secret Moscow meetings with Count Ignatiev's agents, Abdul Rasul had thrashed out a plan to do more than seize the Suez Canal. The high valleys of Kashmir and Jammu were shimmering in their minds, and in Duleep's. The Muslim-populated provinces been sundered from Ranjit's empire by the Treaty of Lahore and 'bought' by the Dogra, Golab Singh, with a million pounds looted from the Lahore treasury.

Aziz's report continued:

At present the Russian military party has asked him that he [the Maharajah] should create disturbances in Kashmir in his favour, and if he can do that, in that case they can force the Czar to go against M. Giers, and give him assistance to attack the English.

To carry this out Thakur Singh's sons are intriguing in India and Abdul Rasul, after looking after his intrigues in Egypt, will go to India to carry it out. Their plan is first to try to win the Maharajah of Kashmir on Duleep's side, and to ask him that he should rise against the British Government, and should say that he is doing that for Duleep, and in that case all the Sikhs will join with him. In the case of their not winning the Maharajah on their side they should try to win one of his brothers, and if they fail in this, too, then they should send large numbers of Sikhs to Kashmir and Jammu.

These men should remain in hiding, and when the Maharajah starts for Kashmir, and is on the middle of the road, these men should simultaneously rise up and loot the treasuries and arsenals, and thus they will have money and arms, and will be in a position to arm the other Sikhs, who will rise up against the British Government.

There is another plan which Duleep and his advisers are now planning to carry out, that is, that he should go in disguise to Amritsar, and there should collect some Sikhs, and then should suddenly throw off his disguise, and should proclaim himself that he is the true incarnation of the deity and rightful sovereign of the Sikhs; in this too the Russian military party supports him, and they say that in that case they will furnish him with any amount of officers to lead his men.

'A brilliant plan,' Colonel Henderson noted.

Whatever he called himself – 'Lambert's Man', 'agent L. M.' – the utility of Aziz-ud-din as a spy seemed at an end. The Calcutta police were flashing messages to Simla that Duleep's partisans believed he had murdered Thakur Singh. The Foreign Secretary told the Viceroy on 18 April: 'I wish the little chap would be a little more judicious in some ways. He might do so much. In the Punjab I fear he will never never be of use again.' Just who was in charge of agent L.M. had meanwhile become problematic. Sir John Lambert, his former boss in the Calcutta police, seemed to be running some freelance intelligence operation against the Maharajah. The Foreign Secretary was warned from London 'some communication from Lambert mentioned that an intended trip to Moscow had got wind – a caution ought to be conveyed'. Aziz did not go to Moscow; instead, he went to Constantinople, then via Berlin to London, with a mission to hunt down the mysterious 'Bengali Fenian'. He lodged 'with friends' in Kings' Road, Clapham Park, in south London where, so he said, 'he would be quite safe'.

Latif Rahmann, the 'Bengali Mohammedan' law student, turned out to be 'quite harmless', but Aziz indulged in some bruising bureaucratic in-fighting while in London. He wanted to be made head of a new 'Foreign Intelligence Department' in Simla, something 'no native Indian could be allowed to do'. He refused to work under Colonel Henderson, finally threatening in August 1888 'to go to Russia'. 'He may go to Russia – or the devil for all I care,' noted Sir Henry Mortimer Durand. He was sacked from the Special Branch in 1890.

Presented meanwhile with the evidence of Abdul Rasul's overarching Islamic conspiracy, the India Office dithered. Should they arrest him now or allow him to proceed to India? Let him proceed, it was agreed in the now well-proven pattern of allowing the conspiracy to mature in order to implicate others. But 'he might evade the police at the port of debarkation', it was noted. In mid-May another Special Branch detective was sent to Cairo to make up to the so-gullible Abdul; his codename was 'A.S.' and this time he was a Sikh.

The Sikh detective's real name was Amrik Singh. He wore a huge floppy headdress (his contacts in Cairo quickly dubbed him the 'father of the turban'). His undercover intelligence-gathering was almost as sharp as that of Aziz. Throughout the last week of May 1888, agent A.S. sent a stream of reports with several sparkling nuggets of information to be shared between Whitehall and Simla.

The Maharajah now distrusted Gurbachan Singh and 'suspected them of showing all letters that come from himself and of writing with knowledge of the British Government', he reported. Of course it was Our Correspondent who was merrily steaming open every Pondicherry–Moscow letter and copying the contents to London.

Duleep meanwhile was 'in great pecuniary difficulties and has not money even for food. He repents deeply what he has done at the instigation of Sardar Thakur Singh and remains night and day in solitude weeping ... very little would induce him either to commit suicide or return to London.'*

Abdul Rasul revealed that the Kashmir project had been worked up by the Muslim General Alikhanov, governor of Pendjeh. 'The first attack on India by the Russians will be made by way of Kashmir by the Russian force which is 60 miles from Gilgit,' the Sikh detective reported. A feint would be made around Herat but the real target of the attack would be the Gilgit passes. The Maharajah of Kashmir meanwhile was proving unreceptive – he would have to be subverted.

And there was this: a Russian agent had been sent to India to feel out the ground. He had been given letters of introduction to Thakur Singh Sandhanwalia. The agent was apparently 'working for the Russian Foreign Ministry. His name is Nicholas Notovich'.

The Sikh detective had also fallen on Ada's potential to avert mischief against England. Colonel Henderson noted on the report: 'A.S. has discovered, no doubt from what he heard from Abdul Rasul, that Duleep's female companion has already prevented him from carrying out some of his schemes in the Caucasus and even appearing in India. She could be easily influenced to prevent him going anywhere ...'

Should the British mobilize for a war in India, or would Ada Wetherill bring down the whole conspiracy for them?

---

* The Consul-General in Egypt was disparaging of Amrik Singh's efforts. Baring told Durand on 23 May 1888: 'Your Sikh came to me this morning. He had a long cock and bull story about Moukhtar Pasha being about to block the Canal etc all of which is trash. He asked for £50 which I refused to give him. The waiter of the hotel in which Abdul Rasul lives is in my pay and I have got the key of the desk in which he keeps all his papers.'

# 33

# The Cockney Empress

❦

*Hotel Billo, Bolshoi Lubyanka, Moscow, January 1888*

PRINCESS PAULINE ALEXANDRA DULEEP SINGH was a day old. The Maharajah did not cradle Young India for long. Muffled against the falling snow he trudged from the Hotel Billo to the telegraph office on Mjassnizkaya Street to send one line to Our Correspondent: 'Failure. I leave for Paris.'

The Maharajah followed the message a week later with a despairing letter: 'I have washed my hands of the whole affair and, after writing one more letter to my cousins, will not trouble myself with India again. There are many thousands of these loyal, good, but ignorant people who are I know willing to sacrifice their lives for me and many of them will be uselessly hanged. My God! My God! why can I not reach them in India at this moment.'

It was the 'Executive of the Indian Liberation Society' proclamation that had done the damage, that and the secret societies rumpus stirred up by Casey and Davis in the *New York Star*. The 'Maharajah on the war-path' story printed in the *Sunday Mercury* on 8 January just made things worse – why could he not keep quiet? The governor of Moscow came to the point, enough was enough, there would be no interview with the Czar, the Maharajah must please go away. Kiev, the capital of the Ukraine, might be acceptable, out of reach by English reporters and spies, but certainly not Tiflis, or anywhere in central Asia. England was Russia's friend, all was to be peace. Had the Maharajah not read the papers?

Our Correspondent was told the glum news and consulted with Cyon in Paris. The doctor was blunt. 'It is as we supposed; we could manage him before, he has got into bad hands. He is to all intents and purposes under surveillance, and the best thing he can do is to keep quiet: try to keep him so but he is such a fool – *il est si bête.*'

Mr Hornstedt, the Moscow vice-consul, evidently did have a shadowy source of information in the Maharajah's depleted camp. He sent a stream of telegrams to London relayed via the St Petersburg embassy which quickly reached Lord Salisbury's desk. There was this on 28 January: 'I have to inform you that the Maharajah Duleep Singh has applied for an audience to the Emperor and has been refused, and I have reason to believe that he was then requested to leave the country. At all events he told a friend of mine that the audience had been refused to him, that he found he could do nothing in Russia, that his mission was therefore at an end, and he would leave in a couple of days.'

The 'friend' knew about Duleep's gambling debts, even the state of his bank balance. 'When the Maharajah first came to Moscow he deposited Rs. 50,000 at the Moscow Branch of the Imperial Bank where the money is still lying, and Rs. 10,000 he placed with a private banking house here: Of the latter amount about Rs. 2,000 are still to his credit, the remainder he has successively drawn to cover his expenses,' the vice-consul messaged. And the 'friend' reported at the end of February: 'When the Maharani, who is very ill after *accouchement*, is sufficiently recovered to enable her to bear the fatigues of the journey, he will leave Russia for good and return to France.'

Frugality became an increasing necessity. At the end of February the couple departed the Hotel Billo for 'a kind of private hotel or boarding-house, called Paris, for the sake of economy,' so London was told by the omniscient Moscow informant.

Duleep's realm had come to this, a shabby boarding-house on Tverskakaya Street near the Smolensky station, the Zenkers' money-box all but empty, his listless wife attended by coarse-faced Babushkas, the baby swaddled like a mummy in layers of cloth in the Russian style. Someone close was betraying him. 'He knows he is under espionage, one or two of his faithful servants will arrive here early in the spring, and that it will go hard with any spy that gets into their clutches,' Mr Hornstedt reported.

The spies were proliferating. Since Aziz-ud-din's infiltration of the Cairo conspiracy, the Indian government was reading Duleep's increasingly desperate communications with Abdul Rasul. The Muslim agent's reports of Duleep's condition were gleefully circulated in London throughout the spring. He was indeed brought low.

'Duleep himself is now at Moscow living with his mistress, a cockney girl, on about ten shillings a day. All his money is gone and he is now selling his Maharajah's dresses. He also the father of an illegitimate child since December last,' Aziz reported. 'Even in Moscow too he sleeps with all the doors securely closed, a sword by his side, and a revolver under his pillow and two dogs which he has imported from England watching his bed.*

'Duleep is now living in a fool's paradise. Himself as a sovereign of the Sikhs. Cockney girl as Empress of India. Thakur Singh's son as a Prime Minister for Sikhs. Bengali Babu of Calcutta as a Prime Minister for the Hindus [Mr Mukerji, the money-grubbing editor of *The Beaver*] and Abdul Rasul as a Prime Minister for Mohammedans.'

A 'cockney Empress of India'. That would not do at all. The pressure must not slacken. The Viceroy cabled Lord Cross in London on 4 April: 'Have you arranged or can you arrange to watch Duleep Singh's movements? He may be contemplating something more than move to Kiev. We hear of a wild scheme of his coming to India.'

## Hotel de France, Kiev, Ukraine, Summer 1888

The royal family of Lahore was spirited into Ukrainian obscurity. Duleep was told not to communicate with anyone – 'your letters are intercepted'. Newspapers were forbidden to mention his name. The British Foreign Office stayed on his trail: 'May 7th. Following from Consul General at Odessa: Your Excellency. Duleep with lady and baby has been some ten days at Hotel de France, Kiev.'

The Maharajah wrote to Our Correspondent on 30 April, care of the St Petersburg International Commercial Bank, Kiev: 'You will at once observe from the above address that I have left Moscow. This has come about on account of the publication of that unlucky proclamation and I am informed that I am not in future to be trusted for were I allowed to reside at Tiflis I might from there find means through my countrymen of sending "seditious documents to be issued in India." Nor am I permitted to visit St Petersburg and the journals are

---

* The Elveden spaniels who crossed the Russian frontier with M. and Mme Casey.

requested to ignore my presence in the country entirely. So you see my position in Russia has become anything but a pleasant one. I am going to settle down in this neighbourhood until the autumn as the season is too hot to start for Algiers or the South of Italy.'

He ended the letter: 'I can not tell you how disappointed I am at not being allowed to reside at Tiflis for the rest of my life as I had hoped to have had some of the best sport that Russia affords.'

The great game the Maharajah had his sights on were those hopping around Caucasian oases. Lady Login received letters from his new residence, a country house at Boyarka, seventeen miles south-west of the Ukrainian capital. 'They were extraordinary effusions,' she recalled in her memoirs, 'some of them madder than others but all of them bearing evidence of an unhinged mind. In the same sentence he would speak of "dying as a patriot in compassing the overthrow of British rule in India," and the prospects of the opening of the pheasant-shooting season.'

The family settled down to rural boredom amid the wheatfields. Duleep wanted to attend Kiev's Orthodox cathedral but 'was only allowed to spectate at the solemnities because of his religion'.

'The English girl with whom he lives and who last winter had a child by him, is apparently recognised as his wife and he himself is known in Kiev as the Indian Prince,' Mr Edward Fitzgerald Law, a nosy British commercial attaché, reported in July: 'He has a Russian-German somewhat vaguely attached to him as a kind of secretary, interpreter and general factotum.'

All was by no means lost, however. In St Petersburg the eclipsed pan-Slavists were creeping back into the imperial fold. At the end of May 1888, General Evgenii Bogdanovich, Duleep's rail-ticket into Russia, was suddenly rehabilitated, given a job at the Interior Ministry, and Count Ignatiev was elected president of the Slavonic Benevolent Society. The German newspapers were outraged, insisting that Katkov's policy was coming back from behind the grave. Sir Robert Morier urgently sought out de Giers for assurance that Russian policy was not lurching back to war. The ambassador sent the results of the conversation to Lord Salisbury in an extraordinary report dated 16 May 1888:

Seeing the circumstances under which General Bogdanovich

had been dismissed, M. de Giers was not pleased. His reinstatement to office ... was naturally a slap in the face to himself.

The following was the exact state of the case – the Emperor's anger against General Bogdanovich had been originally roused by the Duleep Singh incident.

That the Maharajah should have been allowed to slip into Russia without the knowledge either of his police or of his foreign secretary who only became aware of the fact by my calling attention to it ...

With the Imperial anger thus aroused, had coincided the revelations respecting the intrigues of Monsieur Katkov at Paris the previous winter with General Boulanger ... Both Katkov and the incriminated General [Bogdanovich] had emphatically declared that the latter had never seen or had personal intercourse with General Boulanger and enquiries were made at Paris to ascertain if this was the fact.

A certificate to the effect that General Bogdanovich had not seen General Boulanger was obtained from General Saussier, the Governor of Paris, who as he observed, is a perfectly respectable man.*

Sir Robert had stumbled on (or rather he knew all along) the heart of the matter. When, eight months earlier, the ambassador and de Giers had been piling up enough Casey–Duleep dynamite to blow Mikhail Katkov out of Gatchina on 30 May 1887, their efforts, so Sir Robert said, had 'coincided with the revelations respecting the intrigues of Monsieur Katkov at Paris with General Boulanger'.

Not just that. The forged 'Floquet letter' and the authorship of 'L'Alliance Franco-Russe', attributed to 'General Bogdanovich who had smuggled Duleep Singh across the border', had all reached the imperial ear at the same critical time. The exquisite coincidences had smashed the ambitious editor and saved the German alliance. They might be said to have averted a war.

The Maharajah had unwittingly travelled with some heavy company. Sir Robert had told Lord Salisbury in a 'Very Secret' dispatch of 15

* The 'old sabreur' could not know the full extent of the war minister's secret diplomacy. In January 1887, as the British military attaché reported, he was sleeping under armed guard should Boulangist plotters try and abduct him from the Château de Vincennes.

June 1887: 'If what I am told is true, the sudden dismissal of General Bogdanovich was connected with the equally sudden and till now unexplained journey of Count Paul Shuvalov to St Petersburg.' This was when the Russian ambassador to Berlin, brother of Count Piotr Shuvalov, had returned to the imperial capital to impart Bismarck's very secret offer of the Reinsurance Treaty.

'The Count it is said, or to speak more correctly, it is whispered, brought convincing proofs from Prince Bismarck for delivery direct to the Emperor Alexander, establishing beyond doubt that General Bogdanovich, acting on behalf of Monsieur Katkov, had been implicated in an intrigue at Paris, the object of which was to urge General Boulanger and the War Party to take the offensive and attack Germany under the most positive assurances that if they did so, the pan-slavist party was strong enough to force the Czar and the Russian Government to side with France in the struggle.

'Other important personages besides General Bogdanovich were, it is said, implicated. Amongst them is Monsieur Saburov, late Russian Ambassador at Berlin [a long-time bitter rival of de Giers]. That Monsieur Saburov belongs to the elite of the Katkov circle is generally asserted.'

Morier mentioned another visitor to Paris that previous January, another Katkovite, Sergei Spiridonovich Tatischev, Paris editor of *Russki Vestnik*, former Ambassador to Vienna. He now had a job in the imperial archives and thus access to a panoply of diplomatic secrets.

Thousands of miles away, meanwhile, in Thakur Singh Sandhanwalia's house in Pondicherry, British agents had burgled letters from the Maharajah saying 'a General Buzgovitch has arrived here' – who carried an invitation from Constantine Bonodovostzeff and M. Katkoff asking me to come over to Russia'. The Maharajah had to have written that letter in January 1887. It compromised another very powerful figure in the conspiracy: Constantin Pobedonostsev, the Ober-Prokuror of the Russian Orthodox Holy Synod himself.

It was clear that Bismarck had intimated to the St Petersburg Foreign Office what German intelligence knew of the Boulanger–Katkov contacts. It was equally apparent that British and German ministers were colluding at the highest level. Lord Cross had cabled the Viceroy from Balmoral on 9 June 1887: 'You ask about a Franco-Russian alliance. Bismarck has done all in his power to help us.'

It was also clear that, as much as Cyon claimed in his memoirs that the smear was all cooked up in Berlin, it was substantially true. Why else would the *Moscow Gazette* editor's *faiseur* and his conspiratorial companions have come to Paris? Not just to give the truculent ex-King of Lahore an invitation to 'come over' from Paris.

Now, a year later, it seemed as if all was not undone. Madame Bogdanovich had come to the Singer's Bridge to appeal for her husband and 'starving children', so Sir Robert informed the Prime Minister. The Ober-Prokuror and interior minister, he said, had backed her plea at the time the Czar was 'performing his Easter devotions'. De Giers had described how 'Madame Bogdanovich had come to him and, sitting in the very armchair I was then occupying, with many tears and much sobbing, had implored him to use his influence on her behalf.' De Giers's heart was obviously touched; he interceded for the Czar's forgiveness and it was granted. Sir Robert seemed unconvinced that it was simply the tearful pleas of the general's wife which had melted the imperial heart. Something was up.

The ambassador was right to be suspicious. Powerful figures, it seemed, were seeking out the Maharajah at Boyarka. General Dreteln, governor of Kiev, paid several official visits. The Ukraine was no military backwater – the general was commander of the Podolia and Volhniya military districts, the front-line in any war against Austria-Hungary. It was Aziz-ud-din (a formidable spy) who picked up the intelligence that: 'Count Ignatiev introduced Duleep Singh to all the Russian noblemen who are now staying at Kiev.* They have promised to befriend him and also undertaken to obtain help for him from the Czar. They have given him pecuniary assistance and advised him to go and settle down at Merv or Pendjeh.'

On 24 October Lord Salisbury received a one-line enciphered message from Morier. 'My Lord, the *Kievskoe Slovo* reports M. left Kiev for Odessa on the 10th–22nd instant.' Where was he going? Was it a descent on the Punjab at last, a miraculous visitation to Amritsar to proclaim himself the deity reborn? Duleep was slouching towards a different destination.

---

* The July 1888 ceremonies in Kiev to mark 900 years of Christianity in Russia were whipped up into an orgy of pan-Slav, orthodox nationalism by Count Ignatiev. The Czar refused to attend.

# 34

# The Cossack

❦

WHILE THE MAHARAJAH sulked in Moscow in the autumn of 1887, someone at least had been moving with ease through his lost dominions. His name was Nicholas A. Notovich and he was the kind of Russian who dressed in a way Rudyard Kipling was wary of. In his short story 'The Man Who Was',* a Russian officer turns up at a remote British outpost on the north-west frontier. Brandy is drunk and talk flows. 'The Russian is a delightful person till he tucks in his shirt,' wrote Kipling, 'it is only when he insists on being treated as the most easterly of western people instead of the most westerly of eastern that he becomes an anomaly.' Sir Robert Morier, sitting in Palladian St Petersburg surrounded by Byzantine intrigue, would have sympathized.

Kipling's fictional Russian, 'Dirkovich', was clearly based on the Cossack 'journalist'. He 'earned his bread by serving the Czar as an officer in a cossack regiment . . . and corresponding for a Russian newspaper with a name that was never twice alike . . . he was decorated after the manner of the Russians with little enamelled crosses and would unburden himself by the hour on the glorious future that awaited the combined arms of England and Russia when the great mission of civilizing Asia would begin.'

Notovich had already been turning up in secret Whitehall reports. Sir Donald Mackenzie Wallace, the Viceroy's secretary, gave the *Novoye Vremaya* correspondent an interview in Simla in August 1887. His visitor wanted to speak alone and in Russian. Wallace reluctantly agreed when Notovich 'suddenly developed a scheme for supplying

* Written in London in 1890 but inspired by the then 21-year-old Kipling's time on the staff of the *Lahore Civil and Military Gazette* in Lahore three years earlier.

the India Office with confidential information from Central Asia and from the Foreign Office in St Petersburg'. This would be supplied by Prince Dolgorouki and a certain Princess Kleinmichael.*

The civil servant was suspicious; he knew Notovich of old from Constantinople where he had been at the embassy at the height of the Bulgarian crisis, when the Russian had turned up bearing (forged) compromising letters from the Czar for Prince Alexander. His black-propaganda talents would later emerge at the heart of the Maharajah affair.

Just whom Notovich was working for at any one time is highly problematic. Arur Singh had confessed in the Calcutta police cell: 'He was to take round a Russian officer for the purpose of verifying the information obtained and given to the Russian authorities by Duleep Singh as to the favourable disposition of the princes in India.'

Aziz-ud-din had reported: 'Arrangements were quite completed to send a Russian officer in disguise with Abdul Rasul to India to test Duleep's influence among his countrymen, but after Katkov's death everything fell to the ground.'

And Amrik Singh, the Sikh detective, told Colonel Henderson shortly afterwards: 'The military officers are favourable to the Maharajah and have assured him that one day he will certainly receive aid from Russia, but the Foreign Minister would not consent and said that the Czar had aided the king of Bulgaria and the Amir of Kabul but the English had turned both against the Czar and no good result has been attained by aiding them. How then could aid be given to Duleep? The Foreign Minister also said that his spies had travelled over India and ascertained beyond doubt that no one wanted Duleep Singh there and that Duleep Singh could be of no use even if there is any intention of invading India.'

Notovich was clearly already serving multiple masters – Katkov, de Giers, the war ministry – and, like a good journalist-spy, spinning his reports to order to please his masters.

---

* The same Prince Vladimir Dolgorouki who had telegraphed the border-station allowing Patrick Casey to enter Russia. Princess Kleinmichael would have proved useful to British intelligence. Notovich had accompanied her 'as personal photographer' on a trip to the Caucasus. Later in Paris, the cossack challenged de Giers's son to a duel after the embassy-secretary told the French police that Notovich was blackmailing the Princess over sexual relations with, it seemed, half the Russian court.

Lieutenant-Colonel Ivor Herbert, military attaché at the St Petersburg embassy, sent a long report on Notovich to London in August 1887. It was important enough to go straight to Lord Salisbury.

> Made acquaintance of M. Notovich last November who introduces himself as having known my brother in Teheran.
>
> He describes himself as a Cossack and secret agent of the military party. In proof he shows a scar on his arm which he says he received in Bulgaria where he earned the St. George's Cross which he wears.
>
> I believe him to be of Jewish origin deriving his principal means of existence from the *Novoye Vremaya* though I have no doubt that he is one of that numerous class in this country who carry on political intrigues, at their own risk, receiving payment by results, that is to say decorations and official rank if successful and disavowal under other circumstances.
>
> He gave to me to understand that he was in a position to furnish me with valuable information, books, maps etc. frequently promising the latter to look at.
>
> In the meantime by a simple expedient I learned myself that his object in coming to me was as much to obtain as to give information and I accordingly discouraged his visits.
>
> I learn from my brother in Teheran that Notovich had access to documents in the Russian Legation and that he furnished H.M.'s minister with valuable information for which he was well paid.
>
> He had already been in India when he knew him and talked of going there this year [1887] 'on a secret mission'.

The mission was a badly kept secret.* On his way east Notovich turned up again in Constantinople where the British Ambassador, Sir William White, 'declined to see him'. White messaged Lord Salisbury on 27 June 1887: 'A Russian whose name is Nicholas Notovich called at the Embassy . . . I have heard that a person of that name left for Bombay and there is a strong presumption that Notovich is a Russian agent who has been sent to India.'

---

* Notovich's arrival was in the papers. The subject was interesting enough for the German consul in Bombay to send cuttings to the foreign ministry in Berlin. The report dwelt on the fact that the French consul in the port seemed to be sponsoring the mysterious Cossack.

Two weeks later he had arrived very publicly in Bombay and headed promptly for Simla, then the Punjab, beyond to Kashmir and the frontier with Tibet. At the Zoji pass he met the English adventurer and mystic Francis Younghusband.

The *Akhbar-i-am* newspaper of Lahore got an interview on Notovich's return:

> The editor, accusing the Russian Government of religious intolerance, M. Notovich laughed and said that the Czar had himself built two large mosques in Central Asia for the use of Musselmans, but that not a single Christian church was yet to be found there: on the contrary, there were Christian churches even in small native states in this country. He added that forty natives of Central Asia held high posts in the Russian administration.
>
> When the editor asked M. Notovitch how far the Russian boundary was from Ladakh, he replied that next year the Russian boundary would be extended to Chitral. The editor then, smiling, asked him when the Russians would invade this country: he replied with a laugh that, as they had already advanced so far, they would now have no great difficulty in approaching the Indian frontier.
>
> [And the Maharajah?] M. Notovitch laughed the English newspapers to scorn for representing him as being a bastard. He said that the British at first accepted Duleep Singh as the legitimate son and heir to Maharaja Ranjit Singh, and concluded treaties with him, and that the Queen and the Princes showed respect to him so long as he lived in England.
>
> Now that he has left England and gone over to the Russian Government, he is called a bastard! M. Notovitch also said that since his arrival in India all natives, with whom he came in contact, made enquiries about Duleep Singh, and that he was consequently justified in thinking that the natives held the Maharajah in high respect and sympathized with him.

Notovich returned to Russia at the end of 1887. Now, six months later, with the stream of warnings coming from Cairo of an over-arching Islamic intrigue, it was not his activities in the Punjab that were exciting British intelligence – it was whatever he had been up to in Kashmir.

Kashmir was vulnerable, its ruler Maharajah Pratap Singh 'weak and opium addicted'. Letters of intrigue with Duleep Singh (including those contracted with Mr Drew as the SS *Verona* steamed towards Aden) and evidence of plots to murder the British resident Sir Trevor Plowden were in the hands of blackmailing courtiers. In March 1888, the wazir, Diwan Lachman Dass, known to be in contact with Duleep's Pondicherry partisans, was dismissed under British pressure and set off on new conspiratorial paths. The point of danger were the Gilgit passes, gateway to the Karakorams and Hindu Kush, the line of march of an invasion from the north.

The new intelligence from Cairo revealed that the Kashmir project had been worked up by the Muslim General Alikhanov, governor of Pendjeh. 'The first attack on India by the Russians will be made by way of Kashmir by the Russian force which is 60 miles from Gilgit,' the Sikh detective Amrik Singh had reported. 'A feint would be made around Herat but the real target of the attack would be the Gilgit passes.'

Colonel Henderson noted in July: 'When Mons. Notovich was in India it is understood that he was much interested in the Gilgit passes. It is rather noteworthy from these papers that great stress seems to be laid on the importance of securing the adherence of Kashmir by Duleep Singh and his advisers, and corresponding exasperation is shown by Duleep Singh at his failure in this respect. The foreign minister is represented to have told Duleep Singh that according to his information Kashmir is not favourable to his cause.'

Notovich, meanwhile, was making very different noises in St Petersburg. The British military attaché met him again in July 1888. 'He talked a great deal about his travels in India ... he explained that maps of the Gilgit districts made by the British Q.M.G.'s department had come into his possession having bribed a Babu, he photographed them and returned them through Sir Mackenzie Wallace [the Viceroy's private secretary] in order to show how easy it was for Russia to obtain secret information in India. The War Office had paid him 12,000 roubles.'

Next, Notovich published an article in *Grajdanin* (a nationalist and anti-Semitic journal), foaming with war fever:

When the natives of India learnt that Duleep Singh had openly broken with England and established relations with Russia, they saw him as 'the long expected friend' soon about to appear for their deliverance.

Russia of late is advanced three-quarters of the way to India and now the whole country looks on Duleep Singh who has gone to Moscow, as sent by Providence as a deputy from Hindustan to ask from us that which all the subjects of Russia enjoy: i.e. freedom and equality.

To understand these two last words one must see for oneself the arrogance with which the English treat the natives.

Meanwhile Duleep Singh's partisans wrote to him as follows: 'Go to the White Czar and beg him to protect our lawful prince. The White Czar in his justice will not abandon you or us, when the moment comes for his mighty army to advance to the gates of Hindustan . . . the Sikhs will conduct his victorious troops across the Hindu Kush, if you, our hope, are in their ranks.'

I have travelled through the whole of the land of the Sikhs and seen nearly all their principal chiefs and everywhere they begged me to assist Duleep Singh that their hearts would begin to beat and their blood to run quick as soon as he appeared among them.

### *Khaf Oasis, north east Persia, Central Asia, 27 July 1888*

Some Sikhs could not wait that long. Reports began to flow into Simla that summer of mysterious emissaries from the Punjab turning up in Russian central Asia.

General Maclean (the British consul in Meshed) cabled on 15 June: 'It is reported that Sikhs recently arrived here in search of Duleep Singh, forwarded letters to Moscow through Russian agent and afterwards left for Askabad. They said they had letters from Kashmir and Nepal.'

Sir Henry Mortimer Durand cabled back: 'Please endeavour to obtain further information regarding number, names and movements of Sikhs. If they return, inform us of their names, route and destination with view to their being intercepted if possible. The matter is important.'

An agent called Malik Marwaid in the scruffy little oasis of Khaf south of Meshed filed a bizarre report to General Maclean on 27 July. A wanderer had turned up, described as 'a puny Hindustani': 'I asked him where he was going now and he said he was going to Bokhara. I asked him his object in going there. He said that the son of Ranjit Singh, Duleep Singh, had been a prisoner in London with the English but that two years ago he had escaped to Russia and that he was going to join him in Russia. He kissed my feet and hands and begged me not to show him to the Duffadar [cavalry NCO]. After an hour he asked for water and drank it. He was then quite well. Little by little I saw that he was ill.'

The Duffadar, Rajman Ali Khan, was General Maclean's orderly sent to take charge of the prisoner. He reported: 'Malik returned and told me that he found the man lying crouched up in his numdah, with his limbs stiff and contorted and froth and saliva coming from his mouth. Some of the people said that a djinn had taken possession of him, others said that he was shamming, and some said that he had taken opium. Water and salt were given to him to cause vomiting, but he resolutely kept his mouth closed.'

Reports continued through the autumn: from Askabad of 'Sikhs in Turcoman disguise riding with cossacks'; from Meshed of 'a sturdy man, with a beard and twisted moustaches turned round his ears and long hair on his head ... The Russian agent's men came to him and took him to the quarters. My emissary again had a chat over the wall. They told him that their chief had arrived and they were leaving at once. He asked them casually the name of the chief, but they evaded the question and told him they called him ... "Maharajah".'

# 35

# The Alliance

❦

THE MAHARAJAH had vanished from Russia like a wandering fakir. Duleep, Ada and the ten-month-old Pauline departed Boyarka without ceremony, taking the train for Odessa in the south to embark on a Messageries Line steamer heading for Marseilles. He had had enough of waiting for His Imperial Majesty. He was going back to Paris. Duleep messaged Our Correspondent tersely before departing the Crimea: 'I am returning to Paris on private pecuniary business.' They arrived back in the city on 3 November 1888, shutting themselves away at the Hotel des Iles Britanniques on the rue de la Paix. The Elveden spaniels seemed, astonishingly, still to be part of the ménage.

Paris had changed. A succession of political crises had seen Charles Floquet at last installed as premier, while the venerable President Jules Grévy had resigned after a family scandal (his son-in-law had been caught selling government favours). In March 1888 General Georges Boulanger had been court-martialled for insubordination and sentenced to 'retirement'. He embarked on a messianic political campaign which would set the republic teetering on the edge of a military coup for almost a year.

Any idea of a Franco-Russian alliance was on hold; France was too chaotic to ally with anyone. But the old Maharajah gang sought out their flawed hero – Madame Adam, Elie de Cyon, Patrick Casey and interesting new partisans sniffed round the returnee to see what could be salvaged from the turbanned wreck.

One of their number was the exotically-named Baron Anatole Arthur Textor de Ravisi, Egyptologist and orientalist, who had published works on the cult of Krishna and the archaeology of Hindu temples.

He had financial interests in the newly-acquired colonies of French Indo-China and acted as agent for Prince Min Goon, deposed and exiled by the British after the 1886 conquest of Upper Burma.* He presented himself as something the Maharajah sorely needed: an expert on the clandestine international movement of money.

The second interested party was Félix Volpert, the young *chasseur à pied*, born in Wissembourg in sundered Alsace, who seems to have met the Maharajah in Paris during the winter of 1886–87. He was a fervent revanchist and, something else, a Roman Catholic convert to Islam. British intelligence had first noticed him in late 1886 when the French lieutenant headed off to Pondicherry just as the Sandhanwalias were flying into exile in the colony. It was Aziz-ud-din who picked up the trail. Volpert was, he reported two years later, 'deputed to visit native states, and to conclude an arrangement by which Russia after the conquest of India would engage to leave them free and undisturbed, on condition that they should refrain from assisting the British Government when India was invaded.' The *chasseur* travelled to Baroda and Oodeypore where his interpreter introduced him as 'the son of one of the French President's "Wazirs"'. Later he posed as a 'travelling artist'.

'When at Baroda he talked a great deal about the "Revanche" and the location of the French and German troops on the frontier,' Special Branch in Simla reported. 'Although nothing very precise has been ascertained regarding his proceedings, his movements have not been those of in ordinary tourist and he left India very suddenly. Agent L.M. who first reported that M. Volpert was sent to India as a Russian agent, latterly inclined to the opinion that he was acting on behalf of Duleep Singh, whom he had met in Paris.'†

Her Majesty's Foreign Secret Service also resumed their abiding interest in the Maharajah. Our Correspondent went live again, reporting on 14 November 1888 that Duleep was 'seeing him frequently – but suspicious of everybody and, if he fancies he is watched, he will break off relations or remove elsewhere. He admits that he was refused

---

* The whole of Burma was annexed to British India in May 1886 after a campaign in which many Sikh troops were engaged. The Prince Min Goon fled under French protection via Saigon to Pondicherry to be taken up by the Sandhanwalias.
† Volpert's mission seems to have been sponsored by Boulanger's war ministry in great secrecy.

naturalization in Russia, but he hopes to obtain it eventually and for that purpose is preparing to join the Greek Church provided that after attentive study his conscience will permit him to do so!

'He has moved with his wife and child from the Hôtel des Iles Britanniques to 24 rue Marbeuf. He is noted at the Préfecture de Police as a "subsidized Russian agent".' The spy, naturally keen to secure his renewed HMG payments, was not about to disagree. Duleep was still acting 'in accordance with instructions', he messaged.

'The Russians hope to keep England out of any European war by showing how they could injure by helping agitation in India. Duleep Singh is a tool to be disavowed if in the way. He is encouraged to let as much noise be made about him as possible so that Indians may know him to be still alive.' But under those instructions was Duleep 'acting'? Was he an instrument of Count Ignatiev's die-hard pan-Slavs, or of the imperial government in St Petersburg?

Some of the Maharajah's old bluster was returning. He resolved to sell his jewels in a grand public auction to stoke the war-chest. He hired a Paris hack journalist, M. Bertie-Marriot, to produce a eulogistic pamphlet full of the old whinges. The fee was 1,000 francs. Fleet Street also woke up again. 'I have sought acquaintance with the Maharajah Duleep Singh,' wrote the *Standard*'s Paris correspondent on 28 November. 'He will not admit the object of his visit is any other than the sale of his jewels, which he hopes, during the Exhibition year, to be able to dispose of advantageously ... The Maharajah asserted that he was hand-and-glove with some of the Irish leaders. Nevertheless, he affirmed, in the most positive manner, that he had never seen the notorious Patrick Casey.'

Duleep was lying, of course, but whether with an eye to rehabilitation in British eyes or for good conspiratorial reasons was not clear. The Patrick Casey dodge had blown up in his face in Russia, but the old soldiers' revolutionary talking-shop was evidently back on boozy parade in Reynold's Bar. 'A committee of organisation composed of competent military men is on the point of being formed,' the Maharajah told his Pondicherry partisans on 7 January, 'and the head of this is my friend [blank], our future commander-in-chief, and either he or one of the other members will perhaps visit India with letters from me. Is there any use in their doing so? I have a promise of some 15,000 Irishmen at the moment in the British forces in India who will revolt against their masters and join us. Can you not get up another mutiny as in 1857 of the Hindoostan troops, when I land with some 10,000 European volunteers?'

This was truly fantastical. The Maharajah now spoke of 'raising £4 million' to recruit and arm a force who would disembark from some piratical tramp-steamer fleet to wrest the whole of India from British rule. The weapons would come from America. The Russians could bide their time, this was a plan for a general rising, militarily informed by the most case-hardened revolutionaries in the world, the Irish Republican Brotherhood and their US allies – the Clan-na-Gael.

He told the ever-receptive *Standard* correspondent that 'He could get volunteers to join him from Ireland, Hungary, Austria, Russia, France and even Germany, these men would receive no pay till they reached India, but when there he would have no difficulty in raising money by forced loans if necessary.

'In the meantime he pretends to be frightened of assassination,' the *Standard* man reported. 'He was, some considerable time ago, put on his guard against it by a letter, from a Frenchman, formerly in the service of King Thebaw.* "I do not care one jot for my life, but I am a prophet," he said. "I may be beaten but I do not believe it, and I shall either die or be victorious."'

As always there was a new proclamation, carried first by the Paris edition of the *New York Herald Tribune* before being picked up in London. 'Brother Princes and People of India,' it stated portentously. 'It is apparent to the whole world that at this moment the attention of every European great power is entirely occupied with the maintenance of peace in this quarter of the globe. But should a war break out, this state of affairs must certainly undergo a total change, and we believe that it will be to your advantage.

'Both in Europe and America there are thousands of brave men who sympathize deeply and sincerely with you and who would willingly volunteer to form an army to fight for your deliverance. In the opinion of competent military authorities, the sum of between three and four million pounds sterling will be sufficient, and this should be placed at the disposal of the Committee of Organization in Europe.'

---

* The 'Frenchman' was Baron Textor de Ravisi. Thebaw was the Burmese king deposed by a British expeditionary force in November 1885.

He also wanted to square things with Russia. On 25 January he wrote yet another plea to the Czar: 'My most gracious Sovereign. Taking my life in my hand, as it were, and with the earnest desire of my brother Princes and people of India I ventured to reach you in order to lay the crown of Hindoostan at your feet, but it is no concern of mine if Y.I.M. did not condescend to place it on your brow and become the liberator of some 250,000,000 helpless beings although I cannot (as a patriot) but lament their fate.

'That affair having ended, my object in addressing you now, Sire, is to implore that a passport may be granted to me simply as a private individual to return to Russia to which country I desire to return after I have disposed of my jewels and that I may also be permitted to visit the north of Russia for the purpose of enjoying some salmon fishing and other sport and allowed to proceed to Yalta afterwards.'

He was indeed going to sell his jewels – not to go salmon fishing in Siberia, but to fund the mercenary expedition – in a spectacular sale at the Maison Drouot auction rooms where visitors to l'Exposition Universelle were sure to flock. Many of the gems were still in London, in Messrs Coutts' vault. No matter, he would send for them, and write a letter to Queen Victoria with a diamond-sharp new edge. This time he wanted the Koh-i-Noor back. That really would draw the world's attention.

'Madame,' he addressed the Queen on 23 February 1889: 'It will be useless for me to demand the restoration of my kingdom swindled from me by your Christian Government but which I hope shortly by the aid of Providence to retake from my robbers.

'But my diamond the Koh-i-Noor I understand is entirely at your own personal disposal, therefore believing Y.M. to be "She our most religious Lady" that your subjects pray for every Sunday, I do not hesitate to ask that this gem be restored to me out of your privy purse. By such an act of justice Y.M. would acquire a clear conscience before God before whom all of us whether Christians, Mohammedans or Sikhs must render account of deeds done in the body and fulfil the law of Christ, thus washing your hands of at least one of the black works of Y.M.'s Government.

'I demand and reclaim the restoration of my jewel and of my Sovereign rights of which I was defrauded by the perfidious representative of England.'

Lord Cross, the Secretary of State for India, advised the Queen to do the thing that would most enrage the Maharajah: 'Duleep Singh intends to publish his letter and any reply he may get. Therefore Lord Cross advises not to acknowledge it in any way.'

That just made Duleep angrier, but what is so striking about the Maharajah's second wind is the intensity of the planning for the mercenary invasion, the revolutionary professionalism of those involved, and the scale of their ambition. It was not the Punjab he was after; it was now the whole of India. A grand-sounding organization was formed: 'The League of Indian Patriots' (an echo of the Boulangist *Ligue des Patriotes*), which issued a printed manifesto on 1 March. It stated:

ARTICLE 1. Our object is to insure unity of action against the common enemy and which shall have its adherents in every town and village in India.

ARTICLE 2. For reasons of prudence, the head-quarters of the League are, at present, located in Paris. They may be transferred from time to time to other places, as circumstances may require, of which due notice will be given.

ARTICLE 3. The direction of the affairs of the League is vested in a Supreme Council, of which Maharajah Duleep Singh is President. It is at present composed of our members, to whom will be added the four special delegates who will be sent for that purpose from India. All its orders, instructions, and proclamations will bear the signature of Maharajah Duleep Singh, without which countersigned by that of the Executive Secretary, known as No. 1, no communication will be genuine and valid.

Adherents to the League were to be sworn to secrecy, violation of which was 'punishable by death'. Members must contribute to a patriotic fund to buy arms and ammunition, one anna a month. Two 'Ameers' had been appointed, 'one for the Sikhs and Hindoos, one for the Mohammedans' who would in turn appoint chief organizers to be 'the future generals of the National Army'.

'Colonels, Lieutenant-Colonels and Majors' would be raised up: 'men of approved patriotism, honesty, and intelligence. All will be known to the Chief Organiser, but for the present, not to each other,' the plan stated. 'They will be designated by the letter "A".' In turn 'Bs', 'Cs' and 'Ds' were to be recruited, swelling the ranks of the 'Grand Army of Freedom'. In its system of secret cells and cut-outs, the League of Indian Patriots was a straight borrowing from the Fenian Brotherhood.

There were two immediate priorities: intelligence-gathering and money. The 'Bs' were to snoop around British garrisons to find 'the sentiments of the soldiers and officers, their race and religion, their unit number and strength, the number of rifles and cannon, the locations of magazines and drinking water'. Money was to be subscribed by a card coupon system, and loans extracted from wealthy individuals to be sent to Paris via a clandestine banking system to be established in Bombay and Calcutta. Coded acknowledgements of receipts would be placed in European newspapers. Loans (to be guaranteed by Indian Railway stock) would be paid back 'doubled in value after the deliverance of India'.

The plan was signed: 'By Order of the Council. President: Duleep Singh. Executive Secretary: Number One.'

Our Correspondent sent everything to the Foreign Office on 13 March: 'The plan of organisation, all the details of which I forward in the original, is the joint elucidation of Patrick Casey instructed by James Stephens and of Lieut. Volpert,' the spy wrote. 'The Executive Secretary Number One is [blank], the idea of that designation was suggested by Casey. If it should leak out, the British will believe that there really is some connection with the Invincibles.' (Blank was Stephens.)

Lieutenant Volpert's plan was worked out in great detail. It had two components – a secret revolutionary army to be recruited in India itself 'inspired with a violent hate towards the English', and the 'relief army' of mercenaries who would arrive by sea at the critical moment of the uprising. The revolutionary army should 'consist of 120,000 men and, at the last minute, if commanded by intelligent and energetic leaders (Europeans or Americans) it could overcome the 55,000 British soldiers who are guarding India'.

Volpert set out the priority: money 'to buy arms and ammunition and all sorts of munitions'; to recruit, arm and transport the relief army; to pay the European and American officers designated to command the revolutionary army, but, he admitted, 'the Muslims hate the Sikhs as much as the English'. It was Volpert's role to raise them in a *Jihad*.

The *chasseur* added a dangerous new element. Our Correspondent had been deputed at the beginning of the year by Duleep to bring the French lieutenant back into the fold. The spy reported: 'Last year Volpert travelled on leave at his own expense in India where he made the acquaintance of a number of native notables, exclusively Mohammedans, and embraced Islam. He made a report to the Minister of War [Boulanger] on the interior military situation of India. He was afterwards appointed at his particular request to Djalfa [in Algeria] where he can be in constant touch with the natives. His idea is to send missionaries to India to stir up a religious war. His letter shows that he has taken the first step to effect this. Abdul Rasul who was consulted about the plan says it is feasible if the Chief Iman in Mecca will accredit the missionaries.'

James Stephens was also a name to excite the secret servants in Whitehall. He was Ireland's most notorious revolutionary, a name once as famous as Mazzini or Garibaldi – one-time chief organizer and 'Head Centre' of the Irish Republican Brotherhood, rebel against the English Crown for over forty years. Aged sixty-three, poverty-stricken and embittered, he had long lost the battle for leadership of the movement to the American dynamiters. The League of Indian Patriots looked like a last attempt to fulfil his old dream of meeting English force in the open field.*

In spite of his newly proclaimed self-sufficiency, the Maharajah was not yet done with Russia. According to Our Correspondent: 'Duleep sends a copy of his plan through [blank = Cyon] to Ignatiev. Given the secret character of the document I find in this, its communication to an outsider, collateral evidence of Russian connivance. Duleep has also contributed 500 fr to Madame Adam's subscription in aid of the Achinov victims.'†

---

* James Stephens's Paris address, 50 rue de La Rochefoucauld, is intriguingly a few doors down from the address of 'Madame Vallier' written on a cheque stub found on Arur Singh in the Calcutta police cell.

† Achinov was the eccentric Russian Cossack who Mme Adam had taken up in Paris in 1886–87 along with Duleep Singh. Backed by the same pan-Slavist and Orthodox Church interests, Achinov had set off to found the first and last Russian colony in Africa, 'New Moscow' in the deserts of Ethiopia. It lasted a month. His boatload of settlers, including women and children, arrived on the coast of Somaliland in mid-January 1889 and set up camp. A French admiral demanded their withdrawal. The colonists were shelled and several killed. Mme Adam opened a charitable fund for the survivors. De Giers demanded Achinov be sent to Siberia but he was personally pardoned by the Czar a year later. The affair was seized on by General Boulanger and his followers in a last-ditch attempt to bring down the republican government.

The Maharajah's rapprochement with the intriguing Madame Adam was completed with a cordial meeting on 21 March. 'Yesterday in the course of an interview Duleep and Madame Adam made up their quarrel,' reported Our Correspondent, 'and on comparing notes, traced "intrigue" against the former to one Shatoukin, formerly Katkov's secretary and now director of the *Moscow Gazette*.* They claim to have discovered him to be a British spy, principally because he is married to an Englishwoman and visits England every year.'

It was as simple as that. Ada's tea-parties with Mrs Shatoukin had been the golden source of Maharajah intelligence in Moscow. Mrs Shatoukin clearly loved her Russian journalist husband, but she knew her duty as an English woman. Every gossipy scrap was going to the British consulate. Duleep scolded Ada for being so foolish but forgave her. He had a very important proposal to make.

Four days later, on 25 March, a certain M. Maryschkine, a secretary from the Russian embassy, turned up at the rue Marbeuf with stunning news. The Maharajah's old enemy, Prince Kotzebue, had invited him round to collect passports 'Authorized by His Majesty' for 'himself, his wife and the Princess Pauline his daughter, by which he is permitted to go and come within the limits of the Empire, to return there or to travel abroad at his pleasure as a Russian subject.'

Our Correspondent was very excited. This proved the whole League of Indian Patriots wheeze was concocted in St Petersburg, or so he told London. 'Since his residence here Duleep has indulged in a violent proclamation, virtually an appeal to an insurrection and has written to Her Majesty a letter that has been reproduced in a French paper. The fact that the passport now accorded was issued after these manifestations supports my theory that everything has been done by the Maharajah in accordance with orders,' the spy told the Foreign Office. 'It was after the interview with Kotzebue that Duleep ordered the printing of 2,000 copies of the aforesaid letters which will be sent to all the members of both Houses of Parliament and to the principal newspapers of the United Kingdom and India.'

What had caused the Russian change of mind? European power

---

* Shatoukin was eventually appointed editor of the *Moscow Gazette* on the Czar's authority in 1888. Cyon wanted the job but was disbarred.

politics had clanked ponderously on. The old Kaiser had died on
9 March 1888. His son Friedrich III reigned for ninety-nine days
before succumbing to the throat cancer that his wife, Queen Victoria's
daughter, had alluded to in her Maharajah letter. The new ruler of
Germany was the volatile, ambitious Wilhelm II – a 'rascally young
fop', according to the Czar. There would be changes made in Berlin.

Bismarck could see his system collapsing. The German Chancellor
made politely rebuffed overtures to Lord Salisbury for an Anglo-
German alliance, directed primarily against France. Britain instead
poured money into battleships.

The post-Katkov Russian nationalist press kept up their attacks on
the 'Prussian reptiles', but this time they did not use de Giers for target
practice. Even the old apostle of the Bismarckian peace, desperate
to shore up the Reinsurance Treaty, began despairingly to see the
inevitability of a French alliance. The process began almost casually
– an order by the Russian Army in January 1889 for 5,000 French Lebel
rifles. Money, the Rothschild loan, and armaments deals intensified the
deepening embrace.

In France Boulangism had flared and imploded. The League of
Patriots won a by-election in Paris on 27 January 1889 with the slogan
'With the Czar for God and France'. If the moment had come for a
coup, it was now. That night the general was swept from Durand's
restaurant in the Madeleine by a vast crowd with cries of 'A l'Elysée'.
Cyon was there. He wrote: 'I approached the general to offer my
support. He pulled me towards him and said: "Let them know in
Russia that I will not resort to force, public order will not be troubled".'

The general indeed held back. He believed that forthcoming general
elections would propel him to dictatorial power. Kotzebue started
sending highly favourable reports on Boulanger to St Petersburg. He
would 'establish a government modelled on Napoleon's First Consulate'. He would 'purge anti-clericals and embrace royalist exiles'.
Alexander III warmed to the authoritarian theme: 'Boulanger's programme is not bad, but can he do it?' he minuted. It was the Achinov
affair which did for the general. The Boulangists lashed Floquet for
spilling Russian blood. The republican government at last reacted with
unexpected energy, banned the League of Patriots and arrested its
leaders. The general, charged with treason, fled to Brussels on 1 April
to escape arrest but kept up the propaganda. In August 1889 he wrote

with Duleep-like portentousness to the Czar: he was 'the choice of providence', he was 'the only guarantor of a strong France'. All he needed have added was that he was the subject of a prophecy.*

It was against this background of new diplomatic upheaval that the Maharajah's latest posturings were greeted in London. There was immense huffing and puffing at the India Office. The invasion scheme by a European army may have seemed crazier than ever, but how long could the dignity of the British Empire withstand the darts of a martyred self-publicist? Now he was planning to relieve Her Majesty the Queen Empress of the Koh-i-Noor diamond. The £25,000 a year pension was still being paid under the Treaty of Lahore from the tax revenues of the Indian government into a fund (less the allowances to the family) which technically he could demand at any time. Enough was enough. Sir Alfred Comyn Lyall, the scholarly former governor of the North-West Provinces, wrote in a long memorandum for his India Council colleagues on 14 March 1889: 'No European Government other than the British would hesitate to treat him as a political offender and open enemy who at least has forfeited all claim personally upon the indulgence of the state.'

Sir Henry Rawlinson, chairman of the political committee, was in no doubt what to do. He told his fellow-members of the India Council: 'After his outrageous proclamations, steeped in treason, it is surely quite out of place to split hairs as to whether he has or has not been guilty of "disobedience" according to the wording of the "Terms of Lahore". In my view he has been guilty of deliberate High Treason which would justify our shutting him up in a state prison for life if ever he fell into our hands.'

Our Correspondent was becoming almost as testy. On 16 April, like a disapproving schoolmaster reporting on a delinquent pupil, he told London: 'This intense fool is very nearly at the end of his rope. Nothing would please him so much as such a refusal of financial help from India as would free him from what he calls his obligations to the

---

* Boulanger was tried *in absentia* for plotting against the security of the state; 30,000 francs had evidently disappeared from 'secret funds', channelled to a blackmailer and forger named Foucault de Mondion, known to have been a Russian agent in Berlin and Paris. (Mondion was further accused of forging compromising letters from Prince Ferdinand of Bulgaria, just as Lord Dufferin's secretary accused Nicholas Notovich of doing.) The Boulangists were wiped out in the election of September 1889. The general shot himself on the grave of his mistress on 16 July 1891.

sacred cause of his country's emancipation and allow him to treat with England. He is running short of coin. His concubine is extravagant and is deliberately throwing him into the hands of the Jews to whom he now proposes to offer his jewels for sale instead of putting them up for auction as originally intended.'

Duleep needed the money; the King of Lahore had decided to marry his Queen.

## *Mairie of the VIII arrondissement, rue d'Anjou, Paris, 20 May 1889*

The town hall of the *huitième* was the most fashionable place to get married in Paris. Under French law, all marital unions had to be solemnized in the eyes of the republic. Monsieur le Maire Paul Beurdeley had seen many unusual alliances joined in his flower-filled *salle de mariage* in the *quartier* of La Madeleine. A stern moralist with a penchant for speech-making, he had ordered the fleshily allegorical paintings inherited from his predecessor removed for being too provocative. Journalists (and spies) hung round the shabbily elegant old mansion, scanning the wedding notices for potential gossip. Lately M. Beurdeley had been visited by an Indian gentleman.

There was an interesting item in the *publications de mariage* posted for Sunday 28 April 1889, cleverly spotted by *The Times* man: 'Happening to pass by the notice-board of the rue d'Anjou Mairie to-day, my eye caught the English name "Wetherell",' he reported. 'And I found the document to be the banns of marriage between "Duleep Singh: Profession, Maharajah, son of Runjeet Singh, deceased, and widower of Bamba Müller, living at 24 rue Marbeuf, Paris, and Ada Douglas Wetheries [sic] living at 24 rue Marbeuf, no profession, daughter of Charles Douglas Wetheries, deceased, and Sarah Charlotte his wife, of Greeminorn [sic], England".'*

Our Correspondent told Whitehall the news on 2 May: 'I enclose notices of marriage in which Duleep Singh's name appears. Before

---

* The 1881 census gives Ada's mother's birthplace as Bishopstoke, Hampshire. The family are living at no. 41 Great Ormond St, Holborn, London, but there is no Ada in the household. An Ada Wetherill, aged thirteen (the age is out by one year) is working as a 'domestic servant' at a house in Easingwold, Yorkshire.

the Mayor he produced a certificate obtained through the Embassy establishing the fact of his origin and his widowhood, also that his father and mother being dead he may marry whom he likes. He is considered to be a British subject.

'Ada Douglas Wetherill (not Wetheries) was born on the 15th of January 1869 in Kennington, Surrey. Her father is a civil engineer. [The 1881 census says 'chronometer maker'.] The consent in writing of her parents was produced.

'Duleep Singh was married to this woman according to the forms of the Sikh religion some time ago. This marriage has been coming on some time, but the difficulty in the way has been that Duleep Singh has not been able to produce proof of the deaths of his former wives [sic]. Enquiry is being made with regard to the statement respecting the grant of a certificate at the British Embassy.

'This marriage will ruin him in Russia,' the spy added knowingly. He was right.

There was a tremendous flap at the British embassy. How could the Maharajah creep in and get official documents without anyone noticing? It was a repeat of the Arur Singh fiasco. The consul insisted: 'He has no recollection of any such transaction of late and he does not believe that any representative of Duleep Singh came to the consulate. Certainly the embassy have heard nothing of him and have given him no certificate.'

The wedding announcement caused a much more disagreeable diplomatic rumpus at the rue de Grenelle. It was just as Our Correspondent had predicted. On the morning of 6 May, a messenger arrived chez Duleep with a note from the Russian embassy for him to call immediately *'pour prendre connaissance d'une communication importante'*. Duleep showed it to Our Correspondent in a 'state of prodigious funk'. 'He went in the afternoon to Mr. Kotzebue, who requested him to explain the meaning of the marriage announced in the papers,' so the spy told London, 'the passport granted to him being for himself and the Princess Ada on his representation that he had been married to her. Duleep Singh replied that he was married to her according to Sikh law, and that the present marriage is merely a civil one in order to protect the Princess and her children in France and England.'

Somebody, somewhere, was pulling artful strings. Singer's Bridge

The Maharajah's abandoned youngest children Edward and Sophia (front-row right) at a fancy dress party in Brighton – with the children of their guardians, Mr and Mrs Oliphant, *c.* 1888.

Miss Date, the Elveden nanny, with Princes Victor and Frederick, Princesses Bamba and Catherine and the infant Sophia, *c.* 1878.

Maharani Bamba in mid-life, *c.* 1878.

Prince Victor (1866–1918), a miniature country-gent with shotgun, Norfolk-jacket and long hair, *c.*1878.

Prince Frederick (1868–1926), *c.* 1883.

The Maharajah, plump and balding – but with his great rebellious adventure still ahead of him, pictured on a *carte de visite*, *c.* 1877.

Prince Edward, the Maharajah's youngest son, who died in Hastings in April 1893 aged 13. He was buried alongside his parents at St Andrew's Church, Elveden.

Princess Bamba (1869–1957) photographed just before her formal presentation at court, c. 1887.

Lina Schäfer, the Princesses' German governess, engaged by their guardian after the Maharajah's flight to Moscow.

Princess Catherine: formal portrait, *c.* 1889.

Princess Catherine (top right), Bamba, Sophia and Prince Edward (in sailor suit) *c.* 1886, the year their father disowned them with an announcement in *The Times*. Queen Victoria thought it her duty to help the abandoned family.

As well as pursuing the life of a country gentleman, the Maharajah was an ornament of fashionable London society. He can be seen bareheaded with two Indian servants (far right) in the French painter Jacques Tissot's 'Hush! (The Concert)' of 1875.

The Maharajah in a portrait photograph of 1883, looking a pillar of respectable Victorian society. He was already sloughing off his English skin as beguiling calls came from the Punjab to return.

"FILLALOO! OULD INDIA FOR EVER!"

Juliette Lamber (Madame Adam), socialite, beauty and intellectual – publisher of the political journal *La Nouvelle Revue* which championed a military alliance between France and Russia and 'revenge' on Germany for the defeat of 1871. Her Paris salon was the centre for the shifting intrigues which set the Maharajah on his journey to Moscow as 'England's Proud Implacable Foe'.

RIGHT Elie de Cyon, Russian Jewish-born doctor, physiologist and editor of *La Nouvelle Revue*, who was also Mikhail Katkov's chief agent in Paris.

OPPOSITE When the Maharajah fled to Russia claiming to be the Irish rebel Patrick Casey, the British press woke up. *Punch* (11 June 1887) depicted him as a shillelagh-wielding comic Irishman dancing to the tune of the Russian bear, conveniently labelled 'Katkoff' (editor of the *Moscow Gazette*). The Maharajah thought it 'a clever production'.

General Charles Carrol-Tevis.

Mikhail Katkov, ultra-nationalist editor of the *Moscow Gazette*. Hugely influential on Czar Alexander III, he advocated war with Germany (and if necessary with Britain as well) in conflict with the 'peace-party' at the imperial foreign ministry. He was the sponsor of the Maharajah's flight to Moscow, and his protector until his death in August 1887.

Thetford, August 1998: British Sikhs gather for the unveiling of the equestrian statue of the Maharajah Duleep Singh. The statue was later moved to a river island in the centre of the Norfolk town to be formally unveiled by HRH the Prince of Wales.

was in a frenzy over 'Queen' Ada. And news had somehow reached M. de Giers that the detested Elie de Cyon was to be one of Duleep's wedding witnesses. The foreign minister had 'changed the terms of the passports', Kotzebue frostily explained to the chastened Duleep. Any future residence would be restricted to 'Finland or northern Russia', the Caucasus was out of the question. 'As you are not to be considered altogether as a prisoner, leave may be granted to you from time to time to change your place of residence, but before moving you must obtain the approval of the Imperial Government. The petition for the free entry of your baggage and effects is refused.'

Duleep was crushed. The wedding had indeed ruined him in Russia. He wrote a cringing letter to the Czar about his precious baggage-train. 'My Sovereign. I desire to express to Your Imperial Majesty my sincere gratitude for the bestowal upon me of the passport, by which I am authorized to return to Russia, but, at the same time I venture to appeal most respectfully against the refusal to permit the entrance of my baggage free of duty which was communicated to me by the Imperial Embassy in Paris. Everything is destined exclusively to my personal use, principally for sporting purposes and not for sale,' he wrote, lamely informing the supreme autocrat of his housekeeping arrangements.

The Maharajah's boxes could wait. Damn the Russians with their hypocritical prudery. Love would triumph. On the afternoon of 20 May, the wedding party arrived at the town hall. Duleep wore morning-dress, a glittering diamond-studded decoration, 'l'Etoile de Punjab' proudly stuck on his *redingcote noir*, an enormous emerald tie-pin in his cravat. Ada swept up the steps in a lavender travelling costume clutching a bouquet of *muguets*. She was, gushed a French journal, '*une belle miss anglaise – avec une toilette riche et discrete*'.

The mayor, resplendent in a tricolor sash, performed his republican duties. There had been no objection to the marriage notice; Ada's birth certificate was in order; she was aged twenty; her mother's permission to marry had been obtained. Duleep was a widower. Each answered the marital interrogations, a London-born lawyer, M. Augustin Mourilyan, translating. At four o'clock they were declared man and wife in the name of the law.

Four witnesses signed the register: 'Comte Carrol-Tevis, général, officier de la légion d'honneur, age 59, Elie de Cyon, conseiller d'état de Russia, Chevalier de la légion d'honneur, age 46, Anatole Arthur Baron Textor de Ravisi propriétaire, Commandeur de la légion d'honneur, age 67, Fernand Bourdil, ingénieur, age 35.'

Our Correspondent reported intimate details of the ceremony to London. 'Duleep Singh was married yesterday. This is in the newspapers. But what is not known is the legitimation by marriage of the infant Pauline born of Miss Wetherill during their residence in Russia. By this act, according to French law, this child will enjoy the same rights and privileges as his other children. Duleep signed himself "Sovereign of the Sikh nation".'*

The mayor could not resist making a little speech tracing the '*grandeurs et malheurs*' of the last King of Lahore. He had been 'despoiled of his territories by England', he told the guests, 'and found sanctuary in France, as once Venice had sheltered dispossessed kings. That was the privilege of republics.' M. Beurdeley hoped 'the royal union would be propitious'. Ada was already three months pregnant.†

## *24 rue Marbeuf, Paris, Summer 1889*

The newly-weds were broke. The royal court in an apartment on the rue Marbeuf scarcely glittered. Our Correspondent reported the ménage's condition in a stream of detailed dispatches through the early summer. 'Duleep is nearly on his last legs,' he wrote on 25 May. 'The experts yesterday estimated the jewels which he proposes to sell at 150,000 frs. instead of 400,000 frs. as he had valued them. He has confessed to me with tears that besides these jewels his entire fortune consists of £5,000 sterling which: "Is beggary and if Russia learns my penury I am a lost man".'

'This unfortunate is now entirely in the hands of the Philistines, the bride's mother and sister having joined the household in Paris,' the London spymasters were told on 5 June. 'The jewel sale will take place at the end of the month. Duleep has hired a room at the Hotel Drouot

---

* 'And thus history is written!' a unknown civil servant minuted against this dispatch.
† Cyon said in his memoirs: 'I was a witness at the Mayor's office in the eighth Arrondissement where the marriage took place and promised to stand as godfather to his little child whom he wanted to have baptised according to the Orthodox rite, as a compliment to Russia.'

for five days exhibition from 18th instant. The expert Bloche estimated the collection at 759,000 francs.'

There was a poignant echo of lost greatness in the same dispatch. It related to the 'Star of the Punjab' Duleep had worn at the wedding: 'Aided by a daughter of General Ventura,* once military instructor of Ranjit Singh, he is getting up a revival of the order of chivalry created by said Ranjit: this decoration will be distributed in Russia and elsewhere.'

The jewel sale was a flop. It brought less than £10,000. According to *Le Temps*: 'The first day produced 46,086 Francs, the most important piece was a very beautiful brooch of three enormous rubies.' The second day realized 46,758 francs. A collar of fifty perfect pearls, the one the Maharajah had worn in the Winterhalter portrait, was knocked out for 7,210 francs. The financier Baron Hirsch† sought out the Maharajah. He was sniffing round Elveden. According to Our Correspondent: 'The baron first sent to him a "drummer", one Davidson, and then called in person to negotiate for the sale of the Norfolk and Suffolk property. Duleep has written to him that for a £20,000 bonus to himself he would give his consent to said sale, naming £200,000 as the minimum price.'

The King of Lahore was liquidating his birthright, his bride eager to spend what might be left. Wild, empty promises came from Pondicherry: special messengers bearing mountains of cash would arrive in Paris disguised as visitors to the *Exposition*. Gurbachan Singh wrote excitedly in June that the head of the Kuka community in the Punjab had posted presents, and 'though they are trifling in value – yet the spiritual leaders of this community do always give such things to those whom they respect and love highly. This man has offered the services of his disciples to your Majesty and they are really much devoted to your cause. He can muster brave and fighting persons from 80,000 to 90,000 strong.'

At the end of June, meanwhile, Patrick Casey printed up yet another

* Jean-Baptiste Ventura, Italian-born colonel in Napoleon's army, became the hard-fighting commander of Ranjit Singh's 'model brigade' in 1822. He lived in splendour in a palace in Lahore attended by fifty female slaves before retiring to Paris in 1843. His daughter Victorine Ventura was also granted feudal estates in the Punjab.
† Baron Maurice de Hirsch, German-Austrian Jewish financier and railway promoter, was a friend of the Prince of Wales. Before his death in 1896 he devoted his fortune to promoting the emigration of Russian Jews to America.

proclamation, date-lined this time 'Geneva', so it was said, to 'throw the British off the scent' – a dodge as obvious to Our Correspondent as the Eiffel Tower rising in the Champ-de-Mars.

Beloved Fellow-Countrymen

It is with feelings of deep gratitude and sincere pride that we thank you for the offer of your lives to the sacred cause of Freedom, of which we are the champion. But, as you say that you have no money to give, it becomes necessary for us to explain how small a sacrifice is asked of you to enable us to enter India with a European army and deliver you from the accursed British Raj.

Beloved Fellow-Countrymen, you number in all India some 250,000,000 souls, and if each one of you would subscribe only one pice, during eight or nine months, the required sum would be raised, and surely this is within the means of all.

Believe not that this money is for our personal use!

Sri Khalsa ji! For you, our cause is not only national but also religious. You number about 8,000,000 in the Punjab, and we believe that to none of you will it be a great hardship to lay by, in the name of Sri Guru Gobind Singh ji, one anna each month during eight months time.

To our brother Princes also do we address an earnest warning:

Beware of England's perfidious designs! . . . The system of peaceful annexation has already begun in the case of the Maharajah of Cashmere, and unless you all unite in an indignant protest against this outrageous attempt at spoliation, his sovereign rights and dignity, like yours, will soon be at an end.

And in prevision of the future, we decree that from the date of this our present Royal Proclamation:

> 1st. Cow-killing is absolutely prohibited throughout all Hindoostan, and as compensation to the Mohammedans who have hitherto enjoyed this privilege, they will receive from the Hindoos a pecuniary indemnity which shall be paid upon our arrival in India;

> 2nd. The Payment of all taxes to the British Government

is forbidden, and the population is hereby commanded to refuse compliance with every order for their collection.

3rd. The Public Debt of India is hereby repudiated, and all railway and telegraph lines are confiscated.

4th. All debts upon which the interest exceeds 5 percent per annum are abolished, except where the lender can prove that he has contributed liberally to the success of our mission;

5th. All persons imprisoned by the British authorities shall be released from confinement.

6th. All persons who have suffered from the tyranny and injustice of the accursed British Government will be reinstated, as far as practicable, upon their thrones and in their rights, after a scrupulous investigation of their grievances;

7th. As soon after our return to India as circumstances will permit, a plebiscite will be held in every province, and under the rule of any native princes, and the people called upon to select the government of its choice. For example, Bengal will be permitted to try the virtues of a Republic;

8th. All Hindoos, Brahmins, Sikhs, Mohammedans and Christians are invited to offer up prayers to God for our speedy triumph; and upon furnishing evidence that they have so done, all shall be rewarded according to the well-known liberality of our ancestors, so soon as, by the aid of the Almighty, and the material support of Russia, we shall appear again among you as a Conqueror.

Duleep Singh Sovereign of the Sikh Nation and Implacable foe of the British Government.

The 'Geneva Proclamation' may have shown a glimmer of political maturity (a Bengal republic), but it seemed as desperate a plea for money as ever. For good reason. Mallet Frères advanced a trickle of cash on the security of the last remaining jewels but, it was made clear to Monsieur le Maharajah, not for much longer.

Patrick Casey had other business on his mind that summer. In

London, *The Times*'s 'Parnellism and Crime' case had collapsed with the confession and suicide on 1 March of the forger Richard Piggot during the Parliamentary investigation of the allegations. A Scotland Yard detective-sergeant called Patrick McIntyre was employed (with the secret sanction of Sir Robert Anderson) to rake over Paris dynamite conspiracies. He travelled to the French capital with the super-spy Henri le Caron who had sensationally abandoned his cover in the High Court witness-box to reveal he had been a British penetration agent in the Clan-na-Gael for a quarter of a century.

'We opened up communication with Patrick Casey,' McIntyre wrote in his newspaper-serialized memoirs published in 1895. But this time Casey played double-agent. 'He appeared to act with us who were working in the interests of *The Times* but he was all along informing his brother Joseph – who was in his turn repeating it to Mr. Michael Davitt, who in turn was communicating it to the Irish parliamentary party.' Eugene Davis performed a similar service. Parnell stayed unsullied by dynamite smears – it was adultery that would bring him down.

The court on the rue Marbeuf received ever-more baroque ambassadors. Late in July a mysterious Russian arrived called 'Prince Czenicheff of Premszyl' with a promise to introduce Duleep to 'a lady of position and influence who will forward all your letters direct to the Czar . . . Russia has not abandoned her designs in Asia, but her European enemies must be crushed before any move can be made eastward,' the noble visitor confided. 'You must wait the choice of the opportunity when you can be used in Russia's interest. Your restoration is only a question of time.' Nothing was heard of this again.

Ada's hate-figure, Abdul Rasul, turned up in Paris in midsummer. 'He found out Duleep's address and they then embraced and made friends again,' Our Correspondent reported. The visitor bore letters from Zobair Pasha, the Egyptian intriguer, 'Imploring Duleep to throw himself entirely upon the Mussulman element promising an insurrection in Egypt simultaneously with one in India. He begged the Maharajah "not to waste his time in Russia, but to go to Mecca and thence to Burma whence he could enter India in disguise".' Our Correspondent also noted: 'Abdul Rasul professes strong loyalty to his "Sovereign" but he is a fanatic Mussulman, and I judge, at heart, Duleep's enemy. He could never forgive his marriage to the Englishwoman.'

The Kashmir intrigue was back on the agenda. Our Correspondent remained on the secret case. On 7 October Lord Cross gave the Viceroy intelligence gleaned from Duleep's Paris camp: 'Secret and confidential. Abdul Rasul, Duleep Singh's agent, furnished by him with £100 intended leaving Paris for Egypt on 26th September, en route for India. He has letters from Duleep Singh for Zobair Pasha at Cairo, and also for Maharajah of Cashmere and two other natives, one of whom married a daughter of Ranjit Singh's son, Sher Singh. It is, however, doubtful whether Abdul Rasul himself proceeds further than Egypt . . . Rasul is a sharp and suspicious, bigoted Mohammedan, has not been in India for many years. Description – medium height, Arab features marked by small-pox, scar like burn on left cheek diving into closely cut grisly beard.'

Passage was booked (second class) on the Marseilles–Alexandria steamer for 18 October. London knew everything, even the contents of the seditious letters Abdul Rasul would carry to the Maharajah of Kashmir and the Rajah of Faridkot. It was noted on a Whitehall memo: 'Duleep is said to hope much from this mission if it produces money which is the result hoped for, someone known to our informant is to be sent to confer with the malcontents, but if not, the belief is that he will throw in the sponge and ask for terms from England. We are told that he is almost at the end of his resources and that Mallet Frères hesitated much before cashing a cheque for 410 francs by him lately, and that he has been forced to give up some shooting he had hired.'

It was all falling to bits. Arthur Oliphant had turned up in Paris in mid-September to seek out Duleep and seemed to have been treated civilly enough: 'His Highness introduced me to "his young wife" as he termed her,' Oliphant wrote for the Queen's information. 'She is a pleasant-mannered person and spoke English well but with an accent. He is full of plans for revenge and raged in loud tones for God to come out of hiding and crush his enemies. At times he had the appearance of being raving mad.'

Two weeks later Oliphant confided: 'The Queen will be interested to learn that since I saw the Maharajah in Paris I have most trustworthy information [the confidant is not revealed] that he (the MR) expressed during the last few days the following: That if he does not obtain from India the pecuniary aid which he expects he might find himself in extreme poverty in which case he thought the government might show its magnanimity by giving back his rejected stipend on his returning here and <u>apologising all round</u>.'*

The Maharajah was decaying. The plan to go splashing after Camargue duck was cancelled for lack of funds. He resolved to winter in Algiers. Getting back to Russia glowed in his brain like a Muscovite icon. He had been confident enough, apparently, on 10 July to send 'his dogs to Odessa, whither his heavy baggage was forwarded', then uproot again to another apartment at 390 rue St Honoré. Our Correspondent judged the move to be 'preparations for a hasty exodus'.

It was not to be. Parisian summer turned into autumn. The Maharani's confinement was due. On 25 October 1889 she was delivered of a second daughter, Princess Ada Irene Helen Beryl Duleep Singh. There was no renewed call from the east.

A long dispatch from Our Correspondent on 17 November gave London the reason for the silence from St Petersburg. Queen Ada was the problem. 'Duleep Singh is accused by some of his Russian friends of indiscretion, especially since he left the country, and for this reason, the Governor of Moscow [Prince Dolgorouki] and others who supported him at the outset now decline to compromise themselves further in his cause. His marriage with an Englishwoman who is believed to be a paid English agent, is considered as a proof of the insincerity of his protestations in favour of Russia.'

Nevertheless, there were tiny glimmers of hope. 'Count Kotousov, the alter ego of Ignatiev, will take him up on condition that he returns to Russia and accepts the absolute guidance of Russian politicians,' the all-seeing spy reported. 'This accords with the views of the Directors of the Asiatic Department to whom the case has been submitted and the advice that he be kept on hand to be used at such time and place as the course of Russian politics in Asia may dictate.

'This is not the view taken by M. de Giers, who will avoid, at any reasonable sacrifice, any possible cause of difficulty with England. But as the Maharajah may possibly be of use some day, the other opinion has prevailed. The sine qua non of Kotousov's assistance to Duleep is

---

* The 'apologising all round' letter was sent by the Queen's private secretary to Lord Cross. He returned it with the comment: 'He is quite aware that the Maharajah who has sold his jewels is becoming poorer every day, and at the present moment is unceasing in his endeavours to do mischief especially through his agents at Pondicherry.'

complete abdication of personal policy, and his return to Russia where he can be directed and watched. Duleep has consequently decided to return to Russia as soon as possible and take up his residence at Yalta. His letters from India affirm unwillingness to give him money until the people know of his arrival there.'

Another message arrived at the Foreign Office four days later: 'It may interest you to know that Duleep's son, Victor, is about to marry the daughter of a rich New York banker. He is invited to join his father who proposes to make over to him his claim for some private property in the Punjab, salt-mines it is believed, for which he hopes to obtain a million and a half sterling from the British Govt.'

The British government, it seemed, had little to fear from its proud, implacable foe. As he steered the greatest empire in the world from the Elizabethan gloom of Hatfield House, Lord Salisbury could comfort himself with the latest most-secret intelligence received from Paris: 'Duleep has taken to drinking hard, he falls out of his carriage, frequents night-houses and music halls, in which he is encouraged by his wife and is generally going to the bad.'

# 36

# Pondicherry Beach

❦

*10 rue Law de Lauristan, Pondicherry, French India,*
*Winter 1888–89*

THE RAGGEDY GOVERNMENT-IN-EXILE of Gurbachan Singh and his
brothers resumed their daybreak gatherings on Pondicherry beach. The
Maharajah had promised a fleet would arrive off India's shores loaded
with Remington rifles. As they stared out to sea, the smoke smudges
on the horizon were busy British gunboats heading down the coast for
Madras. The condition of the 'government' was becoming more eccentric in the second winter of exile. The fugitive Burmese Prince Min Goon
held court in a nearby dilapidated bungalow off Dupleix Square where
the garrison band played the 'Marseillaise' each morning.

The French governor came to visit to promise, yet again, that a
subsidy would soon be granted from Paris, against the day his government would find this strange collection of England's enemies useful.
A banker, Baron Anatole Arthur Textor de Ravisi, with interesting
connections with France's new-won Asian empire in Indo-China, had
sought them out with extravagant pledges of help. They had advised
him to 'Go and see His Majesty'.

Gurbachan of the blue spectacles had been appointed wazir on his
father's death. But more, he had, according to the letters steamed open
by the Paris spy, been adopted as the Maharajah's son, 'the highest of
all the honours in the world', the young man called it.

'On the night of 23rd [February] a son, by Sri Sut Gurooji's grace
was born to me,' he wrote to Duleep in Paris, 'and I most humbly ask
that Y.M. both as Guroo sovereign grandfather may be pleased to pray
that he may become brave, wise and a true Sikh and may lead a happy
life and die in your service.'

*372*

The baby was more likely to die of hunger. The Sandhanwalias were supposed to be raising a fortune for the cause. Instead they were begging for food, their wives had sold their jewellery, their clothes were threadbare, and their unpaid servants deserting. There had been an unanswered overture for pardon in September 1887, and six months later it was made again: 'We commit our case in your hands and will obey your orders, and we are sure the clemency of the government of India will be extended to us. Our remaining more out of British India is giving much time to our opponents to injure us,' Gurbachan Singh wrote imploringly to Simla. There was no reply. Our Correspondent had reported a letter in which the Maharajah had told his cousins that he understood 'why they must be seen to appear friendly to the British'. The spy told London, who told Simla. The pressure was kept up.

In October 1888, agent A.S., the Punjabi detective who had worked Abdul Rasul in Cairo, turned up in Pondicherry posing as a Sikh soldier, a veteran of the Burma campaign. The Sandhanwalias believed him. He extracted names and designations of disaffected regiments, and intimate details of the Kashmir subversion plan.

In the spring of 1888 Colonel Henderson had sent an agent to interview Mangala, the slave-girl who had been 'minister of pleasure' in the last decadent days of the Lahore court. She had retired 'with great wealth' to Khankal in the North-West Provinces. Mangala had confided: 'The Sakhi prophecies, and the sayings of astrologers have caused a firm belief that Duleep Singh will certainly come to rule over the Panjab, and this will not disappear till his death.'

She named sympathizers: the Rajah of Faridkot, Rajah Amar Singh of Kashmir, and Bawa Budh Singh Bedi. She also said that Jiwan Singh, of Berki, had taken a letter from her to Duleep in Aden. She would say nothing of its contents. Jiwan Singh was a former native police officer of Lahore. Perhaps he could be turned back to old loyalties. Colonel Henderson opened a special file on 'Jiwan Singh alias Karam Singh'.

Hyderabad Special Branch reported in September that a former servant of Thakur Singh Sandhanwalia had left Pondicherry heading for the Sikh shrine of Nander. He had a large sum of money with him on some Duleep-related mission, £300 of which had been robbed on a train. He had boasted to a police informer that: 'He had met Duleep in a fine house in Moscow where he was guarded by Russian sentries.

The Maharajah received money not from the Russians but from some bank which supplies him with funds. Two Sikhs and a one-eyed Mohammedan were with him in Moscow.' The suspect claimed to have been to England with Thakur Singh who, he insisted, 'was poisoned by the English'. It was Jiwan Singh. Colonel Henderson ordered his expedient arrest.

Jiwan Singh was discreetly lifted at Akola on 14 November. Detective Assistant E. J. Stephenson of the Hyderabad police messaged Simla: 'Prisoner is a very clever fellow but extravagant and given to drink. He is very violent, refused food and insisted he was a political prisoner. I have not had time to push him, but, if I was left to work, I could get him to confess.'

Mr Stephenson's interrogation methods were successful.

CONFESSION OF JIWAN SINGH, AKOLA POLICE STATION, 20 NOVEMBER, 1888

I was at Pondicherry from the 31st September, 1887, to the end of September 1888. I met Sardar Thakur Singh's sons there and was employed by them. If I am pardoned and allowed to work, I will agree to do the following:

I can get hold of all the correspondence which has taken place between Duleep Singh and the Sardars at Pondicherry.

This correspondence is in a box in a room where the Granths [scriptures] are kept and read. The box is placed under the Granths. When I was at Pondi, I had free access to this room. The keys of the box of papers and of all other boxes are locked up in one box.

If I were supplied with a lot of keys, I could open this box and then get the keys of the other box and abstract all the correspondence without any one knowing any thing about it.

There is a Granth which is written by Guru Gobind Singh, in which there are many things foretold, some of which says that Duleep Singh will be king of the Punjab.

There are eleven things foretold in this book, all of which refer to Duleep Singh, nine of them have come to pass and there are only two to take place. One is that Duleep Singh will come to Ghazni in Afghanistan and will either by force of arms or treaty get back the Punjab; he will be assisted by a strange king, who this king is, is not mentioned. The other is after two years after coming to Ghazni, Duleep Singh will mount the throne of Delhi and be the king of the Punjab. The original and a copy of this Granth is now at Pondicherry. I could hand it over to one who comes with me.

There is a Mohammedan named Inhodeen, or some such name, with Duleep Singh; this man came to Afghanistan and about 300 Shias [Muslims] from the Punjab have joined him.

Among these papers, there is, I think a copy of a treaty which has been made between Duleep Singh and the Russian Government, but I am certain several of the letters refer to this treaty.

The prisoner admitted that he had never been to Russia. He had made it all up from stories he had heard to sound impressive. But what he said added something new and puzzling. 'Inhodeen' was clearly Djemal-ud-din, but what was the 'Treaty with the Russian Government' kept with the prophecy in the tabernacle of scriptures?

Jiwan Singh's turning was complete. He told the detective: 'Gurbachan Singh, Narinder Singh and Gurdit Singh, all sons of Thakur Singh, are in the habit of going out for drives towards the English boundaries of Pondicherry. If arrangements were made, I could drive them over the border and then entrap them.' The offer was declined. The unfortunate Jiwan Singh was spirited to Asigarh Fort where he was kept in secret detention. It was much better to leave the Pondicherry conspirators where they were. Our Correspondent was already reading every letter – and they were revealing much.

It was an eerie feeling working through Gurbachan Singh's autograph letters sent to Duleep's chief of staff in Paris throughout 1889. Most were originals written on flimsy paper in a sprawling hand addressed to 'Dear General', others were transcribed on creamy India Office letterheads, the addressee concealed as simply [blank]. The last time they had been subject to this kind of scrutiny had been in gaslit Whitehall offices, freshly dispatched across the Channel by Our Correspondent. Like Sir Edward Bradford, the head of the Political and Secret

Department* whose handwritten margin notes they bore, I too scanned them for every nuance of intelligence.

Gurbachan Singh wrote on 1 January: 'Two Sikhs have accompanied to Europe a German Baron lately at Hyderabad, where he bought arms as curiosities, they go on the promise of being taken to the Maharajah. The Rajah of Faridkot, is suspected by the British of loyalty to your Majesty.'

There were more snippets: 'No news of Aroor Singh who must be in Nepal.'†

'Results of much importance are hoped from the "National Congress" of which the British are much afraid.‡ The Congress is a fatal enemy to the British and we will keep on informing Y.M. of this important movement. Special emissaries travel from one end to the other of India telling people of their rights and sowing the seeds of discontent.'

'The Prince Min Goon of Burmah sends his compliments to your majesty and wishes to unite their fortunes,' Sir Edward scrawled in red ink before passing the letter to a colleague: 'I really don't know that such rubbish is much use to you, but I send it for what it is worth and will continue to do so until you say nay.'

There was a particularly poignant touch in one letter: 'My Dear General,' Gurbachan wrote on 26 February. 'Before everything else please accept my thanks for the noble work you have taken in hand to serve our beloved sovereign in his patriotic task of releasing the 250 millions of the creatures of the creator of the universe from the foreign yoke. Pray convey my thanks to your associate too.' He did not know that 'the general' was telling London everything.

In February 1889 the Maharajah's astonishing plan for an invasion of India by a force of European mercenaries had reached Pondicherry. Gurbachan Singh's reaction was sanguine. 'Here are our views of the

---

* Bradford had supplanted Sir Owen Tudor Burne in the job on 10 February 1887. He was appointed chief commissioner of the Metropolitan Police on James Monro's resignation in June 1890.

† Arur Singh was being held in a British prison in Chunar Fort, under Regulation III of 1818 under which the Maharajah's partisans were arrested and held; state prisoners could be detained in secret.

‡ The Indian National Congress was founded in Bombay in 1885 under the benign patronage of the Viceroy, Lord Dufferin. It was largely a collaborationist talking-shop for educated Bengali Hindus – lawyers, schoolmasters and journalists. The Muslims stayed out. Home-rule militancy would take another three decades to foment.

plan. It is the best and well chosen. Difficult but possible,' he wrote. 'Nearly all of the Indian Princes are injured in heart by the English Government, and I can say without the fear of contradiction that all of them are more anxious to throw over the British yoke. But alas! they have been rendered useless and inactive. They are cowards.'

There was more hope in the 'starving people of India', Duleep's cousin said. 'It is our sincere impression that if Y.M. does land in India with a European army of about 20,000 fighting men, the people will join us willingly.'

But how to pay them? 'There is very little hope of raising any money in India,' Gurbachan reported. 'The Calcutta men promised pecuniary aid but the collectors themselves misappropriated it.'

Even the Fenians might desert the cause: 'Your Majesty must be very well satisfied with the Irishmen. They are deadly enemies of England of course but we fear that if they are offered the full liberty and Home Rule in Ireland in the same way as they demand they may change their minds. We do not doubt the sincerity of Irishmen but we only express our thoughts.

'A mutiny of Bengal army can be raised, because the Bengal army chiefly consists of Punjabis . . . but they have neither munitions of war nor artillery all of which are in the hands of European soldiers. If the Irish officers do really join us they can give us much help in this direction.

'Our only enemy in the country is the European [British] army therefore we think that Y.M. must have an army of between 15 and 20,000 Europeans at the time of landing and must appear in India suddenly and surprise the English and capture at once an important town and defeat its small garrison which will be no difficult matter at all. And as soon as this news spreads, certainly all of India would be in a blaze and God willing the enemy would be overcome easily.'

But where was the vanguard of the 'Grand Army of Freedom' to land? The Punjab was hundreds of miles from the sea. Sind was suggested or Bengal. Gurbachan said it should be Burma where 'our Punjabis muster in large numbers and if we could drive the English out of Burmah we will not have difficulty in treading down the English Raj in India'.

There was also the small matter of the Royal Navy. Would not Duleep's promised armada of American ships be blasted out of the water? 'We think our friends will ask us how is it possible for Y.M. to land in India with such an army as all the routes to India are in the hands of the enemy. We solicit instructions in the matter,' wrote Gurbachan. There was no sensible answer from Duleep.

No more might the would-be monarch of India divulge how his liberated dominion would be governed. 'Some people have questioned us about the mode of our government,' wrote Gurbachan Singh in February 1889, 'and as we had not special instructions from Y.M. we have given different answers to suit the questions. The majority like the despotic form of government and really that suits the country. We have told the Princes that they will have their share in the general management of the country on the same footing as the German peoples enjoy. The Congress also demand a Parliament and as Y.M. has not expressed any opinion on the subject and even as they do not know how you like the Congress movement they cannot make up their minds.'

The Maharajah post-liberation politics may have been highly flexible but so, by the summer of 1889, was his reclaimed religion. Since his sojourn in Kiev, he had ostensibly been flirting with the Russian Orthodox Church. Cyon (whom Mikhail Katkov had sponsored on his conversion from Judaism) had offered to be god-parent to Pauline after Duleep's civil wedding.

Gurbachan Singh was horrified. 'As to your Majesty's joining the Russian faith we beg to say that it would produce very bad effect among the Indians and more particularly with Sikhs who believe in you as their Guroo,' he wrote in May. 'According to their idea, you became Christian in accordance with the prophecy ... and not on your own accord. Already the English papers of the Punjab are giving out that you are not a Sikh. If you ever take [Russian Orthodox] baptism they will spread the news at once and the peoples will not trust us.'

He was none the less prepared to be flexible: 'In our humble opinions your Majesty must remain Sikh unless the Russian Government binds itself to help your Majesty at once and get you back to the country. In that event you must remain Sikh outwardly up to the time that your Majesty is firmly established on the throne.'

The Punjabi detective Amrik Singh returned to Pondicherry in May 1889 as the Maharajah was celebrating his Paris nuptials. The conspirators were utterly penniless, he reported, they had received just £100 from the Maharajah. 'Gurdit Singh admitted the correspondence that had been going on with Duleep was entirely useless. "The brothers" he said "wrote nonsense in the hope of getting money, the Maharajah buoyed up by these messages entertains hopes of conquering India." Gurbachan Singh mentions the "Irish major" who proposed to visit India in order to gain over the Irish troops, but there is no immediate intention of sending out this agent.' The 'Irish Major', of course, did not exist – he was Our Correspondent.

The summer weather brought disaster. A delegation of rebellious Burmese arrived off Pondicherry in a French steamer, looking for their deposed chieftain. A storm blew up and they were landed in Madras in British India to be immediately arrested. They carried seditious letters to Prince Min Goon. This became a major diplomatic incident. Why was France openly succouring England's enemies? The Foreign Office brought discreet pressure to bear on their French counterparts – the Sandhanwalia family were caught in the net.

In Paris, Baron Textor stormed round to the Quai d'Orsay to try and undo the damage. But M. Nisard, the political director of the French Foreign Office, told him sternly: 'As in the case of the Burmese Prince Min Goon, Gurbachan Singh is under surveillance and will not be permitted to leave French Indian territory except to British India. The French Government will not tolerate acts of a nature to embroil it with a friendly power and it has been decided to put a stop to all similar intrigues concocted within its jurisdiction. With regard to the granting of a subsidy to the Sikh refugees, the French Government has not yet come to a decision. As a friend of the person entitling himself "Sovereign of the Sikh nation", you would do well to inform that individual of the necessity of prudence and moderation. Otherwise, he is in danger of expulsion from France, in virtue of the same police regulations which were enforced in the case of the Irish agitators in 1885.'*

Expulsion from France, indifference from Russia. Where could the Maharajah turn? 'Duleep is scared out of his senses,' reported Our

---

* In 1885 Patrick Casey, Eugene Davis and James Stephens were expelled from France to Switzerland and Belgium for a year after an outrageous 'dynamite' newspaper interview too far.

Correspondent on Christmas Day 1889. According to the spy, Queen Ada seemed to be leading him by the nose round Paris's night-houses. The conspiracy was falling apart but the Maharajah seemed too drunk to care.

# 37

# Victor

❦

## *Royal Military College, Sandhurst, Surrey, 1887–88*

FOR A GENTLEMAN CADET set to enter Queen Victoria's army to bet on racehorses was to be expected. To owe one's bookmakers £1,390 by the second term at the Royal Military College was not. In the middle of August 1887, just as the Maharajah was boastfully celebrating his official permission to reside in Russia, Prince Victor Duleep Singh faced a howling society scandal.

The committee of Tattersall's were due to meet, as the loudly-check-suited regulators of the turf did on the fourth Monday of every month at Knightsbridge Green, solemnly to ponder the debt-book. If a punter would not pay up, the sanction was 'posting', publication in the sporting prints of the names of defaulting gentlemen for whom the nags had not been running well.

They had not been running at all well for the Queen's Old Etonian godson. Messrs Goodson, Fry and O'Connor, bookmakers to the gentry, were demanding their money. Prince Victor faced disgrace. The family trustees were not that surprised. On Bamba's death, £500 a year had been held back to pay the young man's existing debts 'for champagne and other delicacies'. Thereafter, once the question of whether or not to call him 'prince' had been grumpily resolved, the rules excluding 'natives' from holding officer's commissions had been bent to get him his Sandhurst cadetship. If the trustees had thought that would sort him out, they were wrong.

The Queen knew the fate of an Indian in the flashy elite of her army. She thought Victor 'would be bullied in the Blues [the Royal Horse Guards] or any Household Regiment'. To begin with, the family trustees were equally doubtful. A minute records: 'The trustees recommended that he go into the Scots Greys or some other regiment of that character which does not go to India. In such a regiment he would, we think, be not only contented, but be in a measure removed from the temptations of an idle London life. We are not sanguine that his military career is likely to be a successful one.'

He scraped through the first two terms at Sandhurst. 'Half yearly report on gentleman cadet Prince Victor Albert Jay Duleep Singh, 19th July 1887. Place in order of merit list 155. Probationary examination 554 marks out of a maximum 1250, minimum required one-third of the aggregate. Pass.' His worse subject was 'tactics' – 87 out of 300. Colonel A. S. Cameron VC, commandant of the college, signed off his conduct as 'V. Good'.

It could hardly be described as such. Victor had taken an apartment in Mayfair, at 120 Mount Street, where grand young friends might be entertained. There were card games in which he seemed to enjoy as little success as his father in Moscow. Lord Frederick Pelham-Clinton, heir to the Duke of Newcastle (£120) and Marcus Milner Esquire (£60) were gently pressing for payment of their gambling 'debts of honour'. The bookies were proving less gentlemanly. With days to go before Tattersall's met, the looming scandal blew up at the India Office.

Sir Owen Tudor Burne minuted on 26 August 1887: 'Prince Victor Duleep Singh is due to be "posted" on Monday next. The affairs of the family are giving us much anxiety. I regret to say I do not much trust Prince Victor's character or tone. But we must persuade him to return to Sandhurst from which he threatens to run away and do what we reasonably can to prevent a scandal.' A week later the bookmakers got their money from the revenues of the government of India – and the prince got a stern letter from Lord Cross, the Secretary of State. This was to be the last time

It was not. Victor Duleep Singh left Sandhurst in December and was gazetted lieutenant in the First Dragoon Guards, a regiment with pretensions to being fashionable. The warning of the 'idle London life' enjoyed by a subaltern at Knightsbridge Barracks had been ignored at the India Office's peril. By July 1888 his debts were staggering.

The Political and Secret Department was told: 'Prince Victor's debts as stated by himself amount to £17,721 of which bookmakers and money-lenders are owed £7,277, and a £4,000 gambling debt to someone unknown.' As well as the Maharajah's designs to invade India at the head of a Russian Army, the India Council had now to consider the threats of Messrs Ward and Co. (bird-stuffing), Penhaligon and Jeavons (hairdressers), Bowring Arundel and Co. (hosiery), James Purdey (gunsmiths) and Philip Morris (cigars etc.) to declare the Queen's godson bankrupt. Mr Harris (money-lender) was not going to be appeased by an offer of ten shillings and sixpence in the pound, but Mr G. A. Leslie-Melville (Lord Leven's son), co-lessee of the Mount Street apartment, seemed prepared to wait for a £4,000 gambling debt. The young gentlemen's gas-bill meanwhile went unpaid.

The prince must disappear. Lord Henniker drew up an agreement 'which binds Prince Victor to go and reside wherever he is ordered by the Duke of Cambridge and to give up gambling and betting for at least five years'. The commander-in-chief found a bleak imperial outpost – Halifax in Nova Scotia, supposed to be devoid of temptations (it was not). Sir Owen Tudor Burne noted: 'To clear Prince Victor once more is a hopeless task. He is devoid of all principle or honour. In these circumstances I should let him go, say that he may go to Canada if he wishes to do so. My inward conviction is the trick he has played us will be repeated many times before he dies!' In December 1888 the India Office disgorged another £8,500 and Victor was sent, it was hoped, into snowbound obscurity.

The Oliphants meanwhile had their hands full with the princesses. In spite of the Thorncliff camp drill-sergeant's efforts, rebelliousness still smouldered in genteel Folkestone. Their guardian kept the Queen informed with a string of reports.

Arthur Oliphant wrote to Windsor on 8 November 1887: 'I am very sorry to find that they certainly hold some of their father's views with respect to his grievances and wrongs he believes to have been inflicted on him by the British government.'

Things had improved a bit by the following January: 'Prince Frederick had returned to Magdalene Cambridge after spending three weeks with us here. Victor is evidently disappointed that Bamba and Catherine have not yet been persuaded to do up their hair or to adopt the wearing of corsets. Of the whole family there is one who has any pretension to be anglicised and that is the eldest. Even the youngest girl, Sophy, in her playing with Edward and our own boy speaks of "those *horrid* English who would not let them all go to live in India but stopped them at Aden".'

Sir Henry Ponsonby summarized their condition in a note for the Queen: 'The Princesses get more reserved every day and their manners are abrupt and rude to strangers.'

Supposedly temptation-free Halifax had not dampened their elder brother's enthusiasms meanwhile. Victor took a comfortable house, 7 Spring Garden Road, and had a cavalry charger at livery. He was gambling again. The colonial outpost was also inconveniently close to the United States. There was a flurry of activity in the India Office in October 1889 when Prince Victor seemed to have fallen in love. He wrote breathlessly to Lord Cross from the Hotel Brunswick, New York: 'I am writing to inform you of my engagement to a most charming and beautiful American lady, Miss J. Turnure, daughter of Mr Lawrence Turnure, a prominent New York banker.' Prince Victor wanted money, 'one half to be settled absolutely on my future wife,' adding, 'I must also ask you that the name of my betrothed may be kept entirely secret . . . I have not yet spoken to her father nor can I see how I can do so unless I can tell him what prospects and future position I can offer his daughter.'

Windsor Castle was informed by Lord Cross: 'As to the alleged engagement of Prince Victor, I should be very glad to see him well married. I have been given to understand that he went to New York with the intention of finding a rich wife but that he fell violently in love with some lady or other who was penniless.

'He now writes to me to say that he is engaged to . . . the daughter of a banker, but he has not yet spoken to her father! and eagerly waits an answer as to what allowances can be made to him and what settlement can be made upon her.

'But the difficulty is great owing to the unfortunate action of the Maharajah and the position is still more complicated by the fact that he has already two children by his second wife and may probably have a dozen more – who may all come before the unfortunate Secretary of State!'

The New York banker seemed unimpressed by the Indian Prince's social prospects. The engagement was broken off. What Queen Victoria thought of her godson marrying a Manhattan socialite is not recorded, but her reaction to his continuing embarrassments is. She was told (via Arthur Oliphant) at the end of November 1889: 'Prince Victor Duleep Singh is again in financial difficulties. I trust a lenient view may be taken of Prince Victor's settlements although I see great difficulties in the way. It would be a great calamity if he should have to leave the Queen's Army which he fears will be the case.' Queen Victoria minuted tersely: 'This is most unfortunate.'

## *5 Sussex Square, Brighton, 1889–90*

The princesses' reconditioning was proceeding much more happily. In the autumn of 1889 they were removed to the Oliphants' Brighton house, 5 Sussex Square. A German governess, Fraulein Lina Schäfer from Kassel, Hesse, and tutors for the violin and singing were engaged. They learned to swim. They were bright although they displayed 'Fads, nonsenses and rude ways which so mar their character.' It was deemed appropriate for the two eldest girls to go to Somerville Hall, Oxford, under the watchful eye of its youthful principal, Miss Agnes Catherine Maitland.

The Queen received a stream of progress reports. Lord Henniker wrote in May 1890: 'They are very much improved in every way and are nice presentable young ladies. Catherine is a very pretty child and the eldest, Bamba, is nice-looking. I have great hopes that the management of them, poor neglected children, will turn out well.

'I do not think that Bamba should be out in society yet. She is 20 but her early training makes it difficult for her to join in general society at present i.e. she is very young for her age.'

Arthur Oliphant wrote a month later: 'The Queen will, I am sure, be glad to know that the two Princesses Duleep Singh have made a happy beginning at Oxford. They left us on Saturday 26th with Miss Schäfer for Somerville Hall.'

Off they went that summer with Miss Schäfer to the Black Forest, Cassell and Dresden. Catherine was embarking on a much longer visit to Germany.

# 'The Turks Shall Break Their Silence'

⚜

*Apollo Bunder, Bombay Harbour, Midnight 31 January 1890*

THE SS *MASSAILLA* nosed round the oily waters off Colaba point bearing Duleep's last hope. Landfall was close, the scents of Bombay carried on the breeze from the shore. In his cabin, Abdul Rasul, the Maharajah's Mohammedan emissary, heard the engine revolutions drop and the clanging noises of a ship about to dock. He made his preparations to go ashore and vanish into the midnight alleys of the teeming port. There was a scurry of metal-toecapped boots on the companion-way. Bombay policemen thumped at the door.

Abdul Rasul's mission had been blown from the start by the clever double-agenting in Cairo of the Sikh detective Amrik Singh. The 'bigoted Mohammedan' had indeed taken ship from Marseilles, as Our Correspondent had warned London, landed briefly in Cairo, then embarked on his wild mission to raise Kashmir in revolt. The telegraph wires had been busy from the moment he had transited Suez. There were to be no half measures. 'Send warrant for Abdul Rasul,' the Thugee and Dacoity Department had cabled. 'Viceroy wants him arrested before he lands at Bombay. He may have shipped as Abdulla Effendi, as he used that name at Cairo as his postal address.'

The secret arrest was effected with velvet efficiency. As the pilot boat met the *Massailla* just after midnight, a police steam-launch puffed out from the Apollo Bunder, the Bombay waterfront, bearing Major J. Humfrey, the officiating commissioner of police, a gaggle of plain-clothes detectives and Amrik Singh. 'Immediately the steamer cast anchor, about 1 a.m., she was boarded and Abdul Rasul arrested and removed before any shore boats reached the ship, and without anybody except a few of the ship's crew being any the wiser,' Colonel Henderson reported triumphantly. A waiting carriage spirited the prisoner from the Mazagon Bunder (the monsoon dock) straight to Bombay's raucous central police station. The Sikh detective stayed hidden in the darkness as his Cairo-confected trap sprang quietly shut.

Colonel Henderson himself arrived the next morning. The prisoner's baggage, a 'portmanteau and a bundle' were taken to pieces. They disgorged an envelope with a Moscow postmark, a sheaf of letters in Arabic and some press cuttings posted from Pondicherry about potential trouble in Kashmir and the 'government employing spies in the disguise of fakirs and sadhus'. The interrogation began 'after breakfast'. Abdul Rasul seemed as tough a subject as Arur Singh had been in Calcutta eighteen months earlier. The prisoner 'knew nothing about Duleep Singh, or anyone he communicated with in India'. He had 'never been to Moscow', or maybe he had – and 'by accident had found himself in the same hotel as the Maharajah'.

It was the same story in Paris – he had gone there 'to visit the exhibition and only by chance was in the city at the same time as Duleep Singh'. Why had he come to India? 'Having heard that a just government under a British resident had been established in Kashmir,* he had determined in his old age to return to his native country and endeavour to earn a living by teaching languages,' the prisoner replied.

The Arabic letters were dissected, including a secret message from Zobair Pasha saying that he expected a visit from a person called 'the father of the turban'. The interrogator produced a letter in the prisoner's own handwriting to the flamboyantly head-dressed double-agent (whom Rasul still supposed to be his clandestine ally, 'Jaswant Singh'), urging him to go to Duleep in Paris. The prisoner protested he had 'never seen it before'.

A catch-all warrant under Regulation III was safely tucked in the colonel's pocket. Rasul was promptly heading for Asigarh Fort under orders: 'All communications between him and strangers outside or visiting the fort should be prohibited. I shall be glad to consider any

---

* In 1889 the British resident Sir Trevor Plowden was recalled by Lord Dufferin for over-zealous internal political interference, but the newly appointed Viceroy, Lord Lansdowne, with the Duleep intrigue as an excuse, spurred him back substantially to take over government of the state. There was a heated debate in the House of Commons that Kashmir was about to be annexed outright, just as the Punjab had been.

proposals made by the commandant regarding the necessary expenditure of his diet and clothing. He was a shawl merchant and a man of no social standing, but for years he has been in Europe and Egypt where he very likely has learnt to live as European. I think about Rs. 40 a month will probably be enough.' The 'father of the turban' was dispatched to the Punjab to carry on snooping, while the prisoner was squirrelled away to secret detention. Henderson noted: 'I have no doubt that properly managed Abdul Rasul will tell us all he knows.'

Even confined in Asigarh Fort the prisoner could be useful. Henderson resolved to allow news of his arrest to reach Paris with Zobair Pasha as the unwitting intermediary. 'He was Duleep's last hope,' the colonel told his political masters in Calcutta on 21 February, 'and finding this gone he will sue for terms. Abdul Rasul told me that Duleep is prepared to make his submission and indeed that a Mr Cirblestone or some such name came over to Paris on behalf of the British government to treat with him.'*

A public 'surrender' – what an auspicious way for the civil servants of the India Office to close the Maharajah file. There would be knighthoods in it. A declaration of 'outlawry' in parliament (Sir Owen Tudor Burne's suggestion in March 1887) or Sir Henry Rawlinson's 'put him on trial for High Treason' outburst smacked of heads on pikes at London Bridge, not the orderly running of the empire. A very public scandal would be averted. The Queen would be appeased. Even better for those who had suffered his hubris for so long, the Maharajah's monstrous ego would be denied its martyrdom.

All that was needed was to chip away at what was left of his preposterous rebellion. Queen Ada and her friends would do the rest.

## 4 rue St Roch, Paris, February–March 1890

It was the Maharajah's fourth winter on the run. He had found a wife and lost a fortune. If he had any hope left, it was in Abdul Rasul's Islamic intrigues (he did not yet know that his 'emissary' had been deftly lifted from the P & O steamer in Bombay harbour), the starving

* Probably the freelance Oliphant mission of September the previous year which triggered the 'apologising all round' report to the Queen. There is no 'Cirblestone' in the Foreign or India Office lists.

true-believers in Pondicherry and Baron Textor de Ravisi's increasingly baroque schemes for raising money. The Punjab was a lost cause. Colonel Henderson had cabled the government of India from Lahore: 'The intrigue is dying out. The arrests we made last year have inspired a wholesale terror.'

Cheaper rooms were found, on the fifth floor of a lodging house, no. 4 rue St Roch behind the Tuileries. Ada's mother and sister arrived to fuss over the infant princesses. With a Paris concièrge as its chamberlain, the court of Lahore received a procession of increasingly eccentric visitors and fortune-hunters amid the drying washing. Our Correspondent was ever-more disparaging of the cockney Empress. He had a new name for her as he treated Whitehall to a series of intimate snapshots of Duleep's condition.

'Duleep Singh is constantly drunk. This pretender is now, under the influence of his wife, fast becoming a besotted swine. His only endeavour is to get money out of the Indians to enable him to supply the extravagance of the gas-fitter's child, who has now her family installed with her in their lodgings.'

'He is drinking very hard and his head and face is like that of a defeated prize fighter from a fall while intoxicated,' the spy messaged on 9 February. 'I have seen a note from Duleep to a friend asking him to call any day about 5 p.m. at which hour he says: "I am generally asleep in a chair in my room."'

'He is disposed to sell out for a good sum. He is tired of playing at politics and his wife fairly "eats money" as the Turks put it.'

Mr Villiers cheerfully minuted Mr Maitland: 'Our implacable foe, I expect, is in a very boozy state.'

There were more bruising political humiliations to endure. The Russian Grand Duke Nicholas was in Paris in the first week of February. Duleep 'demanded an interview' and was refused. The French Foreign Office blew hot and cold. The busy Baron Textor told Our Correspondent the news from the Quai d'Orsay. They had agreed a secret subvention for the Burmese pretender Min Goon and spirited him and his family to Saigon because: 'In any quarrel with England, Prince Min Goon can render us material service by getting up troubles for her in Burmah, wherefore, it is expedient to keep at our disposal what may someday be a valuable weapon of offence.' But there was to be nothing for the Sandhanwalias. 'As to the Sikh Princes we cannot see of what use they can be to us at any time, and for this reason the grant to them of any subvention is not recommended.'

The baron set up a complicated system of dummy bank accounts in Pondicherry, Bombay and Madras for remitting money from India. It would be run by a cipher code, which Our Correspondent immediately sent in full to London along with an impression of a 'Royal Seal' which was to be attached to all future proclamations to 'Beloved countrymen and faithful subjects'. But it was fantasy – there was no money. Our Correspondent noted: 'The same cypher will be used between the Burmese Min Goon and the Baron who has persuaded Duleep that his man will send to him 50 lakhs as soon as he re-enters Burmah to put himself at the head of the natives. The details of this alliance are grotesque – Duleep is to aid the other with a European army.'

Letters still arrived from Pondicherry, ever hopeful, ever loyally addressed to 'His Majesty and Her Majesty, the Maharani Sahiba'. At the end of February the message came that 'a certain Mohammedan menial police official has been sent to Paris by the English wicked Govt. to kill Your Majesty'. It was Aziz-ud-din, of course, but he had been pulled off the case after his exertions in Cairo. Nevertheless the Maharajah was frightened. Our Correspondent reported: 'Duleep is vastly scared of the assassination story and is about to put himself under police protection.'

The crisis was approaching. Victor was being 'dunned' again for the Halifax debts and was about to file for bankruptcy. He asked his father for help. The Maharajah replied on 1 March: 'My Dear Son. I once more renounce all my right to the pension that was enforced upon me by the late Marquis of Dalhousie and the India Office if they please can pay your debts. You can make of this what you may desire. Your loving father.' A week later Victor turned up in Paris, setting up at the Grand Hotel on the Boulevard des Capucines on whatever credit could be scraped together.

The Queen's godson was not an emissary of the India Office, although he would now effectively be the conduit for surrender negotiations. Lord Cross told the Viceroy: 'His eldest son has been over to Paris once or twice although they cannot do each other any good. He is a thorough oriental in extravagance.' Duleep had not seen his son in three years. He greeted him warmly enough, and with all the old bluster. He was not going to surrender, he was going back to Russia, that was his 'irrevocable decision'. Victor must take a commission in the Imperial Army to please his protector, the Czar.

Our Correspondent was telling London meanwhile that for £50,000 lodged in a French bank the Maharajah would sign 'a treaty promising his neutrality in any future war between England and Russia'. The gas-fitter's child and Mrs Wetherill had their own opinions: What about us? What about the new little Duleep Singhs?

The family discussions evidently raised the price of submission. Victor was the go-between for an approach to Sir Owen Tudor Burne in a letter dated 9 March. 'I have just seen my father and I wish to say that he informs me that he is returning immediately to Russia,' he wrote in a long letter. 'Can nothing be done to prevent this? Will the India Office not do something to make his return to England and ourselves possible?'

This was his price: a court of inquiry and £100,000 'be given him for settlement on his family,' wrote Victor. 'He would promise (and I think you must know that his word is good) not to agitate or act in any treasonous (sic) way against England again. He insists on the £100,000 as he is now pledged in many various ways: I presume to Russia and probably to some society of malcontents. In order to return to England he must have something to fall back on, something that he could give his second family for certain.'

The following day the Political and Secret Department of the India Office opened a new file: 'Maharajah Duleep Singh – Question of making overtures to him for a reconciliation.' It began with Victor's letter. The members of the India Council fell on the prosaic piece of government stationery with their pens as if sticking needles in a voodoo effigy. 'Absurd', 'What effrontery', 'Take no notice of this or any other communications!' The mention of a 'second family' was scornfully underlined. The Secretary of State was cooler in his analysis but even less forgiving. He wrote on the file:

> This communication contains no expression of regret on the part of the Maharajah at the course of hostility which he has pursued towards this country since he resigned his stipend in 1886, nor is there any recognition of the fact that by his intrigues against the State and by his appeals to H.M.'s Indian

subjects to renounce their allegiance he has incurred the penalties of treason.

The conditions he seeks to impose are absolutely unacceptable. The Maharajah is a rebel and a traitor. Since his departure from England in 1886 he has allied himself with the enemies of England, and has engaged in conspiracies to subvert British rule in India.

In the judgement of the Political Department it would be an abasement of the dignity and honour of the Crown to make any overtures whatever to the Maharajah. If he desires reconciliation the preliminary step should be his complete submission to the Government of Her Majesty. This should be the antecedent condition to any dealings with him. It will be for the law officers of the Crown to advise what course should be followed if he submits.

The Queen was told simply: 'Prince Victor has been to see his father who is leading a disreputable life. Prince Victor fears he has taken up drinking and his health is breaking up.'

It did not matter much right then – father and son obviously had a blazing row. The Maharajah would fight to the end. Victor wrote wearily to London on 16 March: 'Having been so authorized, I, after full consideration, withdraw the letter of the 9th instant, I had the honour to address to you. The possibility of the negotiations which it contained being finally at an end.'

Four days later, the greatest figure in late nineteenth-century European politics shuffled off the stage. On 20 March Prince Otto von Bismarck resigned, weary of domestic and foreign political battles, spurned by the ambitious young Kaiser. The secret Reinsurance Treaty was due to expire in June. The new men in Berlin would let it die. Colonial compacts with Britain rapidly followed – almost an Anglo-German 'entente'. The atheist republic and Holy Russia were perforce being pushed together. There was more diplomacy by dynamite. On 30 May fourteen Russian nihilists were arrested in Paris to the delight of Alexander III. De Giers saw the wreckage of a decade. He feared the new order in Europe would not be for peace, but for the adventurers and revanchists who wanted war. He was right.

How ironic it was. The Maharajah was about to be brought in from the cold, when everything he had been so subtly used to bring about – the destruction of Katkov, the routing of Boulanger – was now irrelevant. The Russo-German alliance was dying unmourned. France and Russia were about to conjoin. Like one of Mr Casey's Peep o' Day alarm clocks, the countdown to the detonation of 1914 had started ticking.

At the beginning of April there was a mysterious new arrival at the rue St Roch. A well-dressed woman came bustling up the stairs, an intimate friend of Queen Ada's. She was going to move in as house-keeper, so the Maharajah was told. Her name, according to Our Corre-spondent, was Madame Parraton and she appeared to have some connection with Russia. Whitehall was baffled and requested more information. It was extraordinary.

'The woman Parraton, who is now ascertained to be a Russian agent, returned at her own expense and without previous warning from Russia on Wednesday,' the spy messaged. 'Mrs Duleep seems to have known of this person's intention, not so the Maharajah, who was obliged to consent to her reinstallation by his wife. Madame Parraton now rules the household and will furnish full information to the Russians by whom Duleep's sincerity is doubted. They are taking a villa in the environs of Paris for six months.'

Mr Maitland noted on the secret dispatch: 'It appears that Madame Parraton, whose name is now mentioned for the first time, attached herself some time ago to Duleep's wife but, as far as could be seen, with no special motive. She left Paris on a visit to Russia, but has now reappeared and her role has become apparent.' Whitehall was told a week later: 'Duleep's wife and her Parraton have taken a villa at Le Vesinet for six months; the poor drunkard is left behind at a boarding house in Paris.'

The Foreign Office seemed surprised by the arrival of a 'Russian agent', a female friend of Duleep's wife. Ada had a woman friend in Moscow with whom she was very gossipy but she provided the British vice-consulate with intelligence. The mysterious Madame Parraton was a friend of Ada's from some time in Paris. If Our Correspondent was correct, someone in Russia was still taking a deep interest in the Maharajah. It was not benign.

# 39

# The General

❦

*Grand Hotel, 21 boulevard des Capucines, Paris,*
*May–July 1890*

IT WAS EARLY SUMMER in Paris and the Maharajah had reason to feel bumptious again. Ada was cavorting with Madame Parraton at Le Vesinet. The baby girls were temporarily in the care of the Queen Mother, Mrs Sarah Wetherill. Restored to the same palatial hotel to which he had first rebelliously decamped four years earlier, he could feel ever-so-slightly monarchical again, even ducking and diving on spurious credit.

'Duleep has removed his quarters to the Grand Hotel and will now no longer keep in such undignified obscurity,' Our Correspondent reported. 'With his wife, his intercourse becomes more and more infrequent, she only visits him when she wants. From the new departures in extravagance of the Maharajah, it looks as if he had received money through Baron de Ravisi from India.'

There were new visitors to revive conspiratorial flames, one with a little enamel cross pinned to a tucked-in Cossack shirt. Our Correspondent messaged on 20 May: 'A Russian, whose card I enclose, recently called upon Duleep Singh.' The card was from an old friend of HM Foreign Secret Service. It read: 'Nicholas Notovitch, 42 avenue d'Antin, Paris.'

'Notovitch pretends to have been sent to India in 1887 by General Vannovksi [minister of war]. He says he has notes affecting the situation in India which he declares were furnished him by a Mr O'Connor who occupies an official position at Simla. Notovitch avers his own affiliation to the pan-slavist war party. He was an orderly officer of Skobolev's in 1877–8 and has the Cross of St George.'

'The spy quickly learned more about the Cossack adventurer. 'He has a traveller's notebook inscribed with the names of the Rajahs whom he knew in India,' Our Correspondent reported to London, 'and of whom he has photographs in most cases, and dedications to him over their signatures. He also has several voluminous ms. books containing, he says, the "secret" reports of English officials in India on the railways, the lines of march to the frontier, the military strength, and enclosed is a memo about India and the Maharajah written by him.'

The Notovich report was addressed to 'Mon General'. He had gone to India, he said, on behalf of the Russian war ministry. He had been advised by friends to see the Maharajah in Moscow before leaving but: 'M. Shatoukin [Katkov's secretary] refused to divulge his secret address.' He regretted this because his Indian journey had convinced him that 'Russia would possess in the Maharajah a beautiful card in the game played with England in Asia'.

Notovitch reeled off a list of secret sympathizers: the Maharajah of Jeypoor, the Maharajah of Kashmir, the Nizam of Deccan, Jeven Singh the Maharajah of Dholpoor – married to a cousin of Duleep's, who was 'ready to give two lakhs of silver' – and a host of *petits khanats* on the North-West Frontier 'on which Duleep Singh or rather Russia can count for support'.

Notovich warmed to his theme: he proposed Duleep should be projected as the 'chef-mogul of the whole of India', under the protection of the White Czar. A campaign of sedition should be launched in the Punjab, the Kukas secretly funded, and Duleep's claims turned into a diplomatic crisis.

'All that was needed,' he wrote, 'was a *casus belli*.' It did not matter where: Persia, Bulgaria, central Asia. Once an Anglo-Russian war was triggered, the chef-mogul would sweep through India.

It was nonsense, of course. Whitehall scarcely blinked when Our Correspondent sent them the hugely seditious plan. Mr Maitland sent the Cossack's calling card to his political master Lord Cross with the note: 'We know all about the rascal Notovitch!'

The 'Black Pamphlet' affair resurfaced when Mr Edward St John Brenon, victor in the 'Fenian libel case', came calling the same month of June 1890. 'Although the results have been nil, it is right you should know that Duleep has been persistently approached by an Irish journalist and politician who wishes to agitate his pretensions before Parliament,' Our Correspondent reported. 'Duleep, after refusing to see him, finally consented to do so and an interview was arranged. Mr Brenon accepted but failed to put in an appearance.'

And there was an outburst of sheer vicious temper at the British Empire and its works. In June, a French newspaper reported an outbreak of Thugee-style murders in India. 'Notices have appeared on trains on the East Bengal Railway,' it said. 'Do not accept drink or food from strangers. Sweets and cooked food bought in the bazaars is being poisoned by fanatics.' Duleep claimed it was part of a scheme devised by him to 'slaughter the English'. 'This is rubbish, he has never, it is believed, suggested anything of the kind,' the spy reported charitably.

His still-loyal friends in England would have been appalled. They hovered unctuously as Victor shuffled to and fro brokering some kind of deal. The madness must end in death or redemption.

On the morning of 13 July the Maharajah was alone in an attic room of the Grand Hotel when he suffered a stroke. He remained conscious. He stumbled into the boulevard des Capucines and took a cab to his doctor's house. The doctor was out, 'so then he drove about Paris in search of another – all this motion aggravated the attack'.

Victor rushed to Paris. Ada returned from Le Vesinet, Prince Frederick was summoned. Dr Forbes Miller, the British embassy doctor, was sent for. Duleep's left side was paralysed. He could barely speak or pick up a pen. Victor pleaded, Victor cajoled – his father must beg for pardon. The boy on the Aden boat who had complained about his 'idiotic parent' had not changed his mind four years on. It is the most poignant of all the many Duleep Singh letters in the Royal Archives. It bears the crowned lion and the crusader's shield and is addressed to Queen Victoria. Written in Prince Victor's open flowing hand it is signed by his father in a palsied scrawl. It says:

GRAND HOTEL PARIS 18TH JULY 1890

May it please your Majesty.

My son Victor is writing this letter from my dictation. I have been struck down by the hand of God and am in consequence quite unable to write myself.

I have been disappointed in everyone in whom I had been led to believe and now my one desire is to die at peace with all men.

I therefore pray your Majesty to pardon me for all I have done against you and your Government and I throw myself entirely upon your clemency.

It seems to me now that it is the will of God that I should suffer injustice at the hands of your people.

I can find no-one to curse Great Britain and in spite of all her faults and her injustices God blesses her and makes her great and when I look at her, I feel that in fighting against your country I have been fighting against God. I would return to England were I assured of your free pardon.

I am your Majesty's Obedient Servant
Duleep Singh

Lord Leven (Ronald Leslie-Melville, Duleep's friend from the 1850s) went urgently from London to the Grand Hotel to see what could be done. He wrote to Sir Henry Ponsonby on the 22nd:

My visit was totally unexpected by him. I saw in the papers that he had had a paralytic stroke . . .

The moment he heard I was there he called on me. He was a pitiable sight. All his left side paralyzed, he held out a trembling right hand, drew me towards him and with floods of tears thanked me for coming – over and over again. He wished to be at peace with everybody, he said, and repeatedly expressed the utmost contrition for all he had done.

It seemed indeed as if his deep religious fervour (and in his youth he was the most truly religious confirmation boy that I ever knew) had returned and I trust it has.

He spoke of the disgraceful way he had behaved towards Her Majesty, and told me had written or rather dictated a letter, in the hope that she might be graciously pleased to forgive him – he also wrote an abject apology to the Prince of Wales. I sat with him for some time on Sunday and he expressed frequently his extreme thankfulness to the Almighty for having struck him down and thus brought him to a sense of his wrong doing – but he was not always very coherent and I think now as I have long thought that he is hardly responsible for his actions. His doctor who attended him a year ago told him he was even then suffering from Diabetes and that he does not doubt that his brain is affected.

The Maharajah's sons are both with him and as far as I understand have succeeded in keeping his former associates from entering the room. He has been moved to a good large airy bedroom – before the attack he was for economising and lived in a small room up many pairs of stairs . . .

The Duke of Grafton also kept up the pressure. He wrote to Windsor Castle: 'What is the result of the poor Maharajah's penitent letter to the Queen? I saw Lord Leven this evening and he has been over to Paris and seen him . . . he knows now he is alone, Russia has not taken him up, but his account of their behaviour to him is very open and says they told him they could do nothing now, but when they go to war with us <u>then</u> they would arrange matters with him.'

The duke, master of Euston Hall, had his own concerns: 'It is high time his estate was put in other hands for it is a disgrace to the country that such mismanagement should be carried on by government trustees, 16,000 acres without one labourer employed . . . game live and dead and eggs are sold and all round poached.'

Lord Henniker wrote: 'I am not very anxious that he should move to England as we have the children in hand, at last, and if he came back he must take charge of them. He is surrounded by all sorts of people who will cling to him if he has money to give them . . . I have seen a copy of the Maharajah's letter to the Queen. It shows most distinctly that the writer is off his head. The end of it is laughable were it not so sad.'

The Queen Empress did as she must; the plea for pardon letter was sent to Lord Cross, Secretary of State for India. Her ministers must reach a political judgement. On the morning of Thursday 22 July it went before cabinet. The mood was forgiving but pragmatic. The Maharajah must make 'a public expression of regret'. The Viceroy agreed, cabling: 'I see no objection to pardon and restoration of allowance if submission is complete.'

*398*

The minister told the Queen: 'A friendly letter might properly be sent by your Majesty to the Maharajah expressing great sympathy to him in his present attack of illness and regret that he should have taken the course of hostility which he has so long held towards your Majesty and this country, and pleasure that he should at last have asked pardon, and thrown himself upon your Majesty's clemency, adding however that as a matter of state, after his open proclamation against your Majesty's Government, it would be necessary to consult your Majesty's advisers.

'Lord Cross is personally anxious that clemency should be shown to this broken-down man, and hears that he may still hope for some public expression of regret for his treasonable proclamations which he has scattered broadcast over India . . .*

'Lord Salisbury is however decidedly opposed to his return to England, though willing to grant pardon and restore allowance, but all these are matters of detail which may easily be adjusted afterwards.'

The Queen replied to Lord Cross from Osborne the next day: 'Please cypher. We have received your letter with satisfaction but cannot agree with Lord Salisbury's objection to this poor unfortunate Maharajah's return to England as he would be far safer under control here [than] elsewhere. Many feel with me that the former government was very largely to blame for what has happened and therefore we should be merciful. VRI.'

The 'poor unfortunate Maharajah' must show remorse. The 'broken-down man' must display public obedience. It was made clear he must do so by application, not to the Queen but to the loathed politicians of the India Office. This was a matter of state. He had changed quarters meanwhile, to the Hotel d'Albe on the Champs-Elysées; perhaps the management of the Grand had presented their bill. From there, via Victor's dictation, he wrote to Lord Cross on 27 July: 'I write to express my great regret for my past conduct towards Her Majesty the Queen Empress of India. I humbly ask Her Majesty to pardon me and I trust entirely to the clemency of the Queen. Should

---

* Lord Cross was telling Lord Lansdowne, the Viceroy, meanwhile: 'I have sent you a telegram today [25 July 1890] about Duleep Singh the elder. He is I fancy hopelessly ill.' In the same letter he instructed the Viceroy to make a plan for the capture of the French Indian Ocean island of Réunion. 'For now assume war with France only, not Russia.'

Her Majesty grant me pardon, I promise obedience to Her wishes for the future.'

Prince Victor was alert to the government's sensitivity to 'obedience'. He added a handwritten gloss to the declaration of surrender: 'By the last sentences in my father's letter to you officially today, he means by obedience, absolute loyalty to Her Majesty the Queen and no more wild plotting against Herself and your Government, but my father thinks it would be too painful to live continuously in England and therefore hope obedience to the Queen will not mean compulsory residence in England.'

It was enough. The Queen was advised to assent. There was no great majestic dénouement between the turbulent King of Lahore and the Queen Empress (not yet anyway). The rebellion was declared terminated by a stiffly formal letter from the Secretary of State. Duleep had been a naughty boy.

'Her Majesty's Government have had under consideration your Highness's letter of 27th July, in which you express your great regret for your past conduct towards the Queen Empress of India, promise obedience for the future, and throw yourself entirely on the clemency of Her Majesty.

'I am now commanded to inform you that on the understanding that henceforward your Highness will remain obedient to the Queen Empress of India, and will regulate your movements in conformity with the instruction that may be issued to you, Her Majesty, by the advice of Her ministers, has been graciously pleased to accord to you the pardon that you have sought.'

The Maharajah was 'forbidden by his doctors to reply personally'. His son promised he would 'write as soon as he is able to express himself his thanks and satisfaction'. He never did. The India Office was jubilant. Edmund Neel of the Political and Secret Department breathlessly told W. J. Cuningham, the Viceroy's private secretary: 'The Maharajah is in a critical condition and had a relapse a few days ago. Prince Victor who is in charge of him, at once denied access to all the adventurers, male and female, who have been sponging off him.

'Ludwig Müller, the father of the first Maharani, has reported that Duleep Singh is a complete wreck. The whole of one side is paralysed, face arm and leg. The dismay of the Duleep Singh conspirator-gang at the unexpected turn of events would be delightful to witness.'

It merely remained to announce the Maharajah's submission to the maximum political advantage. The letters were passed to *The Times* (of course) and Indian newspaper correspondents were summoned to Simla for a special briefing. Of the 'I promise obedience' statement it was noted: 'Its very brevity and the absence of any stipulations regarding Duleep's claim of the sovereignty of the Punjab will do much to detract from His Highness's importance in the eyes of the people of India.'

As old Müller had reported, Prince Victor had indeed taken charge of the Hotel d'Albe invalid. English visitors were admitted; the spongers, male and female, were barred. Mr Burrell of Messrs Farrers turned up to draft the Maharajah's will.

In the critical days between the stroke and the surrender, the conspirator gang had evidently made a last bid to keep the rebellious flame alive. 'One of his friends went to the Grand Hotel and got into the sick man's room,' Our Correspondent had reported on 20 July. 'It seems that on Thursday Duleep had insisted that this friend should be summoned, which was done by the Maharani, contrary to the wishes of Prince Victor. Duleep was very glad to see this friend . . .

'The son, Victor, was sent for immediately after the friend's arrival; he is a cad in manner and appearance and before five minutes had passed informed his father's friend in so many words that he wished him to discontinue his visits.

'This young man is making a mistake in preventing access to his father, as already people are beginning to comment upon the situation. He, the avowed enemy of England is surrounded exclusively by English people and is medically cared for by the doctor of the Embassy of the nation to which he is a rebel.'*

Who was the friend that Victor objected to who was so urgently summoned to the sick-room? It was probably Elie de Cyon. He wrote in his memoirs: 'About a year after his wedding I learned without much surprise that the Maharajah was seriously ill, that in a letter which had been made public he had renounced all his claims to the

---

* A London practitioner, Dr Drewitt of Brook Street, was summoned. He diagnosed 'Diabetes and Bright's disease' (Glomerulonephritis – chronic inflammation of the kidneys inducing high blood pressure). He reportedly commented on Prince Victor's devoted care, but added: 'The wife of the Maharajah is lamentably deficient in the art of nursing.'

throne of Lahore and asked his ancient subjects to stay loyal to Britain!'

Cyon's own affairs had turned dangerous. The Russian loan business had blown up in his face, the feud with the Russian ambassador to Paris, Baron Mohrenheim, had become visceral. Accusations flew over the fraudulent finance for the Panama Canal which had erupted up into a huge scandal. Cyon had turned his pamphleteering venom on his former patron Ivan Vyshnegradski, the finance minister, and his successor, Count Sergius Witte, architect of Russia's economic reconstruction. The Ohkrana foreign agency at the rue de Grenelle were out to get him. The doctor had more information, but he felt it best not to burden the Maharajah. He knew at last the real author of 'L'Alliance Franco-Russe', the little pamphlet which had helped to doom General Bogdanovich, and Duleep with him, on that fateful day at Gatchina three years earlier. It was a 'Cossack' adventurer, a journalist-spy; it was Nicholas Notovich.

The rebellion was over but Whitehall thought it worthwhile to keep up the secret watch. Our Correspondent did not sign off. Perhaps it was the money, perhaps he felt that his own and the Maharajah's fates were now inseparable. The spy seemed suddenly protective towards the man whose fall he had worked so long and secretly to ensure. No great actor (and the spy was the Sir Henry Irving of late nineteenth-century espionage) wants the show to close. The cast of the Duleep Singh drama were shuffling off the stage. It would soon be the agent's own turn to come out of character, for which Prince Victor would be the accidental instrument.

In the weeks following Duleep's submission, the prince had obviously turned trustingly to the man in Paris that he, like his father, believed to be the loyal chief of staff. On 13 August the spy sent Whitehall short bursts of the latest intelligence, all obviously derived directly from Victor:

'Duleep is a wreck. His son says that he kept three women and to excesses there and to drink must be attributed his collapse.

'Father and son say that Her Majesty has graciously pardoned the Maharajah and, they hoped, would ultimately restore his pension.

'It might be as well, now that the "rebel" has returned to his allegiance, to protect him against the harpies who surround him and will make a public scandal if he fails to meet their demands.

'Prince Victor states that his father seems to be in fear of Madame Parraton, but he could not understand why.'

That the Maharajah kept three women was an extraordinary enough revelation; that he should be frightened of Madame Parraton, the 'Russian agent', opened dangerous new possibilities. But in his bumbling attempts to shut down his father's rebellion, the prince was about to bring Our Correspondent himself out of the shadows. He would do so in a letter and some injudicious remarks to a very persistent American newspaper reporter.

First the letter. Victor drafted it on 15 August to Our Correspondent. 'Because you have not come here I am leaving this at your house,' the prince wrote in a covering note, although no address was given. It was a form of words for the chief of staff to send to Pondicherry telling Gurbachan Singh that the rebellion was to be liquidated. It said baldly:

> Prince. In the opinion of His Highness you have no other alternative than to appeal to the clemency of the British Government and to make for yourself and family the best possible terms, without delay.
>
> Every appeal for practical support has met with no response, and disheartened by this apathy and indifference, unwilling any longer to be the dupe of scheming politicians, His Highness has decided to abandon the struggle which he now sees to be hopeless.
>
> I am therefore ordered to inform you that His Highness the Maharajah has asked for and has received the pardon of Her Most Gracious Majesty the Queen of England and Empress of India, and has by this act of submission* retired indefinitely from political life.
>
> His Highness directs you to destroy, immediately, all letters and documents which might in any way compromise yourselves and others. I am happy to add that the Maharajah, although still weak, is recovering steadily from an illness produced by mental tension and anxiety. By order of the Maharajah faithfully yours [name erased].

* The word 'submission' was crossed out then reinserted in the original, signed 'approved Duleep Singh'.

The covering letter to Our Correspondent was addressed by Prince Victor to 'Dear General [blank].'

On 21 August, following a discreet briefing by an India Office source, *The Times* published a short notice of the Maharajah's 'expression of deep regret for his course of hostility' and news of the 'pardon'. There was a media frenzy in Paris, or at least among the American papers who had always cheered along the turbanned puller of the British lion's tale. The London edition of *New York Herald Tribune* (a short-lived but very modern publishing experiment) was on the doorstep first with a fabulously rumbustious won't-take-no-for-an-answer report.

DIFFICULTIES OF A VISIT TO MAHARAJAH DULEEP SINGH.

His Highness an Undesirable Subject to Interview – The Story of His Pardon.
Paris, 23 August:
By the Herald's private wire

'His Highness is ill, and has been peremptorily forbidden by the doctors to receive visitors,' was the reply sent down by Prince Victor Duleep Singh to a Herald reporter who called at the Hotel d'Albe to talk with Duleep Singh, Maharajah of Lahore, on his pardon by Queen Victoria.

And some kindly physician had apparently warned Prince Victor against the danger of receiving a journalist, for it was only after much parleying that I gained access to his room.

'I thought you wanted to interview my father, don't you know,' said Prince Victor, 'and he's ill, and has been forbidden to talk much. He can't see you, you know. We hope to be able to move him on Tuesday. We shall cross to Folkestone and stay the night there, and Claridge's will most probably find us in London.

'I can't tell you anything more. I don't know anything more. I don't know anything about family affairs. I am an Englishman, and don't want to have anything to do with Indian affairs,' concluded this godson of Her Gracious Majesty . . .

'But if you'll go to General Tevis, he will tell you everything you want to know. He's conducted all my father's business. If you tell him I sent you, he'll tell you all. He has all the documents, don't you know.'

General Tevis, the Duc de Guise at Madame Adam's fancy-dress ball. A man named Tevis, 'principal agent of the Irish Republican Brotherhood in Europe', according to James Monro, the chief commissioner of Scotland Yard. General Charles Carrol-Teviss, 'an American soldier of fortune' and notorious dynamitard, according to the 'Black Pamphlet'. Comte Carrol-Tevis, 'officier de la légion d'honneur', according to the Maharajah's wedding certificate. General Tevis who had 'conducted all my father's business', according to Prince Victor Duleep Singh.* The mask had slipped. He was Our Correspondent. I had found 'C'.

The *Herald Tribune* reporter sought out no. 3 rue Daru to confront the man who would 'tell him all'. It was a bizarre encounter. Tevis refused to talk.

> 'But Prince Victor sent me to you – wrote me your address on this envelope; bade me say, you could tell me all!'
>
> Then General Tevis turned to his desk and handed me the following note, which I give verbatim: 'Dear General – The enclosed (a written request for a few minutes' conversation) has just been handed to me. I have sent him to you; please tell him absolutely nothing. I am very truly yours, Victor Duleep Singh.'

The reporter returned to the Hotel d'Albe, sent up to Prince Victor Duleep Singh a note stating the circumstance of his visit to General Tevis, and requesting that the prince would put in writing the assurance he had given by word of mouth to the effect that General Tevis

---

* The way the India Office letter file 'Duleep Singh Secret Correspondence 1887–1892' is bound up confirmed the discovery. The *Herald Tribune* cutting is at the very front, out of the date sequence, loosely held by a rusting treasury tag. Attached is a note from Edmund Neel, assistant secretary at the India Office (Political and Secret Department) to the Minister's private secretary, Mr Maitland: 'Lord Cross may like to read this cutting from the London New York Herald. General Levis (not Tevis) belongs, I believe, to the French Army. He was one of the witnesses at Duleep Singh's 2nd marriage in Paris and has acted as the medium of communication with the Sirdars at Pondicherry.' Our Correspondent handled all the letters with French India.

The secret was very tightly held. Edmund Neel did not know of the existence of the Foreign Office spy Levis-Tevis. But Lord Cross did; he read every dispatch.

was at liberty to supply the reporter with any details of public interest regarding the Maharajah of Lahore.

After an interval, the hotel waiter brought down the information that the prince was too busy to write a note as requested. Just before he left, the American reporter was approached in the lobby by 'a dark-skinned, sparkling-eyed gentleman, His Highness Suchet Singh, Maharajah of Chumba', who told him: 'If the Queen has pardoned Duleep Singh, she thinks he will die soon!'

The frustrations of the Tevis encounter made sense. Of course the general was not going to give an interview, especially with the newspaper published by the 'prince of blackguards', James Gordon Bennett. This was a very dangerous time; the conspiracy was unravelling, much more might be revealed and not all the Maharajah's partisans were under arrest.* Our Correspondent would stay on the undercover case almost until the bitter end. No one would ever doubt his loyalty to the cause. But I had found him.

---

* The General was almost unmasked. In the autumn of 1890, following the collapse of *The Times* 'Parnellism and Crime' court case, Michael Davitt's short-lived newspaper *The Labour World* published a series of exposés called 'Unionism and Crime' claiming that Irish dynamite plots had been cooked up by 'agents of the Secret Service of the British Government'. One article was catchlined 'Duleep Singh and the Secret Service'. It gave dangerously accurate glimpses of the real agenda.

The first proposal for Fenian overtures to Katkov had been made in 1885, so the story stated, by an unnamed agent provocateur in British pay based in New York. (It was General Francis Millen, the 'jubilee bomber' who had simultaneously secretly offered to 'provide H.M.G. warning of outrages should war break out between Britain and Russia'.) Millen, with a second envoy (who evidently believed the mission was real), travelled to Paris where he 'made out one Patrick Casey and called upon General [blank] whose name for certain reasons cannot be given', so the story continued.

General [blank] meanwhile gave 'Envoy No. 2' a 'letter of introduction to Katkov' (the conduit would have been Elie de Cyon). He proceeded to Moscow. The 'second envoy' was clearly General Macadaras – whose mission to Russia early the previous year had been reported in the secret despatch from Louis, Missouri (Macadaras's home town) to Scotland Yard on 2 June 1887.

'Another character now appears in the person of Duleep Singh' so Davitt's story continued – concerning events of mid 1886. 'General [blank] brought about an interview between the envoy [Millen] and the deposed Indian Prince. The result was that a manifesto from Duleep was printed by Patrick Casey.' The story clearly stated that one of the American envoys was acting as an agent provocateur – but not that the mysterious 'General' – clearly Carrol-Tevis – was also a British agent. *The Labour World* cuttings can be found in secret Home Office papers concerning Parnell Commission, neatly pasted on the back of Metropolitan Police Criminal lunacy warrants, each revelation underlined in red ink.

# 40

# The Prodigal's Return

*6 Clifton Gardens, Folkestone, Kent, August 1890*

HE HAD SURRENDERED but the Maharajah was not yet shriven. Duleep slunk back to England on the Calais *paquebot*, wrapped in a blanket against the mid-Channel chill. Ada tended the invalid. The infant princesses added a doe-eyed touch. A late Victorian genre-painter would have adored the scene – it was a promenade-deck parable, the return of the prodigal meets the fallen woman.

On 26 August, Prince Victor had spirited the family out of Paris on the ten o'clock boat-train, away from the 'conspirator-gang' and prying American newspaper reporters. Maybe it was the rebel spirit, maybe it was financial desperation, but Duleep, as he had done for the flight to Aden, insisted the government of India should pay for the tickets.

Victor had informed Sir Owen Tudor Burne: 'My father's money is all in Russia, and, although I have written for it and ordered it to be transmitted to Paris, it has not so far arrived; so he wishes me to ask if the India Office will advance him £1000 for his expenses at Folkestone, where I have taken a house for him, and where we shall arrive on Tuesday evening next if all is well.' They paid up. And further, orders were given to 'allow the baggage of His Highness Maharajah Duleep Singh to be passed through the Custom House without examination'.

The prince told the India Office of the party's arrival. His father had 'stood the journey very well'. An anonymous civil servant, sensing the bathetic tragedy of it all, wrote simply on the letter file: 'It is now more than four years since the Maharajah embarked for Bombay in the Peninsular and Oriental Steamer "Verona" on the 31st March 1886.'

Folkestone was a family affair. Prince Freddie arrived, thirteen-year-old Sophia and her younger brother Edward were summoned to stay in a nearby seaside hotel. Their father sat in the parlour, his hand flapping to make the introductions – this is the Maharani and here are your new sisters. It was the first time they had met. Catherine and Bamba were in Germany with their governess. In the autumn they would be returning to Somerville Hall, Oxford. Should they be summoned? What would they make of Queen Ada, who was herself only a year older than Duleep's eldest daughter?

It was evidently a high matter of state. Lord Cross wrote to the Queen's private secretary: 'I do not want these young ladies to go to D. Singh. They are much better off at Oxford.' The Queen agreed, penning in the margin, 'Think we cd. urge strongly against it.' The royal urgings were disregarded. The princesses arrived in Folkestone to embrace the father they had last seen waving them off at Steamer Point four years before. The Maharajah was 'delighted'.

## *Grand Hôtel, Paris, 22 October 1890*

It was clear that the Maharajah could not stay in England. Nor did he wish to. In late September the couple returned to Paris on the money newly advanced by the India Office. Ada seemed more eager than ever to spend it. Our Correspondent, General Charles Carrol-Tevis, kept up his scrutiny, the Maharajah blissfully unaware that Her Majesty's Foreign Office still thought him worth watching. That knowledge at least might have flattered whatever vanity was left.

The general's reports reappeared in Whitehall in-trays on 18 October. 'I have renewed relations with Duleep Singh. He professes great satisfaction with the arrangement made in his favour by England which he attributes to the fears entertained by her Government of India. Neither he nor his family are likely to cause any further annoyance; he will take and furnish a house in Paris where he proposes to remain till January.'

He had news of Madame Parraton who had been 'thrown out' by the Maharajah in favour of the Baroness Textor de Ravisi, now installed as 'lady of honour and housekeeper'. 'She may get the poor creature into trouble,' he noted, 'her husband being the agent of the Burmese pretender Min Goon.'

Something remarkable happened in Paris later that month which neither the general nor his Whitehall masters had sight of. The archival evidence is scanty,* but on 22 October, at the Grand Hotel, the son and heir of the Queen-Empress met not just the Maharajah, but the gas-fitter's child as well.

The Prince of Wales was making a private continental tour. He left London on 6 October, to travel via the Orient Express to Vienna. There, to the outrage of his anti-semitic Austrian hosts, he entertained Baron Maurice de Hirsch to lunch. The financier, who had approached the Maharajah the previous year with a view to buying Elveden, bore the Prince and a small party of friends (including Lady Randolph Churchill) by special train to St Johann, his 'shooting box' on the Hungarian border. There they slaughtered Carpathian fauna on a Duleepian scale. 'The Prince enjoyed excellent sport,' the papers reported, '11,300 head of game were bagged.' On Tuesday 21 October, the Prince arrived in Paris to stay for two nights at his favourite Hotel Bristol. There was an old friend he wanted to look up.

Who made the overture is not clear. Prince Victor was in the French capital to steer his father once more towards the rue de Grenelle, this time 'to sign papers enabling him to get money he left in Russia . . . he is going to help me pay off my debts,' so he told the India Office by letter on the 24th. He was anxious the visit to the Russian embassy should not be misinterpreted. His father was 'very well', he reported, and had 'a long and pleasant talk with the Prince of Wales'. He did not mention the fact that Queen Ada was in attendance. More details of the encounter would emerge later in most disagreeable circumstances.

The ray of royal warmth did not last long. The general's reports suddenly got very much darker. Ada had evidently not broken off relations with her Russian lady-friend.

'The Maharajah is getting killed off slowly but surely by his wife and her accomplice Madame Parraton,' the general reported on 3 November. Far from being 'very well', as Victor had reported ten days earlier, 'he is now in a state of almost coma', said the general.

---

* The bulk of the Prince of Wales's personal correspondence was destroyed after his death as King Edward VII.

'The woman [Ada] insists upon remaining in Paris, where she and her spouse are surrounded by a set of adventurers.' Among them there was a 'Comte d'Hauterie',* and 'a bogus Prince Tchitchacheff whose nationality is not clearly determined'. Prince Victor was described as 'a fool living for amusement'.

'In order to curry favour with the queer set she begins to know, she represents her spouse as an injured victim, "forced by the councils of false friends to solicit pardon from his spoilators". She goes so far as to state that he did not write to his cousins at Pondicherry to make peace with England notifying them of his intention to withdraw from political life, and that any such letter was a fabrication utterly unauthorized. How far the Maharajah himself is a party to this game it is impossible to say.

'The Maharajah now says that he regrets his reconciliation – complains of the illiberality of the British Government which through fear of a renewal of his agitation has reduced his pittance to £800 a month. He will yet show what he can do, if by the month of April all that he demands be not granted.'

London read these reports with equanimity. If Duleep was claiming his surrender was a sham, that was no matter. He was a burned-out case. But that Ada and her accomplice, the mysterious Russian housekeeper, should be 'killing him off slowly but surely', hardly caused a bureaucratic ripple.

Monsieur le Docteur Elie de Cyon hinted darkly at what he thought was going on. He stated in his memoirs:

In 1891 [no more precise date is given] the Maharajah Duleep Singh came to meet me to explain his change of mind. The once vigorous, energetic man, hardly into his fifties, was nothing but a wreck; half paralysed, he could only speak with difficulty, and could hardly walk. His first words were 'I am poisoned! *I am a dead man!*'

He then told me that he had been betrayed, that all his 'sons' in the conspiracy had gone over to the British government; three thousand followers had been jailed [a colossal exaggeration]. As for himself, as a dying man, they had torn

* A former diplomat, at the time engaged in a scandalous divorce from the sister of Baron de Staal, Russian ambassador to London.

an act of abdication from him, in return for a promise to set free and pardon those who had been compromised in his cause; to recognise his second marriage legally, and for his children to have a pension of £25,000 a year restored.

The poor man had agreed to everything, seeing himself approaching death. Duleep Singh confided many other things to me about this drama about which I must stay silent.

He had tears in his eyes when he spoke about his poor people who had been deprived of their last hope of seeing the heir of their ancient kings and of regaining their independence . . . Sometime afterwards he died.

## *Hôtel des Anglais, Nice, Alpes Maritimes, Winter 1890*

It was healthier to be out of Paris. In November the Duleep Singh household decamped to Nice and took a suite at the grandest hotel in the resort. The bankrupt 'cad' Victor, who by now had resigned his commission in the Royal Dragoons, went with them. The prince and his step-mother ventured down the Grand Corniche to Monte's glittering casino. The Maharajah stayed muffled up in the hotel day-room. He was getting sicker.

The general messaged on 23 December: 'Duleep Singh, who has been at the Hotel des Anglais, Nice, for some time, has had another paralytic stroke but not of a serious nature. Marriott [British honorary consul] went to see him but was refused admission. He, however, saw him on the Promenade des Anglais. Duleep is very feeble and complained to Marriott that he was not allowed to see any letters not previously examined and approved by his surroundings – in fact, he is practically sequestrated and left to the company of a servant, while Madame and Prince Victor amuse themselves at Monte Carlo where they both play heavily. Duleep and his wife have left many debts behind them in Paris.'

Mr Villiers thanked Mr Maitland for the general's telegram and noted simply: 'If the accompanying from "our man" is true, it looks as if Duleep will not last much longer.'

## *Grand Hôtel, Grasse, Alpes Maritimes, 31 March 1891*

It was unlooked for, it was almost accidental, but the turbulent relationship with the woman who was always the real leading-lady in his extraordinary drama was approaching its most theatrical moment.

Queen Victoria was in the habit each spring of making a continental trip, as informally as court protocol would allow. With scant incognito she travelled as the 'Countess of Balmoral'. In 1891 it was to be Florence until an outbreak of typhoid was reported. Her courtiers' eyes fell on Grasse, the French town on an inland hill-top bathed in mimosa, suitably removed from the Riviera with its disreputable connotations. But that spring there was an outbreak of small-pox among the Piedmontese labourers completing the railway-line up from Cannes.

An English sanitary engineer came to inspect the plumbing of Grasse's only suitable hotel – the recently-built Grand.* The local milk was sampled. All was pronounced perfectly acceptable. Monsieur Rost, the proprietor, was delighted when his entire establishment, including gardens and stables, was rented to ensure the privacy of his royal visitor and her sprawling retinue. The royal choice of Grasse was announced in the court circular. Lord Henniker spotted it and contacted Victor who was in Germany. The Maharajah was close by in Nice – could a meeting be arranged? Would HM receive the Maharani? Letters and telegrams began to arrive for the attention of Sir Henry Ponsonby. He discreetly inquired of Arthur Oliphant as to Queen Ada's origins, when she first met the Maharajah, that sort of thing. She was the 'daughter of a general officer', he was informed, so that was all right.

On 25 March the royal party arrived on the mountain railway spur. A military band played, the crowds cheered. 'The life pursued by Her Majesty in Grasse was of the quietest description,' according to a contemporary account. 'The mornings were often spent in rambles round the gardens of Miss Alice de Rothschild, or with the donkey-

---

* The Grand Hôtel's days as a royal resort did not last long. Before the Great War it was turned into apartments. The interior, with brass cage-lifts and Queen Victoria's suite on the first floor, remained substantially intact in 1999 in an edifice of soaringly magnificent shabbiness.

chaise along the ancient mule-paths which run along the side of Mount Rocquevignon.

'During her drives, the Queen was much pained to notice the cruelty displayed towards the horses and mules, and Sir Henry Ponsonby was requested to notify the fact to the president of the branch of the Society for the Prevention of Cruelty to Animals at Cannes.'

The Queen worked in the afternoons on matters of state, and at tea-time received a stream of 'Royal and distinguished personages in audience: – The Grand Duke of Mecklenburg-Schwerin, the Duke and Duchess of Saxe-Coburg-Gotha, the Archduke and Archduchess Reinier of Austria, the Archduchess Stephanie of Austria [with 'the face of a bull-dog' according to the Queen's lady-in-waiting, Mary Adeane], Prince Francis Joseph of Battenberg, their Serene-Highnesses the Prince and Princess of Monaco, Dom Pedro, ex-Emperor of Brazil ['like a monkey'], and his daughter, the Countess d'Eu and the Maharajah Duleep Singh, and his son Prince Frederick.'

There would have been a lot to gossip about at the Grand Hôtel. Archduchess Stephanie was the twenty-seven-year-old widow of Crown Prince Rudolf of Austria-Hungary who had committed suicide with his mistress at Mayerling two years earlier. The Prince of Monaco had recently caused a scandal by having his marriage to the Duchess of Hamilton annulled and marrying the Comtesse de Richelieu at the VIII Arrondissement mairie in Paris. Emperor Dom Pedro II had abdicated and fled the throne of Brazil in 1889. As for the Maharajah ... But there were, in 1891, no paparazzi to intrude on royal misfortunes. Queen Victoria's own words do much better instead. She described in a letter to her daughter, dated 1 April, the moment the once handsome and charming boy shambled back into her sight:

'The poor Maharajah Duleep Singh came to see me yesterday driven over from Nice with his 2nd son Frederick. He is quite bald & vy. grey but has the same pleasant manner as ever. I came in I gave him in my hand wh. he kissed, and said: "Pardon my not kneeling" for his left arm and leg are paralysed tho' he can stand and walk a little.

'I asked him to sit down – & almost directly he burst out into a most terrible & violent fit of crying and screaming (just as my poor fat Indian servant Muhammed did when he lost his child) – and I stroked & held his hand, & he became calm & said: "Pray excuse me & forgive my faults" & I answered: "They are forgotten & forgiven."

He said "I am a poor broken down man" and dwelt on the loss of the use of his left arm as a great trial.

'I soon took leave & he seemed pleased with the interview but it was vy. sad still I am so glad that we met again to say I forgave him.'

The Queen's journal entry was less charitable: 'After a few minutes talk about his sons and daughters, I wished him goodbye and went upstairs again, very thankful that this painful interview was well over.'

Mary Adeane's view was coruscating: 'Old Duleep Singh drove here from Nice to beg forgiveness for all his misdeeds. I believe he is a monster of the deepest dye and treated far better than he deserves.'

The forgetting and forgiving of the Queen-Empress were not enough to still the Maharajah's unquiet soul. After the tears of Grasse, he returned to Paris more angry and confused than remorseful. The general reported on 11 April: 'He is very much broken and says he is losing all his intelligence. During his stay at Nice he received several communications from India and affirms that he directed Victor to send them on to London.

'Duleep complains of the parsimony and bad faith of the British Government, which he will be obliged to prosecute in the law courts, but he is in no hurry as his friends in England are working for him.

'On the whole he regrets his submission which he made only to secure his children's future thinking that he was about to die . . .'

The cosiness of Grasse had rapidly turned sour. A royal snub and a thumping marital row were the reasons. The Queen had refused to receive the Maharani. The Prince of Wales was sent a very rude communication immediately after the Maharajah's return to Paris. It seems not to have survived but the prince's reaction to it has. Albert Edward wrote to Ponsonby from Sandringham on 4 April: 'I cannot do otherwise than send you the enclosed extraordinary letter from the Maharajah Duleep Singh. When I called upon him in Paris [the encounter of 22 October 1890] I made the acquaintance of his wife – who was pretty but appeared to me *de la bourgeoisie*. Beyond being English I never heard who she was but have been told she was an actress. Possibly Lord Henniker may know more about her antecedents but you must advise what to answer. I must say that I think the latter part of his letter is most impertinent, but he is decidedly rather cracked still and not answerable for what he does. I fear if he comes to London this summer he will be troublesome. I have no idea if his wife was received in Parisian society but Lord Lytton [the ambassador] may know.'

The Queen became embroiled. On 6 April she was memoed by her private secretary: 'Sir Henry Ponsonby did not know that the Maharani was at Nice. The interview was entirely arranged by Lord Henniker and Prince Victor. He believes she was an actress but had a good character.'

The Queen reached for the purple crayon to write crossly on the memorandum: 'Mr Oliphant knows all about the present Maharani and the Queen <u>fears</u> that the connection existed <u>before</u> the late Maharani died.'

It got worse. Sir Henry wrote a memo for the Queen the next day: 'The best answer that the Prince of Wales can give to the Maharajah is that he knows nothing of the arrangements for his visit here as they were made by Prince Victor and Lord Henniker. Mr Oliphant told Sir Henry Ponsonby that he did not think there was anything against the Maharani's character, though she was of low origin. There was another, a Miss Ashted [?] who he gave £3000 a year to during his first wife's life.'

Her Majesty minuted: 'It may be so but the Queen has a strong impression that this Maharani has not been correct. Her being an actress would not raise any objection.'

Poor Arthur Oliphant had some frantic back-tracking to do. He told Sir Henry Ponsonby on 13 April: 'I think you may have misunderstood some remark I may have made regarding the lady in question. I believe I stated to you that I was not aware that she lived with the Maharajah *prior* to his visit to Aden and that perhaps may have led you to infer that there was nothing against her up to that time.

'I have been told that she was the daughter of an English General Officer her mother having been the General's housekeeper. She lived with the Maharajah in Moscow after his return from Aden, and the first child of this marriage [crossed out for 'alliance'] was born 3 or 4 months after the late Maharani's death. The second child was born some 2 or 3 months after their civil marriage in Paris about two years ago – I am not aware of any other children of the Maharajah's by her.

'My authority as regards the origin of the Lady was the Maharajah's eldest son, Prince Victor.'

The Queen realized more of the truth than all her ministers and secret agents put together. Never mind the fact that Ada was 'an actress'. Never mind Miss Polly Ash of the Alhambra music-hall. The relationship with Miss Ada Wetherill was contracted in England before the Maharajah boarded the SS *Verona*.

## *Villa de La Celle, St Cloud, Bougival, Seine et Oise, Summer– Autumn 1891*

Queen Ada must have sulked royally after the Grasse snub, but she still had the Maharajah under her well-manicured thumb as they returned to the Paris hotel thinking what to do next. His plans became decidedly odder, her appetites became harder to satisfy. 'He wants leave either to reside in India or to purchase an estate in Poland for which he has asked England to demand authority for him from Russia,' Whitehall was told in early May. Ada would not have liked Poland. 'He might settle in France but fears revolution, or a German invasion. Duleep's general health is good and he looks well, save his left arm which is helpless as he pretends from the effects of a sprained finger, but really from paralysis.

'He is looking for a furnished house at not more than 30,000 francs per annum. His wife insists on a Parisian residence and will not accompany him anywhere. He complains that none of his letters reach him, and that he is not allowed to receive visitors alone.'

By summer Ada had changed her mind. 'His wife, not succeeding in French society, now urges a change of residence,' the general reported in June. 'They would go to England, if easy in their mind over their reception there, idem, the Crimea, the result will probably be Nice.' In the end they took a villa at St Cloud, the agreeable western suburb of Paris on the Seine. It would be the scene of the return into the drama of a character Ada loathed and the Maharajah would much rather forget.

Abdul Rasul, last bearer of the revolutionary flame, had been removed from Asigarh Fort in November 1890, sent under guard to Bombay and dispatched (second-class) in a P & O steamer to London.

His war-chest of '600 francs, three gold sovereigns and some small change' was returned. He took lodgings in prosaic Warren Street where he read the news of Duleep's pardon. In January he wrote to Our Correspondent, wanting to get in touch with his old patron again – for one thing the Maharajah owed him money. The requests continued through the spring of 1891. Ada would have none of it but Duleep could not resist reopening the intrigue. It was a mistake.

The Kashmiri arrived in Paris in late June and first sought out the general who was still, as he supposed, acting as Duleep's secret letter-box. The spy was wary; the two men had last met in the days when Abdul Rasul was promising to bring the Ottoman Empire in on the great plot. He was supposed to be watched by Scotland Yard. How had he got across the Channel this time? The traveller's reply was disarming: 'The authorities had forbidden him to leave London, wherefore he slipped away unbeknown. But his movements will be known to them at once from the Maharani who, as Duleep himself admitted, is their spy.'

Ada was an English spy, said Abdul Rasul. The Maharajah himself had admitted it to him – presumably during their time together in Moscow. The general reported the revelation impassively to London where the news was also received with indifference. Let Duleep believe what he liked about the gas-fitter's child; it masked the real traitor.

The general had no doubts about Abdul Rasul's motives in seeking out his old co-conspirator. 'His designs are on Duleep's purse,' he told London. 'He talks of bringing a claim in court for money, which he has no chance of gaining. He could, however, create a scandal and thinks that he can therefore levy blackmail on Duleep. Rasul has been advised to draw up a statement and to give a list of the documents which he pretends to hold and which he says "will be fatal to the traitor".'

The Kashmiri elicited Duleep's address and headed for the Paris suburbs and a show-down. He wanted no less than 150,000 guineas as compensation for his imprisonment and the 'life pension' the King of Lahore had promised him. It would have been all rather comic were it not for the death threat. The Maharajah reported the St Cloud encounter thus: 'Abdul Rasul came here the other day and having drunk three bottles of beer became rather intoxicated and threatened to shoot me. The Punjabis, as was to be expected at my giving in, are exasperated and therefore desire to find a victim and if they should be successful, are they not right? Now that I am a Christian there will be many fanatic Moslems who will seek my life but I am sure God will protect me, but if not what is better than to die for Christ's sake?'

However he professed to worship his Creator – as a Sikh, a member of the Russian Orthodox Church, or as a communicant of the Church of England – the Maharajah sought a more earthly safeguard. He insisted that the Paris police provide protection.

There was one uplifting arrival that autumn, but it revealed another betrayal. Arur Singh, so faithful, so loyal, was released from Chunar Fort on 15 December 1890 after being held for over three years as a state prisoner. Before leaving India he had been diligent enough to check on the money-raising schemes set up by Baron Textor de Ravisi. The servant, whom Duleep now proposed adopting as a son, arrived in St Cloud almost a year after his release carrying a list of thirty contributors to the patriotic fund. '£5,000 was collected and sent to the Pondicherry banker recommended by Baron de Ravisi, who seems to have stuck to the coin,' according to the general.

A month later he reported: 'Baron de Ravisi evades a reply to the question who was the banker at Pondicherry whom he recommended and to whom it is alleged that a sum of £5,000 was remitted from Hyderabad to the Maharajah's account. Duleep continues to be an almost helpless cripple, he will pass the winter in the South.'

The Abdul Rasul affair was much more serious than the revelation of Baron Textor's avarice. The Kashmiri plotter had had so many secret masters – the Sultan of Turkey, Mouktar Pasha the Turkish agent in Egypt, the French Foreign Office, Zobair Pasha the Mahdist zealot, Count Ignatiev, General Alikhanov – that 'his only occupation is to serve as go-between to further intrigues of one government against the other,' Aziz-ud-din had reported. His portable loyalties were obvious to the general. 'I am sure he would open his mouth wide if paid for it,' he had told London.

Rasul indeed wrote to Lord Cross in London on 3 January 1892 offering to betray the Maharajah who, he said, was still treasonably plotting in spite of his 'pardon'. The Kashmiri related his version of what had happened the summer before. 'I received a letter from Duleep by handwriting of his secretary "General Tevis," who is a native of

Ireland, in which Duleep requested me to come to Paris at once and I arrived on 15 May 1891.

'I had an interview with Duleep at the Hotel d'Albe – he asked me to see Mr. Gearas [de Giers] who at that time was in Paris from Russia, Duleep offering me a salary of 50 guineas per month [to act] concerning very great political matters against the India Government which I refused to undertake, about which I am in a good position to give you now the full particulars in his own handwriting.'

This was dangerous. Rasul knew about Tevis but not his secret role. The India Office tried to buy him off. On 14 March 1892 he was offered 'payment of debts, passage to India and safe conduct to Kashmir' with a deadline of fourteen days to accept. But instead he returned to Paris and engaged a Parisian advocate, a M. Giovanelli, who prepared a 'very damaging case'. The general stayed close to developments, telling London a month later: 'I passed an hour with Duleep yesterday. He arrived in Paris four days ago and called three times before finding me. This showed a certain anxiety to get on good terms again. I touched discreetly on his suit with Abdul. He declared he cared nothing for any scandal which could only do him good, especially in India.'

According to the Maharajah, Abdul Rasul was bluffing: 'If he gave money to Abdul the latter would return to India, where he was sure to be assassinated on landing [by whom he did not make clear]. Besides Abdul has no evidence,' he said.

The general, however, thought differently. 'This is a mistake and Abdul will gain his suit,' he told London urgently. 'I told him also how very disagreeable it would be for me to have my name mixed with a very disgraceful suit. He replied that whether it did or did not injure me was quite indifferent to him and to his family.

'Duleep's general health is good, but he is a cripple and his mind is affected leaving of his former intelligence, only a sort of oriental cunning. He is entirely without moral principles and even now the recipient of British bounty is doing what he can to undermine, through others, British prestige in India.

'He is deplorably surrounded, his wife is vulgar and brainless, his sons beneath contempt, and his chief admirer, Mourilyan, a petifogging lawyer whose father was the intermediary of English Jews with English gentlemen in financial difficulties.'

The case was due for hearing on 16 May 1892. M. Giovanelli had offered the Paris newspapers a series of 'scurrilous articles which they are afraid to publish'. The general became very agitated. He dreaded it coming out in court that the Maharajah's solicitor was acting 'under the instructions of the India Office'.

There was also a juicier scandal brewing – the life and times of Ada Douglas Wetherill. It was all going to come out in a French court-room.

'Duleep plans to go to Egypt or Palestine; His wife will go to England and into the best society. Unless English society be much changed the Maharani will not succeed in her aspirations,' the general messaged.

'I heard enough to convince me that the plaintiff's solicitors are thoroughly posted, especially on points of Duleep's private life which – if aired in court and in the newspapers – must bar the access of all decent continental society to every member of the family.

'If the plaintiffs fulfil their threats, the revelations that they could make about her are such as would close the door upon her of any respectable French kitchen.'

Whitehall held its breath. Duleep's lawyer offered M. Giovanelli 'half the money' to keep quiet, but Abdul Rasul said no. The India Office concluded 'the solicitors involved on both sides are in league to plunder the Maharajah'. The French High Court took five minutes to throw out the case on the grounds they had no jurisdiction in a quarrel between British subjects. Rasul slunk back to London, still demanding money, his secret file marked by the Secretary of State in red ink: 'Have no dealings with this person whatsoever.'

# 41

# The Hawk's Bell

❦

*Albany Hotel, Hastings, Sussex, April 1893*

DULEEP AND ADA saw little of each other after the unpleasantness of the Abdul Rasul affair. In the summer of 1892 the Maharajah went to Royan on the French Atlantic coast to take the waters, the Maharani to Ostend with the children for 'a change of air'. That winter the Maharajah was evidently strong enough to make a journey to Algiers en famille where the 'eldest child of the present marriage [the Moscow-born Princess Pauline Alexandra] was received into the English church, I don't quite know what the means,' according to a dutiful Oliphant report. The two-year-old Princess Ada Irene was also baptised a Christian.

The Maharajah was to return to England one more, sad, time. His youngest son, Prince Albert Edward, was rising thirteen, about to go to Eton like his brothers. The India Office has preserved a few funny, inky letters from him to his sister Princess Sophie. They are written on monogrammed paper 'E.D.S.'. One letter hinted at the snuffling frailty that would claim his life:

'Aspal Hall, Debenham, Suffolk, February 7th 1890. We played cricket against Eye grammar school, I got 44 runs. This letter is for Bamba and Catherine. Give my love to the girls and Miss Schafer. I exchanged my stamp album with the kitchen boy. I have got over 400 penny stamps. I am not going to church because my cold never properly went.'

In January 1893 Edward contracted pneumonia. He was removed from the Oliphants' Brighton home a little way down the coast to Hastings to be under the care of a specialist. Sir Henry Ponsonby was informed: 'Prince Victor and Frederick were both with their father in

Algiers when the little boy's illness commenced and I was commissioned to send a telegram daily to the Maharajah as to the little
one's condition. I mention this to show that the Maharajah has some
sort of feeling for his children though not quite as much as one would
like.'

The Hastings physician, Dr Cecil Christopherson, did what he
could. The boy grew weaker. Oliphant wrote to Ponsonby: 'The little
prince is rapidly failing and the end cannot be long distant. Life is
sustained by brandy, champagne, Brand's essence and nutrient enemas
of egg, milk, etc. He is a dear patient little fellow, so thoughtful of all
around him, so anxious not to be thought ungrateful – when he couldn't
take his food.'

Edward's condition grew critical. On 21 April Victor brought the
Maharajah over from Paris. 'He was very much overcome on seeing
his little son, and wept bitterly and loudly,' wrote Oliphant. 'When
Prince Victor told him he must not do so he was quiet. He told his
little boy he had come a long way to see him and hoped his visit would
do him good. Before leaving the Maharajah wrote on a piece of paper,
the Lord is my shepherd and gave it to his little son.' Three days later
Duleep returned to France.

Edward died a week later. He was buried at Elveden next to his
mother on Friday 1 May. The princesses stayed at Chalk Hall near
Elveden, a shooting lodge half a mile from the main house which now
stood mournfully shuttered and empty. The nursery lawns of their
childhood were covered in weeds. The Queen sent a wreath and telegram of condolence. The Maharajah was too ill to attend.

The elder princesses were growing up fast. Their education was progressing at Somerville Hall and, under Fraulein Lina Schäfer's continuing influence, in all things German, land of their grandfather's birth.
Oliphant told Ponsonby in July: 'The Princesses Bamba, Catherine
with their governess are spending some weeks of their vacation in the
house of a Colonel von Kietzell at Kassel.'

It was now up to Arthur Oliphant to report on the condition of the
Maharajah himself. The secret servants of Whitehall had lost interest
but Windsor had not. Our Correspondent's watch in Paris had expired
when William Gladstone had returned to office for the fourth time in
August 1892 with Lord Kimberley back as Secretary for India and

Lord Rosebery as Foreign Secretary. The general's communications ceased immediately thereafter. Whether or not it was a political move, there was no longer any point in the Foreign Office spying on a dying man.

The Queen learned from Oliphant in July: 'I am very sorry to say that the latest reports on the Maharajah's health are very indifferent. In fact I think he is in a most critical condition, kidney trouble and dropsical symptoms – intense irritability of temper &c and I cannot think that he will be spared much longer.'

## *Hôtel de La Trémoille, rue de La Trémoille, Paris, 21 October 1893*

The last court of the King of Lahore was held in a Paris hotel in a nobly shabby old street near the Pont d'Alma. The Maharajah knew he was dying; he had already drafted letters to Ada and Victor and gave them to Arur Singh for delivery after his death. In the second week of October he had rallied enough to discuss future plans with Prince Victor: he would go to Cairo for the winter. He kept changing his mind; he would go to Algiers. On the 16th, his wife and younger son decamped to London to 'look for a smaller house'. Prince Victor went off to Berlin to visit his friend Lord Carnarvon.

The French capital was in joyful uproar. On 17 October a squadron of Russian warships had dropped anchor at Toulon in return for a visit to Kronstadt by a French flotilla the year before, when even the Czar had to take his hat off for the 'Marseillaise'. Russian naval officers in Paris were greeted like liberators following a long occupation. Queen Victoria asked Lord Dufferin, the ambassador, what was going on. He replied in a detailed and very personal letter: 'When the Emperor of Russia held up his little finger, France has tried to force herself into his arms with the utmost alacrity. For eight days past the thoroughfares have been impassable in consequence of the crowds who accumulated wherever it was thought the Russian cortège might appear, some kissing their hands . . .

'Admiral Avelan [Russian naval commander] has received 19,000 letters, a great proportion of them from ladies asking for a lock of his hair . . . wherever a Russian officer passes the ladies mob him. The coachman of Count Munster [the German ambassador] was called "a German pig".' Queen Victoria would have disapproved.

In his hotel room, Duleep heard the shouts and laughter of *les fêtes Franco-Russes* engulfing the city. The seemingly impossible strategic revolution which, six years earlier, he had been so subtly used to forestall, had come.* He was too near to death to appreciate the irony.

The Maharajah had not been completely abandoned. Princess Pauline and the infant Ada were in a nanny's care and saw their father every day. They came to the Hotel de La Trémoille the day he suffered his last and fatal embolism.

He was alone when it struck. It was Arthur Oliphant who found out what happened: 'This morning the Prince of Wales received me,' he wrote to Windsor on 29 October, 'and was very much interested in all I told him about the late Maharajah and his family. And H.R.H. hoped I would write to you fully that Her Majesty may also be in possession of the facts ... On Saturday the 21st (on the night of which he was taken ill) he had the two little girls to see him three times, and gave them each a hawk's bell† on which other occasions they had been allowed to play with and then only when they were good.

'The elder little girl told her father she had heard from Mummy and was writing to her. The Maharajah told her "to give his love to her mother and ask when she was coming back".'

Around nine that night the fifty-six-year-old Maharajah had a fit. He seems to have lingered unconscious until the evening of the following day, Sunday, 22 October 1833. M. Lafond, the hotel proprietor, grew anxious. Chambermaids came knocking. According to Reuters: 'A physician was summoned without delay, but was only able to pronounce life extinct.'

There was flap at the British embassy late on Sunday night when the news came from M. Lafond. Lord Dufferin, who had been Duleep's *bête noire* when Viceroy of India, had been appointed ambassador to France in 1892. He was roused from his bed and told Duleep Singh was dead. An official was sent to see what would be done. Telegrams went the next morning to the Foreign and India Offices. The trustees

---

* Alexander III approved a formal military convention between France and Russia on 27 December 1893. Count Schlieffen, the new quartermaster-general of the German Army, had already started planning for a two-front war with a first knock-out blow in the west.
† The bell worn on the 'jesses' tied to a young bird's legs during training in falconry.

were informed. Ada was tracked down in London, Victor in Berlin. The Queen was in Scotland. Mr Warren, the royal telegraphist and cipher-clerk, wrote out a stream of telegrams from noon onwards as the Balmoral Morse tickertape chattered. Lord Henniker messaged first from Suffolk, then five minutes later Oliphant from Brighton: 'Telegram just received from Victor Duleep Singh – "H.H. the Maharajah died in Paris last night at 7pm quite suddenly".' An hour later the officials came on the line.*

GOVERNMENT TELEGRAM ... OCTOBER 23RD 1893

From Embassy, Paris 1.31 p.m. Received in Balmoral 1.33 p.m.

Duleep Singh has died suddenly in Paris. The Princess [the Maharani] has telegraphed that she wishes the body to be interred in England. Her address is Berkeley Hotel London.

Dufferin.

GOVERNMENT TELEGRAM ... OCTOBER 23RD 1893

Foreign Office, London. 3.30 p.m.

Following from Lord Dufferin. No. 99. 'The Maharajah Duleep Singh has died here suddenly in the absence of any of his family who will not arrive until this evening – I have recommended to sanction the body being embalmed.'

Rosebery

The British Empire could, in death, reclaim its proud, implacable foe. The Maharajah had died, it seemed, a Christian. He would be embalmed and the body interred in an English grave. There was no post-mortem. There would be no Sikh cremation, it was never even considered.†

The Maharani, Prince Frederick and Arthur Oliphant rushed to Hotel de La Trémoille by the Monday afternoon boat-train. Victor

---

* The Maharajah's death was formally notified to the British embassy by a Mr Reginald Gosling, 'undertaker', of 5 rue d'Aguessau, Paris. No cause of death is given on the death certificate.

† The Maharajah's will made in Paris on 12 April 1892 stated: 'I wish to be buried wherever I may happen to die and that my Funeral shall be as simple and inexpensive as possible.'

arrived from Berlin later that night. There was obviously a row about who was in charge of the funeral. Reuter's telegraphed on Tuesday the 24th: 'The British Embassy has charge of the preliminary arrangements connected with the removal of the remains. The body will be embalmed to-day, and placed in the coffin immediately afterwards.'

The news agency sent a correction the next morning: 'The statement made yesterday that the British Embassy had charge of the arrangements connected with the removal of the body was incorrect, the family of the late Maharajah having sole charge of the matter.' Victor confided to Lord Cross: 'The awful thing is that none of us was with him at the time. But his being unconscious is a very slight solace. We are going to bury him next to my mother at Elveden on Saturday next at 1.00 and there will be special train from St. Pancras leaving at 9.15.'

The Queen wrote to Victor from Balmoral: 'It is with sincere concern that I heard of the death of your dear father which was telegraphed to me by Lord Dufferin . . .

'I need hardly say how I like to dwell on former years when I knew your dear father so well, saw him so often & we were all so fond of him. He was so handsome so charming. But I will <u>not</u> dwell on the few after years which followed which were so painful. It is however a great comfort & satisfaction to me that I saw the Maharajah two years and a half ago at Grasse & that all was made up between us . . .

'Pray accept this expression of my warmest sympathy in your heavy loss & convey the same to your brothers and sisters. Be assured that I shall always take the deepest interest in the welfare and the happiness of yourself and your Brother & Sisters. Believe me always your affectionate friend & Godmother. Victoria R.I.'

There was no mention of sympathy for Ada in the Queen's letter, no mention of Ada at all.

## St Andrew's church, Elveden, Suffolk, 28 October 1893

The body of Maharajah Ranjit Singh, the Lion of the Punjab, had been borne to his funeral pyre in a golden ship. The dark oak coffin of the Maharajah Duleep Singh was placed on the 9.00 p.m. boat-train at the Gare St Lazare in time to catch the midnight Dieppe–Newhaven ferry.

The funerary train arrived at Thetford station at noon the next day, Friday 27 October. The coffin was borne to the church of St Andrew to lie overnight in the piously plain chancel. Mr McArthur, the Elveden head gardener, prepared the brick grave, next to Maharani Bamba's and Prince Edward's, lining it with moss, ferns and ornamental oak, humble plants from the estate. A Great Eastern Railway special brought a trainload of mourners the next morning – a line of black carriages waiting to bear them the five miles through Elveden's autumnal woods to the shuttered Hall. The churchyard overflowed with 'country people who had swarmed to the spot from all the parishes round about' dressed in their respectful Sunday black to send the Old Maharajah off and see the fine people come up from London. At midday, four special constables parted the crowd to make a path for the family. Ada, drenched in the deepest mourning, stepped first from the carriage; the princesses, Bamba, Catherine and Sophie, invisible under veils, Prince Victor and Prince Frederick followed their step-mother. 'The two children of the present Maharani, being very young, were left behind in London.'

Lord Camoys represented the Queen, the Prince of Wales sent his equerry, Lord Kimberley deputed an India Office official. It was all done properly. Sir Owen Tudor Burne turned up in person. The Maharajah would not 'snarl at him in a pleasant way' again. The Reverend St George Walker, rector of Elveden, conducted a service of 'extreme plainness'. There was no music.

The coffin was carried out by estate workers: Mr Alexander McArthur, head gardener; Mr Gant, head woodsman; Mr James Mayes, head gamekeeper; Mr Charles Howlett, Mr T. Trayes, Mr J. Darkens, under-keepers; and Mr A. Ford and Mr H. Flack of Thetford.

A wreath came from Balmoral ('From Queen Victoria' its message said simply), from the Prince of Wales ('For auld lang syne, Albert Edward'), from the Maharani ('Ada' picked out in violets). There were tributes from earls, dukes, lords and ladies, gamekeepers and poachers. Arur Singh placed Suffolk flowers. A mysterious 'beautiful wreath' came from Paris anonymously.

The Maharajah's obituarists had their own distinct viewpoints of their subject. The Exchange Telegraph news agency wired: 'He was man of some power, but intemperate both in action and speech, and very ill-content to remain in the obscurity to which fate had consigned him. He was an amateur musician of some skill, and brought over to London the French system of baccarat with disastrous results to himself.'

To *Land and Water* he was: 'A splendid shot. No man living could change guns more rapidly than he could without interfering with the accuracy and quickness of the act of firing.'

'Ruffler' of *Vanity Fair* wished to 'disinter one bright and qualifying feature in the character of the ex-ruler of the Punjab – his devoted personal attachment to the Queen and to the Prince of Wales. The sentiment never wavered in the midst of all his fancied or real griev-ances against the British Government. Only those who have been brought into personal contact with the Sikh character have any idea to what heights of nobility it can soar, or to what depths of degradation it can occasionally descend.'

The Maharajah Duleep Singh was buried a Christian in a Saxon church laden with the memorials of the great and the good. England had claimed him.

# 42

# The Gas-fitter's Child

❦

*Oriental and India Office Collection, British Library,*
*St Pancras, London, July 1999*

A MILLENNIAL ANALOGY of the Maharajah's story would be extraordinary. It would be as if Mohammed al Fayed, outraged at his treatment by the House of Windsor, had run off with a teenage lover to the American mid-west (Orthodox, pan-Slavist Moscow) claiming to be Gerry Adams with a plan to claim the pharaonic throne of Egypt and unite Ireland. The whole thing is backed by a messianic media magnate working in secret with a survivalist cult to smash the United Nations and let the USA find its true destiny. British intelligence confound the plan by linking Mr Fayed's name with a conspiracy to assassinate the President of the United States.

What were the Maharajah's motives? To understand a boy-prince born in the semi-medieval Punjab a century and half ago was problematic enough, to understand someone reinvented as a God-fearing Victorian gentleman was as difficult. Each persona was a foreign country. He slaughtered animals by the cart-load but was a diligent menagerie-keeper. He was 'a liberal contributor to the village school' yet pursued the village's poachers 'leading to episodes not quite acceptable to English ideas'. He raved at the India Office for not allowing him to leave Elveden to his children – yet abjured his entire family and ran off with a chambermaid. He extolled Indian freedom yet would call off his rebellion for £3 million. His English pygmalion mentors saw it as the unfortunate re-emergence of his 'eastern nature'.

It was simpler to share the view of those who gathered again in Thetford in late July 1999 as the Prince of Wales, grandson of the last Empress of India, formally unveiled the statue raised by the Maharajah

Duleep Singh Centenary Trust (now moved to an island in the river Ouse). The inscription read: 'Bringing History and Culture Together'. It was a dignified celebration of a shared heritage, of the 19th-century Punjabi king who strove to embrace English life. But was he the squire of Elveden, the Tory in a turban, or the proud rebel? The statue's inscription ended with a Duleepian war-cry: 'He died in Paris having re-embraced the Sikh faith while still engaged in a struggle to reclaim his throne. Even today the Sikh nation aspires to regain its sovereignty.' As he pulled the string, the Prince of Wales was observed to blink.

What drove him on? There was always 'the prophecy', first revealed by his mother, reinforced in Holland Park by Thakur Singh Sandhanwalia. It miraculously evolved according to circumstance. The depths of cynicism were revealed in an Our Correspondent dispatch to London in May 1889 bearing intelligence from Pondicherry. 'A letter from Gurbachan suggests another proclamation and Duleep Singh is now writing it. Care is being taken that "the time of the prophecy shall not expire before the plan is realized" and, adds Gurbachan, "our minds are now directed to the correction of dates so that the *period may be extended*"!' [The spy's emphasis.]

The prophecy was a forgery.

What was wanted of Duleep? His smuggling into Russia was not done to boost the circulation of the *Moscow Gazette*. The key to everything was Katkov. As one familiar with newspaper proprietors, the motivations of the Muscovite editor were compelling. He was eaten by cancer, but that just made his ambition to smash the German alliance greater. The Maharajah was the unexploded bomb to be detonated in Central Asia when the newspaper hawks at last toppled de Giers and pushed Russia into war. That had seemed inevitable until the very last moment, 30 May 1887, when Katkov begged forgiveness on his knees before the Czar at Gatchina.

What brought Katkov there? It was all very clever. The editor's *attentat* was turned on itself by the British Foreign Office with more than a little help from Berlin. When he was apparently going native in St Petersburg in late 1886, Sir Robert Morier was being spied on by the Germans – until, armed with reports from Bismarck himself, Lord Salisbury whipped his ambassador back into line. In the subsequent battle with Katkov, Morier proved himself ultra-loyal to the Foreign Office pro-German line – and thus saved his job. Whitehall and Wilhelmstrasse were as one in the cold war of 1887. Sir Julian Pauncefote paid personal visits to Carlton House Terrace at the height of the Duleep-in-Moscow crisis. Berlin supplied a flow of intelligence about the Boulanger–Bogdanovich contacts meanwhile. The venerable Kaiser Wilhelm I himself telegraphed the Czar demanding the obscure railway-general be punished. At the critical moment, de Giers's son at the Russian embassy in Paris added the 'Floquet letter' twist in concert with the Ohkrana forger Katakazi. And so it turned out, as Cyon discovered much later, it was the universal conspirator Nicholas Notovich who had cooked up the 'L'Alliance Franco-Russe' pamphlet that so damned Evgenii Bogdanovich.

It was Sir Robert Morier, the British ambassador, who kept de Giers clinging to office. The diplomat's masterstroke was linking Duleep and Ada, Monsieur and Madame Dynamitard, with threats against the life of the Czar. The Russian foreign minister could use Sir Robert's drip-fed intelligence as he wished, bomb-plots courtesy of Scotland Yard were switched on and off to order. London's apparent incompetence as the Maharajah strutted around Moscow for a month posing as 'the well known revolutionary Patrick Casey' could have not have been scripted more exquisitely. The KGB would have called Duleep 'a useful idiot'.

Whitehall's imperative was not to stop Duleep – it was to destroy Katkov.

It was the great game for the highest stakes imaginable – forestalling a catastrophic war in Europe weighed against the potential loss of British India. Sir Robert Morier and his political master Lord Salisbury played the game like masters – but they were cheating. The all-seeing spy in Paris was reading their opponent's hand. Who was he?

The 'Black Pamphlet' described 'General Carroll-Teviss, member of the Fenian Supreme Council' as 'an American soldier of fortune'. West Point Military Academy in New York state sent me the obituary of a distinguished alumnus from the class of 1849. 'General Charles Carrol Tevis, who died at Paris aged 72, on 29 September 1900, was the most accomplished type of the gentleman and soldier of modern times,' it said. 'An actor in the greater part of the upheavals which marked the second half of the nineteenth century, he had the varied and knightly career so qualified to inflame the imagination of a soldier.'

Indeed he had. Born in Philadelphia, he had graduated to serve as a US Army cavalryman. But his 'adventurous spirit' had compelled him in 1850 to resign the tedium of Carlisle Barracks, Pennsylvania, and offer his services to the Sultan of Turkey.

'Appointed Bim-Bacchi, a rank equivalent to that of Major, in the Turkish irregular Cavalry, Major Tevis took part with that rank in the Asiatic and Crimean Wars under the name "Nessim Bey". Britain awarded him the Crimea Medal. He returned to America to fight for the Union in the Delaware Infantry and 3rd Maryland Cavalry Volunteers.

He next turned up in Rome, offering to serve as a private soldier in the Pontifical Zouaves. 'Touched by this offer, Pope Pius IX appointed the General, on February 22nd, 1868, secret chamberlain of the Cloak and Sword, with the title of Count, inherent to that office,' continued the West Point eulogy. 'During a stay in France previous to this time, General Tevis had embraced the Roman Catholic religion.'

When the Prussian armies fell on France in 1870–71, Tevis was a general leading a fighting retreat of the 20th Brigade, finally pushed across the frontier into Switzerland. There were more foreign wars – *pronunciamentos* in Venezuela, service with the Khedive of Egypt and back to the Sultan of Turkey where he fought the Russians in Bulgaria in 1877. He seemed to have had as many names as battle honours – 'Washington Carroll Tevis', 'Charles Carrol Tevis', 'Charles Carrol de Taillevis, commandeur de St Jean de Jerusalem', 'Nessim Bey'.

There was something missing from the résumé. How could the Philadelphia-born adventurer pass as an Irish republican? There was this, definitely not included in the West Point eulogy. 'In 1865 Tevis was appointed adjutant-general to General Thomas W. Sweeny, secretary of war of the Irish Republic and Commander-in-Chief of the Irish Republican Army.' In January 1866 he had been the armourer for the doomed Fenian raid on Canada. A year later he sent H.M. Minister in Washington a full breakdown of Fenian arms dumps in the US – it was signed 'John Smith'. The diplomat noted: 'The writer is Tevis . . . he is anxious to be employed as an agent of H.M.G. – he asks £100 per month.' Francis Millen was also on the payroll – his condename was 'James Thompson'. The implacable foe of the British empire was betrayed by the adjutant-general of the IRA.

The general had been a Foreign Office 'sleeper' since May 1883. In mid-February 1887 Sir Julian Pauncefote, the Foreign Office spymaster, somehow steered him towards the Maharajah. That somehow remained problematic.

Elie de Cyon had been in contact with Irish-Americans in Paris since 1885. Macadaras made his mission to Moscow in early 1886 'with a letter of introduction to Katkov furnished by General [blank]' according to Michael Davitt's intelligence. Cyon and Tevis clearly knew each other – indeed they were fellow fancy-dress wearers at Madame Adam's bal masque.

'The Irish exiles made contact with the Maharajah soon after his arrival in Paris,' the doctor wrote in his less-than-truthful memoirs, but thereafter, other than letters by 'E.C.' and the first encounter with General Bogdanovich on his mid-winter journey to France, nothing much happened. New militancy was needed – enter Our Correspondent.

It looks like it was Cyon who acted as H.M. Foreign Secret Service's unwitting fool when he suggested Tevis be Duleep's clandestine chief of staff. He did so on 8 March 1887.*

Our Correspondent was already primed by London to jump. The general had been circling the conspirators from the beginning, watching from a distance. But as soon as the general was on the inside, events moved very rapidly. Our Correspondent made his first detailed dispatch to London on the night of 8 March. The written approaches to Czar Alexander III and to Katkov followed within forty-eight hours. The Russia-bound luggage was very soon labelled up as Mr and Mrs Reginald Lorraine, then came the Casey passport dodges on St Patrick's Day, 17 March. Four days later Duleep and Ada were steaming out of the Gare du Nord towards St Petersburg. *The Labour World* exposé 'Duleep Singh and the Secret Service', which had come so close to unmasking Tevis, gave an inside account: 'It was resolved on the suggestion of General [blank] that Duleep should proceed to Moscow. A passport was got from the British ambassador in Paris in the name of Patrick Casey, on the suggestion of General [blank].' On this account it was Tevis himself who propelled the Maharajah towards Moscow and engineered the seemingly mad identity switch. Whether premeditated or opportunistic, it suited the higher political purpose.

What could be more contrived to scupper Katkov than sending a

---

* The date Cyon said a 'senior Irish émigré asked permission to introduce Duleep Singh to him'. He reversed roles to absolve himself from the general's treachery. The doctor never mentions Tevis in his memoirs but obviously knew the truth when he wrote in 1894: 'There remain many accusations and suspicions concerning this affair on which it is best to remain silent.'

turbanned self-obsessive claiming to be an Irish dynamiter into the heart of the impending coup-by-newspaper, accompanied by an attractive teenage girl and a brace of yapping spaniels?

Her Majesty's Foreign Secret Service intended them to get on the Nord Express.

Mr Reginald Lorraine changing trains in pickpocket-infested Berlin would not have had the same impact as the embarrassments of someone claiming to be Mr Patrick Casey. The robbery on the Freidrichstrasse Bahnhof platform seems a genuine accident, grit in the historical gears, brilliantly seized on by the counter-conspirators. Then Katkov died.

That was not predicted. With Katkov extinguished, the conspiracy lost its messianic motor. While the pan-Slavists – Pobedonostsev, Tolstoi and Ignatiev – brooded, waiting for a second chance, what remained for the secret servants of the British Empire was the leisurely mopping-up of the Maharajah's own conspiracy. It was completely penetrated after all. But Duleep never really gave up. As the rebellious dreams of England's proud implacable foe flared and fizzed, the busy Aziz-ud-din was snuffing them out, from Pondicherry, Constantinople, Cashmere and Cairo to Clapham Park. And, even two years after the stroke-crippled Maharajah's 'surrender', Our Correspondent stayed on the case before flitting back into the Paris shadows.

The general still had a lot to report: 'The Maharajah is getting killed off slowly but surely by his wife and her accomplice Madame Parraton,' he told London in November 1890. Every time Mrs Parraton turned up, Duleep seemed to take a turn for the worse. Cyon had his own suspicions when he met the Maharajah again in 1891. The doctor 'was not surprised to find him ill'. Duleep had told him: 'I am poisoned, I am a dead man.' Could Madame Parraton have been a protypical Rosa Klebb, a female assassin sent to kill the Maharajah by slow poisoning? The Paris Sûreté files are full of reports on spies (German and British) – but no Parraton. It comes down to motive, there was no one left in Russia who might want the Maharajah silenced. For the British, as he shuffled round Paris night-houses, he was a warning to other 'rebels'. The overwhelming probability is that Duleep Singh died of natural causes – hastened by the excesses of his queen.

An intelligence report dated 23 May 1889 by Colonel Henderson adds the greatest twist of all: 'According to Duleep's letters to Pondicherry, it was the military party in Russia that pressed him to go to

France and enter into relations with the Irish and American party there, telling him that, if successful, he would receive help from Russia.

The 'St Louis letter' of 2 June 1887 from the mysterious agent Brodie to Scotland Yard also claimed that the 'Fenian General' Macadaras had gone to Russia in early 1886. The wealthy American had returned to Paris, then 'opened up a correspondence with Duleep Singh, which resulted in him leaving England'. On this account, the Casey-Maharajah encounter was no coincidence – it had been pre-arranged by clandestine messages to Elveden Hall. But could the Maharajah 'have been pressed to go to France' – or summoned to Paris by letters – in some cooked up Fenian-Russian war-party plot (the Irish-American part of which was a British secret service operation)? That would make the flight on the SS *Verona*, Bombay-bound with Bamba and the children, a colossal stunt. Did the Maharajah plot the whole thing with his lover – perhaps the most astonishing running off with a mistress in history?

There is evidence that it was just that. If the memoirs of the louche Mr Julian Osgood Field are to be believed, the great *démarche* was a lover's tryst, cooked up by a stream of telegrams to Elveden long before passage for India was booked. Duleep knew the family would be stopped. He expected it. There was a confirmation in the private papers of Lord Dufferin – Sir Henry Ponsonby wrote to the Viceroy from Windsor on 6 June 1886: 'I hear that when he was stopped at Aden he telegraphed to Lawrence his lawyer, "Arrived, Arrested, Delighted!".' (The letter was not copied to Queen Victoria; it is peppered with tasteless jokes.)

The Maharajah got to Paris in July 1886, spectacularly disowning Bamba and the children two months later.

'Marini' arrived in the French capital in early September. He summoned her there. The dates all fitted. Herr Müller suspected it, so did Arthur Oliphant. Poor, sad Bamba must have been aware. Queen Victoria knew it too; she feared 'that the connection existed <u>before</u> the late Maharani died.' But it did not stop in Paris. The Maharajah could, as Sir Owen Tudor Burne had assumed, have 'lost himself among the fair horizontales'. Instead they got on the train to Russia. He really thought he was going to lay the crown of India at Miss Wetherill's delicate feet.

His co-conspirators told him she was a British spy – and then he married her. The last King of Lahore loved the gas-fitter's child.

# 43

# Catherine

᯽

THE MAHARAJAH'S JOURNEY was over. Other journeys were ending – and beginning. Our Correspondent died on 29 September 1900. He was buried in Montparnasse cemetery, Paris, with full military honours. His daughter married a French cavalry officer.

Patrick Casey returned to Kilkenny in 1891 – where he 'associated with leading local Fenians'. A Dublin Metropolitan Police report of 1893 stated 'he has now come down in the world and is employed as a night watchman by the Paving Board of Dublin Corporation . . . He is fit for any villainy when in drink.'

James Stephens, 'Number One' of the League of Indian Patriots, died in Dublin in 1901 and was buried a republican hero in Glasnevin cemetery. Eugene Davis went back to poetry and died in Brooklyn in November 1897.

Abdul Rasul never got to Srinagar. He settled in Cairo in his old business and died in 1915 with seven bales of Cashmere shawls, five children and a mountain of debts. The Indian National Congress passed a motion in his honour a year later.

Djemal-ud-din, Duleep's Islamic rival in Moscow, returned to Persia where he preached revolution. When a follower assassinated the Shah Nasru-ud-din in 1892 the 'Afghan sheikh' fled to Constantinople and died twenty years later. In 1943, in one of the more bizarre episodes of the Second World War, his body was disinterred and flown by the RAF to Karachi – then taken to (neutral) Kabul to be reburied. The heads of the British, Soviet, Japanese and German legations attended, the last, top-hatted, giving a Nazi salute at the graveside.

The Sandhanwalias were pardoned after the Maharajah's 'surrender' and allowed to return to the Punjab. The Governor-General granted them a 'charitable allowance of 33 rupees per month'. In 1966 the government of India paid Thakur Singh's descendants 5,000 rupees in recognition of his 'struggle against the British regime in India'.

Félix Volpert, who tried to stir up a *Jihad* in the cause of *revanche*, finally got to fight the Germans. His military record says he 'fired at the enemy' (in the frontier battles of 1914) before being invalided out of the army aged fifty-four, having fallen off his horse.

Nicholas Notovich gave up spying for literature. He wrote a loopy book, *The Unknown Life of Jesus*, claiming the resurrected Christ lived in the Himalayas. It was a best-seller.

General Evgenii Bogdanovich was arraigned for embezzling the funds of Kazan Cathedral. He died in 1914.

When Elie de Cyon failed to become editor of the *Moscow Gazette*, he turned his pamphleteering venom on the imperial finance minister, Count Sergius Witte. In 1895 he was ordered to St Petersburg. He refused and was stripped of Russian citizenship. He fled to a villa on the shores of Lake Geneva which was burgled in 1897 on the orders of the Paris Ohkrana chief Peter Rachovski. The doctor died, frightened and embittered, in 1912. His personal papers, kept by his widow, disappeared when the Germans entered Paris in 1940 although there have long been rumours among diplomatic historians that his casket of secrets might one day turn up.

In 1894 Elveden was sold by the trustees, snapped up by the brewing magnate Lord Iveagh for £150,000. It remains the property of the Guinness family. Duleep's partridge coverts are now a Center Parc holiday village.

The Maharajah's line did die from the light. Queen Ada stayed in Paris with her children after the Maharajah's death. The visitors' book at Old Buckenham Hall, Freddie's home from 1897, records several visits for family reunions. She drove a French Red Cross ambulance at the Battle of Verdun. Ada came to London in 1919 with £17,000 of debts. Her step-children thought her return 'unfortunate'.

Ada's first daughter Pauline Alexandra married Lieutenant J. S. Torry (died of wounds, Battle of Loos 1915). There were no children.

Princess Ada Irene Helen Beryl married a Frenchman named Pierre Marie Villament. On 8 October 1926 fishermen dragged her body from the sea off Monte Carlo. 'She is known to have had family trouble,' ran a press report 'and the police found a letter in her hotel room stating that she was "tired of life".'

Prince Victor went bankrupt, then married Lady Anne, daughter of the Earl of Coventry. There were no children. On his death in 1918 the Viceroy noted: 'The family of Duleep Singh is almost forgotten in the Punjab, and therefore there is no need on grounds of policy to advocate generous treatment.'

Prince Frederick became the squire of Blo' Norton Hall and a notable Norfolk antiquary. He never married.

Bamba, the eldest daughter, inherited her father's rebel spirit. She insisted on being allowed to visit the Punjab. There was an unseemly incident in October 1905 when she was not invited to a reception for the visiting Prince and Princess of Wales (the future King George V and Queen Mary). The Viceroy's private secretary explained why: 'On the occasion of Lord Curzon's last visit to Lahore the Princess Bamba was invited to a garden party to meet Their Excellencies and appeared in an oriental costume which, to say the least of it, was distinctly improper.' She had apparently worn 'an "anji" stretched across the breasts and the body naked from that down to the navel'. That the Special Branch tagged her is clear from another vice-regal letter to King Edward VII's private secretary.

'I can't resist telling you the following: You recently wrote as to the reasons for the alleged want of courtesies to "Princess Bamba" at Lahore. I did not like to include the report of the Secret Police who have apparently had an eye on the lady, and who informed us as an absolute proof of her unsuitability to mix with the higher circles of Indian society that "she wears drawers under her pyjamas".'

In 1915 Bamba married an Indian Army doctor, Lieutenant-Colonel David Waters Sutherland. There were no children. She died aged eighty-eight of heart failure at her home, 'Gulzar' in Lahore Model Town, Pakistan, in 1957, 'still dreaming of ancestral greatness'. The UK Deputy Commissioner organized a sparse funeral.

The princesses Sophia and Catherine lived together as spinster sisters in a grace-and-favour home granted by Queen Victoria, Faraday House on the fringe of Hampton Court. Sophie was a rebel: in 1911 she became a militant suffragette, placarding the royal palace with 'Votes for Women' and 'Revolution!' banners. 'What hold do we have over her?' minuted an India Office official. 'It is for the King to decide to evict her,' came the reply. He chose not to. In January 1914 her jewellery (pearl necklaces again) was sold by court order for withholding tax. In the First World War, Sophia organized patriotic flag days for Punjabi troops of the Indian Army. Her sister's wartime odyssey was much more mysterious.

## *Office of the Director of MO5(g), War Office, Whitehall, London, 27 September 1914*

Lieutenant-Colonel Vernon Kell, the peppery director of Britain's counter-intelligence service, had a lot on his mind. The British Empire had been at war with Germany and Austria-Hungary for almost a month. His job was to round up spies and traitors, and for the last two years he had compiled a compendious secret register. A diligent officer was installed at Mount Pleasant post office sniffing out treason. A letter arrived from Kassel in Germany addressed to someone apparently living in a royal palace. Kell recognized the sender's name and immediately passed it to the India Office. It read:

Secret

Copy of Letter addressed to H.H. Princess Sophia Duleep Singh, Faraday House, Hampton Court.
Willemshohe 20.9.1914.

Dear Suph

It is awful having no news of you all. We are going to Switzerland in Nov. if it is possible then and from there of course we can communicate.

I am perfectly all right here, you must not be anxious in any way, it is just the same as in time of peace, perfect order everywhere, and no sort of restrictions for me.

There have been no murders or disturbances by Germans in Germany and the destruction of property, etc., in their enemies' countries has simply been the just punishment of civilians who have taken part in the war.

I implore ★ to have nothing to do with this unjust war against Germany.

Please pay the remainder on Harrod's shares when due and any bills etc.

Very much love to all specially B. who I fear may have been worrying.

Your loving sister

[signed] Catherine.

PS I enclose a letter to Coutts, authorising them to [letter torn] on my account. CDS.

An official noted on the transcript: 'This is interesting. "B" is presumably Princess Bamba. The ★ is perhaps a reference to Prince Victor, whose crest, I think, is a starred coronet.'

It looked as if something astonishing was happening – could she be repeating her father's rebellion, with the demon king this time the German Kaiser rather than the Russian Czar? Just as Berlin strove to foment revolution in Ireland, agents prowled Afghanistan and the north-west frontier.* A mutiny of the Sikhs would be as great a strategic prize as the Arab revolt was for the British. The German legation in Berne was the source of seditious funds. The princess mentioned 'Switzerland' in her letter, her instructions to Messrs Coutts tantalizingly obscure. The key to the Maharajah's Box turned a notch.

*Schlossteichstrasse 15, Wilhelmshöhe, Cassel, Germany, 11 November 1918*

German intelligence had a cub of the Lion the Punjab under their noses, but for all their efforts to raise a conflagration in India, it seems they did not know it. Catherine stayed in Germany until the end of the war for her own very personal reasons. The friendship with Fraul-

* An archeologist, Max von Oppenheim, was deputed by the German foreign ministry in September 1914 to stir up revolution in India, funded through Switzerland. In 1915 a committee of exiles moved from Zurich to Berlin, an 'Indian National Legion' was to be formed from POWs with the Punjab its primary target; it was the Maharajah's war plan of 1889 dressed up in field-grey.

In a direct parallel of the Irish Clan-na-Gael, fervent anti-British militancy had already sprung up in the Sikh diaspora in British Columbia and California. The Ghadr (uprising) movement based in San Francisco was its motor, its newspaper's masthead slogan 'Enemy of the British Government', a Duleepian echo. On the outbreak of war many thousands of emigrant Sikhs returned to the Punjab expecting imminent revolution. There was a rising on 21 February 1915 which was crushed. Thirty rebels were hanged. Ninety thousand Sikhs loyally served in the British Army meanwhile, one-eighth of India's total contribution.

ein Lina Schäfer, the princesses' governess so approvingly appointed by Arthur Oliphant, had developed into an 'intimate' one (Sophie's description). I could find no letters between them – perhaps they were lodged somewhere very safe.

The day the war ended, Catherine applied for a passport by letter to the Dutch legation (British Interests Section), Berlin. Red flags flew from the Kaiser's palace. Two days later she wrote to Sophie at Hampton Court who informed the Foreign Office: 'I have had a letter dated November 13th from my sister Princess Catherine Duleep Singh saying that she requires a new passport as soon as possible, the one she has no longer being valid ... The reason she has to remain in Germany is, on account of the serious illness of her friend Frl. L. Schäfer.'

MI5 were consulted and could find no fault.* The India Office considered her case. They decided: 'Quite early in the war we intercepted a foolish pro-German letter from Princess Catherine; but, so far as I know, nothing has been heard of her since. It may be hoped that she has found occasion to modify her views. In any-case, there seems to be no sufficient evidence for treating her as an "enemy".' Catherine got her ticket home.

The love for her governess lasted unto death. Princess Catherine added a codicil to her will: 'I wish to be cremated and three quarters of my ashes to buried at Elveden Churchyard, a quarter of my ashes to be put in a casket and buried as near as possible to the coffin of my friend Fraulein Lina Schäfer at the Principal Cemetery at Kassel in Germany.' Thus it was.†

---

* MO5(g) became MI5 in January 1916.

† Britain was at war with Germany. Princess Bamba took the ashes to Kassel in 1949.

Governess and pupil sustained a lifelong relationship. Princess Catherine returned to Kassel in 1920 where she lived, punctuated by short returns to Princess Sophia at Hampton Court, until Lina Schäfer's death, aged 78, on 27 August 1937. Local police records show Catherine made several trips to Switzerland between 1928 and 1930.

Frau Christina Twelker, who had been a neighbour's child, told the *Hessische Allgemeine* newspaper in July 1997: 'The old Princess would always walk on Fraulein Schäfer's left, out of respect for her teacher – who would say, "We are like two little mice living in a little house." The inside of the Villa am Mulang was full of Chippendale furniture and luxurious tapestries. The Princess worked in the garden but never cooked. They would lunch every day in the nearby Pension Blankenburg.

'The Local Nazis disapproved of the old Indian lady. Her neighbour and accountant Dr Fritz Ratig warned her to leave the country. In November 1937 the Princess sold everything and fled via Switzerland to England.'

# EPILOGUE

## Basel, Switzerland, 3 December 1999

The scramble for the Maharajah's Box was as unseemly as Duleep Singh's grudge-fight had been with the India Office. By the original deadline of March 1998, scores of claims had been lodged. Swiss lawyers grappled with ancestral trees stretching back to the lost kingdom of Lahore.

The Sandhanwalias kept to their claim. In October 1999 the family came to England, were given a warm reception by British Sikhs and a frosty one at the jewel house of the Tower of London. Eyeing the Koh-i-Noor, Beant Singh Sandhanwalia was unstoppable. 'My mission is to take back to India what is rightfully hers,' he proclaimed in the *Eastern Eye* newspaper – which concluded portentously: 'The whole case may hang on the contents of Catherine Duleep Singh's safety deposit box. Until it is opened the whole world waits with bated breath.'

Deadlines came and went as Swiss bankers wrapped their proceedings in secrecy. There was over $750 million to disgorge in all the dormant accounts (including one owned by Vladimir Ulyanov, better known as Lenin). 'The Duleep Singh case is not a priority, it does not concern Holocaust victims,' said a Claims Resolution Tribunal official. But there was a final twist. Fraulein Lina Schäfer also had an unclaimed bank account. She left all her property to Princess Catherine. What strange tryst had the 'two little mice' been planning?

On 3 December 1999 the Swiss declared that the multiplicity of claims meant a further six-month delay before deciding the true heir. But a source admitted this: 'There are only a very few documents in the bank file and these documents do not exceed the normal technical information connected with a bank–client relationship. There are no special documents revealing aspects of the family, political events or the Koh-i-Noor diamond.'

Claiming the lost riches of the Kingdom of Lahore was as wild a dream as Duleep Singh's had been over a century before.

The Maharajah's Box was empty.

# APPENDIX I

# The Prophecy

English translation (made by Punjab Police Special Branch) of the prophecy circulating in the Punjab in spring 1888, claimed to have been made by Guru Gobind Singh in 1725.

1. A Sikh martyr will be born and will reign fearlessly as far as Calcutta.
2. It will then happen that his glory will spread throughout the world.
3. He will be accompanied with his Khalsa army.
4. He, Duleep Singh, will drive his elephant throughout the world.
5. Duleep Singh will shine among the Khalsa.
6. Duleep Singh will overcome all kings.
7. It will then happen that there shall remain no Sikh ruler.
8. A trader, who is my Sikh, will wander in anxiety for the sake of his religion . . .
9. Dissensions will arise at Calcutta and quarrels will be in every house.
10. Nothing will be known for 12 years.
11. Duleep Singh will be Lord since his birth.
12. When Duleep Singh will come, the Vikrami Sambat will be 1899.
13. Rising from the West, the Khalsa will predominate the East.
14. The wicked, the reserved [Englishmen] and the Morji [Muslims] irreligious men will all hide themselves in the hills.
15. The Khalsa will meet together at sunset and will subdue Hindus and Mohammedans who are friends to each other, also the white-faced.
16. The Khalsa will become powerful, the Turks will break their silence.
17. The villages will be plundered, the subjects will suffer and justice will depart.

18. The Sikh women will become unchaste and desire to abandon their husbands.

19. Then will rise the Khalsa, whom the people of four castes will like.

20. All here will rise in the 3rd year, the shamed will plunder the villages and bazaars.

21. First some fear will be felt in Malwa then in other countries.

22. A faithful king will be born in a large town which will be well known in the country.

23. After conquering the country, he will rule it and defeating kings he will then drive them away.

24. Fighting will take place near Delhi – the Bhujangis will then meet.

25. And dressing themselves with arms will plunder the town of Panipat (of rail roads and steam boats).

26. Everyone of you, my Khalsa, will be equally powerful . . .

27. Then my Sikh Duleep will rise whose strength shall be like Teja Singh (or a lion).

28. The Dekkanis, the white, the silent, and the ferangis will be on one side.

29. But when the Khalsa Duleep Singh rises, there shall be no comfort for kings.

30. The manners and customs shall disappear and Duleep Singh will appear in a new fashion.

31. He will die in his native home and the Sikhs will wear arms (or leave Lahore).

32. He will no doubt rule at Lahore and Kashmir for some time.

33. He will rule over the Khalsa and will be helped by me.

34. The person of Ude Singh is for the Guru, the Khalsa Deep or lamp will be illuminated.

35. He will grind down the followers of Christ and of Musa [Moses] and the Hindus.

36. Deep will be the incarnation (of God) and will correct the wrong. My Sikhs will remain for ever, their doings will shine.

37. As new pearls and diamonds shine so the glory of Deep will shine, as soon as Hira Singh dies, Duleep's glory shall rise.

38. Duleep will sit on the throne and the people pay homage to him. When Delhi remains 16 Kos away, the King will cease. Duleep Singh will sit on the throne and all people will pay him homage.

# Elveden, Suffolk, Census of 1881

### Elveden Hall

Maharajah Duleep Singh
Maharani Bamba Duleep Singh
Princess Bamba
Princess Catherine
Princess Sophia
Prince Victor
Prince Frederick
Prince Albert

### Indoor Servants

| | |
|---|---|
| Cracknell, Elizabeth | *domestic servant* |
| Brooks, Helen | *governess* |
| Jay, Arthur | *tutor* |
| Smalley, Mary | *ladysmaid* |
| Candy, Kerzia | *cook* |
| Anderson, Lydia | *laundry maid* |
| Bamstead, Mary | *laundry maid* |
| Bird, Jane | *housemaid* |
| Hiscock, Elizabeth | *housemaid* |
| Farrow, Mary | *housemaid* |
| Boddy, Eliza | *kitchen maid* |
| Downie, Bessie | *scullery maid* |
| Mayes, Margaret | *ladysmaid* |
| Granger, Bertha | *housemaid* |
| Arur Singh | *valet* |
| Hookum Singh | *valet* |
| McLeod, William | *footman* |
| Gems, George | *footman* |
| Baker, George | *usher* |

| | |
|---|---|
| James, Arthur | *groom* |
| Walker, St George, | *rector, St Andrew's* |
| Bonnet, Frederick, | *postman, estate message-taker* |

## THE ESTATE AND FARMS

| | |
|---|---|
| Peebles, John | *farm steward, Red Neck Farm* |
| Powell, Isaac | *bailiff, Summerpit Farm* |
| Gosling, James | *business manager, Chalk Hall* |
| McArthur, Alexander | *head gardener* |
| King, Frederick | *under gardener* |
| Capp, Charles | *woodsman* |
| Mayes, James | *head gamekeeper* |
| Pattle, Absalom | *assistant gamekeeper* |
| Woods, Robert | *gamekeeper* |
| Shillings, Thomas | *coachman* |
| Moore, George | *gardener* |
| Paul, Frederick | *carpenter* |
| Anbon, Frederick | *agricultural labourer* |
| Fuller, James | *shepherd* |
| Turner, William | *labourer* |
| Bailey, James | *gamekeeper* |
| Constable, Mary | *dairymaid* |
| Jeffries, Frederick | *butler* |
| Cooper, Daniel | *labourer* |
| Thurston, Jeremiah | *labourer* |
| Bailey, John | *labourer* |
| Darkens, John | *labourer* |
| Firman, Charles | *garden labourer* |
| Peachey, William | *farm labourer* |
| Bowers, Charles | *warrener* |
| Thorpe, Adam | *farm labourer* |
| Linge, William | *warrener* |
| Cross, John | *gamekeeper* |
| Neal, John | *warrener* |
| Stubbings, Simon | *labourer* |
| Thurston, James | *labourer* |
| Turner, Thomas | *labourer* |
| Smith, Charlie | *labourer* |
| Levitt, John | *labourer* |

| | |
|---|---|
| Cornwell, Samuel | *labourer* |
| Cook, John | *gamekeeper* |
| Hall, Thomas | *groom* |
| Green, John | *shepherd* |
| Green, Richard | *page* |
| Roper, Russell | *labourer* |
| Sparke, Thomas | *labourer* |
| Thurston, George | *labourer* |
| Hunt, Francis | *labourer* |
| Neale, William | *labourer* |
| Elmer, David | *shepherd* |
| Fox, William | *labourer* |
| Baker, George | *carpenter* |
| Baker, William | *groom* |
| Howlett, Charles | *under-keeper* |
| Holmes, James | *shoemaker* |
| Gayton, Richard | *bailiff* |
| Pickard, Albert | *gamekeeper* |
| Charmwell, Jeremiah | *labourer* |
| Cooper, Walter | *labourer* |
| Cornwell, Harry | *gardener* |
| Bijam, William | *labourer* |
| Fox, John | *warrener* |
| Palmer, William | *gamekeeper* |
| Clarke, John | *labourer* |
| Shaylor, Richard | *labourer* |
| Baker, Edward | *groom* |
| Stebbings, James | *labourer* |
| Arbon, George | *labourer* |
| Cornwell, William | *woodsman* |
| Rayner, John | *woodsman* |

# The Franco-Russian War Against Britain

In 1900 the French Magazine *Le Monde Illustré* published a single profusely illustrated issue called 'La Guerre Anglo-Franco-Russe', a fantasy projection of a war between the British Empire and France and Russia in alliance. The war begins with a border spat in Afghanistan. The Russian Army invades the Punjab, the Sikhs and Irish rise in rebellion – it follows exactly the war-plan as cooked up in Paris by the Maharajah Duleep Singh, Félix Volpert, Nicholas Notovich, Patrick Casey et al. in 1888–89. A British expedition to the Cherbourg peninsula is cut off and defeated. The French invade England, fight an enormous battle behind Brighton, and advance in triumph on London. A Russian fleet arrives in Dublin Bay to proclaim the Irish Republic. The war ends with the Treaty of London and the complete dismemberment of the British Empire.

THE TREATY OF LONDON was signed at Westminster on 25 October 1900.

The principal signatories were
*For Britain*: Lord Rosebery, Mr Henry Campbell-Bannerman
*For Russia*: Grand-Duke Serge, M. Mouraviev
*For France*: M. Deschanel, Admiral Caillard

The Treaty agreed:

The Dominion of Canada shall become part of an American confederation with the United States of America.

Newfoundland shall form a French archipelago with the islands of St Pierre and Miquelon.

Jamaica is annexed to Cuba.

The Windward Islands, St Christopher, Antigua, St Dominica, St Lucia, Barbados and Tobago are conjoined to Guadeloupe and Martinique to form the French Antilles.

British Guiana is annexed by Venezuela.

In Africa, Bathurst, Sierra Leone, Cape Coast, and lower Niger are ceded to the French Sudan.

All British territory in Africa north of the Zambezi and to the north-west as far as the equatorial lakes is ceded to Portugal.

The territories formerly known as Rhodesia are ceded to Germany, its northern limit marked by the Zambezi, its southern by the Boer republics. These become the apanage d'Orange and Transvaal with Zululand and Natal become the United States of Africa.

In the Nile Valley, British East Africa is incorporated in German East Africa. Egypt in Sudan to Menelik, also Egypt – in its sphere of influence the entire Arabian peninsula except Perim and Aden – which are granted to France.

The Indian Ocean islands, Mauritius, Rodrigo, the Admiralty islands, the Seychelles, are annexed to the French colony of Madagascar.

The Empire of India, including Burma, forms with Ceylon, Socotra, the Laccadives, and the Maldives, a state the independence of which shall be guaranteed by Germany, Russia and France.

The peninsula of Malacca (Malaya), Singapore and Hong Kong are granted to France.

In the South Pacific, Australia, New Zealand and Tasmania shall form an independent confederation under the name Australasia. New Guinea with the Gilbert and Ellice islands are granted in entirety to Germany.

All other Pacific Ocean territories are annexed by New Caledonia (France).

In the Atlantic, Ascension Island, St Helena and Tristan da Cunha become penal colonies under international administration.

Gibraltar is returned to Spain. Cyprus is given to Greece and Malta to Italy. The Channel Islands are retroceded to France.

Ireland becomes an independent Republic under the protection of the European powers.

# ACKNOWLEDGEMENTS

I wish to thank the archivists and staffs of the Oriental and India Office Collection, British Library, London; The Public Record Office, Kew; The Salisbury Archive, Hatfield House; The National Maritime Museum, Greenwich; The Family Record Centre, London; The Guildhall Library, London; The Tower of London; The Victoria and Albert Museum and National Theatre Museum, London; The Suffolk County Records, Bury St Edmunds; Thetford Public Library, Norfolk; The National Library of Ireland, Dublin, l'Association des Amis des Archives Diplomatiques and the Archives Nationales, Paris. I am grateful to the system managers of the British Library's 'OPAC' and the Public Record Office's 'DORIS' on-line catalogues, without which so much electronically cross-pollinated research would have been impossible.

Special acknowledgments are due to Sheila Biles and Judith Sibley of The US Military Academy, West Point, N.Y., to General A. Bach, Chef du Service Historique de l'Armée de Terre, Château de Vincennes, Paris – and to Lady de Bellaigue, Registrar, and the staff of the Royal Archives, Windsor Castle, material from which is published by gracious permission of Her Majesty Queen Elizabeth II.

I am personally grateful to the following for their help in pursuing the Maharajah and his elusive legacy: Michael Alexander and Sushila Anand, the authors of *Queen Victoria's Maharajah*, Katherine Ardagh, Peter Ashpitel, Amandeep Singh Madra, Peter Singh Bance, Nigel Beaumont of James Purdey & Sons, Bhupender Singh, Oliver Bone, curator of the Ancient House Museum, Thetford, Clare Campbell, Katy and Maria Campbell for advice on medical aspects of the story, Frederick Carlson, Director of Music, Golders Green Crematorium, Dayanita Singh and Ranjit Kaur in Delhi, Harbinder Singh Rana, Project Director of the Maharajah Duleep Singh Centenary Trust, Ian V. Hogg for information on contemporary firearms, Richard Johnson, Janet Law, David Monaghan, Eva O'Cathoir, Margaret Phelan of the Kilkenny Archeological Society, Stephen Rabson of the Peninsula & Oriental Steam Navigation Company, Professor Andreii Raikov of the Lipetsk Pedagogical Institute, Mike Roberts of N16

*Acknowledgments*

Webworks, Beant Singh Sandhanwalia, Jaswinder Singh Sandhanwalia and Sukhdev Singh Sandhanwalia in Amritsar and Amsterdam, Vivienne Schuster, Mary Sharp, assistant secretary of the Carlton Club, Trilok Singh Wouhra of the Maharajah Duleep Singh Project, Alan Walker of Killin, Perthshire, and management, colleagues and librarians at *The Sunday Telegraph* and *The Daily Telegraph*.

I would like to thank my mother, Mrs Mary Campbell of Blackrock Dublin, and her unrivalled collection of books on Irish history – and John O'Dowd, for leading me to the right ones and explaining the term 'Dynamitard'.

# SOURCES

*Abbreviations used in the References including the principal archives used in this work*

| | |
|---|---|
| Cross | The Cross Papers, IOR Mss Eur E243 |
| Dalhousie | *Private Letters of the Marquis of Dalhousie* (see Published Sources, below) |
| DSC | *The Duleep Singh Correspondence* (see Published Sources, below) |
| DSF | Duleep Singh Family Papers, IOR Mss Eur E337 |
| DS-Secret | Duleep Singh Secret Correspondence 1887–92, IOR L/P&S/20/H3–9 |
| Duff | The Dufferin Papers, IOR Mss Eur F130 |
| FFM | French Foreign Ministry, Paris |
| GFM | German Foreign Ministry* |
| HMD | The Durand Papers, IOR Mss Eur D727 |
| IOR | India Office Records, Oriental and India Office Collection, British Library, London |
| JSS | *Journal of Sikh Studies* |
| Login (1) | Lady Lena Login, *Sir John Login and Duleep Singh* (see Published Sources, below) |
| Login (2) | *Lady Login's Recollections 1820–1904* (see Published Sources, below) |
| PP | *The Punjab Papers, Papers Relating to the Punjab 1847–49*, HMSO, *1849* |
| PRO | Public Record Office, Kew, London |
| QV Letters | *The Letters of Queen Victoria* (see Published Sources, below) |
| RA | Royal Archives, Windsor Castle |

* Held on microfilm in the Public Record Office, London.

RAC          The Cross Papers (Richard Assheton Cross, 1st Viscount
             Cross), British Library Mss, London
RFM          Russian Foreign Ministry, Moscow*
WEG          The Gladstone Papers, British Library Mss, London

* Russian material is quoted from compilations by K. S. Thapar, JSS
vol.iv (Amritsar, 1977) and Prof. A. Raikov, *Africa and Asia Today* No. 6
Moscow, 1994).

Material from the Royal Archives at Windsor Castle is reproduced by
gracious permission of Her Majesty Queen Elizabeth II.


*Published Sources*

Memoirs, Collected Correspondence, Pamphlets

Alexander, Michael and Anand, S., *Queen Victoria's Maharajah* (London,
    1980)
Anderson, Sir Robert, *The Lighter Side of My Official Life* (London, 1910)
Bell, Thomas Evans, *The Annexation of the Panjaub and the Maharajah
    Duleep Singh* (London, 1883)
Bertie-Marriot, Clement, *Le Maharajah Duleep-Singh et l'Angleterre* (Paris,
    1889)
Buckle, George Earle, *The Letters of Queen Victoria* (Third series) Vol. 1
    1886–1890 (London, 1930)
Burne, Sir Owen Tudor, *Memories* (London, 1907)
Cyon, Elie de (Ilya Faddeich Tsion), *Histoire de l'Entente Franco-Russe,
    Mémoires et Souvenirs, 1886–1894* (Paris, 1895)
Dalhousie, *Private Letters of the Marquis of Dalhousie*, ed. J. G. A. Baird
    (Edinburgh, 1910)
Davitt, Michael, *The Fall of Feudalism in Ireland* (New York, 1904)
Devoy, John, *Devoy's Post-Bag 1871–1920*, Vol. 2, eds William O'Brien
    and Desmond Ryan (Dublin, 1948)
Duleep Singh, *The Duleep Singh Correspondence*, ed. Ganda Singh, Punjabi
    University (Patiala, 1977)
Ganda Singh, *Private Correspondence relating to the Anglo-Sikh Wars*, Sikh
    History Society (Amritsar, 1955)
Le Caron, Henri (pseud.), *25 Years in the Secret Service, the Recollections of
    a Spy* (London, 1892)
Login, Lady Lena, *Sir John Login and Duleep Singh* (London, 1890)
—— *Lady Login's Recollections 1820–1904*, ed. E. Dalhousie Login
    (London, 1916)
Mallet, Marie (Mary Adeane), *Life with Queen Victoria* (London, 1968)

Pobedonostsev, Constantin, *Mémoires politiques, correspondence etc.* (Paris, 1927)

Anon. *The Repeal of the Union Conspiracy or Mr Parnell M.P. and the Irish Republican Brotherhood*, ('The Black Pamphlet'), pub. W. Ridgway (London, 1886)


GUIDES, DIRECTORIES, TIMETABLES

Baedeker, *West und Mittel Russland 1887*

*Crockfords Clerical Directory*

*Galignani's Illustrated Paris Guide 1887–88*

The Foreign Office List

Post Office London Directory, 1887

GPO Telephone Director (Reading) 1939

*Guide de Voyageur en Russie, St Petersbourg et Moscou*, ed. A. F. Tastevin (Paris, 1887)

Bradshaw's Railway Guide 1887–88

Great Eastern Railway, timetables 1887–93

*Guide to Grasse*, 1891

The India List

Messageries Maritimes timetable, 1887

P & O Steam Navigation Company, *Guide for Travellers*, 1887

Thacker's Indian Directory 1887–89


NEWSPAPERS

GREAT BRITAIN

*The Times, The Standard* (later *Evening Standard*), the *Daily Telegraph*, the *Sunday Telegraph*, the *Sunday Telegraph* magazine, *The Echo, The Globe*, the *Morning Advertiser, Reynolds's News*, the *Daily Chronicle, The Labour World*

FRANCE

*Le Voltaire, Le Temps, Le Journal des Débats, La Nouvelle Revue*

USA

The *New York Herald Tribune* (USA, Paris and London), the *New York Sunday Mercury*, the *New York Times.*

INDIA

The *Times of India, The Hindustan*, the *Lahore Tribune, The Pioneer*, the *Civil and Military Gazette, Akhbar-i-am*

RUSSIA

*Le Journal de St Pétersbourg, Moskovskie Vyedmosti, Novoye Vremaya*

# REFERENCES

Epigraph

'After Flying' *A Wing and a Prayer, the 'Bloody 100th' Bomb Group of the 8th US Army Air Force in Action over Europe in World War II* Harry H. Crosby (New York, 1993)
Author's Note 'How do you spell' IOR R/1/1/44
'Russia has' QV Letters, Vol. II p. 193.

*Part One*

CHAPTER 1   The Maharani of Tunbridge Wells
4 'The death' *The Times*, 8 Aug. 1930
7 'The Maharajah intends' IOR R/1/1/77
7 'the most serious danger' Richard J. Popplewell, *British Intelligence and the Defence of the Indian Empire* (London, 1995)

CHAPTER 2   The Diamond
8 'Dulecp' www.dormantaccounts.ch

CHAPTER 3   The Heirs
16 'Old "Princess"' Paksh Tandon, *Punjabi Century* (London, 1961)
16 'I am the' interview, *The Sunday Telegraph Magazine*, 12 Oct. 1997

CHAPTER 4   The Lion
20 'The artist deliberately' F. S. Aijazuddin, *Sikh Portraits by European Artists* (New York, 1979) p. 29
20 'The break-up of the Punjab' Ellenborough papers, PRO 30/12 (28/12) 11 May 1843
21 'When the Sardar sat' *The Lahore Tribune*, 25 Oct. 1893
21 'The corpse' William Godolphin

Osborne, *The Court and Camp of Runjeet Singh* (London, 1840), pp. 17–18
22 'According to Duleep's four wives' ibid., pp. 223–4
21 footnote quoted in Aijazuddin, op. cit.

CHAPTER 5   The Governor-General
24 'Had I been aware' RA Vic/Add N2/20
25 'Sir, as' *The Times*, 31 Aug. 1882
26 'The Rani's mind' Major W. Broadfoot, *The Career of Major George Broadfoot* (London, 1888), p. 272
27 'Jawahir Singh' Alexander Gardner, *Memoirs* (London, 1898), p. 259
30 'Give us powder' ibid., p. 272
30 'We have heard' *The Lahore Tribune*, 25 Oct. 1893
30 'The Council' *The Times*, 3 Aug. 1882
31 'All went off' Punjab Papers f. (fiche) 76
32 'He is a very' DSC (23)
32 'The young lady' George Monro Smyth, *A History of the Reigning Family of Lahore*, (Calcutta, 1847) p. 94
32 'The half measures' DSC (23)
33 'I had entrusted' Ganda Singh, *Private Correspondence Relating to the Anglo-Sikh Wars* (Amritsar, 1955) p. 489
34 'the rallying point' pp. f. 208
36 'We print elsewhere' *The Times*, 31 Aug 1882

CHAPTER 6   The Fall
38 'Unwarned' DSC p. 63
38 'Your Majesty' QV Letters (first series), Vol. II, pp. 257–9
39 'Terms granted' pp f. 693
39 'I cannot' ibid., f. 703
40 'Lord of the' Login (2), p. 75
40 'I wish you' Login (2), p. 80
41 'The confiscation' DSC (58)
41 'on a table' Dalhousie, p. 172

42 'I have received' Login (2), p. 81

42 'more than five' Khuswant Singh, *A History of the Sikhs* (Princeton, 1963)

42 footnote 'When Runjeet' QV Letters, Vol. II, pp. 286–7

43 'a box of toys' Mrs Helen Mackenzie, *Life in the Mission, the Camp and the Zenana, or Six Years in India*, Vol. III (London, 1853)

43 'Having heard that' RA Vic N14/65

44 'It was sometimes' Login (2), p. 95

44 'I well remember' Login (1), p. 278

44 'My little friend' Dalhousie, pp. 156–157

44 footnote 'List of armour' RA Vic N14/66

45 'He told me' Dalhousie, p. 249

45 'Having at' Login (1), pp. 393–94

46 'The Queen has seen' QV Letters, Vol. II, pp. 278–79

46 footnote 'As my subjects', original printed memo in L/P&S/20/H3–7

47 'I am a little disappointed' Login (1), p. 407

47 'It was hardly' QV Letters (first series), Vol. III, p. 315

47 'The Queen fears' ibid., p. 320


CHAPTER 7   The Shoot

48 'The Reverend' IOR L/P&S/8/1

50 'When the Russian' IOR L/P&S/18/D152

50 'The Government' DSC (162)

52 'Lunch was served' *The Field*, October 1893, Ancient House archives

52 'It did not' RA Vic/Add N2/125

52 'She is' RA Vic/Add N2/126 (minute)

52 'although it' RA 09/32

53 'was in the possession' IOR L/P&S/18/D25

53 '£448' RA Vic/Add N2/11

53 'He may have' RA Vic/Add N2/6

53 'Hire a house' IOR L/P&S/18/D25

54 'hated the sight' RA Vic/Add N2/22

54 'I have learned' RA Vic/Add N2/35

54 'Messrs. Phillips' RA Vic/Add N2/49

55 'Having consulted' *Correspondence relating to the Maharajah Duleep Singh (1849–86) Confidential, Political and Secret Department, India Office, January 1887* IOR L/P&S/18/D25 p. 131

55 'It is little' ibid.

55 'Guru Ram' IOR L/P&S/18/D152


CHAPTER 8   Regina Imperatrix

58 'My Sovereign' RA Vic/Add N2/176

60 'There is a terrible storm' RA Vic/Add N2/167

60 'extraordinary' RA Vic/Add N2/165

60 'My dear Maharajah' RA Vic/Add N2/180

61 'After luncheon' RA *Queen Victoria's Journal*, 1 Jul. 1854

61 'The Queen wishes' RA Vic N14/74

62 'We took a drive' RA *Queen Victoria's Journal*, 21 Aug. 1854

62 'This young prince' QV Letters (first series), Vol. III, pp. 59–61

62 'beautiful clothes' RA *Queen Victoria's Journal* 13 Nov. 13 1854

62 'He had learned nothing' ibid., 14 Nov. 1854

63 'It is very good' Dalhousie, p. 325

63 'The "night-cappy"' ibid., p. 325

64 'She thinks such' QV Letters (first series), Vol. III, pp. 68–69

64 'A good wife' RA *Queen Victoria's Journal*, 14 Dec. 1856

65 'Osborne' ibid., 22 Aug. 1855

65 'presents from' Login (2), p. 118

66 'Went to see' RA *Queen Victoria's Journal*, 10 Jul. 1855

66 'very handsome' Login (1), pp. 340–43

67 'Her Majesty' ibid.

67 footnote 'I do not recollect' Dalhousie, p. 395

68 'It is to me, Ma'am' Login (i), pp. 340–43.


CHAPTER 9   The Green-room

71 'One night it might' Alhambra file, Theatre Museum, Covent Garden, London

71 'The Maharajah' *London in the 'Sixties* by 'One of the Old Brigade' (Donald Shaw) (London, 1908)

71 'Will you kindly' WEG BL Mss Add 4468–77

71 footnote 'grand pantomimic' Alhambra file op. cit.

72 'He strongly denied' RA Vic/Add N2/142

72 'I am bound to say' RA Vic/Add N2/42

73 'I accepted a loan' *Uncensored Recollections* by 'Anonymous' (Julian Osgood Field) (London, 1926), pp. 245–7

73 'Statement from Farrers' JSS, Vol. 2 1979, p. 131

74 'When I told him' Field, op. cit.

# References

CHAPTER 10  The Guru

75 'On the 28th' IOR L/P&S/18/D152 (McCracken)

76 'In April 1884' ibid.

77 'Being asked' *Affairs of Maharajah Duleep Singh* IOR L/P&S/18/D83

78 'My cousins' RA Vic/Add N2/215

78 'The Queen commands' RA Vic/Add N2/243

79 'Private, would you mind.' PRO FO 5/1932

79 'To whom is the General' ibid.

80 'I beg of you' RA Vic/Add N2/205

80 'Depend on it' RA Vic/Add N2/275

81 'I am aware' IOR L/P&S/18/D152 (McCracken)

81 'The time is' ibid.

82 'The question' DSC (187)

83 'I cannot tell' IOR L/P&S/18/D83

83 'May I invite myself' IOR L/P&S/20/ H3–8

84 'just like Leatherhead' the poet Edward Lear quoted in James Cameron, *An Indian Summer* (London, 1974)

84 'I have the honour' DSC (203)

84 'He pesters' IOR L/P&S/3/20/H3–7

85 'Duleep Singh's' Sir Owen Tudor Burne, *Memories* (London, 1907)

85 'The Maharajah intends' IOR L/P&S/ 18/D83

85 'I am strongly' ibid.

85 footnote 'The terms' RA Vic/Add N2/ 29

86 'I do not' IOR L/P&S/18/D25 pp. 151–153

86 'The Secretary' ibid.

86 'Your claims' ibid.

86 footnote 'Mothers' Alexander Burnes, *Travels into Bokhara* (London, 1834)


CHAPTER 11  Bamba

89 'Elveden Rectory' Vic/Add N2/268

91 'I know how dearly' IOR Mss Eur E337/1 (DSF)

91 'She is the illegitimate' Montgomery papers IOR Mss Eur D1019/2

92 'The story of the Marriage' IOR L/P&S/20/H3-7

93 'The Marriage' *The Times of India*, 7 Jun. 1854

94 'To the memory' letter from Mr A. Walker, Killin, Perthshire Dec. 1997

94 'She is not' Login (2), op. cit., p. 234

95 'Her costume' ibid., p. 243

95 'I never beheld' RA *Queen Victoria's Journal* 20 Mar. 1867

95 'All the building' IOR Mss Eur E337/1

95 'The Lord has been' ibid.

96 'Cheer up' ibid., IOR Mss Eur E337/2

96 'Dearest Vickie' ibid.

96 'Our little ones' ibid.

96 'I desire also' IOR L/P&S/18/D83

97 'Secret, the' IOR L/P&S/3/279

97 footnote 'Elveden Hall' *The Times*, 20 Jul. 1883

98 'Grant me' WEG BL Mss

98 'Abstract of Political' DSC (233)

99 'The Viceroy's Powers' IOR Mss Eur E337/2 (DSF)

101 'It is perfectly' IOR R/1/1/46

101 'Duleep Singh's' DSC (277)

102 'My Sovereign' RA Vic/Add N2/328


CHAPTER 12  Casey

104 'English racing gentlemen' *The Echo*, 2 May 1887

105 'the secret-service' Michael Davitt, *The Fall of Feudalism in Ireland* (New York, 1904), p. 436

105 'There also' ibid., p. 437

106 'Last evening' *The Times*, 21 Apr. 1884

107 'Paid up like' Godley papers (Sir J. A. Godley, 1st Viscount Kilbracken) IOR Mss Eur F102

108 'There is not a man here' quoted in Bernard Porter, *Origins of the Vigilant State, the Metropolitan Police Special Branch Before the First World War* (London, 1987), p. 52. See also K. R. M. Short, *The Dynamite War, Irish American Bombers in Victorian London*, (Dublin, 1979)

109 footnote 'On the other plots' Le Caron, *25 Years in the Secret Service* (London, 1894) p. 142

110 'Why were cheers' *The Repeal of the Union Conspiracy*, (London, 1887) p. 21

113 'The next year' Davitt op., cit. p. 613


CHAPTER 13  Jindan

115 'Captain de Horne' NMM, P & O/40 Nautical Records

115 'my idiotic parent' DSC (331)

115 'All the dear ones' IOR Mss Eur E377/2 (DSF)

116 'Duleep Singh left' L/P&S/18/D25
   pp. 167–175
116 'Burmese Party' ibid.
117 'There is nothing' ibid.
117 'The Sikhs fondly' *The Lahore Tribune*,
   17 Apr. 1886
117 'In consideration' L/P&S/18/D25
   pp. 167–175
118 'Maharajah should not' ibid.
118 'I have asked' ibid.
118 'The Queen was' RA Vic/Add N2/335
118 'rarely mentioned her' Login (1),
   pp. 239–40
119 'She is much changed' ibid., p. 450
119 'India is a beastly place' ibid., p. 454
120 'worn over native' Login (2), pp. 213–14
120 'dirty old' Normanby papers quoted in
   Michael Alexander and Sushila Anand,
   *Queen Victoria's Maharajah*, London,
   1980
121 'evil genius' ibid., p. 221
121 'I feel it very difficult' Login (1), p. 466
121 'The arrival of the Maharani' ibid.,
   pp. 464–5
121 'I wish to have' ibid., p. 463
122 'My attention has' *The Times*, 7 Aug.
   1863
123 'most sincere' Login (1), p. 480
123 footnote 'A large number' ibid., p. 477


CHAPTER 14   Steamer Point
124 'The climate' *P & O Traveller's Pocket
   Book*, 1888
124 'I leave this ship' *The Lahore Tribune*,
   1 May 1887
125 'I desire Your Excellency' L/P&S/18/
   D25 pp. 167–75
125 'It is my desire' ibid.
125 'Clear the line' ibid.
125 'I have made' ibid.
125 'I shall have great pleasure' ibid.
126 'On further reflection' ibid.
127 'After the Maharajah' RA 09/50
128 'The Empress thanks' RA 09/52
129 'Sardar Thakur' DSC (325)
130 'You may have seen a report' DSC (346)
130 'My first cousin' DSC (333)
131 'The book begins' IOR L/P&S/18/
   D152 (McCracken)
131 'His Highness' IOR Mss Eur F130
   (Duff)
132 'You can allow' IOR L/P&S/18/D25

132 'The Pahul is the' R. W. Falcon,
   *Handbook on Sikhs for Regimental
   Officers* (Allahabad, 1896)
133 'You may leave him' IOR Mss Eur
   F130/24 (Duff)
133 'We thought we had' IOR Mss Eur
   F130/25 (Duff)
134 'Some kind and firm' RA Vic/Add N2/
   358


CHAPTER 15   'A Sikh Martyr Will
Be Born'
135 'Although I am' *The Times of India*,
   6 Jul. 1886 in IOR L/P&S/18/D25
137 'I have returned here' PRO FO 146/
   2817
137 'Paris, 26 June' RA Vic/Add N2/360
138 'His Highness is' IOR L/P&S/8/1
138 'I send you' PRO FO 146/2817
138 'Duleep Singh talks' RA Vic/Add N2/
   363
138 'As to the Maharajah' RA Vic/Add
   N2/364
139 'Who is looking' RA Vic/Add N2/363
   (minute)
139 'That he was sorry' RA Vic/Add Mss
   N2/363
139 'Having received' IOR L/P&S/3/293
140 'To the Earl of Rosebery' PRO FO
   27/2797
140 'In your letter' IOR L/P&S/8/1
141 'Dear Maharajah' RA Vic/Add N2/368
142 'Gracious Sovereign' RA 010/39
142 'The person' PRO FO 146/2844
143 'The Queen got' RA Vic/Add N2/374
143 'I style myself' Scott family papers,
   courtesy of Peter Ashpitel


CHAPTER 16   The Dancing Mouse
144 'I think it better' PRO FO 146/2844
145 'A man came to me' ibid.
145 'I return the letters' PRO FO 146/2820
145 'Enquiry into the man Smith's' PRO
   FO 186/2420
145 footnote RAC BL Add 5127
146 'Proclamation No 1.' IOR L/P&S/3/
   278
147 'By the grace of' ibid.
148 'I enclose' RA Vic/Add N2/376
148 'It is now too late' RA Vic/Add N2/
   415 & 417
149 'The Russian' IOR L/P&S/8/1

149 'The Minister told me' IOR L/P&S/3/
279
150 'From where does the Queen' RFM/
JSS pp. 77–8
151 'Highness, The Imperial' ibid., p. 79
151 'has come again to see me' ibid., p. 80
152 'Should you M. le President', FFM,
Memoires et Documents. Asie, vol. 80
pp. 326–329
153 'With regard to' DS-Secret
13 Feb. 1887
153 'The Maharajah called' DS-Secret
8 Nov. 86 pp. 4–5
153 'You may tell' IOR R/1/1/62
155 'presents his compliments' L/P&S/3/
278
156 footnote *'Spatial perception'* Elie de
Cyon *Le Sens de l'Espace Chez les Souris
Dansantes Japonaises* (Paris, 1900)

CHAPTER 17   Revenge
158 'Madame Adam is delightful' Claude
Vento, *Les Salons de Paris* (Paris 1891),
also *Le Voltaire* 27 Feb. 1887
161 'Private and most secret' Mss Eur
E243/19 (Cross)
162 'Care of British signaller' ibid.
164 'Statement of Pierre Georgevich' PRO
HD3/70
166 'the information you gave' PRO HD3/
70

CHAPTER 18   The Editor
168 'Le Siècle' George F. Kennan, *The
Decline of Bismarck's European Order*
(Princeton, 1979), p. 216
168 footnote 'Soon after' GFM Russland
82 Nr4, secr. Katkow
169 'In 1885' Cyon, op. cit., p. 276
170 'conduct foreign' Robert Blake, *The
Unknown Prime Minister, the Life and
Times of Andrew Bonar Law* (London,
1955)
171 'Spy of the Russian Monarch' IOR
L/P&S/18/D152 p. 24
172 'My tale would' L/P&S/18/D83
173 'My first duty' ibid.
173 'My Dear Watson' IOR L/P&S/3/278
174 'I beg to say' ibid.
174 'do so to die' RA Vic/Add N2/423
174 'Proclamation No3' (handwritten
original) IOR L/P&S/3/278
174 footnote 'He is mad' RA Vic/Add N2/
423, *Mail on Sunday* 18 Jun. 2000

CHAPTER 19   Winter
177 'he thought it stupid' Quoted in
Kennan, op. cit.
178 footnote 'the Bell system' 'The
Telephone in Russia', *The Times*
report, 4 Sep. 1884
179 'The intrigues of' V. N. Lamsdorf,
*Dnevnik* quoted in Kennan, op. cit.,
p. 262
179 'It has more than once' PRO FO
Paris, 25 Jan. 87
179 'The fate of France' Kennan, op. cit.,
p. 275
180 *'maladie des yeux'* Cyon, op. cit., p. 330
180 'It was all' ibid.
181 *'Bataille de Navarin'*, E. V.
Bogdanovich (Paris, 1887)
182 'bent on revenge' DS-Secret, 13
Feb. 1887
183 'Cause a receipt' IOR L/PS/3/278
183 'Secret.' ibid.
184 'Information' IOR Mss Eur E243/22
184 'Sir Owen' PRO FO 146/2903
184 'Can you give' PRO FO 146/2797
184 'Ought not the Russian' RA 010/42
185 'I heard from my cousin' 13 Feb.
DS-Secret, 1887
185 'Dear Sir Owen' DS-Secret, 15
Feb. 1887
188 'a firm supporter' Kennan, op. cit.,
p. 296
188 footnote 'one of the most' Fritz Stern,
*Gold and Iron, Bismarck, Bleichröder and
the building of the German Empire,*
(London, 1977) p. 443
189 'With reference to' IOR L/P&S/3/279
190 'I beg now to report' IOR L/P&S/8/2

CHAPTER 20   Our Correspondent
192 'Maharajah' DS-Secret, 8 Feb. 1887
194 'Monsieur. By the advice' ibid.,
10 Mar. 1887
195 'May it please' ibid.
195 'plenty of money' ibid
196 'All foreigners' PRO FO 65/1329
197 'St Petersburg is' PRO FO 65/1296
197 'a cloud of detectives' ibid.
198 'young English girl' DS-Secret,
15 Mar. 1887
198 'Before leaving Paris' ibid.
198 'Duleep Singh said' IOR Mss Eur
E243/22 (Cross)
198 'we have reason' FO 146/2908

244 'write and ask' ibid.
245 'All now knew' PRO FO 65/1310
246 'Mr K. is still' DS-Secret, 25 May 1887
246 'The Times Correspondent' DS-Secret, May 18 1887
247 'When I entered' The Times 2 June 1887
248 'Your Highness' DS-Secret, 30 May 1887

CHAPTER 24    King Over the Water
249 'Would it not be' DS-Secret, 31 May 1887
250 'I do not believe' IOR R/1/1/62
251 'With regard to' ibid.
251 'I do not think' ibid.
252 'Rs 60,000 in gold' ibid.
253 'The enclosed memorandum' DSC (445)
254 'The behaviour of the Sikhs' IOR L/P&S/18/D152
254 'Some curious information' IOR R/1/1/62
255 'When Colonel Olcott' ibid.
255 'But for the native' IOR L/P&S/18/D152
256 'It might be a good thing' ibid.
256 'These £3 million sterling' The Lahore Tribune, 11 Jul. 1887
257 'the idea of a Sikh force' L/P&S/18/D152 (Lyall)
258 'An aerial car' The Lahore Tribune, 17 Aug. 1887
258 'a well known American' The Lahore Tribune, 29 Jun 1887
259 'In the first place' IOR R/1/1/62

CHAPTER 25    The Snare
260 'I hear that' DS-Secret, 30 May 1887
260 'I hear privately' IOR Mss Eur E243/14 (Cross)
260 'I am told' ibid.
261 'Madame Adam' DS-Secret, 10 May 1887
261 'I am sincerely' DS-Secret, 12 June 1887
261 footnote 'Duleep Singh appeared' GFM Englische Besitz in Asien 2, Britisch Indien Vol. 2
261 footnote 'very amusing' IOR Mss Eur E243/22 (Cross)
262 'My dear [blank]' DS-Secret, 12 June 1887

263 'Mr K. returned here' ibid.
263 'Freycinet eliminated' Kennan op. cit., p. 325
264 'How can Katkov' ibid., p. 326
264 'It is reported' PRO FO 65/1297
266 'In the course of conversation' IOR L/P&S/3/282
267 'Accordingly, the emperor's first exclamation' ibid.
268 'He is still at the Dussaux' ibid.
268 'Things move here' DS-Secret, 30 June 1887

CHAPTER 26    Fenian Fire
270 'I don't mind telling you' The Morning Advertiser, 28 May 1887
272 'I transmit a confidential letter' PRO HO 144/275
273 'As you are aware' PRO HO 144/275/A6005/2
274 'I enclose a memorandum' PRO FO 5/2044
274 '[French] Minister of the Interior' ibid.
274 footnote 'Dear Sir Charles' New York Times 3 Jun. 1887
275 'I have just had' The Morning Advertiser, 17 June 1887
277 'This clergyman must' PRO HO 144/190/A64470B
277 footnote 'The handsome' RA Queen Victoria's Journal 21 Jun. 1887
278 'One of the principal agents' Sir Robert Anderson, The Lighter Side of My Official Life (London, 1910), pp. 117–18
278 'The Fenian agent' PRO HO 144/1357
279 'Millen forthwith' ibid.
279 'The following information' PRO HO 144/275/A6855/9
280 'sickened by dynamiters' Fenian Brotherhood Vol. 44, PRO FO 5/1931
281 footnote gold mines PRO ADM 1/8274/61

CHAPTER 27    Proud Rebel and Patriot
282 'Alas' IOR R/1/1/66
283 'Besides he' DS-Secret, 14 June 1887
283 'I cannot go' RFM/JSS pp. 82–3
284 'Mr Katkov's dangerous' ibid.
284 'Although I am' DS-Secret, 31 Jul. 1887

284 footnote 'It is my firm belief' ibid., 12 Aug. 1887

285 'The great and powerful' ibid., 2 Aug. 1887

285 'You cannot trust' ibid., 19 Aug. 87

285 'Yes my reply' DS-Secret, 2 Aug. 1887

286 'I have just' ibid., 11 Aug. 1887

287 'I know that' DS-Secret 19 Aug. 1887

287 'Her Imperial Highness' RA 010/44

288 'My beloved Mama' RA 010/45

288 'I think it is now' DS-Secret, 19 Aug. 1887

289 'I do not think' ibid., 23 Aug. 1887

289 'I regret to say' ibid.


CHAPTER 28   The Prisoner

291 footnote 'a whole consignment' IOR L/P&S/18/D152 (McCracken)

292 'Another is a copy' IOR R/1/1/65

292 'Leaving Duleep Singh at Moscow' ibid.

293 'In a pocket book' ibid.

293 'We send our faithful' ibid.

294 'I have this afternoon' ibid.

295 'object was to go' ibid.

296 'The Commandant may suggest' ibid.

296 'I have been directed' ibid.

297 'I cannot help thinking' IOR Ms Eur 243/23 (Cross)

297 'On the 10th August' IOR L/P&S/R/1/1/67

299 footnote 'Inform editors' 10R/L/P85/R/1/1/67

300 'While Henderson' IOR L/P&S/R/1/1/65

300 'The news of his death' ibid.

301 'I should be glad' IOR L/P&S/R/1/1/67

301 'I have taken steps' IOR L/P&S/R/1/1/67

302 'It is well known' PDH April 88

302 'One thing more' DS-Secret, 4 Feb. 1890

303 'Duleep Singh sent Aroor' RA 010/66


CHAPTER 29   Princesses

304 'I, the undersigned' *The Times*, 31 Aug. 1886

305 'Calling the children Princes' IOR L/P&S/3/278

305 'No objection to' ibid.

305 'If you don't call' ibid.

306 'some women insulted' *The Hindustan*, 6 Oct. 1887

306 'Regular hours and habits' RA Vic/Add N2/428

306 'The Maharani had a long' RA 010/49

307 'The Maharani's funeral' RA 010/53

307 'The poor Maharani' RA Vic/Add U32 29 Sep. 1887

307 'Under other circumstances' RA 010/60

308 'Setting aside all' RA Vic/Add N2/428


CHAPTER 30   The Confession

309 'Sohan Lal of Delhi' IOR R/1/1/67

310 'Sohan Lal is down' ibid.

310 'Thakur Singh and' ibid.

311 'I picked out the Egyptian' ibid.

311 'When they reached Pondicherry' ibid.

312 'It is pretty clear' ibid.

312 'Under arrest' ibid.

313 'It will be well' ibid.

313 'I am thirty-six' DSC (521)

313 'I was sent to Pondicherry' DSC (522)

314 'We have more authentic' DS-Secret, 30 Oct. 87

314 'We are in a foreign land' DSC (504)

315 'Send me some money' IOR R/1/1/62

315 'General Buzgovitch' ibid.


CHAPTER 31   Wretched Peace

318 'Abdul Rasul is more' DS-Secret, 21 Oct. 1887

318 'My secretary's name' ibid., 28 Oct. 1887

318 'This individual' IOR L/P&S/3/280

318 'Two or three' IOR R/1/1/66

319 'Duleep was quite' IOR R/1/1/77

319 'Duleep Singh is in high favour' DS-Secret, 16 Sep. 1887

319 'The political situation' ibid., 8 Nov. 1887

320 'I have commenced' ibid., 22 Sep. 1887

320 'Mr [blank], whom' ibid., 2 Oct. 1887

321 'Brothers' *The Lahore Tribune*, 9 Nov. 1887

322 'I hope you will lose' L/P&S/3/284

323 'The Maharajah would have' GFM *Englische Besitz in Asien 2 Britisch Indien Vol 2.*

323 'The *Untersekretar*' ibid.

323 'Please send me a copy' DS-Secret, 17 Oct. 1887

323 'It would be absolutely pointless' RFM Raikov op. cit.

323 'It is all very fine' DS-Secret, 24 Oct. 1887

324 'were illegal' ibid.

324 'I do not see' DS-Secret, 2 Dec. 1887

324 'Yes the ball' ibid.

325 'India's Deliverance' *The New York Sunday Mercury*, 8 Jan. 1888

326 'We came to live' DS-Secret, 17 Oct. 1887

327 'My Lord, I may mention' IOR L/P&S/3/285

CHAPTER 32   The Mohammedan Detective

328 'Aziz-ud-din' IOR L/P&S/3/288

329 'Abdul Rasul is the' ibid.

329 'as a loyal servant' ibid.

330 'His only occupation' IOR R/1/1/77

331 'These men await' IOR L/P&S/3/288

331 'The day England' ibid.

332 'At present the Russian' IOR R/1/1/77

333 'I wish the little chap' ibid.

334 'some communication' HMD IOR Mss Eur D727/15

334 'to go to Russia' ibid., 10 Aug. 1888

334 'in great pecuniary difficulties' IOR R/1/1/82

335 'A.S. has discovered' ibid.

335 'The first attack' ibid.

335 Footnote 'Your Sikh came' IOR HMD Mss Eur D727/15

CHAPTER 33   The Cockney Empress

336 'Failure' DS-Secret, 2 Jan. 1888

336 'I have washed my hands' ibid., 7 Jan. 1888

336 'It is as we' ibid., 22 Jan. 1888

337 'I have to inform you' IOR L/P&S/3/286

337 'When the Maharajah' ibid.

337 'When the Maharani' DSC (531)

338 'Have you arranged'

338 'Duleep himself' IOR R/1/1/77

338 'Following from Consul' DSC (540)

339 'You will see' ibid., 11 Apr. 1888

339 'They were extraordinary' Login (1) p. 521

339 'The English girl' IOR L/P&S/3/290

340 'Seeing the circumstances' PRO FO 65/1330

341 'If what I am told' PRO FO 65/1297

342 'Madame Bogdanovich' PRO FO 65/1330

342 'You ask about' IOR Mss Euv E243/23 (Cross)

342 'Count Ignatiev' IOR L/P&S/3/292

CHAPTER 34   The Cossack

343 Rudyard Kipling, 'The Man Who Was', *A Treasury of Short Stories*, (New York, 1957)

343 'suddenly developed' Cross IOR Cross Mss Eur E243/23 (Cross)

344 'The military officers' IOR R/1/1/82

344 Footnote 'Princess Kleinmichael' les Memoires de Nicolas Giers, Canadian Slavic Studies no. 3 (Montreal, 1967)

345 'Made acquaintance' PRO FO/65/1298

345 'A Russian whose name' PRO FO 78/3998

345 footnote 'French consul' GFM *Englische Besitz in Asien 2 Britisch Indien Vol. 2*

346 'The editor' *The Akhbar-i-Am* (Lahore), 29 Oct. 1887

347 'The first attack' IOR R/1/1/82

347 'When Mons. Notovich' ibid.

347 'He talked a great deal' PRO FO 65/1381

348 'When the natives' IOR L/P&S/3/291

348 'It is reported' IOR R/1/1/99

348 'Please endeavour' ibid.

349 'a puny Hindustani' ibid.

349 'a sturdy man' ibid.

CHAPTER 35   The Alliance

351 'deputed to visit' IOR R/1/1/90

351 'seeing him frequently' DS-Secret, 14 Nov. 1888

352 'A committee' ibid., 1 Feb. 1889

353 'He could get volunteers' *The Standard*, 13 Feb. 1889

353 'Brother Princes' original in DS-Secret, p. 270

354 'My most gracious Sovereign' DS-Secret 25 Jan. 1889

354 'Madame' printed letter in DS-Secret 23 Feb. 1889

355 'Duleep Singh intends' RA 010/84

355 'Article 1.' DS-Secret, 1 Mar. 1889

355 'Colonels, Lieutenant-Colonels' ibid.

356 'The plan of organisation' ibid., 13 Mar. 1889

356 'consist of 120,000 men' ibid., 11 Mar. 1889

357 'Duleep sends a copy' ibid., 13 Mar. 1889

358 'Yesterday in the course' ibid., 22 Mar. 1889
358 'Since his residence' ibid., 27 Mar. 1889
359 'I approached the General' Cyon, op. cit., p. 394
360 'No European Government' L/P&S/3/294
360 'After his outrageous' ibid.
360 'This intense fool' DS-Secret, 16 Apr. 1889
361 'being too provocative' *La Huitième Arrondissement, Souvenirs d'hier et d'aujord'hui*, ed. P. Jassy (Paris, 1938)
361 'I enclose notices' DS-Secret, 2 May 1889
362 'He has no recollection' ibid., 6 May 1889
362 'He went in the afternoon' ibid., 15 May 1889
363 'My Sovereign' ibid., 17 May 1889
363 *'redingcote noir'* Le Temps, 22 May 1889
363 *'une belle miss'* newspaper cutting in DS-Secret, 22 May 1889
363 'Comte Carrol-Tevis' DS-Secret, p. 338 (undated)
364 'Duleep Singh was married' DS-Secret, 21 May 1889
364 'Duleep is nearly' ibid., 26 May 1889
364 'This unfortunate' ibid., 5 Jun 1889
364 'grandeurs' cutting in DS-Secret 22 May 1889
364 'despoiled of' ibid.
364 'Duleep is nearly' DS-Secret 26 May 1889
364 'This unfortunate' DS-Secret 5 Jun. 1889
364 footnote 'I was a witness' Cyon op. cit.
365 'The first day' Le Temps 26 Jun. 1889
365 'The baron first sent' DS-Secret 4 Jul. 1889
365 'though they are' DS-Secret (undated)
366 'Beloved Fellow-Countrymen' DS-Secret 25 Jun. 1889
368 'We opened up' Reynolds's Newspaper 12 May 1895
368 'Prince Czenicheff' DS-Secret 30 June 1889
368 'He found out' DS-Secret 7 July 1889
369 'Secret and confidential' ibid. 7 Oct. 1889
369 'Duleep is said to hope much' ibid.
369 'His Highness introduced' Oliphant mid Sep 1889

369 'The Queen will be interested to learn,' RA 010/87
370 'his dogs to Odessa' DS-Secret 10 Jul. 1889
370 'Duleep Singh is accused' DS-Secret 17 Nov. 1889
370 'This is not' ibid.
370 Footnote 'He is quite aware' RA 010/88
371 'It may interest you' DS-Secret 21 Nov. 1889
371 'Duleep has taken to' ibid.

CHAPTER 36    Pondicherry Beach
372 'On the night of 23rd' DS-Secret, 26 Feb. 1889
372 'We commit our case' DSC (534)
373 'The Sakhi prophecies' IOR R/1/1/95
373 'He had met Duleep' ibid.
374 'Confession of Jiwan Singh' DSC (587)
376 'Two Sikhs' DS-Secret, 1 Jan. 1889
376 'My Dear General' ibid., 26 Feb. 1889
376 'Here are our views' ibid.
378 'Some people have' ibid.
378 'As to your Majesty's ibid., 7 May 1889
379 'As in the case' ibid., 25 Dec. 1889

CHAPTER 37    Victor
381 'The trustees recommended' IOR L/P&S/3/283
382 'Half yearly report' ibid.
382 'Prince Victor' ibid.
383 'which binds Prince' ibid.
383 'To clear Prince' IOR L/P&S/3//290
383 'I am very sorry' RA 010/65
383 'Prince Frederick has' RA 010/74
384 'The Princesses' RA 010/89
384 'I am writing' BL Mss Add. 51278 (Cross)
384 'As to the alleged' RA Vic/Add N2/510
385 'Prince Victor' RA Vic/Add N2/514
385 'This is most' RA Vic/Add N2/515
385 'They are very much improved' RA Vic/Add N2/521
385 'The Queen will' RA Vic/Add N2/541

CHAPTER 38    'The Turks Shall Break Their Silence'
387 'government employing spies' DSC (639)

387 'All communications' DSC (638)
388 'He was Duleep's last' DSC (639)
389 'The intrigue is dying' IOR R/1/1/90
389 'constantly drunk' ibid., 3 Apr. 1890
389 'He is drinking' ibid., 9 Feb. 1890
389 'Our implacable foe' ibid., 20 Jan. 1890
389 'In any quarrel' ibid., 28 Jan. 1890
390 'The same cypher' ibid., 9 Mar. 1890
390 'a certain Mohammedan' ibid., 4 Feb. 1890
390 'Duleep is vastly scared' ibid., 28 Feb. 1890
390 'My Dear Son' IOR L/P&S/3/300
390 'His eldest son' IOR Mss Eur 243/27 (Cross)
391 'a treaty' DS-Secret, 9 Feb. 1890
391 'I have just seen' IOR L3/P&S/3/300
391 'This communication' ibid.
392 'Prince Victor has been' RA 010/92
392 'Having been so' IOR L/P&S/3/300
393 'The woman Parraton' DS-Secret, 4 Apr. 1890
393 'It appears' ibid.
393 'Duleep's wife' DS-Secret, 12 Apr. 1890

CHAPTER 39   The General
394 'Duleep has removed' DS-Secret, 7 June 1890
394 'A Russian whose' ibid., 20 May 1890
395 'He has a traveller's' ibid., 24 May 1890
395 'M. Shatoukin' ibid., DS-Secret (undated) pp. 443–446
395 'We know all about' ibid., 2 June 1890
395 'Although the results' ibid., 1 June 1890
396 'Notices have appeared' ibid., June 1890
396 'so then he drove' RA Vic/Add N2/552
396 'Grand Hotel RA Vic 010/94
397 'My visit' Vic/Add N2/552
398 'What is the result' RA Vic/Add N2/551
398 'I am not very anxious' RA Vic/Add N2/536
398 'I see no objection' IOR L/P&S/3/303
399 'A friendly letter' ibid.
399 'Please cypher' RA 010/97
399 'I write to express' IOR L/P&S/3/303

399 footnote 'I have sent' IOR Eur E243/19 (Cross)
400 'By the last sentences' IOR L/P&S/3/303.
400 'Her Majesty's Government' ibid.
400 'The Maharajah is in' IOR L/P&S/8/2
401 'One of his friends' DS-Secret, 20 July 1890
401 'About a year after' Cyon op. cit., p. 300
401 footnote 'The wife' RA Vic/Add N2/560
402 'Duleep is a wreck' DS-Secret, 13 Aug. 1890
403 'Prince. In the opinion' ibid., 15 Aug. 1890
404 'Difficulties of a Visit' *New York Herald Tribune*, DS-Secret, 25 Aug. 1890
405 footnote 'Lord Cross may like' DS-Secret, 23 Aug. 1890
406 footnote *The Labour World* 1 Nov 1890 cutting in PRO HO 144/926 A4 9982

CHAPTER 40   The Prodigal's Return
407 'My father's money' IOR L/P&S/3/303
407 'It is now more' ibid.
408 'I do not want' RA Vic/Add N2/574
408 'think we cd. urge' (minute) ibid.
408 'I have renewed' DS-Secret, 18 Oct. 1890
409 'to sign papers' IOR L/P&S/3/20/H3–7
409 'The Maharajah is getting killed' DS-Secret, 3 Nov. 1890
410 'In 1891' Cyon op. cit., p. 300
411 'Duleep Singh, who' DS-Secret, 23 Dec. 1890
412 'The life pursued' *A Guide to Grasse* by an 'English Resident' (London, 1891)
413 'The poor Maharajah' RA Vic U32, 1 Apr. 1891
414 'After a few minutes' RA *Queen Victoria's Journal*, 31 Mar. 1891
414 'Old Duleep Singh' Marie Mallet (Mary Adeane), *Life with Queen Victoria* (London, 1968), p. 48
414 'He is very much broken' DS-Secret, 11 Apr. 1891
414 'I cannot do otherwise' RA Vic/Add A12/1768

# INDEX

*Index*

# Index

# Index